# TOUCHLINES
## OF WAR

THE
UNIVERSITY
OF HULL
PRESS

Cover Design by Michael Cox
Portrait by Sally Tomlinson
Maps drawn by Keith Scurr

# Touchlines of War

Peter Tennant

THE UNIVERSITY OF HULL PRESS
1992

© **The University of Hull Press**

**British Library Cataloguing in Publication Data**

Tennant, *Sir*, Peter
   Touchlines of War.
   1. Title
   940.5335

ISBN 0 85958 603 0

All rights reserved. No part of this publication may be reproduced in any form or by any means, electronic, mechanical, photocopy, recording or otherwise, in accordance with the provisions of the Copyright Act 1988 without the prior permission of The University of Hull Press.

Phototypeset in 11 on 12 pt Times, printed by the Central Print Unit, the University of Hull, and bound by Khromatec Ltd.

*To Gallie with love*

The following is a translation of a poem by Frans G. Bengtsson in the summer of 1944 when an RAF bomber crashed in Skåne and was found to have been hit by Swedish anti-aircraft shells. It is a satirical suggestion for a speech by a Swedish official at the burial of the crew.

You saved us from the tramp of Hitler's boot,
We're safe and sound while neighbours pine to death.
And now we bury you with thanks and shoot
To consecrate our neutral shibboleth.

This evil Hydra will e'er long be slain
And so our now secure neutrality
can well afford to shoot to kill and gain
Credit for helping you into eternity.

The original read as follows:-

Ni frälste oss från Hitlers stövelklack
Vi sitta tryggt bland grannar som försmäkta
Och här begrava vi Er nu till tack
För vår neutralitet, den strikt korrekta.

Snart är ondskans Hydra lyckligt fälld
Den alltmer säkrade neutraliteten
Har därför övergått till verkningseld
Och den har hjälpt Er in i evigheten.

# Contents

| | | |
|---|---|---|
| List of Maps and Illustrations | | ix |
| Preface | | xi |
| Acknowledgements | | xiii |
| I | Introduction | 1 |
| II | Sweden 1939-45 | 12 |
| III | Our Life in Sweden | 38 |
| IV | The British Legation - Stockholm | 49 |
| V | Allied Journalists in Stockholm | 60 |
| VI | The Swedish Press | 65 |
| VII | Swedish Personalities | 73 |
| VIII | Propaganda | 105 |
| IX | The Rickman Affair | 126 |
| X | Grey and Black Propaganda, SOE, Intelligence and all that | 133 |
| XI | Cops and Robbers | 153 |
| XII | Germany | 174 |
| XIII | The Invasion of Britain | 196 |
| XIV | Blockade Running | 200 |
| XV | How We Failed to Buy the Italian Navy | 229 |
| XVI | The Russians | 252 |

| XVII | The British Council | 262 |
|---|---|---|
| XVIII | Visitors | 265 |
| XIX | Epilogue | 270 |

| | |
|---|---|
| Who's Who | 273 |
| Bibliography and Sources | 285 |
| Index | 291 |

# LIST OF MAPS AND ILLUSTRATIONS

## Maps

| | |
|---|---|
| Western Europe | xiv |
| Stockholm | xv |

## Illustrations

Facing Page

| | |
|---|---|
| *Valkyrian*, drawing by the author | 38 |
| The author and Anna-Lisa Leadbitter with a party of Russians and Americans sailing on United Nations Day, 1944 | 42 |
| Three Press Attachés - The author, Alexandra Jartseva (USSR) and Carl Jensen (US) sailing on United Nations Day, 1944 | 46 |
| Sir Victor Mallet with Crown Prince Gustav Adolf at the memorial service for the Duke of Kent in the British Church in Stockholm, 1942 | 56 |
| Woodcut of Amelie Posse by Czech diplomat Vaňek | 74 |
| The author distributing copies of *Pow-Wow* to British POWs at the exchange of British and German prisoners in Gothenburg | 86 |
| One of many propaganda shop windows, Vasagatan, Stockholm, 1941 | 116 |
| British publications and weekly newspaper, December 1939 | 120 |
| Christian Günther, drawing by the author | 154 |

| | |
|---|---|
| Bill Waring, drawing by the author | 164 |
| Harry Söderman, drawing by the author | 170 |
| Sir Victor Mallet, drawing by the author | 182 |
| Sir George Binney | 200 |
| Brian Reynolds (alias Bingham) in command of his flotilla of motor cruisers | 214 |
| *Dicto* steaming down Göta Älven | 220 |
| *Gay Viking* under repair in Gothenburg | 226 |

# Preface

Some secrets, even nowadays, are worth keeping forty or fifty years; this book gives plenty of examples. (Sir) Peter Tennant was a young don at Cambridge at the end of the nineteen-thirties, and got caught up in the intelligence world by the accident that he had been at Marlborough with Gordon Welchman, the mathematician. Welchman became one of the brightest stars at Bletchley Park; Tennant worked near him in the earliest stages, for his knowledge of modern languages gave him some advantages for decipher. As one of these languages was Swedish, and he had a Swedish wife, he was moved across from decipher to propaganda, and became press attaché at the British legation in Stockholm just after the war against Hitler began.

This book describes his five and a half years in the Swedish capital, where his ostensible task was to persuade the Swedes - in the teeth of the evidence, for the first half of the war - that the anti-nazi side was the correct one to back, and would eventually win. He was also, much more secretly, SOE's man in Stockholm from July 1940; and was widely, though wrongly, thought to be the head of the British Secret Service on the spot. He recounts, with full knowledge and a keen sense of fun, what work he did and did not carry out; unravelling plot after plot of skulduggery and subterfuge, ranging from the incompetent sabotage efforts of Section D in April 1940 (the now well-known Rickman affair) to the smuggling of special steels that earned George Binney his knighthood, the subversion of German soldiers travelling across Sweden, the recruiting of an informant inside the German legation, the unmasking of double agents, the security of the premises, and the successful planting of deception plans on the Germans.

His minister for most of the war, Sir Victor Mallet, as a godson of Queen Victoria and the son of one of the old Queen's ladies-in-waiting, was a diplomat of the old school, who strongly disapproved the storing of limpet mines on legation premises, and was regarded in the Foreign Office as altogether too friendly to the neutral Swedes; but Mallet's fits of temper never lasted long. He knew when to look the other way, and when to stand up for his staff if they came under threat from plots hatched by nazis or their sympathizers; of whom the local secret police had sometimes too many for comfort. Tennant got on quietly with his work, and was promoted to Paris in March 1945.

No one could be better placed to write this book, which makes a valuable addition to our knowledge of the secret war.

M.R.D. Foot

# Acknowledgements

I am deeply indebted to the following for their help over this book:-

George Alexander who has jogged my memory over our joint propaganda activities; Dr Christopher Andrew for permission to reprint the chapter on the Italian Navy which appeared originally in *Intelligence and National Security*; Barclays Bank for the help given me over typing the original typescript, especially Jean Windsor, Rita Collins, Jean Cawley and Ruth Neville; the late Patrick Beesley; Marcus Binney and his late mother for access to Sir George Binney's papers; Fru Nora Bohman, Frank Martin's daughter, for details about her father's life; Captain Henry Denham who was our Naval Attache in Sweden during the war for invaluable advice; Henry Lambert of Barclays Bank for his support as a director and a naval historian; Leif Leifland, the Swedish Ambassador, for access to his research on Anglo-Swedish wartime history; Maj Lorents for the loan of her wartime diary on board the *Patricia* with the convoy of destroyers bought in Italy and held up by the British in the Faroes on their way to Sweden; John and Philip Mallet for access to their father's, Sir Victor's, unpublished memoirs; Craig Graham McKay of Uppsala for his untiring detective work on Swedish wartime records; Sir Archibald Ross for the history of the British Embassy residence which he occupied as Ambassador; Gösta Sandström, now in Spain, who edited our weekly newspaper *Nyheter från Storbritannien* from 1940 to 1945; Professor Alberto Santoni, the official historian of the Italian Navy, for his research into the Walter affair; Peter Seckleman, now in Switzerland, who acted the part of Der Chef in Tom Delmer's 'black' radio programme 'Gustav Siegfried Eins': Fru Karin Sköld, Harry Söderman's sister, for information about her brother; Harald Wigforss, the former editor of *Göteborgs Handels- och Sjöfartstidning*, one of the few survivors of our supporters in the dark days before El Alamein; Jean Smith for her meticulous editing of the whole text of this book; Arthur Spencer for the invaluable index.

Western Europe

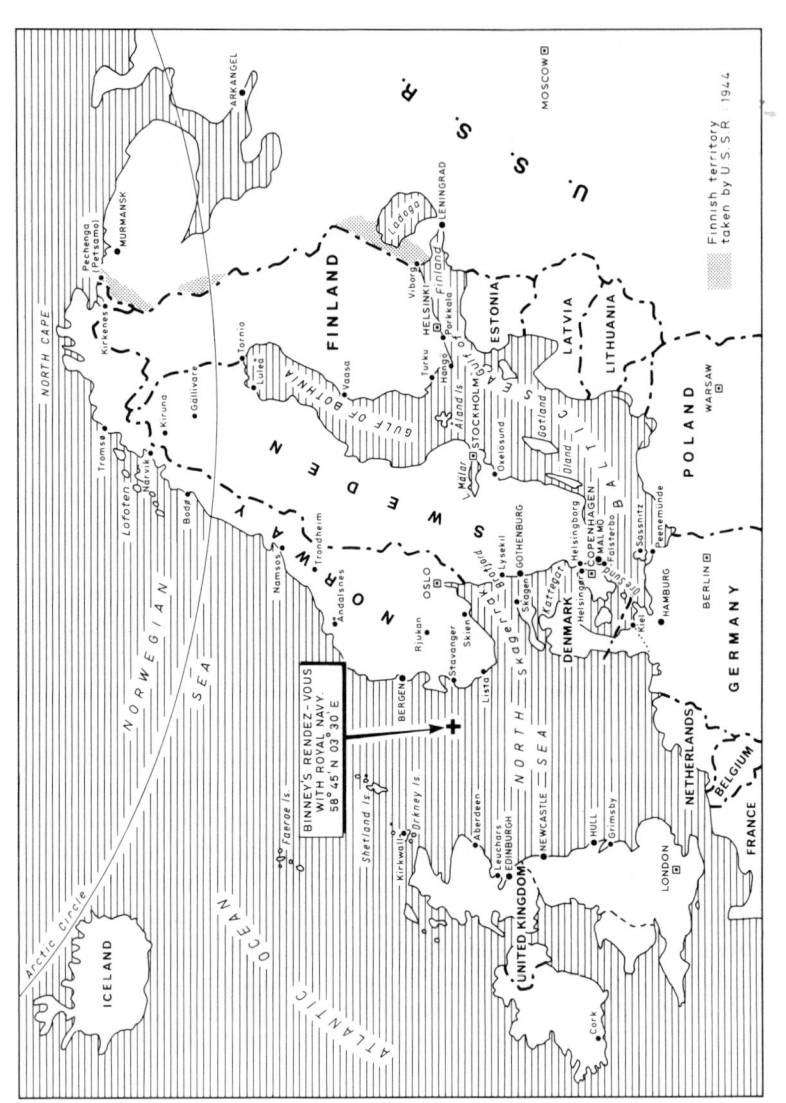

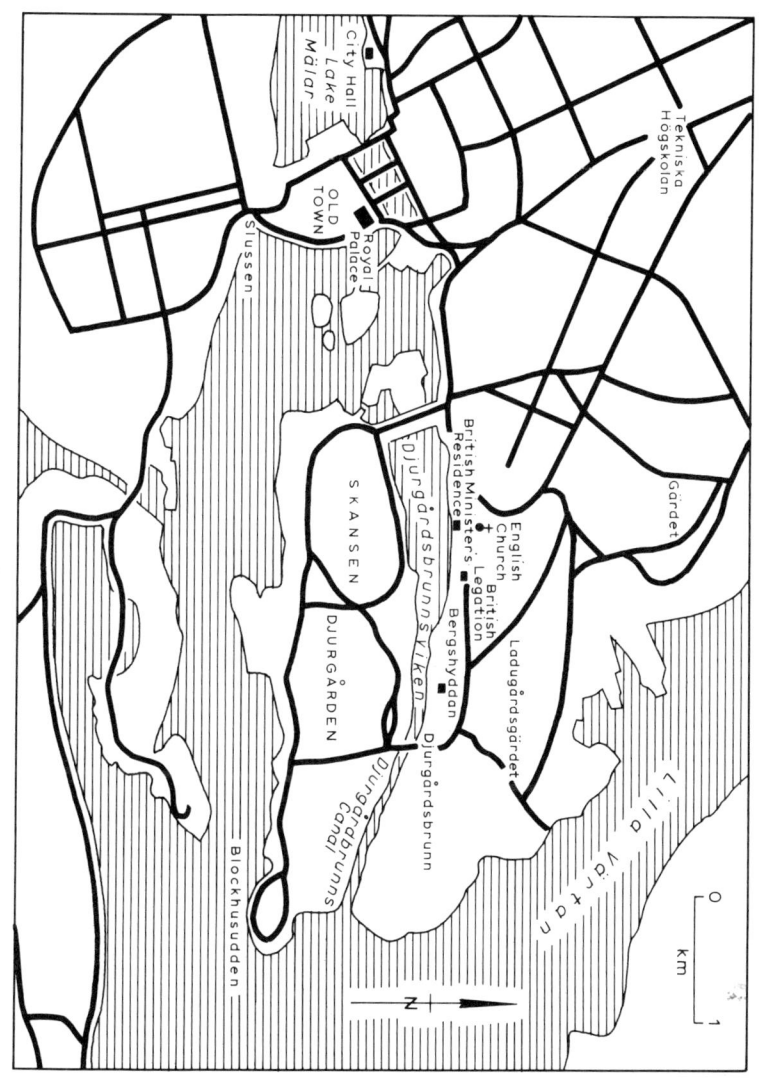

Stockholm

# 1
## Introduction

From the end of September 1939 until March 1945 I was Press Attaché at the British Legation in Stockholm and was lucky, as my knowledge of Scandinavia, in particular of Sweden, the languages, literature, history and people, and a wide circle of friends eased me into the job without much difficulty. The key to my love of Scandinavia was Anna Paués (26 September 1867-2 September 1945). She was a mountain of soft flesh with the face of a kindly, smiling cat. An old maid to the last she loved the young and was loved by them. She was an unselfconscious nudist on her annual holidays in the Black Forest where she propelled her giant form along the well-marked paths around the Kuranstalt, equipped only with a spiked stick and sensible boots. The daughter of a great peasant family of thirteen brothers and sisters, all eminent academics and public servants, descendants, as all good Swedes are, of Stormor i Dalom, the great mother in Dalarna. I got to know many of her family over the years and one of her nephews, Wilhelm, was detailed by Swedish intelligence to keep an eye on me when I was in Sweden during the war. We have remained firm friends ever since. Anna was a Fellow of Newnham and university lecturer in Anglo-Saxon. In 1934 she was given the honorary title of Professor in Sweden, the first Swedish woman to achieve this distinction.

As an undergraduate at Cambridge I read modern and mediaeval languages. My main languages were French and German and I was only acquiring a reading knowledge of others. But I got bored with old German which seemed to consist almost entirely of disconnected fragments. This led me to search for someone, not only a philologist, but interested in literature and social history who could get me reading Icelandic where there was a wealth of poetry and prose completely preserved from the earliest traditions in Scandinavia to the Viking expansion East and West and the discovery and settlement of Iceland in the 9th century.

I found Anna Paués quite by chance and she agreed to give me extra tuition in Icelandic. This she did in the evenings in her house in the Huntingdon Road. After a year she suggested I should learn modern Swedish in which she also gave beginners classes. I attended these and went on with private tuition, learning Swedish from Swedish translations of Icelandic sagas, rather as though one were to start learning modern English from translating the Anglo-Saxon of Beowulf. Anna introduced me and many of my friends to Scandinavian girls staying as paying guests with Cambridge families and it was in this way that I met my future wife, Hellis Fellenius, on her 18th birthday at the Coggins' who had a house at Fulbourn. All this led to visits to Sweden and I finally took an examination in Swedish in my fourth year when I was reading law and researching into Henrik Ibsen. I applied for, and won, a studentship for a year in Scandinavia during which I hoped to complete a fellowship thesis for Trinity. I read Ibsen's manuscripts in Oslo University Library under the supervision of Professor Francis Bull, that endearing omniscient man whose brother said of him 'Francis knows everything but that is all he knows'.

Francis played a heroic part in the Norwegian resistance when, as a prisoner in Grini concentration camp, his talks to his fellow prisoners were a major factor in maintaining morale. Having gone through theatre records in Oslo and Bergen and then in Copenhagen, I moved over to Stockholm to experience another genius in the history of literature, Professor Martin Lamm, who invited me to his seminars and introduced me to the world of Strindberg, the perfect antithesis to Ibsen.

During this time I received a telegram from Queens' at Cambridge to ask if I would accept a Fellowship in Modern Languages. Knowing little of the College I took the advice of two friends who had recently been elected to the governing body. They recommended me to accept and so I did, giving up any pretensions to Trinity.

*Introduction*

On my return to Cambridge that Autumn I was invited to take on a new university post as Assistant Lecturer in Scandinavian Languages and Literature. A year later Hellis and I married and settled down in Cambridge. This was the beginning of much activity in the university on the Scandinavian front.

The years up to the outbreak of war were spent building up interest in Scandinavia, writing and lecturing and travelling and getting Scandinavian plays put on in Cambridge and London, including an effort with Nancy Price and her People's Theatre to stage Pär Lagerkvist's *The Executioner* (*Bödeln*) which Eric Mesterton, the Swedish Lecturer in London University had adapted to the stage from the original short story. I got the producer Pelle Lindberg, a friend of Pär Lagerkvist's, to come over and produce the play together with some more conventional Ibsen plays for Nancy Price. *The Executioner* was a disaster and only ran for a week. Anti-Nazi plays had no appeal at that time.

The Scandinavian countries were only of marginal interest in pre-war politics and the well-meaning efforts of Rickard Sandler, the Swedish Foreign Minister in the League of Nations, and with his Nordic colleagues were of little avail; but there was no doubt that the Germans were taking a deep interest in these countries.

One of my many friends in the context of Scandinavia was Commander Frank Stagg, an expert on Denmark who had been deeply involved in subversive activity in that part of the world in World War I. One of his more amusing exploits was to have tins of Norwegian sardines filled with croton oil shipped to the Germans with dire results for their troops at a critical moment of the war.

In 1938 I spent the summer in Iceland and quite by chance ran into a group of German anthropologists and geologists, so called, engaged in anthropometric research on behalf of Rosenberg in order to prove that the Icelanders were the perfect Nordics. Of course they are not, being largely mixed in their origins. The geologists were concerned with proving that Vatnajökull, the great glacier, was proof of the validity of Wegener's theory of the floating continents. In reality they were teaching the Icelanders to glide which gave them cover to survey air and submarine bases. All this I gathered in evenings round their camp fire singing Nazi songs. When I came back I asked Stagg what to do with my information and he sent me to a Royal Marine Major in the Admiralty who was courteous and disbelieving but, nevertheless, kept my notes and rather detailed sketch maps. It was not until 20 March 1939 that the report which I had made in the Autumn of 1938 was passed on by the Intelligence Division of the naval staff at the Admiralty to the Under Secretary of State at the Foreign Office. I heard nothing more from the Admiralty until the war had broken out and I was in the British Legation in Sweden. A message reached me through the Naval Attaché asking me to join a trawler which was to proceed on a hush hush survey expedition to Iceland. They were somewhat disturbed when I pointed out that I was no longer a free agent but employed by the Foreign Office in Sweden. Later when we occupied Iceland I was approached again for information about railway facilities. I replied that there was no railway, but learnt later that in spite of this our expeditionary force was accompanied by a railway party which remained in Iceland throughout the war.

In 1938 Hitler got away with one villainy after another and, there being very little sign of any reaction from our own government or our French allies, it was difficult for individuals to know how to prepare for the inevitable conflict. I did two things. The first was to dig an air raid shelter in the garden. This provided the necessary physical outlet for my sense of outrage. The second was to try and find out how to volunteer for something or other where my languages and knowledge of some of Europe's countries could be of use. My friend Frank Stagg put the word round and so did Ivison MacAdam of Chatham House. Suddenly I received a summons with two friends of mine, Charles Seltman, a classical archaeologist at Queens' and Gordon Welchman, a Fellow of Sidney Sussex, a mathematician with whom I had been at school at Marlborough. We reported, with a number of people, on 20 March 1939 at 10.15 a.m. to Commander Denniston on the fourth floor of Broadway Buildings. We discovered that this was the Headquarters of the 'friends', or MI6 and were given an induction course in cipher breaking.

Our inquiring minds enjoyed betting on the various options. When one thinks of the sophistication of Enigma and Ultra, to which Gordon Welchman contributed so much, our do-it-yourself methods were incredibly primitive and yet reasonably effective.

After signing the Official Secrets Act for the first of many times, we were put through a course and then let loose on intercepts. The first examination was done by mathematicians who worked with

Introduction 5

miles of ticker-tape in long corridors until they identified a repeat and finally presented the message in its original form of alphabetical or numerical groups more or less intact. Then came the deciphering of the language using the repeats as clues, the vowels or consonants until one finally broke the cipher. Some were relatively easy and one became adept at reading them. Others were infinitely complicated and some were impervious to our efforts. As we improved so we gave up regular attendance and came in for weekends to keep our hands in. Hellis and I had some nights away from home at the expense of HM Government at the Cumberland Hotel, the height of luxury for a penurious university don. We would have an enormous breakfast. I would go off for the day cipher breaking and we would meet in the evening for a theatre and go home on the Sunday morning. In fact this was my last experience of cipher breaking except for a revival of my interest when I got to know Rickard Sandler who had earlier been Swedish Foreign Minister. He was a keen cryptographer and was the first person to introduce me to the commercial enigma machine about which he was well-informed and helpful. I had no idea at that time of how the Poles and the French and we had acquired one of the German military machines which was the basis for the intelligence work done at Bletchley.

At the outbreak of war I received a summons to report to Broadway again but before that the Foreign Office had decided they needed me for something else. I had no idea that this other task was not connected with the first but had learned to ask no questions. I was told to report to 32 Chesham Place on 25 May 1939 where some twenty of us were informed that we were the planning staff for a future propaganda ministry in the event of war. We were issued with identical slim black bags without any identification or royal cipher, signed for the keys, signed once again the Official Secrets Act and then were told that we were to be concerned with information. To start with I thought this was intelligence but it turned out, of course, to be propaganda. While nominally under the wing of Chatham House, the Royal Institute of International Affairs, we were the responsibility of Lord Perth who had just retired as Ambassador in Rome after distinguished service as the first Secretary General of the ill-fated League of Nations. I had no idea what Lord Perth's function was. He could have been the Head of the Secret Service for all I knew but the identity of my companions was different from that of those with whom I had signed on at Broadway. Many of them were colleagues of mine during the war and have remained firm friends in different incarnations in later years. Con O'Neil, the bottom of whose black bag burst one day and revealed a beautiful newly caught trout, had just resigned, for the first of many times, from the Foreign Office, this time over Munich and was writing for *The Times*. Enid McLeod was in charge of us all and it was she who sent me to the Embassy in Paris at the end of the war. Joe Parrott who later joined us in Sweden was another. He had been tutor to King Peter of Yugoslavia, was concerned with Slavonic studies at Edinburgh University and was our Balkan expert. My area was Scandinavia.

Another friend was Michael Balfour who was closely associated with von Moltke and the Kreisauer Kreis. In the meantime Toby O'Brien, who was running the press side of the British Council, assured me that Lord Lloyd was determined that the British Council should be the propaganda arm of the Government in a future war and that I had been picked for a job in Scandinavia. In fact I nearly joined the British Council when I went down from Cambridge as did many of my friends and was attracted by Toby O'Brien's stories of world tours with Lord Lloyd in a flying boat of Imperial Airways.

A further confusing development was to be instructed to report to Rowland Kenney of the Foreign Office News Department who told me to pay no attention to anyone else as the Foreign Office would be responsible for all information work if a war came. One day the secrecy of our group was shattered when we arrived in Chesham Place to find a letter addressed to The Ministry of Information, London, with the following words scrawled across it in pencil by the Post Office 'ask the German Embassy'. They were asked to explain this breach of security and replied 'Oh, if ever we are in doubt about an address we always ask them, they always know. So we then became aware that one of the Abwehr offices of the German Embassy was opposite our headquarters. What with identical black bags and our furtive toings and froings it was not difficult for them to put two and two together, particularly as some of us were undoubtedly on their files. I was well-known to them through Karl von Abshagen, a Canaris man who used to come and stay with me in Cambridge. He was ostensibly the representative of some German provincial papers and acted on behalf of various German wine growers, supplying us with some excellent Piesporter Lay for the cellar at Queens'. His nephew, Helmut Lindemann, hung around throughout the war in the Grand Hotel in Stockholm to be available to me in case of need. The need never arose.

Our Chesham Place meetings were moved to Belgrave Square and continued until the long vacation. Then we all set off on special tasks. Mine was to go to Scandinavia and report to Rowland Kenney of the Foreign Office News Department on local media, the press, radio, films, publishing and communications in general and to make contact with the opposite numbers of Chatham House in Sweden, Norway, Denmark and Finland. I was given introductions by Rex Leeper to our Ministers in the British Legations in Stockholm, Helsinki, Copenhagen and Oslo. Lord Perth insisted that my recommendations should be agreed by each Head of Mission (PRO/FO 395/643). My letter to Rowland Kenney of 16 June 1939 suggested that I should be referred to 'as a member of the Planning staff of the proposed Ministry of Information' and that I was visiting Scandinavia in order to examine the effectiveness of British propaganda, to make recommendations for its extension or modification in peacetime and to prepare an effective plan of action in wartime. These objects would cover my investigations in all fields (press, industry, banking, entertainment, politics, etc.).

I left for Scandinavia on 24 June and took Hellis and the children with me to stay with her parents in Sweden in their lovely country house Viksberg near Södertälje, where we had spent so many happy holidays in summer and winter over the years. The information I collected was public knowledge but my reports and recommendations were not. My task was known only to one person in each of our four legations. My reports were written in the security of the legation offices and were sent home by diplomatic bag together with my notes. When I reported to Rowland Kenney of the Foreign Office on my return at the end of August, he asked me what I had been doing all these months as he had received no reports. My reports had all been sent off by safe hand with the Masters of British ships of the Ellerman Wilson line but never arrived. I had to sit down and re-write them all out of my head without any notes.

Another instance of poor communications was when I reported to the Chancery of our Stockholm legation to receive instructions about my return. I overheard a telephone conversation with London about the travel arrangements for William Strang's party returning from negotiations with the Russians which had been aborted by the Ribbentrop/Molotov Pact. Questions were being asked about the time of arrival of HMS *Sheffield* at Bergen to take them home and about me joining the party. I begged the officer concerned (Urquart) to break off the call and send a most immediate cypher telegram to the Foreign Office asking whether this call had been originated by them. I suspected it came from Hamburg where most of this traffic was routed and listened to by the Abwehr. A very prompt reply confirmed that no such call had originated in the Foreign Office. I myself decided not to return by HMS *Sheffield* but to take my car back by the normal Swedish Lloyd service from Gothenburg, leaving Hellis and the children with their Swedish grandparents in the country until the situation was more certain.

While I was re-writing my report I saw a lot of my friends in the British Council, in particular Toby O'Brien who assured me that the British Council was going to be responsible for the new Ministry of Information and that I was being posted to Stockholm as Press Attaché but that I must not tell the Foreign Office. In the end neither the Foreign Office News Department nor the British Council had any responsibility for the work of the Ministry of Information. Nevertheless when I finally did leave for Stockholm at the end of September I was asked to hold a watching brief for the British Council in Sweden. This I did but when I returned to London for the first time in the Autumn of 1941, I asked to be relieved of British Council responsibilities as I had quite enough on my hands on the political and press side. I suggested to the British Council that they take on a poet friend of mine from Cambridge, Ronald Bottrall, who was unhappy as a principal in the Ministry of Aircraft Production. This they did and he carried out his work with great success though the Swedes never completely believed that he was a poet and not a pugilist and remained convinced, as others do still in other parts of the world, that the excellent cultural work of the much maligned British Council is really, as is so often the case with our French friends, merely a cover for political or intelligence activity. People, I found, also had difficulty in distinguishing between the British Council and the British Consul.

I got back to London and Cambridge at the end of August and reported to Rowland Kenney in the Locarno Room of the Foreign Office. This had been divided into a clutter of hen coops in which we worked. I was in Cambridge on Sunday, 3 September when war was declared, dashed into our College air raid shelter in Walnut Tree Court when the sirens sounded a false alarm and then went to London to report for duty. Assuming wrongly that the Foreign Office was the co-ordinating arm of the activities in which I had been involved, I reported again to Kenney. I explained that full term began in Cambridge on 10 October when I would be expected to undertake my College and University duties unless otherwise required. The answer was that I would be otherwise required but could not be told. In the meantime I should wind up my affairs in Cambridge and make myself useful. I let my house to the President of the College, Dr Venn, as he was full of admiration for my home-made air raid shelter, put my books and papers in my rooms in safekeeping and squared my bank manager who had been accustomed to my overdraft since undergraduate days. He accepted my assurances that someone would replenish my account when it was going to pay me what. He was a very understanding fellow and it was not until the end of the year that I was, in fact, paid anything at all.

I made myself useful by compiling a card index of people I knew would be helpful to the war effort in Scandinavia and was surprised to find that the Foreign Office records were deficient. It was this list which became the main source of many of the appointments in the Scandinavian field in the course of the war. Then, suddenly, I was told that I was no longer the responsibility of the Foreign Office but should now move to London University in Russell Square where a Ministry of Information was being set up. The place soon filled with people hanging around waiting to do jobs to which they had been vaguely allocated. I was left to see what I could usefully do.

One day I called in on a charming Admiral who was the Chief Censor and told him that I had heard lots of complaints from foreign correspondents that the use of English and French as the only languages for cables was an unnecessary restriction. I suggested that teams of multilingual censors could easily cover at least the main Indo-Germanic languages. He bet me a bottle of port that I could not organise such teams. I took on the bet and won, although I was never able to claim my bottle as I was whisked off to Sweden before I could. But I got some teams together. They were all security checked, and I did some trial runs with one team for a succession of nights in the Central Telegraph Office. Our Censor was a retired Colonel from Kent who tended at the start to treat us as enemy agents, but he warmed to the task and was most generous with his flask of whisky in the bleak night hours. We had to read out translations of the press telegrams in English. He then taught us how to use the blue pencil and we soon became quite good at understanding the routine.

Then suddenly I was told to hand over my passport for diplomatic visas for Norway and Sweden as I had been appointed Press Attaché in Stockholm and must report forthwith. I had a good talk with Björn Prytz, the Swedish Minister on 20 September and also with Villgot Hammarling, the Swedish Press Attaché, the successor to Oscar Thorsing who I was to meet again as Head of the Press Department in the Swedish Ministry of Foreign Affairs throughout the war. I said my goodbyes to the Foreign Office and the Ministry of Information, asked for a briefing and got none except to be told that while a Press Attaché was attached to his legation, he was also expected to be attached to the Press as a reliable source of information and help. It was the usual pragmatic British approach to learning on the job. I reported to the good ship *Iris* at Tyne Commission Quay at Newcastle at noon on 23 September. She stank of fish and would obviously be no great loss to the Norwegian Merchant Navy if the Germans sent her to the bottom. As my car was swung on board and I went up the gangway I saw a familiar face. It was my favourite cousin Ernest Tennant who was going over to call on Tennants in Oslo who handled the supply of ferro-silicon to the British steel industry from their works at Bjølvefossen. Tennants had a major shareholding in this company and they had been regular suppliers since the 20's. It was vital that this source should be secured and Ernest was going over to make arrangements for his own firm and the British Government.

Ernest and I parted in Bergen where we docked on 25 September. He went on by train and I drove on by car. Ernest had another objective in his visit to Oslo in which I became involved later. He had many German connections from his time in Berlin as an officer in the occupying army after World War I and from his subsequent business with the German steel industry. He had also been involved with Ribbentrop and the Anglo-German Fellowship and was vilified publicly for being a Nazi which he was not. Like so many who had gone through the First War at the front and seen the

*Introduction* 11

horrors of starvation, inflation and revolution in Germany afterwards, he did his best to avoid a repetition. He had many anti-Nazi friends and one was a German naval officer in the German Legation in Oslo who was a Canaris man. He provided Ernest with valuable intelligence which to start with was wrongly evaluated, including the allegation that the Germans had a highly placed agent in the Admiralty and that they were reading our naval ciphers. It was not until some time before the invasion of Norway on 9 April, 1940 that this officer provided us with evidence by giving us the details of our Admiralty's plans for mining Norwegian waters on 8 April. We never knew whether there really was a German agent in the Admiralty or whether their intelligence was the result of competent cipher breaking. It could have been either or both.

The Germans were still reading our naval ciphers at that time as a result of indiscreet radio chatter in the Red Sea during the Abyssinian war and we did not change them until later.

I arrived at my father-in-law's home on 26 September to join Hellis and the two children Frank and Lotta. The next day I reported to the legation in Stockholm and started house-hunting.

I called on Bill Montagu-Pollock, our Counsellor, who had helped me on my mission in the summer. He introduced me to the Minister, Sir Edmund Monson, who received me with great courtesy but hoped that my vulgar propaganda would not compromise the legation. A combination of luck and chance had landed me in Sweden, but I was without any briefing on British policy if there was any, whether political, military or economic and in particular on the supply of Swedish iron ore to Germany.

Sweden was in a state of shell-shock after the German victories in Poland. I discovered my task was not as straightforward as I had thought and that there were other forces in the field of which I had not heard, shading my white activities to grey and black from time to time. This book is about my experience of Sweden on the touchline of World War II. When I showed some draft chapters to Sir Christopher Warner, my Foreign Office boss in 1945, he laughed and said, 'Peter, for God's sake we have got to live with these people. You cannot publish now. Wait for 40 years.' This I have done and trust my own relations with Sweden will not suffer. My impressions are entirely personal and in no way implicate any British Government past or present.

# II
## Sweden 1939-45

Sweden at the outbreak of World War II was regarded as an enviable socialist paradise which had grown peacefully by avoiding all the European wars since Napoleon, beginning with the benign rule of the Marshal who turned against him and founded the Bernadotte dynasty. Sweden was 'Sweden, the middle way' of Marquis W. Childs, the country whose European empire had covered the whole of northern Europe, retreated into its shell and re-emerged as one of the small powers. The loss of Finland had, to some extent, been compensated for by the Union with Norway until these two countries agreed to separate in 1905. This crisis was solved without armed conflict but it left much bitterness. The picture of Nordic unity and brotherly love between the northern peoples was sadly shattered by the events of the last war, although the Nordens Frihet movement in Sweden became a solid bastion of resistance to Nazi penetration of the Nordic countries and support for their neighbours under German occupation. Sweden with Rickard Sandler as Foreign Minister was a strong supporter of the League of Nations and was held up as a paragon of virtue. Sandler was a great admirer of Eden and insisted on wearing an Anthony Eden hat which was too big for him. He finally left the Government in December 1939 on the failure of his so-called Stockholm plan to remilitarise the Åland Islands so as to help Sweden and Finland resist attack by Germany or Russia. Russia always regarded with deep suspicion any getting together of the Nordic countries. The Social Democrat Prime Minister, Per Albin Hansson, was a solid right wing socialist and Sweden had for so long been under Social Democrat rule that the party had almost become tainted with patriotic conservatism. In December 1939 the socialists went into a coalition with the other political parties except the communists.

With the world struggling to extricate itself from the Wall Street crash, Swedish socialism, with its successful attempts to solve unemployment by the setting up of the Labour Market Commission, was held up as an example to be followed. Relations between employees and labour were orderly and rational and the mix of public and private enterprise was exemplified by the influence of the Wallenberg family of the Enskilda Bank. The two brothers Jakob and Marcus controlled most of the big companies and either chaired them or sat on their boards. The Socialist government made use of them in the fulfilment of their plans for economic development. The elder brother, Jakob, held the portfolio for Germany and throughout the war had the most friendly relations with the German resistance group headed by Goerdeler which came to grief with the Stauffenberg plot of 20 July 1944. Marcus was in charge of relations with Britain where his first wife had married the banker Charles Hambro, who played a leading part in S.O.E. and M.E.W.

The Swedish Co-operative and Trades Union movements, having their roots in England in the 19th century, also had close relationships with their opposite numbers in Germany, and had achieved maturity and economic muscle with very little of the vicious militancy associated with the class struggle elsewhere. Labour relations with their annual national negotiations between employers and labour were considered a model of good behaviour. Swedish economists, such as Heckscher and Ohlin, were respected internationally. Gunnar and Alva Myrdal had begun popular education in family planning, while Gunnar had alarmed the south in the USA with his monumental study of race relations and their future in that country. The Swedish alcohol monopoly was regarded as an enlightened success in dealing with the curse of alcoholism. Low cost housing had almost eliminated slums, while state-owned industries, especially in natural resources, forests, mines, water power and railways, lived happily side by side with private enterprise. An enlightened education system which had also borrowed the Danish people's high school idea of further education resulted in a well-educated and well-informed society. Sweden, with its tradition in arts and crafts, had also become a world leader in modern industrial design and functional architecture. This was exemplified by the Stockholm exhibition of 1930 in the work of Asplund which superseded the more traditional and nationalist style of Östberg and Tengbom, the sculpture of Carl Milles and the painting of the King's brother, Prince Eugen. This was the stereotype the Swedes promoted up till the New York World Trade Fair at the outbreak of war. But the Swedish idyll of the middle way was a stereotype which did not always match reality. It seems to have lingered long in the minds of labour politicians in this country who nearly always failed to go to Sweden to find out.

Ludwig Nordström, the rumbustuous writer from the north of Sweden, wrote a devastatingly cynical corrective to this virtuous self-presentation of his country in a book entitled *Lortsverige* or *Muck Sweden*. In it he revealed slums, poverty, ill health, particularly tuberculosis, paratyphoid and insanitary conditions such as the absence at that time of any sewage purification system for Stockholm for which Lake Mälar and the Baltic on either side were regarded as adequate cesspits. He of course exaggerated, but the old idyllic image persisted and tended to give Sweden a dull, smug and self-satisfied appearance. The proletarian writers of the thirties made a great contribution to their country's literature and showed a far from idyllic picture of the social scene in town and country.

The Swedish image emerged from the war of 1939-45 much tarnished and again the stereotype was one-sided and exaggerated. Sweden started the war as a pro-allied neutral, but became disillusioned by the disasters that befell the allies after the terrible defeats of Poland, Norway, Denmark, the Netherlands, Belgium and France, and then the German successes in North Africa, the occupation of Greece and Yougoslavia and the absorption of Hungary, and Rumania and Bulgaria prior to the initially successful German attack on Russia. Sweden's concession to the Germans for the transit of their troops to and from Norway, and of the Englebrecht or 163rd Oslo Division to Finland against Russia, the use of Swedish territorial waters for German troopships and warships and air space for so-called German courier flights, of which there were 3,157 from 1941 to 1944, and the supply of iron ore and ball bearings to the German war effort, all blackened Sweden's reputation, particularly in the USA. She even cut a canal through the toe of Sweden at Falsterbo between the Baltic and Öresund which provided the Germans a short cut for vessels on their way to and from England, whereby they also avoided some thirty miles of British mined waters. That she conceded too much to the Germans is not in doubt, but in fact there was an identity of interests between Germany and the allies in keeping Sweden neutral however much ignominy she might suffer in consequence. She provided a valuable window for intelligence, a base for political warfare and propaganda, white and black, and in our case a support for our help to the resistance in occupied countries.

What were the main orders of dimension we faced in Sweden? A vast country of 486,661 square kilometres, larger than the combined areas of present West Germany, Switzerland, Austria and the Netherlands. Its population was 6.3 million in 1938, double that of 1840, by comparison with 8.3 million at the present day. Stockholm had a population of 570,800 and Gothenburg of 481,600, and both have grown greatly since. In 1840 Sweden had been an agricultural country with 80.9% of the population on the land and in forestry and fishing, but by 1936 this figure had dropped to 36.7%, with industry and mining at 36.6%, trade and transport at 19.5%. In 1938 the increase in population was 3.9 per 1,000. Lost working days from strikes and lockouts had steadily decreased from the beginning of the century, from 11.8 million in 1909 to 861,000 in 1937. Unemployment was high, at 10.9% in 1938 in all trades unions. The most important industries in 1937 were iron ore and its derivatives, iron and steel manufactures, machinery and apparatus, both electrical and non-electrical, timber, pulp and paper. Sweden's most important imports were coal and coke, mineral oils, food and feeding stuffs, rubber, machinery, and automobiles and parts.

A testimony to the shortage of fuel and the need for imports and substitutes was the use of wood for heating and power. Some expensive automotive fuel was distilled from wood, as was some of their snaps. The streets of Stockholm and other towns were stacked with 3 metre high rows of logs, while cars and lorries were converted to gas generators, run either directly on wood or on charcoal. As a diplomat I had a special ration of petrol, but I converted my old Chrysler to run on a charcoal gas generator, fitted on the back like a large trunk. Spare fuel was stored in a roof rack in paper sacks full of charcoal. I became sufficiently adept to remain immaculate when lighting and fuelling my generator even in white tie and tails. The authorities set up defence zones which were forbidden to foreigners. The Swedish Foreign Office however gave me a splendid pass to navigate the defence zone of Djurgårdsbrunnsviken to our Legation in a canoe I kept in my garden. That was however a manually propelled vessel, as was also my cherished skerry cruiser *Valkyrian*, which I was allowed to sail on Lake Mälar.

Oil became the key to the survival of the Swedish defence forces in maintaining their neutrality. The War Trade Agreements with Germany and Britain depended very largely on the import of fuel, while the belligerents more and more used the Gothenburg traffic to extort concessions from the Swedish government. The British insisted on the Swedes cutting back iron-ore exports to Germany while the Germans always exerted pressure for more and often succeeded in exceeding their quota.

A rationing system was instituted, but there was rarely any great shortage of food, though I do remember rather disgusting cellulose substitutes for beef, coloured with beetroot, while coffee substitutes made the Swedes feel even more the need for their favourite drink.

The Swedish government's first act on the outbreak of war was a declaration of neutrality on 1 September 1939, after the German attack on Poland. This was followed on the 3rd, after the declaration of war by Britain and France, by a similar declaration applying to all belligerents. Neutrality for Sweden went back to the Napoleonic wars. In 1809 Sweden lost Finland which became a Grand Duchy of Russia. In 1810 Napoleon's Marshal Jean Baptiste Bernadotte was elected Crown Prince of Sweden, and subsequently King Carl XIV Johan. Sweden had lost all her European possessions and his task was to rehabilitate the stricken country and either regain Finland, or detach Norway from Denmark and establish a personal Swedish/Norwegian union. After Napoleon's defeat in Russia, there was no question of Finland being recovered and instead Carl Johan turned against Napoleon, fought the French in Germany and then attacked Napoleon's ally, Denmark. Denmark surrendered, and Bernadotte achieved the separation of Norway and Denmark and the setting up of a personal union with Norway. The two countries had joint foreign and defence policies while retaining their own autonomous legislature and domestic policies. Since then Sweden has not known war. Bernadotte concluded an alliance with Sweden's arch enemy Russia; but under his son Oscar I the old anti-Russian feelings surged up. With the Royal Navy in the Baltic in the Crimean war, and their bombardment of the Åland Islands, Oscar was tempted to join the British and French against the Russians and regain Finland. In 1855 he concluded a Treaty with Britain and France, but at the Treaty of Paris in 1856 Sweden gained nothing but the neutrality of the Åland Islands, which they looked upon as a pistol pointed at them by Russia. But Scandinavian brotherhood became the order of the day, and this was put to the test by the non-participation of Sweden in the Danish/Prussian war of 1848. Scandinavianism as sponsored by the Swedes was treated as a threat by Russia, and while the Danes were disillusioned and turned against Germany as their arch enemy, the Swedes more and more looked to Germany as their protector against Russia. Swedish-Norwegian non-intervention in 1863-64, when Denmark was attacked and defeated over the Schleswig issue by the Germans and Austrians, was the death knell of any meaningful, political and military integration of the Scandinavian states.

Henrik Ibsen's reactions reflect the mood of the time. He left Norway on 5 April 1864 and did not return to live there for 27 years. His Scandinavian idealism was destroyed by the Austro-German defeat of Denmark and the failure of the Norwegian and Swedish governments to live up to their promises in student meetings, speeches and newspaper articles to turn words into action. The Norwegian parliament voted on 29 March 1864, to come to Denmark's rescue only if one of the western powers sided with them. This resolution confirmed Ibsen in his disillusionment over his countrymen whom he condemned as phrase-makers and masters of compromise. 'The spirit of compromise is Satan' are the words of Brand. In Copenhagen he got news of the Danish defeat at Dybbøl. Passing through Berlin on his way to Rome, he saw 'the populace spitting in the mouths of the cannon from Dybbøl and for me it was a sign of how history will one day spit in the eyes of Sweden and Norway because of this affair'. It was the end of the hopes of reviving the mediaeval union of the Scandinavian kingdoms and Scandinavianism survived only as a cultural concept deeply mistrusted by the Russians.

In the Franco/Prussian war of 1870-71, upper class opinion in Sweden was Francophile, but the bulk of the population was indifferent or neutral. The German victory however set the seal on the old French influences and the new German empire became the example to be followed in politics, the army, the Civil Service, in architecture, to some extent in literature, the arts, even in trades unionism and the socialist movement. Sweden's neutrality became firmly rooted in pro-German soil, in anticipation of German support against an attack by Russia. The Russian spy mania, with its sighting of Russian saw sharpeners in every corner of the country, developed into a form of mass hallucination before the First World War.

1905 brought the Swedish-Norwegian union crisis to a head with the risk of war between the two countries. The situation simmered down to a peaceful solution, but animosities remained latent, and in Norway grew during the German occupation in World War II.

World War I led to a common interest in neutrality. The three Scandinavian Kings met in Malmö in 1914 and in Oslo in 1917 to underline their common policy. They pressed for intervention to rescue Finland from Russia, but their efforts were far outweighed by those in favour of pro-German armed neutrality. Sweden was tied to Germany economically by the exchange of Swedish iron ore for German coal. They refused the transit of allied war material to Russia across Sweden in 1915, and mined the Kogrund leads in Öresund in 1916, which confined many allied vessels to the Baltic and made entry to the Baltic from the North Sea impossible. Gustav V, who was as pro-German then as he was to be in World War II, endeavoured to mediate as unsuccessfully as he did in the last war. Pro-allied feeling grew, helped by the effect of the allied blockade of Germany. Finally, in 1917, the Conservative right-wing government was replaced at a general election by a liberal-social-democrat coalition under Edén and Branting. This was largely due to the entry of America into the war, thanks to the exposure by 'Blinker' Hall of room 40 in the Admiralty of the Zimmerman telegram and the so-called 'Swedish roundabout', which consisted of the use of Swedish diplomatic bags and ciphers by the Germans to communicate with their missions in Washington, the Argentine and Mexico. One beneficiary of this roundabout seems to have been the Swedish Chargé d'Affaires in Mexico, Herr F. Cronholm. The German Minister wrote to the German Chancellor, von Bethmann-Hollweg, recommending him for the Kronenorden second class as a consolation prize for otherwise only having a minor Chilean decoration. One consequence of the fall of this government was a switch of emphasis of Swedish trade from Germany to the allies in return for essential supplies from the West and the reduction of Swedish iron-ore exports to Germany.

World War I resulted in the independence of Finland and the return of north Schleswig to Denmark. Swedish volunteers took part on the white side against the Reds in the civil war in Finland side by side with the German-trained Finnish Jäger batallion. The Swedes and Finns nearly came to blows over the Åland Islands in 1921, but the conflict was settled without war, though Finnish suspicions of Swedish neo-colonialism were not conducive to Nordic unity.

Sweden joined the League of Nations in spite of opposition by pro-Russian socialists and pro-German right wingers. Branting, leader of the Social Democrats, believed that small nations had an important role to play in the preservation of peace through the new organisation, but they were soon to be disillusioned, not least by the alarming rise of Hitler and his ruthless policies at home and abroad. Rickard Sandler, the Swedish Foreign Minister, did not believe in passive neutrality and tried to resuscitate the idea of a Nordic military alliance to preserve Scandinavian neutrality and remilitarise the Åland Islands in what was known as his Stockholm plan. He failed and was replaced in the coalition government in December 1939 by Christian Günther, a diplomat who had been Swedish Minister in Oslo. His gentle naivety was quite inadequate to cope with the bullying tactics of the Germans. Sweden made the first of many futile gestures of mediation between Germany and the allies with an appeal from King Gustav and King Leopold of the Belgians. The Nordic Prime Ministers and Foreign Ministers met in Copenhagen on 18 and 19 September 1939, and issued declarations of Nordic solidarity and neutrality. They appealed to the Soviet Union on 12 October to respect Finland's independence in the current Russo-Finnish negotiations, and repeated this appeal at the meeting of the Nordic heads of state in Stockholm on 18 and 19 October, when they also received messages of sympathy from the neutral United States. Then came the brutal Russian attack on Finland on 30 November, exposing the weakness of all the assurances of Scandinavian and Nordic solidarity. Swedish public opinion was pro-Finnish and in favour of intervention but the Swedish government, while giving support in war material and volunteers, remained formally neutral.

The British and French had ferried war material to Finland from Norwegian ports and across Sweden camouflaged as agricultural and other equipment, thanks to the splendid efforts of Andrew Croft and Malcolm Munthe. But the Swedes were afraid of allied intervention, particularly as they suspected, rightly, that the allies were more concerned with preventing Swedish iron-ore exports to Germany than giving any really effective support to Finland. The Swedish and Norwegian governments refused the Anglo-French request for the transit of troops on 12 March, and the Russo-Finnish armistice that night put paid to any such enterprise.

As early as April 1939 the Swedish Ministry of Foreign Affairs had sent a circular to its main missions abroad pointing out that the dangers facing Sweden in the event of war would be far worse than in 1914-18, and that their hope of survival lay in convincing the belligerents that it was in their interest that Sweden should remain outside the conflict. Sweden was a more secure source of iron ore to the Germans as a neutral than as an occupied country, and to the British it was a valuable window on Germany and the occupied countries. It took three years for allied pressure to terminate the transit of German troops to Norway and bring to an end the export of iron ore and ball bearings. The Swedish ideal of neutrality fell from its pedestal and became a practical opportunist device for keeping Sweden out of the war at almost any price. The price paid was often far too high. After El Alamein and Stalingrad, Swedish public opinion ceased to be cowed by German threats. It was expressed more and more openly in spite of German protests and efforts by the Swedish government to suppress it. The Swedish government could not be tempted into the war on the side of the allies, but to a large extent hoped to expiate its sins by aid to the occupied countries and the rehabilitation of the victims of the concentration camps and of children who had suffered from the war.

The iron-ore question at the beginning of the war was uppermost in the minds of the British Government, which believed that if exports to Germany could be terminated by negotiation or force the German war machine would grind to a halt. This issue had been a major one in World War I, and was so in this war. At the outbreak of hostilities, Germany was Sweden's most important trade partner. Britain was Sweden's largest export market followed by the USA and the other Nordic countries. Swedish exports to Germany were mainly of raw materials and semi-manufactured goods; German exports to Sweden mainly of finished manufactures, coal and coke. Iron ore was Sweden's principal export to Germany, representing about half all exports in value. Swedish ore was preferred because of its high ferrous content (60% Fe). The low phosphorous content of some Swedish ores was also important for the German armaments industry. Swedish iron-ore exports to Germany dropped as a percentage of exports to Germany from a peak of 50.1% in 1939 to 24.6% in 1944, and eventually stopped altogether. As exports to Britain and the West fell away after April 1940, so exports to Germany increased from 371 million kr. in 1939 to 558 million kr. in 1941, dropped to 345 million kr. in 1944 and ceased in 1945. Timber, paper and pulp formed a larger percentage of Swedish exports to Germany once the UK market had disappeared. On the other hand the export of ball bearings grew from 1.9% to 8.4% of total exports in 1943, dropping to 2.9% in 1944 before ceasing altogether.

After the invasion of Denmark and Norway on 9 April 1940, the Germans established a blockade of the Skagerrak. Apart from the high value exports of ball bearings and special steels and machinery, with which George Binney broke the blockade, Sweden was cut off from trade with the west. The Swedish merchant marine was split in half with one half confined to the Baltic. The only opening to the west after 9 April, 1940 was through the Finnish port of Petsamo connected by a long narrow 600 kilometre arctic highway to northern Sweden. It was never possible to develop this trade to any extent. The most important link with the west, however, became the Gothenburg safe-conduct traffic, in which Swedish vessels were able to pass through the blockade in both directions. The agreement with the British and Germans stipulated that there must be an exact balance of the number of vessels entering and leaving Sweden. Both powers exercised control over this traffic and used it from time to time to exert pressure on the Swedes. Sweden was allowed to import vital necessities such as oil and petrol for the defence forces, food and feeding stuffs, and certain supposedly psychologically important goods such as coffee and bananas. The total number of incoming vessels from 1941 to 1945 was 234, as against 225 leaving Gothenburg, but the main weight of Swedish trade was with Germany.

Trade in Germany had come under state control as early as

1934 and Sweden benefited from the Germans' desire to import raw materials and export finished goods. In this 'clearing' arrangement there was a balance between Swedish iron-ore exports and imports of coal and coke from Germany. Later in 1939 the Swedes negotiated War Trade Agreements to continue 'normal' trade with each set of belligerents and a figure of 10 million tons of iron-ore exports to Germany was accepted by the allies. Sweden was classed Grade 1 by the Germans as a country of importance for delivery of raw materials, i.e. iron ore. A German study dated 10 April, 1940, the day after the invasion of Norway and Denmark, concluded: 'One might say in principle that the advantages of incorporating Sweden into the Reich would be greater than the disadvantages'. Sweden had been excluded in the planning for the invasion of Norway and Denmark; but in spite of invasion scares from time to time the Germans never decided to incorporate Sweden into their system for fear that this precious source of valuable raw material might be less secure under German occupation. The high ferrous content of Swedish ores was important since it cut labour, energy and transport costs and shortened the time factor by comparison with low grade ores of 30% Fe. Swedish iron ore-exports in 1939 were 13,650,000 tons, presumably including exports to the UK for which Hudson, our trade minister, had been negotiating at this time. Desmond Morton, Winston Churchill's 'industrial adviser', had been considering sabotage and the organisation of strikes in the ore mines. In 1940 the figure was 10,137,000 tons, almost wholly to Germany, although Narvik for a time ceased to operate altogether owing to British demolitions. In 1941 the iron-ore export figure was 9,539,000 tons; in 1942 8,625,000 tons; in 1943 an increase to 10,257,000 tons; in 1944 down to 4,598,000 tons and 1945 1,229,000 tons, when it came to an end altogether. Although the Narvik traffic resumed after 1940 it never amounted to more than 15.4% of Swedish shipments throughout the war. The declared policy of not exceeding pre-war shipments was not strictly adhered to in face of German pressure.

    The ball-bearing situation was critical. The British depended on Swedish ball bearings and special steels and machine tool supplies until production took over in Canada and the USA.

    George Binney's blockade-breaking exploits, plus small cargoes of ball bearings carried by air, made up the deficiencies in our own production during this period. While SKF in the UK was one of the main manufacturers of ball bearings for our armaments industry, this was also the case in Germany where SKF's subsidiary, Vereinigte Kugellagerfabriken AG (VKF) in Schweinfurt, Erkner and Canstatt, provided 50-60% of German production. Before the war SKF in Sweden sold only 9.1% of its exports to Germany and 34.2% to the allies, while what became occupied Europe took 34.9%. During the war occupied Europe took less and less dropping to 18.4% in 1943, Germany took more and more, rising to 64.9% in 1943, while the allies who, after 1940, could only rely on Binney's efforts, dropped to 2.5% in 1943. Germany's largest import of ball bearings came from Sweden. In 1943 it was 70% of German ball-bearing imports at a value of 24.3m Reichsmark or 10% of German production.

The crisis with the allies came with the American daylight raids on Schweinfurt which resulted in appalling losses of crews and machines. Speer, in his memoirs, expresses the opinion that if the raids had continued they could have brought German armaments production to an end. However, the damage was made good in a fortnight and production continued with the help of imports from Sweden. The American press launched a virulent campaign against the Swedes for their support of German ball-bearing production and their complicity in the death of so many American airmen. On 13 April 1944 the Americans, backed by the British, handed a threatening note to the Swedish Government. The Swedes were given to understand that the Americans might bomb the SKF works in Gothenburg, a threat made explicit later by Stanton Griffis. But on 22 April the Swedes replied, refusing to be bullied into breaking the War Trade Agreement, the terms of which were well-known to the allies. On the 28th Boheman, the Secretary General of the Swedish M.F.A., had an off-the-record conversation with the US Minister Herschel Johnson in which he defended a neutral state's right to maintain the sanctity of contract with a belligerent party. In the end agreement was reached two days after 'D' Day, to end ball-bearing exports by October 1944. This was offset by a massive pre-emptive purchase by the allies. The discussions were between Griffis and Waring on our side and Harald Hamberg of SKF, so the Swedish government was still able to sit on its moral high horse and pretend it had nothing to do with this breach of neutrality. Even though Swedish ball-bearing exports may not have represented a high percentage of German consumption, their importance was, as in our case, in special types, special steels and special machinery.

The Swedes however got round the termination of ball-bearing exports by delivering ball bearing steel and machine tools which were not included in the agreement with the allies. Neutrality in trade matters depended on not being found out.

Part of Sweden's ability to protect her neutrality was her capacity to defend herself. The Convention of 1921 had demilitarised the Åland islands. If these islands fell into the hands of Russia or Germany this would, with modern air power, certainly be the proverbial pistol pointed at the head of Sweden. Swedish and Finnish proposals to change the Convention and remilitarise the islands were agreed by all the signatories to the original Convention, including Germany, but in May 1939 the USSR refused to agree. This of course scotched all the plans for Finnish and Swedish defence cooperation in the islands and the Baltic and Gulf of Bothnia. While the Swedes had plans for two eventualities, that of a Russian attack or a German one, the Ribbentrop/Molotov pact of 23 August 1939 faced them with the grim prospect of Russo/German cooperation. With the outbreak of war there were the two declarations of neutrality and partial mobilisation while units of the army and navy stood by to be sent to Åland at short notice.

By the end of September the situation became critical, with the Soviet Union leasing bases in the Baltic states (later to be incorporated into the USSR between 15 and 17 June 1940) and facing Finland with demands for bases in the Gulf of Finland and frontier revisions in the south east of the country. The Finns began protracted negotiations with the Russians and Finland took defence measures in the Åland islands without Sweden however agreeing to any cooperation. In spite of Sandler's pleas, the Swedish government was not willing to bind itself by an alliance but was only prepared to help Finland with the delivery of arms. Suddenly the USSR attacked Finland on 30 November and took everyone by surprise. Against the wishes of Sandler and on the recommendation of Thörnell, the Commander-in-Chief, the Swedish government refused the Finnish request to send troops to Åland and delayed laying a minefield for the time being. They only moved one division to the north instead of the two they had planned in order not to appear to be provocative, an excuse frequently repeated by the Swedish government. Swedish public opinion was united in favour of intervention. The slogan was 'Finland's cause is ours'. Sandler resigned on the issue to be replaced by the gentle, soft-spoken diplomat Christian Günther in a new coalition government of all parties, except the communists. The minefield was finally laid on 6 December in Swedish territorial waters in the sea of Åland to be joined by a Finnish minefield on the Finnish side. In January 1940 another Swedish division was moved to the north. A corps of Swedish volunteers with Swedish army equipment under the command of Colonel Ehrensvärd finally took over the defence of northern Finland at the end of February 1940, amounting in the end to some 12,000 men, although the official figure was about 8,000. The Swedish volunteers never saw action nor did the few hundred British who eventually reached Finland. The Russo/Finnish armistice of 12-13 March had been brought about by Günther's mediation. Finland still retained her independence but the Åland Islands were demilitarised again. The Russians obtained a forward base at Hangö and the Finnish railways were joined to Russia at Salla thus enabling the Russians to move more rapidly towards northern Sweden if they desired.

But peace for Sweden was short-lived. Hitler began the planning of 'Weserübung', the invasion of Denmark and Norway on 21 February and on 2 April decided to carry out the operation on 9 April. The British and French warned the Norwegian and Swedish governments on 5 April that they reserved themselves the right to take the necessary measures to protect their vital interests and on 8 April they mined Norwegian waters and waited for German reactions. Unfortunately the Germans were forewarned and had jumped the gun. Hitler had not, as Chamberlain said, 'missed the bus'. The Swedes were also forewarned largely through Jakob Wallenberg from his German resistance friends. They told the Norwegians, Danes and British, none of whom took any notice. But in spite of advance intelligence the Swedes themselves did not act on it, for fear of appearing provocative. They merely called up reserve officers. But at 5 o'clock in the morning of 9 April, the German Minister, the Prince zu Wied, called on Günther to tell him how they were acting in Denmark and Norway for their protection but that Sweden need have no fear. The Swedes were however told not to commit such unneutral acts as to mobilise. Swedish warships were to be confined to their own territorial waters south of Landskrona and on the west coast while the Germans were to have unimpeded telephone and telegram connections across Sweden. This turned out to be a considerable bonus for Swedish intelligence. The Germans also insisted that ore deliveries should continue unimpeded. Nevertheless, the Swedes did mobilise very discreetly to full strength by 15 April and orders were given to shoot down any foreign aircraft entering Swedish air space without warning shots. Allied soundings regarding Swedish intervention in Norway were rebuffed and no corps of Swedish volunteers was allowed to be formed for Norway as had been the case with Finland. The Swedes watched with anxiety as the allies landed on 14, 17 and 18 April at Åndalsnes, Namsos and Harstad, and saw our retreat and withdrawal from the first two southern landings. But while the troops at Harstad moved very slowly on Narvik, the Germans there were completely cut off as we had sunk the destroyers which had transported the German troops and a large number of merchant ships. The Germans demanded the transit of war material to Narvik but this was refused, though food and medicines and later doctors and nurses were allowed. 600 German merchant seamen were evacuated from Narvik across Sweden to Germany. On 15 and 16 April a high level Swedish delegation flew to Berlin to convince Hitler that they would resist any English violation of their neutrality and this was backed by a letter to Hitler from King Gustav on 19 April declaring Sweden's determination to resist any attempt by any of the belligerents to cross her frontiers. This declaration was repeated to England and France. Hitler replied on 26 April that Germany would respect Swedish neutrality. Admiral Tamm and Gunnar Hägglöf, the head of the Swedish Ministry of Foreign Affairs Trade Department, flew to Berlin on 11 May and met Goering at his headquarters 100 kilometres west of Berlin. He was to be told that there was no question of allowing the transit of war material to Narvik. It was the beginning of the German offensive in the west, but the Swedes resisted Goering's threats though they were surprised on their return to Stockholm to find that the Germans had not attacked. The Swedes agreed however in May to allow the shipwrecked crews of the German destroyers to leave Narvik across Sweden. But the

Narvik problem solved itself for the Swedes by the allied withdrawal on 7 June and the end of hostilities in Norway on the following day.

Finally, in view of the capitulation of France, and the mistaken belief that the British were on the verge of suing for peace, the Swedes gave way to German demands for the transit of troops and material to and from Norway. This marked the final breakdown of Swedish neutrality as conceived at the outbreak of war and from now onwards it was a matter of manoeuvering between the belligerents to keep Swedish territory intact. On 8 July 1940 the transit traffic was agreed on the lines of one train daily in each direction on the railway from Trelleborg to Kornsjö and Oslo and one a week in each direction to and from Narvik and Trelleborg. There was also a verbal agreement for the horseshoe or loop transport between Trondheim and Narvik via Storlien in Sweden. The transit traffic continued until 20 August 1943 during which period 2,100,000 Germans were safely transported to and from Norway secure from allied attack.

The justification for equivocation was that the war in Norway was over. While it took time for people to recover from the national humiliation of concessions to the Germans, the government was unable to prevent entirely the press and more and more leading figures from expressing their support for the Norwegians against the Germans.

With the outbreak of war between Germany and Russia, Sweden was faced with further pressures and feared others which never materialised, but the most important demand which was finally agreed, was for the German division from Oslo to cross Sweden to Finland. Other demands, which were not known publicly and were much more important, were also conceded, such as the use of Swedish territorial waters to transport German troops to Finland, escorted by Swedish warships and the use of Swedish air space for German transport aircraft which were allowed to land on Swedish aerodromes. The Swedes agreed to German warships remaining in Swedish territorial waters longer than was permitted by international law. All these concessions were met with strong protests by the British but diplomatic pressure, the entry of the United States into the war and allied victories, stopped the Swedes sliding further down the slippery slope. The reduction of all forms of transit traffic was helped by German breaches of the agreements, the transfer of weapons and armed men in their 'Courier' aircraft and the discovery by the Swedes in the spring of 1944 of cases on the trains containing large consignments of Swedish maps destined for Norway. This led to the cessation of German army postal services under German supervision using the Swedish railways.

The Swedish declaration of 29 July 1943 abrogating the transit agreement, was handed to the Germans by Günther in Stockholm and Richert in Berlin. The Swedes called up 300,000 men, the biggest mobilisation since the spring of 1940. German faces were saved by a short joint Swedish/German communique on 5 August 1943. Oil transport to Norway came to an end on 1 October 1943 but not until September 1944 did the Swedes end all German transit through Sweden except for the sick and wounded. Finally all passage of foreign merchant ships was stopped in Swedish territorial waters in the Baltic. Sweden's neutrality was now publicly washed clean again.

During this Swedish 'Munich' period of tarnished neutrality between 1940 and 1943 they re-armed and strengthened their defences. German protests led the Swedish government to do its best to suppress free speech but this was less and less successful. Fuel for the forces was imported by the safe conduct ships from 1941 onwards. By the beginning of May 1941 Finnish/Swedish relations were less and less close and Finnish cooperation with the Germans more and more obvious. The Swedish Prime Minister, P.A. Hansson, told the Commander-in-Chief that Sweden must observe strict neutrality in any conflict between Germany and Russia. More and more German troops were in transit to the north and sea transport in Swedish waters began to be intensified. The Swedes strengthened their defences in the south but on 22 June the German attack on Russia began. After the British attack on the Lofotens in March 1941, the number of Germans moving north noticeably exceeded the number returning south. The government refused requests of the Commander-in-Chief Thörnell to occupy the Åland Islands and make preparations for intervention in Finland. On the day of the German attack on Russia, 22 June, the Germans made a number of demands, all of which were conceded, although only the movement of the division from Oslo was made known. But they did finally refuse the invitation to join the Three Power Pact, or to participate symbolically in the 'crusade against Bolshevism'. A further demand for the transit of another division at the end of July was refused and they also refused a request for leave trains to cross Sweden from Finland in spite of a second appeal by Hitler in a letter to King Gustav.

While the German offensive ran out of steam in front of Moscow, they became more and more nervous about allied action in Norway. Two successful British raids on the Norwegian coast in December 1941 led, early in 1942, to the reinforcement of German troops in Norway and the movement of strong naval forces including the *Tirpitz* to the Norwegian fjords.

The Swedes feared a preventive attack by the Germans. The Commander-in-Chief warned the government on 18 February 1942 that the Germans thought an allied offensive possible in the spring. He feared they might attack as they believed that the Swedes were unreliable and wished to bring their lines of communication through Sweden under their direct control. The Commander-in-Chief saw little prospect of defending Sweden successfully against the Germans and advocated political action to mollify them. Once again he feared mobilisation might provoke an attack. He also recommended allowing the transit through Sweden of 6,000 Germans on leave since the ice prevented them from being transported by sea. The government turned down these recommendations, no further transit of troops was allowed and there was no question of political concessions. Instead mobilisation was ordered in Skåne and Värmland and round the great lakes of central Sweden which were frozen over and provided a good landing ground for German parachutists. For the Germans frozen in front of Moscow it must have been difficult to have considered sparing the 100,000 men that they calculated would be needed to bring Sweden to her knees.

To assure the Germans that Sweden would resist any allied invasion in Northern Sweden, Gustav V wrote to Hitler to persuade him of Sweden's firm neutrality and determination to resist, to which Hitler replied on 16 April that Germany had no intention of violating Swedish neutrality. At the same time Russian submarines began to sink Swedish shipping, even in Swedish territorial waters, while their escort of Swedish warships scored no hits with their depth charges. The tide was now turning against Germany. El Alamein followed by the 'Torch' landings in North Africa, the capitulation of von Paulus at Stalingrad and pressure to end the transit traffic and strangle Swedish

German trade, all combined to make the Swedes think where their interests really lay.

But the Swedes were still nervous that a German attack might pre-empt an allied landing in Norway. In the autumn of 1942 they believed that the Germans would have 20 new divisions available to invade them. But by now Swedish morale had recovered and while thinking they would suffer severe defeats in the initial stages of a Blitzkrieg, an order was issued to the effect that 'Any order to give up resistance was invalid'. Sweden had about as many men mobilised in the army as in April 1940 (1940 - 225,000; 1943 - 201,350) with almost twice as many in the navy and coastal artillery (22,000 - April 1940; 37,900 - July 1943) and a large increase in the air force of men (6,200 - April 1940; 17,170 - July 1943;) and aircraft (170 - April 1940; 430 - July 1943). The Swedes had also begun the secret training of a Norwegian police force and a Danish brigade. These measures were a precaution against violent German reaction to the end of the transit traffic which in fact passed off peacefully.

Secret peace negotiations began at the end of the winter of 1943 between the Finns and Russians, the reaction to which was that the Germans occupied Åland on 15 February 1944. After 'D' Day there were further alarms of an allied landing in Norway and troops were concentrated on the Norwegian frontier to intervene and stop a massacre of civilians, but again no landing took place.

The Finnish armistice was concluded on 19 September 1944 and Mannerheim became President. The Germans retreated northwards into Norway pursued by their former Finnish co-belligerents, subjecting northern Finland to a grim scorched earth policy as they withdrew. The Swedes manned the northern frontier and gave refuge to 50,000 Finnish fugitives. Sweden held her troops in readiness to intervene in Norway and Denmark in case the Germans did not capitulate but once again no action was needed. Sweden gradually cut off shipping to Germany and the use of Swedish territorial waters by foreign vessels. Ten American DC3s flew from northern Sweden from 30 December 1944 onwards to transport the Swedish-trained Norwegian police units to northern Norway, together with supplies of food and medical equipment for the slave labour employed on the construction of Hitler's proposed arctic autobahn. At the end of the war the German troops, Russians, Yugoslavs, and other prisoners were repatriated across Sweden.

Sweden ended the war stronger and more confident than at the outbreak, but the Germans had no regard for Swedish military ability and were confident they could achieve by threats more than by invasion as Swedish independence depended on Sweden's compliance with German requirements for iron ore, ball bearings and the transit of troops to and from Norway and Finland. But a change in the Swedish high command with General Helge Jung replacing the pro-German Thörnell, as Commander-in-Chief, and General Ehrensvärd taking over as Chief of Staff, did much to stiffen Swedish morale. Under this new leadership the Swedes would undoubtedly have given a good account of themselves if the Germans had attacked. In spite of the often defeatist attitude of the Foreign Minister, the pro-German sympathies of the King and the lack of courage of many other members of the government, public opinion and the press gradually followed the example of the few men and women who resisted Nazi domination from the outset. Sweden was also fortunate in its Civil Servants and the Wallenberg brothers whose intelligence and skill as negotiators did so much to preserve the country's integrity even if the pure milk of neutrality as proclaimed at the beginning of the war was curdled in the course of time.

One factor which helped Swedish defence was the gradual improvement of their intelligence and security services. Swedish security activities were heavily biased against the allies. The number of agents arrested for working for the Germans was 284 while those working for the Allies added up to 935. Some 618 other arrests were recorded but there is no trace of the interests they represented.

When it came to the collection of intelligence this relied very largely on two factors. One was that on the invasion of Norway and Denmark, they allowed the Germans to use and lease their telecommunications to and from Germany and across Sweden to and from Norway and later Finland. The other factor was the very efficient decrypting which they applied to the wealth of material from the tapped and intercepted German telephone and telegraph messages, which gave a good insight into German plans. It seems however that their interpretation of this material was not very sophisticated at the start and the political or military decisions they took as a result were few or late until towards the end of the war. Thörnell, the Commander-in-Chief, and Günther, the Foreign Minister, always tended to justify their failure to mobilise in time for any eventuality by the fear that this might provoke the event they were trying to avoid. The key man in this interesting story was Professor Arne Beurling who, by the autumn of 1940, had constructed a machine to decrypt the German Geheimschreiber messages and print them out *en clair* for the Swedish General Staff and Ministry of Foreign Affairs. How far the Swedes were reading us we do not know but we suspected they were as Boheman occasionally warned our Minister Victor Mallet not to use proper names in our telegrams. For a period of time also Colonel Björnstjerna, who was in charge of Foreign Intelligence, was visited by our Naval Attaché, Captain Henry Denham, very regularly and gave him verbal accounts of German naval dispositions off the coast of Norway until he was summarily dismissed and retired by the Swedish Commander-in-Chief. Another leak of their precious decrypts was when a messenger stopped off at home on his way from the deciphering department at Karlaplan 4, to the Ministry of Foreign Affairs and photographed the intercepts in his care, selling the copies to the Russians. Another serious spy scandal was when a Swedish engineer sold the Russians the drawings of the Swedish Kalix defences in northern Sweden. Most serious of all however was the leak to the Germans by the Finnish Military Attaché in 1942 of the whole Swedish intercept secret with the result that the Germans re-routed their communications, laid a cable on the seabed and introduced more complicated combinations into their encyphering machines. But the Swedes still managed to keep going and at the end of the second Finnish war, they participated in the Stella Polaris operation under the authority of General Ehrensvärd whereby the whole staff and apparatus of the Finnish 'Sigint' with 1,000 refugees under the command of Colonel Hallamaa in four vessels found refuge in Sweden.

In December 1942, 32 Swedish 'bombes' deciphered the messages of 33 German Geheimschreibers. The total length of these messages in 1942 was 2,100 kilometres carried out by 178 individuals working around the clock. In 1940, 26,660 messages were deciphered and forwarded to the General Staff and Ministry of Foreign Affairs of which 7,100 originated from Geheimschreiber activity.

For a long time the Germans dominated the Swedish security services. The intelligence services however became more independent and concentrated on the more real threat of German invasion combined earlier with fear of Russian action, rather than on the more remote risk of an allied attack. In 1937 Adlercreutz, who was the first head of the wartime service, had, with the authority of the Swedish Ministers of Defence and Foreign Affairs, been in touch with Canaris. In return for a Swedish officer being trained in security matters and routines, he reached an understanding that the Germans would not place their own agents in Sweden, presumably because the Swedes would do as good a job for them. They kept the bargain until the end of the first year of the war, when they placed Dr Hans Wagner in the German Legation as head of the Abwehr. His task was to operate against the British and other allies with and through the Swedish security services and not against Sweden. In 1936, Lt. Col., later General Helge Jung, the successor to Thörnell as Commander-in-Chief, had been in touch with Canaris in Berlin and made arrangements for co-operation with the Abwehr on Russia and the Baltic states.

In 1937 the new defence organisation was set up with a common staff for all three services with nine sections, of which No.2 was intelligence. Adlercreutz, a stodgy unimaginative Colonel, was put in charge and told to get on with it without any experience or instruction. He had few resources and had to use mainly published material and reports from service attachés abroad. He did not trust other departments, in particular the civilian ones, such as the Ministry of Foreign Affairs. He maintained such secrecy that his reports were too restricted in circulation to be of any real value. Another informal rival intelligence service, nominally under Adlercreutz, was set up at the outbreak of war by Major Carl Petersén with extensive financial resources which finally led to his downfall. Unlike Adlercreutz he was a highly sophisticated person, much travelled and experienced and a very good linguist, having been an officer in the Persian Gendarmerie and taken part in the civil war in Finland in 1917-18. He was also a close friend of Marshal Mannerheim. The Swedish intelligence services however were caught unaware by the Russian attack on Finland on 30 November 1939. They were fairly well informed in advance of the German invasion of Denmark and Norway both by Juhlin Dannfelt, their military attaché in Berlin, and by Jakob Wallenberg. Although they passed the information on to Oslo and Copenhagen and informed us, neither the Swedes nor the Norwegians nor the Danes nor ourselves reacted in any way until the horse had bolted. The Swedish government took a very long time to learn how to evaluate intelligence and use it operationally. The many wolf-wolf threats of German attacks in the west from November 1939 onwards had lulled them into a state of false security. Only later did the Swedish government begin to appreciate the importance of intelligence for national policy decisions.

The Swedes however were very well-informed in advance of the German attack on Russia on 22 June 1941. In addition to the radio traffic they had a wealth of material from decrypting ciphered telegrams and telephone conversations, particularly with the German C-in-C in Norway, General von Falkenhorst. Björnstjerna, before his forced retirement in 1942, had developed the foreign division of the intelligence department into a more or less self-contained unit with access to Ministers. Poor Adlercreutz was left with internal security and the unofficial G or C Bureau run by Petersén who paid little attention to him. Adlercreutz was sent back to his old post as Military Attaché in Finland in 1942 and Commander Daniel Landquist succeeded Björnstjerna, later to become head of the whole service. Landquist was very helpful to us and after a visit to the Admiralty in February 1943 when he met Commodore Rushbrook, he took home a code book for direct communication in case of need. He was reprimanded by Thörnell and the book had to be returned without explanation. But Landquist did well and overcame the old inter-departmental jealousies by putting himself at the head of a well coordinated intelligence service which had the support of Colonel (later General) Ehrensvärd, the new chief of the General Staff. He initiated a wider distribution of information to users at the centre and in the field with an improved evaluation of the material. Landquist had instituted weekly meetings with the Ministry of Foreign Affairs. In 1944 he started to report to the Government as a whole. At the end of the war Landquist was succeeded by Colonel Juhlin Dannfelt who had been Military Attaché in Berlin where he had served since 1937. Erik Boheman, the secretary General of the Ministry of Foreign Affairs, redressed the balance which had been heavily in favour of the Germans by telling Ehrensvärd 'To put an end to the favouring of axis service attachés that had hitherto been the practice and to pay attention to the allied attachés who had good excuse to feel they had been cold shouldered'.

The Swedes also became the involuntary victims of our

deception operations against the Germans culminating in 'Fortitude 2' and 'Graffham'. The object was to make them keep as many troops as possible in Norway in the belief that major allied landings were going to take place. When I returned from a visit home in December 1943 I let the Germans know that I had instructions to start a propaganda campaign about British landings in Norway. Wagner swallowed the bait, hook, line and sinker and I have a Swedish intercept of one of his cipher telegrams reporting my preparations to the OKW. Then early in 1944 our former Air Attaché, Bill Thornton, was sent to Sweden with the spurious rank of Air Vice Marshal equipped with a large expense account. He was to be seen wining and dining his old friends in the Swedish air force, in particular General Nordenschiöld, its Commander-in-Chief, so as to make it appear that high level talks were under way. At the same time we sent out a Brigadier to talk to the Swedes about rail transport. We also installed two additional radio operators in the Legation to baffle the Germans with increased meaningless traffic. How far all this deceived the Swedes we will never know. But it certainly helped to keep the German troops in Norway away from the Normandy beaches.

The Swedes suffered from leaks and the expulsion of their service attachés from Russia, Germany and the USA. A serious crisis was that of Commander J.G. Oxenstierna who had taken over as Naval Attaché in London in 1942. He was recalled at the request of the British authorities who discovered that his reports were being relayed to the Germans under the cover name of 'Josephine' by a Doctor Karl Heinz Krämer of the Abwehr. The latter had joined the German Legation Press Department as Wissenschaftlicher Hilfsarbeiter in October 1942 and was later given the rank of Secretary. He communicated with Berlin through the air attaché's cipher which we intercepted and cracked. Krämer was a man about town and a great social success with the girls. Two girls in the Swedish General Staff slipped him copies of Oxenstierna's reports unknown to Oxenstierna. All conceivable sources for these 'Josephine' reports were investigated including one of Sir William Strang's domestics. But finally Oxenstierna was asked not to return when he went home on leave and was unable of course to understand the mystification. From post-war interrogation it was thought that much of the material was concocted by Krämer from the reading of recent numbers of British technical journals which by then were arriving regularly in Swedish bookshops. We succeeded in penetrating Krämer's office and obtained copies of his messages which seem to have been appreciated by the OKW but were not regarded by us as of any real significance. With the imminence of 'D' Day all diplomatic communications from Britain were cut off, but Krämer was not deterred and continued his Josephine messages. Krämer did us the service of concocting a Josephine report from Stockholm to the Abwehr at 1910 hours on 9 June 1944 confirming our deception that the landings on the Normandy beaches were merely a diversion from the main landing in the Pas de Calais. Unfortunately when it came to 'Market Garden' (Arnhem) later on he nearly guessed right. It was a sad experience for Oxenstierna who was unaware of the reasons for the British action which was never explained at the time.

Swedish intelligence activities reached a very high standard in the course of time and the Swedish government became converted to the use of intelligence as an instrument for making policy decisions.

The last weeks of the war present a confused picture as far as Sweden was concerned. There were appeals from the Norwegians and Danes for her intervention and preparations made to intern the German troops in Sweden. There were curious communications from Himmler to the British and Americans via his masseur Kersten and Walter Schellenberg and Bernadotte. Finally there were the admonitions from the allies to the Swedes not to interfere and the relatively peaceful and well-disciplined capitulation of the Germans in Norway and Denmark. The war was over and the Swedes were now able to do much to alleviate distress in Norway and Denmark and other countries which had suffered from the German occupation. Many victims of German concentration camps were nursed back to life by the good offices of Count Bernadotte and the Swedish Red Cross. Although the Swedish government was not allowed to interfere by the allies, individual Swedes did some remarkable things, like Nordling, the Swedish Consul General in Paris, who played a part in the German capitulation, and saving Paris from destruction. There was the brave young man Raoul Wallenberg who was lost without trace by the Russians after saving the lives of thousands of Jews in Hungary. There was Harry Söderman who was responsible for training the Norwegian and Danish police troops in Sweden. Single handed and much to the annoyance of the allied High Command, he went over to Norway before the capitulation to stop the Germans taking reprisals against the Norwegians. He released Norwegian prisoners in Oslo jails and the concentration camp of Grini. Swedish humanitarian action during and after the war did much to erase the ignominy the country suffered from the gymnastics of its neutrality policy.

# III

## Our Life in Sweden

We were very fortunate in having a country base in my father-in-law's house Viksbergs Säteri near Södertälje. We lived in various flats in Stockholm. First in Furusundsgatan on Gärdet, a little modern one, a development of the 1930s. Then we had a rather dingy Victorian flat on Valhallavägen 46 and finally one on Styrmansgatan, within easy walking distance of our Legation. For the summer we moved out into Djurgården, first to a dilapidated fretwork summer villa called Fridhem down the Djurgårds canal near the lovely old house Brunnsgården which Bill Pollock, our Counsellor, had rented from Countess Edle Leuhusen. We had strange visitors at night and discovered that it was formerly a seamen's brothel and that our children's nanny was welcoming clients through her bedroom window. I remember mid-summer 1940 when our fortunes were at their lowest and we invited British, American and Swedish friends to a bonfire party. Gunnar and Alva Myrdal were with us, having just returned from America, and were bewildered at our refusal to accept defeat, as we stood alone. I can see Gunnar now on that cool summer evening, wearing an overcoat and a Homburg hat, dancing in the twilight like a slow motion gloomy bear round the dying embers. The next summer, 1941, we moved into one of the green wooden cottages on the right of the road to Djurgårdsbrunn's restaurant by the bridge over the canal. Bill Pollock, our Counsellor, had occupied the house before and we stayed in this cottage till the autumn of 1941 when we

*Valkyrian*, drawing by the author

moved into Bergshyddan and the painter Bo Beskow and his American/Italian wife Ted (Zita) took over. The cottage opposite belonged to Alf Sjöberg, the Theatre and Film Director, and his wife. We rented Bergshyddan that autumn for two years, leasing it from Ingrid Bergman's dentist husband, Petter Lindström. We had very little furniture and were grateful to her for letting us borrow and buy some of hers. Viksberg, however, was always a standby in summer and winter and in the last year when we were back in a flat in Stockholm, my father-in-law let us have the south wing of the house which up till then had been rented by the Lindfors family. He was a retired cavalry captain and publisher whose daughter Viveca made a good career as a film actress in America.

Viksberg was a welcome refuge from the hectic life of Stockholm. The house was on Lake Mälar in a bay at the mouth of the Södertälje canal. It stood on high ground looking west over the lake with Stockholm to the east and Södertälje to the south. It was surrounded by forest and farmland with a huge granite cliff, Korpberget, towering above it to the east, and on the south in the valley were the farm buildings, a brickworks, a well-sheltered harbour and boat house and my mother-in-law's poultry farm with her flocks of white turkeys, white geese and white ducks. The 17th century white stone house had originally been a one-storeyed hunting lodge belonging to Queen Kristina whose name survived in a spring of clear water by the roadside called Kristina's Källa. I often sailed out to Viksberg from Stockholm and based my boat *Valkyrian* there when we were on holiday in the summer. I had bought her from Gösta Sandström, the editor of our weekly newspaper *Nyheter från Storbritannien*, and I made her over to SOE as we often used her for planning, briefing and de-briefing sessions out of range of tapped telephones and microphones.

*Valkyrian* survived and was passed on to new owners after the war. Sailing was confined to Lake Mälar as the sea coast was a forbidden defence area, but the lake is big and you can explore it for days without repeating yourself. One of my most memorable outings was with T.S. Eliot in an earlier boat called *Undra*. He had come over to lecture and jumped at the opportunity of a sail as he had never sailed in his life. We had a fascinating afternoon in very stormy weather. I steered and he baled and talked of the poets who had most influenced him in his life - Kipling, Lear and Lewis Carroll. I took him home to dry and have tea in front of our open log stove and he charmed the children with stories and sent them later what he said was his best book, *Old Possum's Book of Practical Cats*.

Viksberg harbour was also, over the years, the base of operations for a most remarkable craft *Ahto*. She had been bought by my thrifty father-in-law at a Customs' auction, having been confiscated for smuggling alcohol from Finland. She was a large tub with a canoe stern, an open cockpit under a Victorian awning with room for some twenty passengers and deck space above the cabin inside which we could sleep half a dozen.

Ragnar, the chauffeur, handyman, gardener, was in charge of the engine which was continuously under repair. *Ahto* was often arrested by the Customs' cutters when we sailed through Stockholm under the bridges into the sea before the war, but they gradually got used to the fact that she was a reformed character with Professor Fellenius at the helm. Expeditions were usually mounted on the spur of the moment, often in the middle of a house party late at night when we would decide to make for the family island Skälvik in the Stockholm archipelago, or go fishing round Möja or the reefs of Gillöga far out in the Baltic. Less frequently but, with equal spontaneity, we would sail over to Åland and the harbour of Mariehamn with its splendid fleet of Mr Eriksson's tall ships. We once had to abandon ship in a fog on the Swedish coast on the way back, make our way to the shore in the long boat and accept the hospitality of a delightful smuggler who helped us recover *Ahto* before the Customs' men could claim her as salvage. He housed us for the night and entertained us with songs to his accordion. His summer guest that evening, and for many years before, was the police chief in Uppsala who regularly had him sent down every autumn so that he could spend a comfortable warm winter in prison. Each year he built a Customs' cutter so designed that it drew far too much water to follow him over the reefs round his island. Our smuggler became a firm friend, as also were Oscar and Petrus - two fishermen from Möja. Having met an old seal hunter dressed in his pelts and armed with a long spear with which he despatched his victims on the ice in the winter, I wanted to go to Gillöga with them and see some seal. Once we were fishing there and sleeping in the hut on the shore by the old

World War I mine which was used as a sea mark when they woke me up at dawn telling me there was a seal on an outlying rock. I stalked it carefully upwind and crept up the rock only to find that my fishermen friends had rigged up a splendid practical joke in the shape of a drowned pig which they had propped up with driftwood to look like what it was not. From then on I was known as the English seal hunter.

But back to the house at Viksberg. The south wing overlooking the farm was used as a guest house. The north wing was inhabited by Inspektor Hurtig, the farm manager, who also managed the forest and knew all about where to find mushrooms, elk, roe deer, hares, foxes, badgers, capercailzie and blackcock. The fish in the lake were not all that plentiful, but in the days before pollution we found crayfish in the streams. Gös (best translated pike perch) one caught at sundown, while pike occasionally became plentiful. Ragnar, the handyman, was also the chauffeur and mended and maintained everything including the two cars. One was an antique Willys Knight saloon with wooden spoked wheels which transported the whole family with a pack of dwarf pinchers, pet birds, luggage, milk and food to and from Stockholm. The other car was a T Ford which bounced its way to and from the station and other friends' houses. Another of Ragnar's responsibilities was ice which he cut from the lake in the winter. This was stored in the huge ice cellar on the north slope below the house mixed with plenty of sawdust for insulation. When he was cutting the ice and loading it on his sledge, we used to make holes in the ice and catch the occasional pike. Ragnar also drove the farm horses, carts and machinery supervising sowing and harvesting. The elk, in spite of an annual national cull of thousands, do much damage to agriculture and horticulture in Sweden and their presence was felt around Viksberg. One spring the Professor found a little elk calf abandoned by its mother in the bullrushes of the harbour. It was promptly christened Moses and brought up on bottles of milk. It became a domestic pet, walked into the house and followed the Professor on his daily walks round the farm until it grew too big and had to be given to the zoo at Skansen where we used to visit it regularly.

The main house, the *corps de logis,* had been added to with another floor in the 19th century. The Professor had been born there but his father had to sell it as the result of financial disasters. Later in life the Professor bought it back, having restored the family fortunes by judicious investments in property in Stockholm. He had made a name for himself as a hydraulic engineer and in the course of designing and building a stretch of the Narvik-Luleå Railway, he met and married Emy Janse. Her Walloon family had settled in Norrland in the 17th century when Louis de Geer imported skilled workers to help expand the industry. The Professor's family took their name from the little town of Fellingsbro in the province of Västmanland, some 150 kilometres west of Stockholm. As was the habit in the 17th century the family name was Latinised to Fellenius.

Wolmar Fellenius was an engaging eccentric. Competent in his field of hydraulic engineering, he had made his name in the construction of railways, dams and harbours. Honoured in Germany and America with honorary doctorates, his academic fame as Professor at the university was enhanced in the eyes of his pupils by his habit of going to sleep in the middle of his lectures; but the young were devoted to him and he showed great kindness to students who were poorly off. His family of two daughters and three sons and many grandchildren competed with his cattle for his interest in genetics and procreation. He divided his time between handling his investments and running his farm which had to provide all the fuel and food for the family and employees. At moments he burst into paroxysms of rage at the sight of imported food such as oranges and bananas, but in the end he was reconciled to the fact that the younger generation had grown out of living in a medieval economy of only home-grown food stored for the winter by drying, salting and smoking. This huge, benign patriarch with his bald pate, his halo of white hair, white beard and spectacles, walked round the estate with his stick followed by his pack of diminutive dwarf pinchers. When he sat down they would climb all over him and get inside his shirt. His dress was the bare necessities, old cotton trousers, plimsolls with holes in the toes, and an old striped shirt without a collar. His more formal clothes were a quick-change act into a pair of dark trousers, a morning coat and a dickey to conceal the shirt he still kept on, equipped with a collar and made-up tie and detachable shirt cuffs to round it all off. He loved the produce of his farm. There were the peas which we picked as släpärter, eating them as mange touts,

The author and Anna-Lisa Leadbitter with a party of Russians and Americans sailing on United Nations Day, 1944

dipping them in hot, salted butter and drawing them through our teeth. We were always given the first milk of a cow after she had calved and he delighted in milk products of all kinds, sweet and sour, particularly filbunke, the delectable Swedish yoghurt. He kept up a running commentary on the performance of his farm and garden produce inside his bowels and one day, when we were staying on the island of Möja with my parents and had feasted the day before on cranberries we had picked in the woods, he swam out to sea to perform his morning ablutions. He suddenly shouted to my mother on shore to notice the cranberries floating on the surface as proof of his assertion that they were indigestible and were rapid movers through the digestive tracts.

Wolmar had very fixed ideas about life. On the whole we got on reasonably well, in spite of his conviction that the British were no good because we had no engineers, which meant of course that we never gave him an honorary degree. When he came to stay with us in Cambridge I took him to a Queens' College feast and he could not understand the convention of not talking shop. He found himself sitting next to a professor of engineering who would only discuss rowing and cricket and refused to comment on Wolmar's fame as a consultant for the Boulder Dam or his honorary doctorates in Germany. He enlivened the party afterwards in the long gallery of the President's lodge by flinging his arms round the President's wife, thanking her for the meal with a smacking kiss, bursting open the studs of his hard shirt front revealing his hairy chest and doing a Viking war dance. When I got back to Sweden at the beginning of the war we had a tumultuous altercation one evening when he compared Hitler with Jesus Christ. I said I was taking my family back to Stockholm immediately and never wished to see him again. Overnight, however, we both simmered down and were persuaded to keep our cool. This we did, though he remained pro-German till the invasion of Norway and Denmark. This shocked him but he still felt the Germans were superior, as the British were driven back to their island fortress and left to fight alone. But then he had news of a Norwegian colleague who had been arrested and shot by the Germans. He was deeply shocked and bade me come into his study, told me the whole story and asked whether I really believed other stories of atrocities committed by the Germans. I told him I did and gave him evidence of what we knew. He took a long time to digest this ghastly information but, in the end, came round to the view that Hitler was a villain and had misled the German people whom he still believed not to be wholly evil, but misguided. By the end of the war he was able to concede that British engineering had, to his surprise, largely been responsible for defeating Germany.

His wife Emy was eccentric and unstable but she was a superb cook and between working on her loom and chasing her white poultry, she would conjure up unbelievable meals at irregular times. On feast days such as mid-summer, weddings and christenings, the tables were loaded with summer produce, or at Christmas a dinner of dried cod, boiled in lie (lutfisk), followed by boiled ham and wort bread dipped in the pot of greasy water in which the ham had been boiled. The meal ended with boiled rice in which there was an almond which brought marriage the following year to the girl who found it. Emy was also, as a Norrlänning, an artist at preparing surströmming (Baltic herring fermented in a barrel and stored in tins which often exploded) in some twenty different ways which she and I, and sometimes Harry Söderman, ate together in a sealed room by the kitchen because the foetid stench was impossible for the rest of the house. She was famous for her less folksy lunches and dinner parties beginning with a huge smörgåsbord on a long table in the garden or the hall and then, when one was unable to eat any more, faced her guests with a five-course sit-down meal.

Time was not accelerated at Viksberg by war and the seasons followed one another unaffected by the hectic pace of the world outside. There was mid-summer feasting and dancing, harvesting and haymaking with the children riding behind the horses on top of the farm carts. There were bathing parties on the rocky promontory across the bay and in the autumn came the shooting stars in the clear night skies and later the shimmering curtains of the Northern Lights. With winter and snow came skiing and sledge rides at night with flaming torches and huge meals in front of blazing open fires in the hall. Time seemed to have stopped hundreds of years ago. It has all gone now. The estate was split up and sold soon after Wolmar's death and friends and farmhands came to pay their respects to him on his death bed when he lay for four days on a *lit de parade* in the hall and closed the book on the life of the friendly old house.

The house which for two years was our home in Stockholm was one of our happiest. It was Bergshyddan in Djurgården overlooking Djurgårdsbrunnsviken which was connected with the Baltic by the Djurgårds canal. It stood on a bluff looking south over the bay which led to Stockholm to the west. Halfway to town was the British Legation overlooking the water from the east end of Strandvägen. The Legation was easily accessible by road on skis in the winter through the woods or by boat. Our charming saffron yellow Regency house with its white frame, windows, shutters and balcony and its roofline picked out in white had been built by the royal shoemaker to Karl XIV Johan, the first Bernadotte King. His name was Nils Malmquist and he received permission in 1838 to build this villa in the Italian taste on crown land. My friend Otto Järte, Foreign Editor of *Svenska Dagbladet*, who lived not far away in another beautiful old house, told me it had been built by the King's French chef and that his royal master visited him when he rode over the pontoon bridge from his new castle Rosendal on the south bank every morning to inspect his dragoons and discuss the menu for the day; but he was mistaken. The present owner of the house, Bror Cedercrantz, tells me the visits were to an earlier house built in 1836 nearby called Lido which belonged to the senior royal housekeeper Charlotte Piper. So the King did his menus with her. The house was completed with outhouses by the next owner in the mid-1840s. At this time Karl XIV Johan did visit Bergshyddan which was let for the summer to the Swedish actress Emilie Högkvist, a beautiful courtesan, to persuade her to break off her relationship with Prince Karl, the son of Crown Prince Oscar. In 1861 the house passed into the hands of the Bendixson family, jewish merchants who had settled in Sweden in the 18th century. One of them, Harald, at the end of the 19th century, became a partner in Hambros Bank in London and Chairman of the Swedish Chamber of Commerce in World War I. Ivar Bendixson, who was born at Bergshyddan in 1861, became one of Sweden's leading mathematicians and the first rector of Stockholm's Högskola, the predecessor to the present university. In 1888 the house was bought by a poultry merchant Olaf Hansson and in 1902 by a sea captain Carl Blomgren.

As the years went by and communications to the outer archipelago improved, Djurgårdsbrunn ceased to be a fashionable summer resort for rich Stockholmers and the value of the house gradually declined. But the house's fortunes revived in 1917 when it was taken over by Dr Harald Brising, an outstanding art historian, who proceeded to renovate the building and modernise it with electricity, running water and drains; but Brising died of Spanish influenza in 1918. His wife Louise was the niece of the Norwegian poet Welhaven, a sculptor of distinction and pupil of Carl Milles. Bergshyddan became a meeting place for writers and artists both before Brising's death and afterwards when Louise later married John Landquist, the psychologist and literary historian. Their guests included such writers as Sigfrid Siwertz, Anders Österling, Ludwig Nordström, Marika Stiernstedt, Tor Bonnier, the publisher, his wife Greta, Yngve Larsson and Kjell Strömberg whom I first met later in Paris. Pär Lagerkvist visited it often and also with us as he had become a close friend from the early 30s. It was a port of call for Norwegian writers many of whom returned to Sweden as refugees during the war. Many Finnish literary personalities called in when they came over to Stockholm.

In 1937 the house was leased to Anders Österling who had formerly been a guest, the poet and secretary of the Swedish Academy. All the members of the Academy came there after one of their Thursday meetings during the restaurant strike of 1938 when they should have met in their favourite haunt, the cellar of Gyldene Freden in the old town. In 1939, after a vain attempt by Österling's wife Greta to get the Swedish Academy to buy the house, it was leased to Ingrid Bergman with option to purchase during the four years' lease. But she and her then husband decided in 1941 to emigrate to America and that autumn we moved in for two happy years. Ingrid Bergman's collapsible baby's bath came in very handy when our youngest daughter Susie was born there in 1942 on the first anniversary of the Battle of Britain. She was promptly nicknamed Spitfire, which she was very nearly christened had it not been for the objections of her godparents, our Naval Attaché, Captain Henry Denham, and Countess Amelie Posse. Our son Frank and Patrick Waring very nearly burnt the house down one day when they started a fire against one of the outhouses. We managed to put it out with the help of the fire brigade and the commander did a splendid job with the little boys who were told how children who burnt down houses in

Three Press Attachés - The author, Alexandra Jartseva (USSR) and Carl Jensen (US) sailing on United Nations Day, 1944

Sweden were sent to prison for life, living on bread and water and loaded with a heavy ball and chain.

One very cold winter's night there was a sudden alert and precautions against German parachute landings. Our house and outhouses and garden were occupied by the military who took it in turns to warm up indoors in front of our beautiful blue tiled Gustavsberg stove, drinking hot coffee and stuffing themselves with hot buns. We had lodgers whose identity we never knew but explained them to our friends as our Norwegian gardeners. Long afterwards Jean Marin invited me in Paris to the premiere of a film about the sabotage of the heavy water plant at Rjukan in Norway. To my delight one of my 'gardeners' came up and hugged me as an old friend. Not until then had I the remotest idea what he was up to - so good was our security in SOE even when we were all in it together.

I used to ski to the Legation in the winter and in the summer I made use of my special pass provided by Oscar Thorsing, the head of the Press Department of the Ministry of Foreign Affairs, to paddle my canoe to the Legation on the strategic waterway of Djurgårdsbrunnsviken. We enjoyed the garden and apart from the flowers, we grew vegetables in one corner, including early potatoes.

Bergshyddan was a very happy home, a country idyll only half an hour's walk from town. It was always open to our Swedish and allied friends, artists, musicians, actors and journalists. It was here we started our Thursday evening open house parties for the British press. For many of them it was their home from home. Bo Beskow, the artist son of Elsa, the famous author of children's books, with his wife Zita, started with us a new parlour game of communal painting when all the guests had a free-for-all with brush and paint to produce some remarkable works.

We were visited by many Danish friends like Ebbe Munck who led the Danish resistance in Sweden and numerous Norwegians including old friends from Cambridge days such as Professor Ragnar Nicolaysen, the nutritional physiologist from Oslo, who, with his wife and boys, escaped to Sweden. He later did much to restore the health of his own starving countrymen and the forced labour slaves of the Germans in Norway.

We cherished the warm comradeship of our Swedish, British and allied friends in a Sweden hemmed in on all sides by the Nazi armies. Bergshyddan was a creative house which enjoyed providing hospitality and shelter in those dark days.

It was taken over by Bror Cedercrantz, the present owner, and his painter wife Mary. They restored and renovated it and the garden and continued its tradition of being a home for artists and writers. He also unearthed the details of Bergshyddan's history which he published in 1985 in a charmingly illustrated book.

# IV

## The British Legation - Stockholm

The Legation was like a set from the *décor simultané* of a mediaeval mystery play with hell in the basement, home of printing and photography. The reception and chancery offices were on the ground floor, with the Press Department in the kitchen and the Minister upstairs on the first floor landing with the Commercial and Service Departments. Up in the attic was the secret compartment of heaven with the radio operators and people one did not mention. The residence was situated, as it is still, on Laboratoriegatan. It originally housed the Legation offices as well. It had been designed for the Office of Works by R.J. Allison ARIBA at the beginning of the century, and built between 1913 and 1915 under the supervision of a Swedish architect, Count Cronstedt. Unlike any Swedish house, but conforming to the upstairs/downstairs London standard of the time, the kitchens were located in a half basement or area.

Well before the war expansion had begun and the offices were moved from the residence to Strandvägen 82 looking out over the water of Brunnsviken, one of the many Italianate private villas in an attractive thin Roman brick much influenced by Östberg's Venetian town hall. The walls of the hall downstairs and upstairs on the landing were decorated with pale frescoes of flowers and plants.

The Consulate General and the Passport Office were located downtown. My Press office moved to Linnégatan leaving me with a small *pied-à-terre* in the main building while Joe Parrott's Press Reading Bureau, The Parrott House, had separate offices from late

1940 on Strandvägen. George Binney and Bill Waring ran their blockade-busting operation from a minute watchman's cubbie-hole in the Minister's residence. When George was knighted in 1941 for his remarkable exploits, Victor Mallet offered him more prestigious offices, but he begged to be allowed to stay in his 'set' for which he had developed a deep affection. Across the road from the Legation offices was waste ground leading to the old military parade ground of Ladugårdsgärdet. The bank opposite was dominated by a barn from which all comings and goings were watched and photographed by the Swedish Security Police.

The entrance to the Legation was through an arch leading to a courtyard surrounded by the offices. The main door was guarded by Strandberg, the Swedish Chancery messenger, who, with his son, looked after us throughout the war. He was an imposing figure with the courteous manner of the stereotype diplomat, frequently mistaken by newcomers for His Excellency.

To the right of the hall were the Chancery offices presided over by Mr G.A. Urquhart, the archivist, longest serving British member of the staff. For him the war came as a personal shock as one of his closest friends was an equally long-serving member of the German Legation; but he gritted his teeth and introduced such severe security that his holy of holies became an impregnable fortress. This was helped by the arrival from London later of our security officer, Mr Battley, a giant from Scotland Yard. He was a fingerprint expert and made us change our safe combinations so often that it was difficult to remember them. On the left of the hall looking out over the water of Djurgårdsbrunnsviken were the offices of Bill Pollock (Sir William Montagu Pollock), our Counsellor, and nearby Archie Ross, our Second Secretary, who had been in our Embassy in Berlin at the outbreak of war (later Sir Archibald Ross who ended his career as Ambassador in Sweden). Apart from the Minister these two were the only career diplomats, added to which was the Commercial Counsellor who was a DOT man and the Consul General, Ken White. We were later joined by George Labouchere as first secretary, an eligible bachelor from Rio. He disconcerted his many lady admirers by slipping away to England one day and returning with his lovely bride Rachel whom he had stolen from a hush-hush job in the Admiralty. Bill Pollock ran the Legation with charm and firmness, enhanced by his engaging eccentricity and his interest in the arts, cars, non-conformist dress and cooking. He frequently organised expeditions to collect edible fungi and snails. He was also an expert on the plethora of Christian and other creeds to be found in this otherwise secular country. Much of this talent mystified the Swedish establishment.

Once Bill puzzled the Foreign Minister by calling on him barefooted in sandals, an old jacket over one of his specially made green linen shirts sewn for him by Malin Munck with her glow of Titian hair and the other ladies of Svenskt Tenn from the lining of their packing cases. His collar sported a leather woven tie made by another admirer. Early on he earned a reputation as a lady's man as he was reported to have been seen driving round Stockholm in his three wheeled Morgan with a blonde on either side. These turned out to be his two Afghan hounds. Once during a threat of invasion I reported to him early one morning that the sand in our fire buckets had disappeared and he confirmed with a smile that he had taken it all himself to clean a large collection of snails he had picked on the waste ground of an old Benedictine Monastery. Bill gave the most delightful parties, when junior members of the staff mingled with Swedish artists, actors and musicians. He fed them with gravlax which he had prepared himself, raw salmon steaks sprinkled with saltpetre, bedded in dill and pressed for forty-eight hours under a heavy weight of books. He played records of modern music on his remarkable hand-made gramophone with its giant papier mâché horn. He performed on the piano or showed off his various party tricks which included the nose flute, playing the piano upside down or mirror writing with both hands two totally separate messages. With all his unusual accomplishments and eccentricity, he was a stimulating person to work with. Behind this mask of talented comedy there was a quiet and analytical brain, hard commonsense and ability not only to understand, but to make himself understood.

As two old Marlburians and Trinity men from Cambridge, Bill and I were outnumbered by a formidable band of Wykehamists and Oxford graduates, including Victor Mallet, Archie Ross, Jack Mitcheson the Commercial Counsellor, Graham Sebastian our Consul General in Gothenburg, and two entertaining journalists, Ralph Hewins of the *Daily Mail* and Ossian Goulding of the *Telegraph*.

Upstairs on the landing were the Minister, the Commercial Counsellor, and the three Service Attachés.

Jack Mitcheson headed the Commercial Department and probably carried a heavier load than anyone. He had responsibility for the implementation of the War Trade Agreement, rationing of Swedish imports with the safe conduct ships, navicerts and all the thousand and one problems that arose after the German occupation of Norway and Denmark. From then on we were mainly concerned with preventing the Swedes from supplying the Germans with iron ore and strategic goods. He gave full support to George Binney in his brave efforts to break the German blockade with cargoes of special steels, so vital to our war effort. In his quiet modest way he made a great contribution.

There was a large turnover in air attachés. The first one broke down suffering from delusions of being bugged by the Abwehr day and night at home and in the office. He was relieved by 'Bottlenosed' Bill Thornton, an extrovert socialite, who got on famously with the Swedish Air Force and alleged that he had been on a special mission to Italy early in the war to bribe them to remain neutral but that when the figure topped £80m His Majesty's Government refused to go any further. He was replaced by 'Dickie Bird' Maycock, a spritely little man who stayed on in Sweden as the Rolls Royce representative. The Air Attaché's staff had two main assistants, one was Don Fleet, who came from Finland, and Sir Richard Boord, Bt. or 'Switch' of the Gin family. He came from the Air Ministry Intelligence side and married a delightful Swedish/American, Ethel, the private secretary of the American Minister, Herschel Johnson. The Military Attaché, Lt. Col. Reggie Sutton-Pratt, stayed throughout the war though he was nearly expelled for involvement in the abortive Rickman plot to blow up the Oxelösund ore loading cranes. He was a cheerful and helpful colleague who was always ready to lend a hand in promoting our less diplomatic activities. His standby was the impeccable Sergeant Wright, who was a faithful friend to all of us and the father of Dinky, his beautiful dark haired daughter, a brilliant pianist and one of the team of lady cypherines. Assistant Military Attachés came and went. Malcolm Munthe, the son of Axel Munthe, was expelled by the Swedes for his excellent work in supporting the Norwegian resistance. He was replaced by the arctic explorer, Andrew Croft, with whom he had worked earlier in the war ferrying war material to Finland across Norway and Sweden.

Andrew we had known before the war in Cambridge and he

was very much a member of our family during the years he was in Sweden. Then there was Ewan Butler who headed the German section of SOE, formerly of *The Times* in Berlin, of the British Military mission in France and SOE in Cairo. He was an engaging Bohemian practical joker with a talent for subversive activity, whose knowledge of Germany and the Germans was invaluable to us. He was also deeply appreciated by the American OSS when they joined us in Stockholm with George Brewer whose sense of humour and intelligence were a great support to allied activities. But of all the Service Attachés, Henry Denham was my closest friend. He arrived on the scene in June 1940 relieving his predecessor, Commander John Poland, who retired home to be the mace bearer of the Lord Mayor of London. Henry had been Naval Attaché in Copenhagen, was captured by the Germans and repatriated with the whole Legation. Then he was sent out to Sweden via Norway which we were in the process of evacuating. After a most adventurous journey via northern Norway and Finland, he took over and remained with us throughout the war. His whole life had been in the navy having gone to sea from Dartmouth at the age of 16 to fight in the Dardanelles. Then, after World War I, a year or so at Magdalen, Cambridge, was followed by touring the world in the *Renown* with the Prince of Wales and Lieut. Mountbatten. He then spent two and a half years patrolling the Rhine and after a year as Flag Lieutenant to the Commander-in-Chief, Portsmouth, he moved to the Mediterranean Fleet where he could indulge to the full his favourite sport of sailing. He took over as second-in-command of the new light cruiser *Penelope* policing the Mediterranean and covering the Spanish civil war. At the outbreak of war he was organising a section of NID. He then went out to Denmark, back to London and finally out to Sweden and here we met and worked and sailed together for the rest of the war. His office was above mine in the kitchen department wing. He was my youngest daughter's godfather and he enjoyed the company of my friends. His most spectacular achievement was on 20 May 1941 when he informed the Admiralty of the sortie of the *Bismarck* which led to her ultimate destruction. This however was just one of a mass of well-evaluated detailed information with which, without the use of any paid agents and solely through his overt contacts with Swedes and allied nationals, he became a major source of valuable naval intelligence. The Germans pressed the Swedes frequently to expel him. A key figure in Swedish Intelligence, Colonel Björnstjerna, was dismissed by the Swedish Commander-in-Chief, General Thörnell, for being too close a friend of Henry's and providing him with invaluable information on the German navy. This was one of the eight occasions on which the Swedes demanded his recall but he stayed on and had equally good relations with Björnstjerna's successor, Landquist. On one unfortunate occasion SOE obtained cover for an agent in the Naval Attaché's office on the strict understanding that he would not indulge in any *sub rosa* activity. He was caught in the act of preparing to sabotage a German ship in Gothenburg harbour, was sent home, and Henry, who was totally unaware of the man's activities, was immediately accused by the Swedes as responsible. But he rode out this crisis and had the full support of the Foreign Office and the Admiralty and our Minister, Victor Mallet, who just ignored the Swedish requests for his withdrawal.

We started the Press department in a modest enough way with my assistant, Jasper Leadbitter, and Charlie Montagu Evans. Gradually the department grew into the largest in the Legation and had to be moved over to new quarters on Linnégatan. I kept my office in the old building in order to remain in touch with the other departments and SOE which had taken over my kitchen. Joe Parrott (Sir Cecil) who had worked with me in the shadow Ministry of Information in London, joined me as a refugee from Norway where he had been assistant Press Attaché. He took on the Swedish provincial press but since the Swedes were suspicious of any allied activities in the provinces, he set up his Press Reading Bureau in late 1940 and provided London with the coverage of hundreds of German and other papers from occupied Europe. With a team of some thirty refugees of different nationalities, he was ably assisted by Herbert North of Mather and Platt in the management of these strongly nationalistic individuals who never forgot the claims they had on one another's territories. Another interesting addition to our Legation staff was the distinguished art historian, Roger Hinks, an old friend of Bill Pollock and Jim Knapp Fisher, who had unjustly been dismissed from the British Museum for scrubbing the Elgin Marbles for which he had no responsibility. His particular job description was never revealed. He shared an office with Herbert North in the Parrott House and just managed to squeeze into a minute cubbie-hole in the kitchen quarters which had been taken over by SOE. It was rare to have the luck to find him in either of these locations. He was a good linguist and had many civilised German friends. When questioned about his activities he told us he was researching into the architecture of Sans Souci and Prussian Baroque art. He was a brilliant, witty 18th century conversationalist. Occasionally he showed one a page or two in his tiny notebooks, written in a neat microscopic hand, which were to form the basis of the book which alas he never wrote before he died as British Council representative in Paris in 1963. Only now have I discovered that he was appointed to oversee the activities of SOE and the Parrott House. None of us was aware of this at the time. Roger, like his friend and admirer, Kenneth Clark, professed a dislike of Sweden while he was there, but in later life as head of the British Council in Amsterdam, Rome, Athens and Paris, he spoke of it as his favourite country.

SOE gradually moved into operation in 1940. Ronnie Turnbull and others took over the original holding operation from Malcolm Munthe and myself. He had been Press Attaché in Copenhagen and built up and ran the Danish section with the help of Pamela Tower who had also been in Copenhagen where her stepfather had been Minister. Tommy Nielsen, ex-Shell Norway, took over the Norwegian section with the help of Anne Waring. Ewan Butler headed up the German section with the support of Janet Gow whose orderly mind produced a tidy office out of the chaos that would have resulted in leaving it to the mercy of Ewan.

Outside the Legation building there was of course the Passport Office or the 'Friends' under Commander Martin who pursued the work of MI6 without anyone asking any questions or knowing the answers. When Finland entered its second war with Russia on the German side we were joined by the Helsinki station and finally, when we lapsed into a state of war with Finland, Harry Carr, the head of the station, came over. Unlike the more shadowy figures of MI6 he and his assistant, Rex Bosley, took part in the social round and Harry distinguished himself as a tennis player. He was so security minded that nobody ever knew what he was up to and he was even reported to have shut himself in a cupboard in his office in order not to overhear his own thoughts.

Presiding over this team of professionals and irregulars was the Minister with his office on the left of the first floor landing above that of Bill Pollock as one looked out over the water. At the beginning of the war the post was held by Sir Edmund Monson, Bt., described by Gunnar Hägglöf as 'Sir Edmund St. John Debonnaire Monson (Baronet) not a Wodehouse character - something much better and more genuine?' On 5 November Hägglöf noted that Monson was to leave Stockholm. 'A good thing from the Swedish point of view' he wrote. 'If only we now get an intelligent British Minister. His successor is called Mallet, he has been Counsellor in Washington and it appears that he is considered outstanding by the FO.' We looked up Victor and questioned those who knew him and his wife. His mother, whose letters Victor edited later in life, had been a Lady-in-Waiting to Queen Victoria and Victor was one of her many godchildren. His father, Sir Bernard Mallet, had been a Treasury official. His wife, Peggy, was the daughter of the banker, Herman Andreae of Kleinworts, whose mother was a Kleinwort. He had been a keen yachtsman and passed this on to his daughter who loved to sail with those of us who had boats. She was extremely amusing, elegant and a very good hostess taking a lot of trouble as the lady of the manor with the problems of the endlessly extending family of the Legation. Once she arranged for one of the wives, married to a Polish refugee, to have her baby in the residence so that there would be no question of its British nationality. Victor was less of the village squire than he should have been, and rarely, if ever, had a 'prayer meeting' in the office to discuss problems of the day with his staff. He preferred to see us one by one and got on very intimate terms with the Swedes, some thought too intimate. Both were lovers of music and art and they transformed the residence with many of their beautiful possessions. Victor was as clumsy as a sea-lion in a boat, but he enjoyed tennis, bridge, shooting and fishing. On his 47th birthday on 9 April 1940 they were both on a visit to Gothenburg. On the night of 8 April they were dining with Gunnar Carlsson, the shipowner, and celebrated what looked like a British naval victory over the Germans with the sinking of the *Rio de Janiero* troop ship by a Polish submarine. They woke up next morning to find the Danes had capitulated and the Germans had invaded Norway by sea and air while the Royal Navy had failed to intercept them. At the age of 47 Victor had a good career behind him, Winchester Balliol - the Cambridgeshire Regiment as a second lieutenant in 1914, then in 1916 a captain on the staff of the GOC of the BEF. After the war he joined the Diplomatic Service, was posted to Teheran in 1919, then to

Sir Victor Mallet with Crown Prince Gustav Adolf at the memorial service for the Duke of Kent in the British Church in Stockholm, 1942

Buenos Aires and on to Brussels and back to the FO in 1932. Again he went to Teheran as Counsellor and from 1936 to 1939 was Counsellor in Washington under Lord Lothian, often standing in as Chargé.

So when he took over in Stockholm we heaved a sigh of relief and soon found it easy to get on with this burly, friendly man. He could at times be infuriating, obstinate, short-tempered and for a man of his experience he was sometimes alarmingly naive, especially in his readiness to plead the Swedish cause and give the Swedes the benefit of the doubt.

He was however faced with the problem of maintaining good relations with the country to which he was accredited and also being in command of a band of irregulars, many of whom were using their diplomatic cover to fight their war in their own way for purposes of intelligence or action against the enemy. He lost his temper with many of us but forgave and forgot very quickly. These situations from time to time drove him to the devious practice of reporting to London behind our backs and this did not endear him to London. His relations with George Binney were fraught with bouts of fury at George's effrontery in running the blockade and duping him and the Swedes by smuggling arms and demolition charges to defend his ships. But they always ended up as friends and Victor admired George's courage. He often got annoyed with my criticism of his uncritical trust in Boheman and Marcus Wallenberg. Although his nervous outbursts earned him the nickname 'Windy Vick', his close friendship with the Foreign Minister, Günther, Boheman and Wallenberg paid off in the end to our advantage. I had two major battles with him, first when Boheman wanted to declare me *persona non grata* for my alleged implication in the Rickman case, and the second explosion, which lasted only a matter of hours, when I published the photographs of members of the Swedish Secret police who had been watching the Legation.

It is only fair to say that he mellowed as the war dragged on. He came out fully briefed on His Majesty's Government determination to deny the Germans their supplies of Swedish iron ore either by negotiation or strong-armed tactics. He was not prepared for the incredible incompetence of Section D in their failure to blow up the ore cranes at Oxelösund about which he had not been informed either by London or his Military Attaché. The disaster of Norway, which turned the Swedes from potential co-belligerents to frightened rabbits, made him cautious until the tide turned. In spite of our humiliation, he kept on good terms with the Swedes and earned their respect.

He disliked subversive activity but towards the end of the war turned the tables on his Swedish friends who had so often pulled the wool over his eyes by taking a lead in the deception operation 'Fortitude 2' and 'Graffham'. He was over in London early in 1944, saw Winston Churchill, stayed at Chequers and was dismayed at being told by the Foreign Office he was to be posted as Ambassador to Brazil. He begged to be allowed to stay on in Sweden till our final victory. This was agreed and he was sent on a week's secret course in deception. None of us irregulars had the faintest idea what he was up to, but he seems to have put across a convincing story to the Swedes about our impending landings in Norway instead of Normandy. He became for a while Sir Henry Wotton's Ambassador 'the honest man who is sent to lie abroad for the good of his country'. He had been upset at George Binney being knighted in the middle of the war for singeing Hitler's moustache when he had only recommended him for a CBE, but in the end his own knighthood came through in 1944 and he was able to celebrate VE Day in Stockholm forgiven by all for what might have appeared sometimes a lack of enthusiasm for the activities of those of us who were less than diplomatic in our work. His friend, Marcus Wallenberg, was distressed that his honorary KBE was delayed until Victor's successor, Jerram, had replaced him, while the Americans went to the lengths of putting him on their black list. While there was a certain amount of social life, the inevitable number of love affairs, heartbreaks, broken marriages, a few homosexual relationships and one case of transvestism, the security of the various departments of the Legation was such that we did not know or ask what everyone was up to. I suppose I knew as much as anyone. As my job was to promote the British cause publicly it was also important to know what not to promote and this meant keeping in touch with everybody. I needed help from all the departments in talking to the press and politicians.

The general impression one had was that the individuals in the different departments of the Legation fought the war in their own ways with a certain amount of inter-service rivalry, rivalry between professional diplomats and the army of amateurs and between SOE and MI6. There were inevitably lonely people, in particular girls working late at night as cypher clerks who were not looked after and who were not helped with transport or food, tea or coffee to sustain them over the long hours. While some had the money to eat out in restaurants, go to the opera, theatres, cinemas, concerts and travel to the country for holidays, life was too expensive for many to do so. But most people organised their own amusements with parties in their homes, picnics, sailing, music, painting, amateur theatricals and gardening. By and large the Legation was a happy, efficient place where most people worked hard for long hours but always found time to mix pleasure with business.

# V
## Allied Journalists in Stockholm

A silver cocktail shaker given to us when we left Sweden by the correspondents in Stockholm of British newspapers has inscribed on it the names and signatures of many of these friends for whom we kept open house. The signatures include Wallace King of the *Daily Herald*, a wise old bird who followed the temperamental Ronnie Matthews who had been moved to Moscow and there married his intelligent and attractive wife Tanya whom we got to know later in Paris. I shall never forget him on the night of the Russo/Finnish armistice on 12 March 1940 when he and many other correspondents were gathered together in our flat. His call kept being broken off and re-connected as he talked at dictation speed about the crowds waiting outside the newspaper windows in the arctic winter temperatures. Again and again we heard the words and joined in the chorus 'fur-capped men and fur-booted women press their noses against the windows of the newspaper offices . . . .' Cyril Marshall of the *Exchange Telegraph* and *Sunday Times* was a quiet and well-informed loner. Denis Weaver of the *News Chronicle*, a hardened war correspondent, suffered deeply from the horrors of battle which he had experienced in Poland, Finland, Norway and France, and treated us as his home from home. Gordon Young of the *Daily Express* I knew first as the Reuters correspondent. He was an only child and looked Chinese but had not a drop of Chinese blood. His disarming manner of a country curate and very precise way of talking did not match his daring adventures and lively writing, nor did his primness fit his surprise marriage to the beauty queen of the *China Revue*. Walter Farr of the *Daily Mail*, a splendidly imaginative journalist, followed the war on all fronts and Walter Taub, a refugee Czech actor, had various assignments for the Czech Telegram Bureau, the *Observer* and the Overseas Press of New York. A charming and amusing man he was imprisoned by the Swedes for a while as a spy. Later, on his return to Czechoslovakia, he suffered the same fate from the new regime. His blond bombshell wife Lux worked for the Associated Press of America, was a KGB agent and later the announcer on the Swedish broadcasts from Moscow.

R.O.G. (Olly) Urch, who looked exactly like Mr Punch, the well-informed correspondent of *The Times*, had for years lived in Riga from where he irritated the Russians by posing as their Moscow correspondent. He had been through the Russian revolution and was a graduate of the Lubianka about which he wrote a most entertaining book *We Usually Shoot Englishmen*. His knowledge and judgement of things Russian was profound. Till the German invasion of Russia in June 1941 he helped out in the Parrott House in reading Russian papers. He knew better than anyone else how to read between the lines. With the entry of Russia into the war, he was replaced in the Parrott House by the white Russian Prince Lieven, who was shortly afterwards arrested and imprisoned as a Soviet spy, probably the price he had had to pay for being allowed to leave Russia.

Norman Lamming was actually a member of my staff with special responsibilities for Trades Unions and the Co-operative movement. As such he was correspondent of *Reynolds News*. He later became Labour Attaché and finally joined the ILO. Yves du Guerny worked for the *News Chronicle*, a free Frenchman, married to a beautiful and talented Finnish wife. He enjoyed the title of Vicomte as one of a family of minor Normandy nobility and held forth volubly on the proper conduct of the war.

Ralph Hewins of the *Daily Mail* and *Sunday Despatch* was one of the more amusing and colourful correspondents, mixing a Bohemian existence in a small seaside cottage at Saltsjöbaden with gallant affairs with the most decorative beauties to grace the Grand Hotel and restaurants of Stockholm. One of the Wykehamist and Oxford mafia, a keen historian and Olympic hurdler, he started the war as Press Attaché in Helsinki and then remained with the *Daily Mail* for the rest of his working life. He covered the Finnish and

Norwegian wars at the front while his despatches from the Russo/German front were mostly concocted propping up the bar of the Grand Hotel. With many other journalists he was jailed by the Swedes in the early part of the Norwegian campaign because reporting by a foreigner could be construed in Swedish law as espionage for a foreign power. This applied also to Ossian Goulding and the Hungarian refugee Edmond Demaitre of the *Daily Express*, for which he wrote as Edward Masterman. He carried out anthropological expeditions among the Dyaks in Borneo and some of his remarkable collections were donated to the Musée de L'Homme in Paris. He found it easy to adapt himself to writing for the *Express* and never failed to get into the thick of any battle that was available. He was an expert cook with a passion for innovation. Once I remember him serving a meal backwards beginning with brandy and coffee and ending with hors d'oeuvre and soup.

Tom Harris took over Reuters after Gordon Young while Ossian Goulding, a not so neutral Irishman, another member of the Wykehamist Oxford mafia, took responsibility for the *Daily Telegraph* and *Colliers Magazine*. His wife Yasuko was the daughter of the former Swedish Naval Attaché in Tokyo and his Japanese wife. She was a constant source of delight as a society beauty and witty gossip. Robert Rieffel was the former Havas representative who promptly joined the Free French and worked for British United Press and the beginnings of Agence France Presse in French Africa. He was the channel to the *Cahiers des Interdits* in Vichy, the secret information circulars which provided news editors and others with all the news it was forbidden to print, a very useful way of penetrating occupied and unoccupied France. Bernard Valéry was another French correspondent, a white Russian who had lived long in Japan and worked in Stockholm, partly for Reuters and partly for Columbia Broadcasting and *France in London*, the free French newspaper.

Besides the signatures on my cocktail shaker, there were many others who forgathered in the Grand Hotel where the Swedish Ministry of Foreign Affairs had a branch of its Press office under Count Otto Cronstedt and Sven Grafström, two close friends who were unfailingly helpful to all of us. There was Norman McDonald of the BBC who joined us later in the war and George Axelson, a tall and gangly Swedish/American of the *New York Times*. Martha Gellhorn, the fair-haired beauty in her blue denims, the girl from

Galveston, Texas, as she was called by Walter Duranty, was one of Ernest Hemingway's great passions. Elliot Elisofon, made his mark as a brilliant photographer for *Time and Life*. There was Jack Fleisher of *UP* and Karl Frahm, the Norwegian, better known as the German Willy Brandt and future Chancellor of West Germany; Bruno Kreisky, the future Chancellor of Austria, who wrote for *Tribune*; and Ebbe Munck of *Berlingske Tidende*, the head of the Danish resistance in Sweden. Misha Kossov of Tass we got to know very well when we became allies. We sang and drank and sailed with him. The little Swiss hunchback, Dr Regensburger of the *Neue Zürcher Zeitung* was remarkably well informed and Norbert Zaba, the brave and humorous little Pole, fought his war of words with the gallantry typical of his countrymen. Ed Shanke of A.P. finally settled in Stockholm for good. John Scott of *Time & Life* had lived in Russia and was a friend of Eddie Page and Chip Bohlen, the Kremlinologists of the American Embassy in Moscow. His knowledge of the USSR was very sound. There were many others, including the Germans and their allies on whom we played endless practical jokes.

The Grand Hotel has still not found the author to write its colourful war history. Perhaps the man who could have done it best would have been another neutral Irishman, Jack Geddes. With no experience whatsoever, unable to read a word of music, he persuaded the hotel management he was the band leader they needed to enliven their otherwise dreary night life. He carried off his bluff with immense success, putting bubble and sparkle into the otherwise dull Victorian palace.

Editors in London and New York were convinced that Stockholm was the source of all the most interesting news until the landings in Normandy. Apart from a constant interest in North Africa, this remained so, regardless of where the events took place.

The way in which the Russian front was covered thousands of miles away from Stockholm was quite remarkable. Stockholm also became a source of news from inside Germany particularly the results of our bombing only hours after it had taken place. This puzzled Bomber Harris who read the results of the night's sorties in despatches from Stockholm over his breakfast table before he got the photographs. This was finally explained by the fact that Tom Delmer's black radio team at Woburn, beginning with 'Gustav Siegfried Eins', were able to build stories on a priority sight of the air reconnaissance photographs immediately after raids and before Harris saw them himself. This gave verisimilitude to their transmissions. They were monitored by correspondents in Stockholm who telegraphed them to London as information supplied by the German resistance. At least two of the correspondents gained a reputation for reliability on news of the Russian front, by building up detailed records of Russian and German Generals and formations and developing a sound knowledge, in the course of time, of the terrain over which the campaigns were fought. This knowledge, backed by some inspired guesswork, often resulted in some remarkably accurate assessments of the situation.

The correspondents were also targets of rumour spread by the British and the Germans but they became fairly adept at smelling out such plants. Many of them were also helpful in seeing that the Germans were disinformed. In the siege atmosphere of wartime Sweden we naturally saw a lot of one another and many of them have remained friends for the rest of my life. My job was to brief them as well as I could on the situation or help them to find out what I did not know. I had to trust them to observe the rules on off-the-record briefings and I cannot remember a single occasion when my confidence was abused. We disagreed frequently on the reliability of information or its interpretation, but I tried to apply the principle followed by Rids (Sir William Ridsdale) the head of the FO News Department. He told all to his trusties, confident that they would never let him down because if they did he would never see them again. Our correspondents were a trustworthy lot and did their best to keep the British public informed of what they saw and heard without too much fabrication.

# VI

# The Swedish Press

Sweden shared the honour with Switzerland and the United Kingdom of being among the few remaining European powers still to possess a free press in World War II. Soviet Russia had inherited the traditions of the controlled press of Tsarist days. Between 1922 and 1928 all freedom of the press had disappeared in Fascist Italy. Nazi Germany had followed suit in 1933. In the Baltic States the press has long been state controlled, in Lithuania since 1926 and in Estonia and Latvia after the *coups d'état* of 1934. Rumania legalised already existing censorship on 13 April 1938, and the Greek press had already become state controlled in 1936. The temporary press control introduced in Bulgaria in 1934 continued unabated, and the same was the case in Yugoslavia between 1925 and 1929. Hungary introduced press control after the Austrian Anschluss, while our gallant Polish allies never since World War I enjoyed the benefits and inconveniences of a free press. Spain and Portugal were the same and Finland maintained the censorship introduced since the war of 1939 with Russia. What press remained in the countries of occupied Europe was naturally entirely under German control, and alone the clandestine press of these countries maintained the great traditions of liberty of this fourth estate of democratic government.

The Swedish press therefore represented an interesting phenomenon as one of the few remaining cases of free expression still left in Europe, and in a country where tradition of individual liberty, independence, and popular government are as old as our own. While, however, these traditions are deeply rooted in the people as a whole, the Swedish Government in pursuing its neutrality and endeavouring to avoid being embroiled in hostilities was subjected to repeated pressure by the Germans and other Axis powers on account of the anti-Nazi attitude of the greater part of the Swedish press. The pressure was one-sided, and the balance was not adjusted by similar pressure on our part. Our policy as a democracy upholding the freedom of the press had been not to protest officially against the free expression of opinion or misrepresentation of facts against us, even though the liberty of this form of expression was in many cases fictitious and usually attributable to agents in the pay of Germans.

As long as the scales of military fortune remained weighted in favour of our enemies, the Swedish Government rightly or wrongly considered that anti-Nazi utterances in the Swedish press might lead to economic or military reprisals by the Germans. The Government then pursued a policy of acceding to German demands for reprisals against the papers in question. This was followed by the elaboration of a system by which the Government forestalled such protests either by issuing regular instructions to editors through the State Information Board regarding what was or what was not desirable to publish, or by taking summary action against offenders who disregarded the wisdom of these instructions by confiscating the offending article before the Germans had time to lodge a protest. This procedure perhaps satisfied the Germans and calmed the conscience of the Swedish Cabinet, but it did not suppress the liberty of the press, and stimulated many political writers to a sustained effort which they might otherwise not have maintained. It had the effect of increasing the curiosity of the public, steadily raising the circulation of papers which were victimised and encouraging the clandestine circulation of confiscated or unpublishable information. One publisher, Johan Hansson of Natur och Kultur, made such a success of his confiscated books that he evolved a special technique of outwitting the police, selling copies by subscription or under the counter in advance of publication, and advertising the possibility of confiscation of works included in his publication list in order to assure their immediate sale. He had no less than seven editions of Rauschning's *Gespräche mit Hitler* confiscated and was deeply disappointed when a list of books which he had circulated to customers as liable for confiscation met with no attention whatsoever from the Swedish authorities.

As far back as 1935 a proposition was tabled by a Riksdag Committee for a bill maintaining the security of the State and envisaging the dissolution of associations aiming at the overthrow of the State by force. The intended bill remained in abeyance but was aimed at Nazi and Communist activities. One 4 March 1940, an ordinance was promulgated concerning the prohibition of transport for certain forms of printed matter in the event of war, danger of war, or an exceptional situation caused by a state of war. The Riksdag gave its consent to this ordinance which purported to prevent abuse of the freedom of the press without changing the written constitution which specifically guaranteed this freedom. The constitution provided in the ordinance of 16 July 1812 for the freedom of the press, its freedom from censorship and all forms of official intervention, editors only to be answerable to courts of law and only liable to be convicted when a point of law could be clearly proved against them. The press was also guaranteed free access to news. The ordinance of 4 March 1940, was clearly a contravention of the constitution in that summary sanctions could be taken against the press without reference to a court of law. The application of transport prohibition for newspapers showed itself to be ineffective, as this did not prevent the publication and circulation of the papers in question. It would have been more satisfactory to apply the law as it existed for cases of libel or treason which could have been dealt with by the law courts.

The practice of confiscating newspapers without legal prosecution, which became common in 1940 after the Cabinet decision at the end of 1939, was based legally on a paragraph of the constitution which had remained a dead letter since the first half of the last century. This law provided for the confiscation of printed matter which by its contents in any way endangered Sweden's good relations with a friendly foreign power, whether as the result of 'a misunderstanding with a foreign power' or because the newspaper, periodical or book in question 'had been notified by the representatives or governments of one or more foreign power as containing such matter as might cause the displeasure of other powers'. When, after 1933, the Nazi regime in Germany began its series of protests to foreign governments regarding any unfriendly observations in the press of the countries concerned, the Swedish Government, quite rightly and with dignity, produced the regular reply that in Sweden with its free press the Government had no power over the press and could not accept responsibility for its expression of opinion or presentation of news. Nevertheless, with the examples of German aggression in Austria and Czechoslovakia before their eyes and the increasing tension of the European situation, in the autumn of 1938 the Prime Minister and Foreign Minister sent a circular to chief editors asking them to exercise greater moderation in their handling of foreign affairs, in order not to give the impression abroad that Sweden was in any way wishing to take sides in any coming conflict, especially as public opinion in Sweden, as in all the other Scandinavian countries, was unanimous in insisting on a policy of neutrality.

After the outbreak of war in 1939 German protests about the Swedish press rained thick and fast and the Swedish Government decided on its policy of appeasement and confiscation, the first confiscation taking place in September 1939 and gradually being followed on an increasing scale. Newspapers and periodicals were followed by books, among which in particular was the HMSO publication on German concentration camps, Harold Nicholson's *Why Britain Went to War* and Herman Rauschning's *Gespräche mit Hitler*. The Government in such cases needed to give no explanation for its action, and the publisher in question could not appeal to any court. The Swedish Government had by this concession to the Germans placed itself in the position of appearing to accept the German thesis demanding that a neutral state is not neutral unless it pursues ideological neutrality, i.e. that its citizens should think and express themselves, if not in favour, at least not against Germany. The Swedish Government had in fact in the eyes of the Germans accepted responsibility for the opinions of the Swedish press, a responsibility which they could not effectively undertake in a country so imbued with the traditions of individual liberty as Sweden. The decision of the Swedish Cabinet, however understandable it might be in the minds of the rulers of a small country exceedingly vulnerable to German attack, was based on the false assumption that the German general staff would justify offensive action against Sweden on the basis of articles or books published in the country. However friendly Swedish opinion might have appeared to be to Germany, the Germans would have had no scruples about invading Sweden if they so desired.

In fact this policy of press control had on occasions placed the Swedish Government in an exceedingly ignominious and ludicrous position. Protests were on one occasion received from the Iranian Government because Iran was loosely alluded to as Persia in the Swedish press. The Swedish Government dutifully informed all editors of the grave consequences such a misnomer might have on Swedish-Iranian relations. No sooner had this crisis been satisfactorily overcome than it was followed by another. A small west coast newspaper, *Varbergs-Posten*, determined to initiate its readers into world affairs, signed a contract with United Press for a series of feature articles. The first to be printed was an article on Iran which was very properly not confused with Persia but which unfortunately contained a somewhat colourful portrait sketch of the Shah, who was described as having the neck of a bull. This blasphemous simile was duly noted by the Iranian Government, the Shah himself took umbrage and threatened war unless the Swedish editor was duly punished and executed. War was averted, but the Shah then threatened to take reprisals against the Swedish engineers building the Iranian railway unless satisfaction was given. In due course the editor was neither executed nor punished but received a warning to be more careful in future, and the Shah was pacified. This incident could have been avoided if the Swedish Government had refused to accept responsibility for what was printed in the Swedish press and which, on this occasion, was not even written by a Swede but by an American.

  The sense of responsibility of the Swedish press compares most favourably with that of other countries, in fact one might almost complain that this fact makes the Swedish press on the whole somewhat academic and dull. The Swedish Government may have felt a sense of consolation in the fact that those pro-Allied papers with which they interfered from time to time were those which, ironically enough, spread the opinion in Britain that Sweden was still a free and democratic country.

  Other restrictive measures regarding the press were the ban on the publication of information regarding national defence which was introduced on 12 April 1940, the only exception to this being when an official communiqué was released for publication. Preparations were also made for the introduction of a pre-censorship system in the event of war. Sweden, like the democratic belligerent powers, followed the example of the Germans at the beginning of the war by setting up in the autumn of 1939 a State Information Bureau which the following year was enlarged and re-christened the State Information Board and placed in the hands of a phlegmatic and urbane bachelor, Professor Sven Thunberg, the Rector and professor of modern history at Stockholm University. He pursued the unenviable task for a man of his profession of becoming, in the main, a purveyor of news and historical truths which the press was asked to suppress. It had a certain similarity to the *Cahiers des Interdits* which were circulated in occupied France listing the news which must not be published.

Intervention by the State in the affairs of the press resulted in the following balance sheet. From the outbreak of war in 1939 until the end of the year, twelve newspapers were confiscated in accordance with the procedure of legal prosecution and conviction in a court of law. Two prosecutions did not lead to convictions. Not until April 1940, do we meet with the application of the new method of confiscation without trial. Twenty-five confiscations were carried out in accordance with this procedure in the course of the year. Twelve prosecutions were undertaken, of which nine resulted in acquittals. In 1941, eighty-seven newspapers were confiscated without trial, there were ten prosecutions, five resulting in convictions. In 1942 the curve rose sharply and one hundred and thirty nine papers were confiscated without trial. In March alone thirty eight papers were confiscated, the majority on the 12th or 13th March for having published articles on German atrocities in Norway. There were three prosecutions, two resulting in acquittals. The papers acquitted were the notorious *Göteborgs Stiftstidning* edited by the Nazi clergyman Rhedin who had permitted himself the liberty of calling Stalin 'a mass murderer', and another Nazi 'rag' *Veckans P.M.* The Minister of Justice, K.G. Westman, a farmer's party politician and anti-semite, did not evidently consider that such utterances justified confiscation without trial or that they in any way endangered Sweden's relations with a friendly foreign power. In 1943 the curve sank steeply, only one prosecution was carried out, twenty nine papers were confiscated without trial, and of this total only two confiscations took place in the latter half of the year. My officially sponsored British weekly *Nyheter från Storbritannien* had the proud record of being one of the first papers to be confiscated without trial on 27 April 1940, for printing an article illustrated with photographs of ruined Norwegian towns entitled 'German Cultural Monuments in Norway'. My propaganda window in Kungsgatan was closed down for exhibiting photographs of gaunt chimney stacks and rubble. The use of irony of this nature was not approved by Günther, the Swedish Minister for Foreign Affairs. He later committed himself to paper on the case of the brilliant foreign leader writer, W. Johannes Wickman of *Dagens Nyheter*, whose dismissal he demanded on 21 April 1941, as the result of repeated German demands because of his use of irony in quoting the Germans against themselves rather than attacking them direct. While the paper refused to dismiss Wickman he was, in fact, silenced for a period against his protestations. He finally resigned so as to retain his independence but continued to write his satirical commentaries on foreign affairs.

Professor Torgny Segerstedt, the editor of *Göteborgs Handels- och Sjöfartstidning*, never ceased to attack the Germans and the supine policies of the Swedish Government in spite of personal pleas by the Foreign Minister, the Prime Minister and the King and the repeated confiscations of his paper. Figures for prosecutions and confiscations without trial can be broken down in the following manner. Out of a total of 300 confiscations without trial or successful prosecutions, only 36 were against Nazi papers. These figures, I think, on the one hand are a good indication that the sympathies of the press and public opinion were heavily weighted on the side of the Allies, while at the same time they provided an indication of the compass-bearing being followed by the neutral Swedish Government. The figure for 1939, the period of the 'phoney war', was insignificant and related mostly to prosecutions of Communist papers attacking Finland during the war against Russia. The figure increased proportionately with Allied reverses in 1940. There was a lull during the period of British successes in North Africa and the Mediterranean in the winter and spring of 1940-41, and then with the British retreat in North Africa and the German offensive in Yugoslavia and Greece the curve mounted upwards again. This steepened with the German invasion of Russia, the successes of Japan in the Far East, and the British retreat in Egypt in 1942. Then the tide turned with El Alamein and the Anglo-American landings in North Africa, while simultaneously the Russians annihilated the German armies at Stalingrad and Allied forces began the slow but sure march to final victory. Stalingrad and El Alamein turned the tide in Sweden also as far as the control of the press was concerned, and many were those among our former opponents in Sweden who joined the crews of so-called post-Alamein 'oarsmen' who sculled hectically to join the throng so as not to be missing at the finish. It is significant that in the latter half of 1943 only two papers were confiscated.

The Swedish press, on the whole, had an honourable record in contrast to that of the Swedish Government in its attitude to the freedom of the press which was too compliant in the face of the bullying tactics of the Germans. We never protested to the Swedes about the blatant disinformation and threats of the German propaganda machine which was most effective early in the war when it was backed by military success but died a natural death when the truth of German defeat could no longer be ignored.

# VII

## Swedish Personalities

One of the stereotypes people cherish of Sweden is of a dull, clinically sterile, conformist society which has achieved nearly all the material benefits of socialism without mastering the three Bs of boredom, bureaucracy and brutality. The Swedes are no more brutal than any other nation, but are high on the league table for boredom and bureaucracy. Yet the very fact of such monotony seems to produce as many gifted eccentrics per head of the population as any other country. With all their passion for statistics, this is probably the only one the Swedes have never recorded. A high proportion of these individuals who swim against the current are women, perhaps again because Swedish society is so male-dominated in spite of an apparent equality of the sexes. A friend of mine, who had lived long in Japan, found a great similarity between life in both countries. In each of them males dominate, and women, in spite of their emancipation, are almost a different race. Swedish women, beginning with St. Bridget, have always asserted themselves strongly.

The closest of all our friends in Sweden was Countess Amelie Posse, Tant Amelie or Tamelie, as the children called her. I was introduced to her by Gustaf Stridsberg of *Svenska Dagbladet*, who had been in love with her since 1910. She out-did most of our friends in originality and with her, life was never dull. Before she put on her massive weight she had been a beauty, a radical aristocrat with the poetic genes of Gunnar Wennerberg and the political instincts of her conservative prime minister grandfather. She wrote, spoke and battled in the cause of freedom and individual liberty all her life. Like a true aristocrat she was only rude when she meant to be. She was the terror of authority and the pillars of Swedish neutrality. When she was born she was thought to be dead and her father, in a fit of mad depression, put his pipe in her mouth. She sucked it, coughed violently and began to live. This she did in full measure till she died in March 1957 at the age of 73. With her aristocratic Skåne drawl she fought for the underdog and quite unashamedly pulled rank with the authorities by exploiting her long-standing friendships with royalty, such as the painter Prince Eugen and Prince Wilhelm the writer. I rang her up after Gustaf Stridsberg had told her who I was and was promptly ordered to present myself for an audience. This I did in her tiny flat on Gärdet which was full of a noisy gathering of Czech refugees and other nationalities overrun by the Germans. She was sitting up in bed surrounded by typescripts, a typewriter on her knees. She asked me if I was any good at cooking and what I thought of her latest concoction, a savoury rocquefort ice cream mixed with chives, sprinkled with paprika and divided into segments by slices of pumpernickel. In the course of telling me how I could be useful to her, she ate and interjected instructions and questions to her guests with whom she was plotting the overthrow of the Nazis. Her vitality was infectious and so was her humour. Her hair was either loose or bundled into a string bag which kept coming undone, and, like Mary Kingsley and other Victorian lady missionaries, she went to war with an umbrella as her only weapon, which she always mislaid. She had fled to Sweden from Czechoslovakia, ill and penniless in 1938, escaping from the Nazis escorted by John Walter, a Swedish businessman, who later tried unsuccessfully to sell us the Italian navy. Her first husband, a Swede named Bjerre, died and she married the Czech painter, Oke Brazda, a refugee in Italy in World War I. She was interned with the leading Czechs as enemy aliens and pleaded their cause with brazen effrontery with the Italian authorities in Rome. She had them released as allies and finally after the war settled in the new state of Czechoslovakia in the dilapidated castle Ličkov. A close friend of Mazaryk and Beneš, she threw herself into politics, defied the Nazis and finally escaped their clutches as they invaded her home. She started life again in Sweden, regained her Swedish nationality and wrote and lectured and promoted the cause of her beloved Czechs and

Woodcut of Amelie Posse by Czech diplomat Vaňek

of all other occupied countries, especially Norway and Denmark and those of her Finnish friends who were not involved with the Nazis. Her little flat on Furusundsgatan was always full of a motley crowd of journalists, writers, musicians, painters, politicians and, at times, some of her old Italian friends. Vittorio Gui, the conductor, called on her and unburdened himself of his unhappiness for his beloved country. One character who turned up during the first Finnish war was Prince Ferdinand of Liechtenstein, kitted out as a volunteer in a Swedish army sheepskin cap and coat and later marrying the daughter of General Nordenskiöld, the Commander in Chief of the Swedish Air Force, an outspokenly pro-British officer. She had a life-long friend in Alexandra Kollontay, the Russian Ambassador. The Russians at that time were the hope for Czechoslovakia - hopes only to be dashed on her return after the war, when she had to flee a second time as a refugee from Soviet terror. The last time I saw her was in April 1955 when she came over to see her painter son Jan's stage sets at Covent Garden for one of Janáček's operas. She took charge as usual when she left at Haslemere Station. We had to get her over the bridge to the up line while the train waited. Her panting body had to be manoeuvred on board with the help of the station master to whom we told the lie that she was Swedish royalty travelling incognito so that she should receive the appropriate courtesies. Her escape from Czechoslovakia in the company of the kind J.H. Walter, was also eased by his whispers to the German guards that she was a member of the Swedish royal family. She was always a most convincing royal person. She confided to me on this visit her plot to rescue Beneš with the help of her son Slavo whom we had flown back to England during the war to join the Czech air force. Slavo had drowned a Nazi who had tried to murder him in Stockholm's dockland. Malcolm Munthe dyed his hair and changed his identity to get him on one of our planes past the Swedish passport control officers. On this latter occasion in 1948, Slavo was to fly a plane from an airfield in Czechoslovakia and lift Beneš out to Germany. In the event the plot came to nought because Beneš died before he could be rescued.

    On one occasion she triggered off an evacuation plan for the British colony and their families in the event of a German invasion. She rang me up one morning in a state of great excitement while one of my colleagues, Charlie Montagu Evans, was in my room. She described Swedish army manoeuvres she could see on Ladugårdsgärdet. The army was out on manoeuvres simulating the mopping up of invading paratroops and she was carried away with their excellent performance. Her comments were punctuated by the crackle of rifle and machine-gun fire and the crump of mortars. My friend left the room as we talked. Shortly afterwards the Legation was invaded by an orderly queue of fathers, mothers and children with dogs, parrots, canaries, hamsters, white mice and one piece of luggage each. Charlie, believing the invasion had actually started, had given the signal for the evacuation plan and we had to send them all home disappointed.

While Amelie was very much one of the family she was also a public personality and, as such, shunned by the official establishment until the war turned in our favour. She kept the secret police on their toes by her indiscreet telephone talk and party conversation and lived in a world of plots and conspiracies, many of which were imaginary. She and her friend, Countess Ebba Bonde, the sister of the Wallenberg banker brothers, shocked her family by their open support of refugees and their opposition to the Nazis.

Ebba was a close friend of Malcolm Munthe and helped him in every way with welfare and subversive activity on behalf of the Norwegians. She was strikingly elegant and kept a variety of coloured wigs in her bath. Ebba's kindness was extended after the war to starving German children whom she brought to Sweden by the hundreds. Amelie was equally selfless in her help to refugees and her fearless visits to friends in prison who were arrested as spies by the Swedish secret police. She fought valiantly for her friend Walter of the Italian navy story and Vaňek of the refugee Czech Legation, in the course of which she got on good terms with the spy-catcher Inspector Danielsson.

Amelie was determined to see to it that Sweden was prepared with a resistance movement in the event of a German invasion. She set up her own movement in her Tuesday Club which, by the end of the war, had ramifications all over the country with radio transmitters and printing equipment in place to provide underground communication. I was excluded from these meetings as it was important that they were not contaminated by foreigners. I was in on the first meeting by accident. I had been invited one evening to dine with Johan Hansson, 'Kulturjohan' the owner and founder of the publishing firm of Natur och Kultur. He was a remarkable self-taught, self-made man who had come into the publishing world by printing broadsheet ballads to recruit emigrants in Malmö for the United States before the First World War. He published Amelie's books and a whole stable of anti-Nazi books which got good publicity because they were confiscated.

On 28 March 1940 I took Amelie out to their house at Äppelviken in my car which I often did as she liked the protection of my CD plates which, in fact, drew even more attention to her movements. The dinner was a lively one with only right-minded people round the table, including Gustaf Stridsberg, Maj and Yngve Lorents, Torsten Fogelkvist and Bertil Stålhane. The talk then got down to the subject of how to prepare and organise resistance to Nazi propaganda and to the possible occupation of Sweden. At that point I was asked to leave the room. Finally I was allowed to return and Amelie explained that I had been in on the founding of the Tuesday Club which, for obvious reasons, must be wholly Swedish and in no way suspected of being a tool of the allies. So I never attended any meetings though I got a good deal of gossip from Amelie and many other friends who were members. They were a very distinguished group of writers, academics, professional men and women, doctors, lawyers and politicians, who lectured and led discussions in all corners of Sweden. Gustaf Stridsberg was an indefatigable debater and writer of information material. One day he told me that he had turned up late for a meeting as he had gone to the wrong address. He thought it was on Kungsgatan and innocently asked a policeman who showed him where a Tuesday Club was meeting. He arrived to be courteously received by people he had never met before. They appeared to be young males dancing with one another to soft music under dimmed lights. After receiving some friendly propositions, which seemed out of context with resistance to Nazism, he reckoned it was one of Stockholm's many homosexual clubs and excused himself to his kind hosts.

The first formal meeting of the Club was at Årstaklubben on 9 April 1940, the day of the invasion of Norway and Denmark - a day to remember as proof of the Nazi menace for those complacent Swedes who consoled themselves with the conviction that 'it can't happen here'. With Gustaf Stridsberg as commentator and treasurer taking a lead in each meeting, the Chairman was usually Anders Örne with Amelie seated on his left as the 'club mother'. Örne was a person of considerable weight, respected in the social democratic party, deeply involved in the co-operative movement, the post office and the public debt office. The Club began with only some thirty people present but later more were added. The problem of security was difficult as Nazi agents and secret police had a way of procuring cards and pieces of paper which could masquerade as introductions.

The meetings took place every week of the year, except two or three. Speakers were drawn from many sources: Swedish visitors from occupied countries, England and Germany, while organisations like the Foreign Policy Institute, the Swedish equivalent to Chatham House, and Nordens Frihet helped. Gunnar and Alva Myrdal took it in turns to attend the meetings and Swedes like Maj Lorents, Greta Hedin and Asta Kihlbom spoke of their experiences on visits to wartime England.

One foreign journalist, John Scott of *Time and Life*, who was a friend of Chip Bohlen and Eddie Page of the U.S. Embassy in Moscow, was once invited to speak as he was writing a book on Russia and knew the country well. Another foreigner, Margaret Sampson, who ran the Swedish service of the BBC, was herself half Swedish, and was also invited to attend when she flew over to visit us from London. Apart from gathering information from abroad, the Club was preoccupied with the treatment of refugees and the growing tendency towards anti-semitism, but above all they were concerned with revealing and countering Nazi subversion, Swedish officers joining the German army, Swedish Nazis organising propaganda campaigns and Swedish congratulations to Hitler. Sven Hedin presented Hitler with a statuette of Charles XII on his fiftieth birthday 'From Swedish men and women who saw the saviour of Europe in the German Führer and people's Chancellor'. The Club kept an eye on the public utterances of Swedish politicians like the Minister of Defence, Sköld, and his successor, Alan Vougt, who wobbled in their neutrality in favour of a 'realistic' acceptance of Germany's dominant position. Headmasters, headmistresses, university professors and teachers helped to counter subversive propaganda in schools and universities. The sister clubs in the provinces sent representatives to meetings and reported on Nazi penetration. Many leading academics came to speak, such as Yngve Lorents, Maj's historian husband, Folke Lindberg, Carl-Fredrik Palmstierna and Professor Nils

Ahnlund. There were outstanding women also who were strong supporters, like Anna Lindhagen, Professor Lydia Wahlström, Hanna Rydh, Elin Wägner, Emilia Fogelklou and Elsa Cedergren. There was Karin Koch and her lawyer husband, Hugo Lindberg, who defended the victims of the secret spy trials. There was also Marika Stjernstedt, the elegant authoress with her interesting French background. There were military experts like Colonel Willy Kleen and Emil Boldt-Christmas, the outspoken former Swedish naval attaché in London, who ruined his career by his public reaction to the Nazi sympathies encountered in the Swedish navy and their almost total ignorance of the world outside Germany.

Other good friends who took part in these meetings were Ivar Harrie of *Dagens Nyheter*, Harald Wigforss of *Göteborgs Handels- och Sjöfartstidning* and its future editor. There was Bo Enander, the editor of *Nu* and the most effective broadcaster on current affairs, his partner in journalism, the historian Åke Thulstrup, and Victor Vinde, who knew France well and had been right through the collapse and occupation by the Germans. There was Ragnar Svanström, the eminent historian and publisher, Sven Rinman and Frank Martin. One of the old faithfuls was Ture Nerman who had founded the anti-Nazi group the Fighting Democrats and ran the anti-Nazi paper *Trots Allt*. He did a three months' prison sentence for an article on the Bürgerbräukeller bomb incident in which he insulted Hitler and referred to the Nazis as gangsters and their régime as a reign of terror. There was Fredrik Ström of the Stockholm Municipal Council and members of Parliament, such as Knut Petersson, Bertil Ohlin, Ivan Pauli and Kerstin Hesselgren. The list of participants is unending and reads like an *Almanac de Gotha* of Swedish anti-Nazis, a splendid mix of people drawn from all walks of life.

It is fashionable in some quarters to underrate the importance of the Tuesday Club in maintaining Swedish morale and resistance to Nazism, just as it is to write off Amelie as a somewhat laughable old lady. I do not share this view. Her activities inside and outside the Tuesday Club may not have been more than an irritant to the government and an infuriating challenge to the Nazis, both Swedish and German. But they reached out across the whole country by word of mouth and the distribution of information sheets provided a focus for morale which was otherwise deeply shattered by government concessions to German threats. The ripples of its activities spread into Norway and Denmark, helped not only to sustain their morale in the dark days, but also to remind them that these eccentric Swedes were far more representative of their country than the drab weak-kneed men who did so much to lower Sweden's reputation in Scandinavia and the world. When Günther, the Foreign Minister, spoke in defence of Swedish neutrality policy at the banquet of the Foreign Policy Institute on 31 October 1944, it was members of the Tuesday Club, led by Knut Petersson of *Göteborgs Handels- och Sjöfartstidning* and Professor Herbert Tingsten, who demolished him.

The Tuesday Club came to an end officially on 10 April 1945 honouring the memory of Torgny Segerstedt who had just died. A man who had given courage to so many by his pen and his unforgettable 'To-day' articles in *Göteborgs Handels- och Sjöfartstidning*. When Amelie died there were moving demonstrations of affection and admiration in the press and at her funeral. Her splendid autobiographical books, like her life, bore witness to a lovable nature disdaining all the advantages of her birth. She lived a life of risk, poverty and increasing sickness to fight with cheerful courage for justice for her lost country Czechoslovakia, for her Scandinavian neighbours and for hundreds of refugees in Sweden who were afraid of the long arm of the Gestapo. She had the peasant cunning and common sense of good breeding. She was insolent and fearless, putting her Swedish secret police interrogators in their place by telling them to mind their own business. She was typical of the culture of Victorian and Edwardian Sweden so rich in poets and painters and great women, such as Selma Lagerlöf, Ellen Key and Elin Wägner. This culture she defended with a remorseless opposition to the brutality of totalitarian dictatorships. She was in many ways a reincarnation of Selma Lagerlöf's fantastic and forceful lady of the manor of Ekeby in Gösta Berling's saga. Her books were memories of her life since childhood in Sweden, then in Italy and Czechoslovakia. She was an entrancing story teller and wrote as she spoke, evoking striking portraits of people and descriptions of town and country filled with a love of nature, poetry and music and painting. Her ebullient sense of humour was matched by a kindness and generosity second to none, giving away her last penny to help the sick and oppressed. Her old friend who had spent twenty years in Stockholm, the Czech diplomat and artist Vladimir Vaňek, who was given a two years' jail sentence by the Swedes for 'espionage', described how he said goodbye to her in the hospital chapel 'surrounded by lilies of the valley'. Her funeral in the Holy Cross Chapel was conducted by her friend Emilie Fogelklou. Her coffin was flooded with flowers and tributes were sent by the Czech resistance, literary and charitable organisations and old friends like the author Gabriel Jönsson, who described how she came as a child to his father's shop in Skåne to buy sweets which she promptly gave to all the children in the village. She remained cheerful and generous to the end.

At the last meeting of the Tuesday Club, the name of Gustaf Stridsberg was coupled with that of Segerstedt as the man who gave Amelie the greatest inspiration in her resistance activities. He was a hunchback with a weak heart and lungs but, like Amelie, he defied illness and devoted his war years to fighting Nazism with his pen and his phenomenal memory as a self-taught historian. A man of encyclopaedic learning, he was omniscient and had a widow's cruse of quotations for every eventuality. At the age of seven he had had a serious accident to his spine which forced him to lie on his back for five years. Unable to go to school except for short spells, his education was helped by private teachers and his mother who read to him aloud from Dickens, Goethe and Victor Hugo. His command of English was impeccable but incomprehensible as he spoke it. He had learned it by reading *Punch* for a year while lying on his back. His knowledge of all things English was astonishing and so was his memory of the topography of London which, however, was entirely derived from his reading of Dr Johnson and Boswell. He had never been to England but he had read *The Times* and the *Manchester Guardian* since the beginning of the century and one of my special tasks in the war was to see that he was supplied as well as possible. When he could not get the original I got him the miniature airmail copies of *The Times Weekly*, supplemented by my own daily press review based on daily telexes from London. I saw him several times a week to listen to his comments on events. His tortuous style which he described as 'mystice et enigmatice' was interlaced with quotations and a dazzling range of apt historical anecdotes. This not very prepossessing cripple was an enormous success with the ladies who adored his elegant eighteenth century courtesies and the way in which he would mark his approval of them, one being the beautiful Peggy Mallet, by taking a patchbox from his waistcoat pocket and printing a patch on the cheek of the lady of his choice. He had been in love with Amelie since 1910, he as a political conservative, she as a non-political young woman absorbed in painting, music and literature. In World War I he was pro-German like so many conservatives, while Amelie, in her second marriage to the Czech painter Brazda, was a ferocious supporter of the allies. They kept in touch in her self-imposed exile in Italy and in her fourteen years in the new state of Czechoslovakia. Her political radicalism infected him in his battle against the bestiality of Nazism. Although he retired from *Svenska Dagbladet* in 1935, having worked for them since 1901, he was active in the office of Otto Järte, the foreign editor. On his death, the editor of the paper, Ivar Andersson, described him as the paper's conscience. Uppsala University wished to confer on him an honorary doctorate but the government intervened to prevent it. Instead he was described by Professor Nils Ahnlund as Doctor *Honoris Causa de facto*, if not *de jure*. Gustaf loved the country and came to us in our house Bergshyddan with Amelie, enjoying the beauties of the park. He discoursed on nature and sailing and navigation and the sea of which he knew as much as he did about the land masses of the world. He was too crippled to travel much but his travels were in his books and the books of all the great travellers. In spite of his preoccupation with the war and its horrors, he never forgot his love of literature regardless of frontiers. Carl Linné's work and writings he knew by heart. Amelie described how Prince Eugen organised a surprise picnic with 'Strittan' one summer's day in 1943 at Linné's home at Hammarby and how the two men vied with one another in bringing alive the great man's work in the idyllic setting of the trees and wild flowers he had loved and named for all the world. It was in November of that year, 1943, that Strittan died. This was a severe blow for the Tuesday Club. He was a man of outstanding moral courage who all his life had fought for justice and decency from the Dreyfus case to all the obscenities of Nazism.

Otto Järte (1881-1961) I met on my first visits to newspaper editors. He and Stridsberg shared the same room in *Svenska Dagbladet*. Otto was a cherubic little man with a very keen intellect and profound knowledge of Germany. His father was an engine driver and he had been brought up as a socialist. After school he went to university at Uppsala, Munich and Berlin. He was concerned early on with local and national politics in Stockholm, especially with social and unemployment problems. His wife Esther, who died during the war, was a woman of great charm and learning who had also been involved in local politics. Otto had been both civil servant, politician and journalist and he was a leading former of opinion. He took sides with Germany in 1914 because of his fear of Russian policy in Finland. In 1915 he was expelled from the Social Democratic party and in the early twenties he joined the Conservatives, became a member of parliament and joined the staff of the paper for which he worked as foreign editor and a member of the board. We became close friends and on walks in Djurgården and evenings in his and Esther's beautiful eighteenth century house overlooking the harbour entrance, he spoke of his many friends in Germany and those who had fallen victim to Hitler's brutality. Not only was he a stalwart supporter of the allied cause in his articles, but he and his editor, Dr Ivar Andersson, were close to dissident German generals, to Goerdeler and others such as von Trott and von Moltke who remained for him the representatives of another better Germany. Otto was not a flamboyant demagogue in his opposition to the Swedish government and its concessions to the Nazis. He was a well-informed and solid protagonist of military and psychological defence against aggression and subversion and in support of the occupied Scandinavian countries.

Dr Bo Enander was the first journalist I met. I wanted to thank him for his radio talks in the first weeks of the war when Sweden was swamped with German propaganda about the victories in Poland. Hellis had stayed behind in Sweden with the children when I went home at the end of August and Bo's talks rescued her from being submerged by the flood of Nazi victory propaganda during the Polish campaign. He and his brave Finnish wife, Inga, were staunch allies and Bo as editor of *Nu* and a founder member of Nordens Frihet at the time of the Finnish armistice on 13 March 1940, was a brilliant opponent of defeatism, punctuating his hilarious sarcasms with the pipe from which he remained inseparable. He and Åke Thulstrup, two distinguished historians, ran the weekly periodical *Nu* as a well-informed and caustic commentary on current events throughout the war.

Johannes Wickman, the foreign editor of *Dagens Nyheter*, had been the paper's Paris correspondent in World War I. Not only was he very well-informed on international affairs, but he had for long campaigned against the Nazis. He, with Segerstedt in Gothenburg, was the cause of much of Hitler's carpet biting. He was silenced and banned for a time in deference to the Swedish government by his stolid editor, the retired naval commander, Sten Dehlgren. His brilliant shafts of gallic irony and sarcasm and his parodies of the Nazis were unmatched in Swedish journalism.

There were also the memorable evenings with the author Alice Lyttkens and her lawyer husband Yngve on Artillerigatan, when we met many Swedish and Norwegian writers. One of these was the monumental figure of Sigrid Undset in her homespun dress hung with a giant Viking medallion on her bosom. It was the day on which she lost her son in the war.

The figure of Professor Torgny Segerstedt, the editor of *Göteborgs Handels- och Sjöfartstidning*, overshadowed all others as the champion of individual freedom, free speech and a free press against all the obscene manifestations of Nazism from 1933 to its eclipse in 1945. He died on 31 March on Easter eve, 1945, just before the Twilight of the Gods. A latter-day Jonathan Swift, he was a theologian who detested religious ritual and dogma. He was steeped in Kierkegaards Either/Or philosophy and an admirer of Ibsen particularly his play *The Enemy of the People* with its scathing attack on the cant and political humbug of so-called democracy. Dr Stockmann's 'The minority is always right' was very much his motto as a lonely individualist. He wrote with the weight of an Old Testament prophet and the light touch of the satirist whose irony and wit sent Hitler into repeated paroxysms. A proximate pessimist and ultimate optimist, he fought his war with his pen every day without ever taking a holiday.

His prodigious production included his daily 'I dag' or 'Today' weekday articles, his commentaries on current events, leading articles, reviews and books. 'All things have their time', he wrote in the darkest days of the war. 'The dread winter which wraps the world in its pall of death cold snow will not last forever. Mankind will once more see the heavens turn blue.' His stubborn individualism reminds one of Luther at the Diet of Worms. 'Hier stehe ich. Ich kann nicht anders. Gott helfe mir. Amen.' Segerstedt was time and again attacked as an enemy of the people for his unrelenting exposure of his government's neutrality policy which he considered to be no more than cowardice in face of the enemy. For him those who are not for us are against us; those who are not anti-Nazi are Nazis.

Segerstedt was descended from a long line of churchmen and scholars who made their mark as theologians, teachers and writers. He was born on 1 November 1876 in Karlstad and after studying at Lund University took his degree in theology in 1901. In 1903 he was turned down for a lectureship in Uppsala by all, except the future Archbishop Nathan Söderblom, for his heretical liberalism. Finally, after securing a doctorate in theology in 1912, he moved from his teaching post in Lund University, where he had had to withdraw his application for a professorship because of his free-thinking views, to a new professorship in Stockholm in 1913 in comparative religion.

He became involved in journalism as editor of the liberal periodical *Forum*. In 1917 he became editor of *Göteborgs Handels- och Sjöfartstidning* which he remained for the rest of his life. He had a son and two daughters by his Norwegian wife who died in 1934 but he was no gloomy widower and led a lively social life in his beautiful 18th century home protected by two strong dogs, a Great Dane Garm the mythological Hell hound of Vóluspá and a burly bulldog Winston. While they frightened off his enemies they were so affectionate to his friends that they frequently knocked them down with their greetings. His conversation was sparkling, his wit barbed, his humour kindly and he was a most generous friend, especially to the young. When the Swedes organised an exchange of British and German prisoners of war in Gothenburg, he printed for me, as a gift, an English paper, *Pow-Wow*, which was distributed to our prisoners for them to have the latest news. He flouted all convention and protocol. On one occasion I well remember dining with him, with Fru Forssmann presiding as hostess, and Sir George Binney as chief guest dressed in full RNVR uniform. He was visiting Sweden with his motor coasters after having been expelled as *persona non grata* as a civilian for smuggling arms and demolition charges on to our merchantmen which broke the German blockade. The Nazis accused him of every conceivable crime in their Who's Who of anti-Nazis, but regretfully confirmed that the man was incorruptible. When the German press accused him of being bribed by the British, he retorted that he wished he knew how to lay hands on the money as it was not right that it went astray. He was insulted as a madman, warmonger, a threat to national security and was the victim of floods of menacing anonymous letters accusing him of every conceivable form of immorality. He retorted

'Why do they make such a fuss about me, I am such a modest person' and on another occasion he burst out - 'only gutless imbeciles are not slandered and vilified'.

For his twenty-eight years as editor of *Göteborgs Handels- och Sjöfartstidning*, he refused to compromise with the forces of evil. Up till the war his stand against Nazism made him almost a folk hero, but with the outbreak of war and the German victories up till El Alamein and Stalingrad, he was anathematized as a threat to Swedish neutrality with his refusal to observe the government's watchwords of community spirit, watchfulness and silence. Few publications, other than Ture Nerman's *Trots Allt*, Selander's *Eskilstuna Kuriren*, *Nordens Frihet* and Bo Enander's *Nu*, dared to follow his example and all of them suffered the same fate of confiscation and abuse.

He caused a sensation before the war by his attack on Swedish universities for accepting the invitation to celebrate Heidelberg's 550th anniversary in spite of the dismissal of forty-four of their academics for their Jewish blood or dangerous thoughts. He was attacked on 18 December 1939 in *Göteborgs Posten* by three leading businessmen and replied 'it is not wise to act against one's conscience'. This was followed by attacks by seven leading Gothenburg shipping magnates and floods of anonymous letters. In June 1940 he protested against the transit of German troops through Sweden to Norway and attacked the Swedish government for the hypocrisy of its excuse that the war in Norway was now over. On 13 September his paper was confiscated because of his revelations on the transit issue. It was confiscated again for mocking the Swedish Commander in Chief, the comic-opera General Thörnell, for accepting the Nazi decoration of the Great Eagle. In March 1942 his was one of seventeen papers confiscated for publishing information on the torture of fourteen Norwegian patriots by the Gestapo in their infamous Victoria Terasse headquarters in Oslo, in the Grini concentration camp and the death and torture prison of Møllergaten 19. It was confiscated for revealing German plans for recruiting Norwegian youth into a Hitler Jugend and the government seriously considered the possibility of putting an end to his activities by a policy of pre-censorship. The business world declared an advertising boycott on the paper and caused severe financial damage, but Segerstedt refused to budge. His workforce and the employees of the City of Gothenburg all stood behind him in his battle.

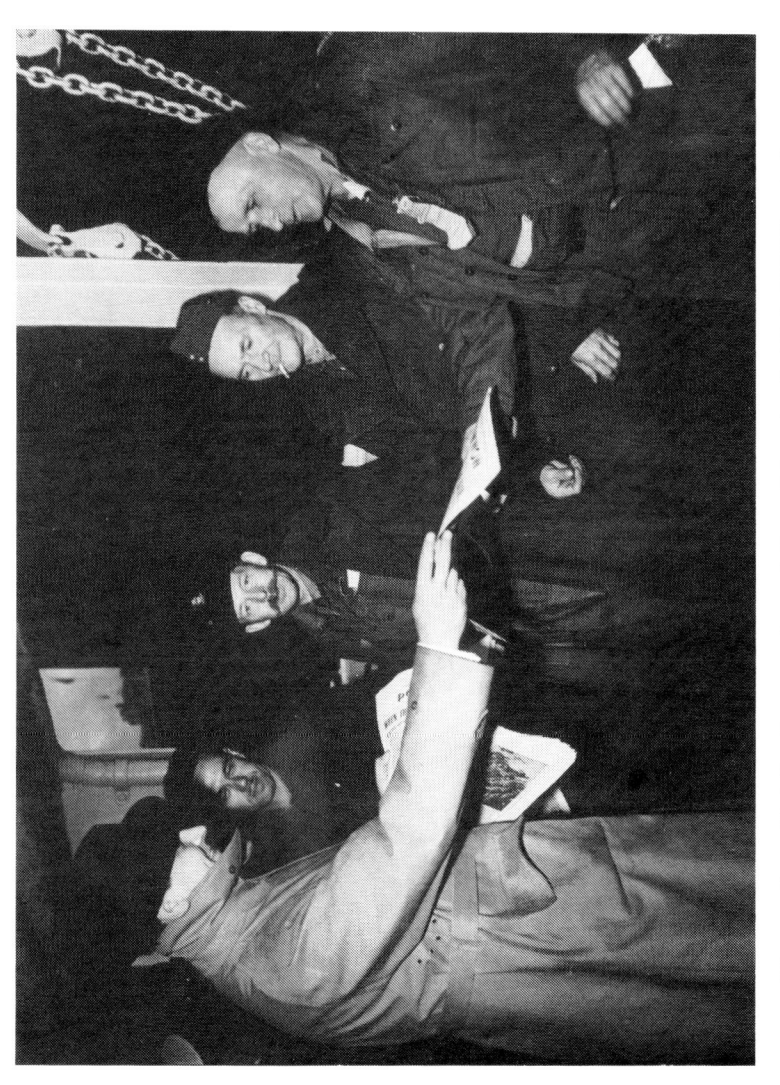

The author distributing copies of *Pow-Wow* to British POWs at the exchange of British and German prisoners in Gothenburg

He only once left Gothenburg during the war to go to Stockholm, which he regarded as enemy-occupied territory. This was when he received a summons from the King, having refused to heed the pleas of the Prime Minister and of the Foreign Minister to moderate his language. On 9 October 1940 he received an invitation from the 1st Marshal of the Court to call on the King. He was to arrive by the west entrance to the palace wearing informal dress. Both Segerstedt and the King gave their own accounts of how they had scored over each other. But Segerstedt's tone never changed. He received warnings from the Press Council, a body composed of so-called responsible editors, but took not the slightest notice. On 9 September 1942 came his last confiscation. Then followed El Alamein and the turn of the tide. The press regained its freedom, the advertising boycott was lifted and Segerstedt was overwhelmed with letters of congratulation. Not only had he given hospitality in his columns to writers whose articles were refused elsewhere, but copies of the paper were regularly smuggled to Denmark and Norway where they became part of the 'underground' press. It was said that Segerstedt promoted Sweden's spiritual hygiene in those dark days of moral sickness and provided a healthy breathing hole in the ice. He was a giant of a man by any moral standards, a brilliant stylist and publicist. He fought his war with courage and died with his pen in his hand a few weeks before the final victory. He had never doubted of the outcome, even when the outlook was darkest.

Our contacts in the film and theatre world were extensive and there was very little doubt where their political sympathies lay. We received great help in special showings of British war films and documentaries and one of the great events was Noel Coward's *In Which we Serve* which did not give much joy to our pro-Nazi friends in the Swedish navy. Commander Tony Kimmins, who had been involved with the production of the film, came over for the occasion and this gave us an opportunity of meeting leading film personalities and fooling around with them on the sets of Svensk Film Industri. The fact that the film was a thinly disguised story of Dicky Mountbatten and the *Kelly*, was not lost on the Swedes who had great affection for his sister, the Crown Princess Louise.

One of our great allies in the theatre world was Karl Gerhard, a Swedish mixture of Noel Coward and Maurice Chevalier, impresario and author of revues, who kept the Swedish public in fits of laughter at the expense of Hitler. He was a friend and admirer of the Soviet Ambassador, Alexandra Kollontay, but when he was invited to one of her receptions after the Ribbentrop/Molotov pact, he made a demonstrative entry, sprang to attention, clicked his heels, gave the Hitler salute and, at the top of his voice, roared 'Heil Hitler'. On 31 July 1940, immediately after the occupation of Norway and Denmark and the beginning of the German transit traffic to Norway and the fall of his beloved France, he opened his revue *Gullregn* (*Golden Rain* or *Laburnum*) at Folkan with his famous Trojan Horse song where a huge wooden horse from Dalarna, painted with flowers and with a fifth leg as a fifth column, opened its belly and out jumped little Tyrolean girls with guitars which turned into sub-machine guns. Karl Gerhard emerged from the fifth leg and sang the trojan horse song which immediately became a popular hit. The Swedish Ministry of Foreign affairs protested in advance and to appease them the shaving brushes on the Tyrolean hats were removed. The Germans protested. Per Albin Hansson, the Prime Minister, rang him up and asked him to remove the act, but he refused. Günther, the Minister of Foreign Affairs, asked him to come to the Foreign Office and sing him the song which he did much to Günther's delight, but this did not stop Zetterquist, the police chief, from forbidding the performance as an offence to public order. Karl Gerhard was prosecuted but this only gave him more publicity and the scene was revived with the horse wearing a muzzle and a nightcap. Karl Gerhard was a tonic in a time of depression. His home, Kråkslottet, (Crow's Castle) in Saltsjöbaden, with its frescoes by Isaac Grünewald, was a happy meeting place for artists, writers and musicians. On one occasion it was the place in which he got his friend Gustav Möller, the Minister of the Interior, with his wife Else Kleen, to meet secretly one night with Alexandra Kollontay, the Soviet Ambassador, and begin the talks which led to the end of the first Finnish-Soviet war.

Stig Järrel, the actor, and his Danish lady companion, the singer Karin Juel, were close friends and he suffered the misfortune of being my look-alike so we often got mixed up. Karin Kavli, the redheaded actress wife of the Norwegian cheese magnate, Knut Kavli, was a hospitable and amusing hostess. She was worshipped by Conrad Pineus, the wealthy Gothenburg average adjuster and art collector, who followed her faithfully every summer as she toured the provincial theatres with *La Dame aux Camélias*. He burst into tears every night as she died on stage and was revived off stage by a champagne supper. One evening in the Kavli flat the party had gone on very late, too late for Frank Martin. His last train to Lidingö had long since gone, so the Kavlis bedded him down for the night on a sofa in the drawing room and we all left. Next day I asked Frank how he had slept. 'Well enough', he said 'but I was wakened early by Karin walking round the room humming to herself and feeding her tame birds, but I had to pretend I was still asleep as the young goddess was stark naked and I thought it might be presumptuous to wish her good morning.'

Norman Lamming was our contact with the Trade Unions and I made through him many friends, chief of whom was dear old Charlie Lindley, the retired boss of the Swedish Transport Workers Union. His father had anglicised his name and he had been a seaman on a coaster on the east coast of England. He was also a friend of Keir Hardie and the founders of our National Seamens' Union. Charlie was born in England and followed his father to sea and as a leading Trades Unionist in his mother country, Sweden. I got to know him as he was the intermediary between the TUC and a mysterious man with the iron mask, as we called him, by the name of Knüfken who, like Wollweber, the notorious future head of the East German Security Police, was held in prison mainly for his own protection from the long arm of the Nazis. Letters and presents from his friends in England used to be taken to him in Långholmen prison hospital on regular visits which Charlie undertook. Early in our friendship I took him out to lunch and asked him where he would like to go. He named the Hotel Continental which I did not know at all. So we met and I ordered the meal and Charlie called the wine waiter. He said 'I think I know more about this than you do and I don't have to look at the wine list as they keep some special bottles for me only'. A claret was produced which he nosed and sipped knowingly and approved. Then I asked him how he had become such an expert. 'As a lad' he said 'I was on the Bordeaux/Bristol run and my job was to test the wine barrels every day with a pipette and add a tot of brandy where necessary. I got to love claret and I suppose I know more about it than most people in Sweden; even the Wine and Spirit Monopoly who are the largest buyers in the world ask my advice from time to time.' We talked a lot of the sea which was his great love and I told him of my boat and where I had her moored at Smedslätten. 'Ah, but that is just below my house so drop in for a bottle whenever you feel inclined.' So from time to time I combined my messages for Knüfken with my sailing and a visit to Charlie's house which had an incredible cellar with the clarets he had laid down over many years.

The Swedish Royal family was very much part of the daily life of the country. The Monarchy has played an important part in Swedish history with its law makers, warrior kings, intellectuals and artists. In this century, with the rise of social democracy, trades unionism and the decline of the aristocracy, the royals became less and less figureheads and more and more citizens in their own right. In spite of the strong vein of republicanism in Swedish politics, the Monarchy is cherished, if not revered, and it was always said that if Sweden were to become a republic its first president would have been the then Crown Prince and later King Gustaf VI Adolf. He and his English wife, Louise, Lord Mountbatten's sister, moved unprotected among the people. She could go shopping and visiting friends without being mobbed by the crowds who always respected her privacy. The Crown Prince was a teetotaller in a country where alcoholism has always been a problem, but he never forced abstinence on others. He was a scholar whose knowledge of the art of China, Persia and classical antiquity was renowned all over the world. There was no doubt where his sympathies lay in World War II. He and the Crown Princess kept clear of politics and were free agents. Prince Eugen, the painter, while keeping quiet in public, felt strongly about the intolerance of the Nazis to artists and modern art. He did much to help refugee artists from Czechoslovakia and Norway and to arrange for some of the victims of persecution to take refuge in Sweden. He was a devoted friend to Vaňek, the Czech diplomat and artist, who was jailed for espionage for two years. He kept in touch with him in prison and attended the celebratory lunch on his release with Vaňek's other close friends, Bill Montagu Pollock, of our Legation, and Countess Amelie Posse whose friendship with the Prince dated from their youth. When the union of Sweden and Norway was dissolved in 1905, he was strongly pressed by many Norwegians to become their King but he had to give way to the objections of the old King Oscar and to reconcile himself to the fact that he really preferred painting to kingship.

Prince Wilhelm was an equally forthright supporter of freedom for the spoken and written word. The old King, or Mr G as he was popularly known at home and on the tennis courts of the

Riviera, was a different proposition altogether. He was determined to exercise what little authority was still left to the Crown and in those days he still had some constitutional leverage. Treating his ministers with fatherly condescension he presided over the meetings of the Council or Cabinet with stubborn determination. Having little or no experience of Britain he was an example of how the Swedish establishment had drifted away from the French influence of the 18th century and the earlier Bernadotte generation to that of Germany which prevailed in the latter half of the 19th century through to the first World War. He was proud of his sporting prowess and even on one occasion astonished a meeting of his Council of Ministers by showing off his double joints and sitting on the table with his legs hooked behind his neck. Considering himself the elder statesman of Europe, he believed his prestige was sufficient to bring the belligerents together to settle their differences. When Sir Edmund Monson, the British Minister, took leave of him in the New Year of 1940 and when Victor Mallet presented his credentials afterwards, he expressed the hope that the allies would settle their differences in a peaceful manner. He achieved the unique record of infuriating both Hitler and Churchill when he offered his good offices in the summer of 1940. He forbade King Haakon of Norway to take refuge in northern Sweden after the German invasion. In the summer of 1941 he was alleged to have threatened to abdicate unless the Swedish government acceded to the German demand for the transit of the Engelbrecht Division to Finland in the war against Russia. Prince Eugen was asked if the story was true and said the King denied it and that he had merely told the Prime Minister, Per Albin Hansson, he must accept the consequences if the Germans were refused. He tried without success to bring Professor Segerstedt to heel to stop him publishing his daily articles. He was, of course, an old man and suffered from the weaknesses of old age. The one weakness, however, which became more and more a cause of embarrassment to his family and his government was his sexual deviations. One of his old brothers, Prince Oscar Bernadotte, a leading light of the Salvation Army, once approached me at a party and said 'They tell me you know everything. Is it true my brother is a homeopath.' Dr Axel Munthe, his personal physician, who had been the late Queen Victoria's lover and occupied her apartments in the Royal Palace, spent much of his time steering the King away from his temptations.

The Germans exploited the situation by sending him his tennis partners on visits. Towards the end of his life he was blackmailed by a Hungarian valet. Undoubtedly his weaknesses and autocratic manner were factors which later led to the Monarchy being divested of most of its residual powers, with the Monarch only functioning as a figurehead as his great grandson does today.

The main contact with government Ministers was Christian Günther, the Foreign Minister, who held down the job throughout the war. Mallet used to see a lot of him and he also saw the Prime Minister regularly as a bridge player without really ever getting to know him. Günther had been Minister in Oslo up to the outbreak of war and was appointed Foreign Minister in succession to Sandler. He was an official, not a politician. After the war he was posted to Rome where he and Mallet saw much of one another. While Günther was a kindly, sensitive man, he was miscast as Foreign Minister, a job which required far more psychological insight, toughness and stamina than he had got. Foreign policy was really run by the Secretary General of the Foreign Office, Erik Boheman, a strong, intelligent man who could measure up to top civil servants anywhere in the world. He had a lively sense of humour and much charm as well as powers of persuasion which could make even the weakest policy of concessions to the Germans appear to be a machiavellian *tour de force*. He became a good friend of Victor Mallet's and obviously impressed Churchill who saw him in London and had him to stay at Chequers. Churchill gave him a special recommendation to President Roosevelt which unfortunately did not give him the entrée he had hoped for in the course of tough negotiations with the Americans. There is no doubt that his sympathies were with the allies, but his belief in Swedish neutrality was certainly reinforced by our bungling of the Norwegian campaign.

He experienced our naivety in April 1940 when he was in London after the German invasion of Norway. He was taken to the holy of holies in the War Office and shown a wall map of Sweden and Norway on which a British staff officer demonstrated how our landings in the north of Norway were to join forces with the British and French troops moving in on Trondheim. When Boheman asked how the troops in the north were to get down south he was told 'by railway'. Boheman replied 'That line is not a railway, it is the frontier demarcation between Norway and Sweden'. He was horrified at the danger to Swedish neutrality in George Binney's exploits breaking the blockade, but when it came to seeing him before declaring him *persona non grata*, his reaction was that it was exactly what he himself would have liked to have done if he had been in the same position. My own dealings with Boheman were only sporadic as my contacts were with the press department headed by my old friend Oscar Thorsing. Apart from meeting Boheman at meals and receptions, I rarely saw him officially; in fact only once as far as I can remember when he wanted to throw me out of the country because of the Rickman affair. On another occasion he attended the memorial service for the Duke of Kent in the English church when all our regular diplomats and service attachés were in uniform. Having no such finery myself, I decided to join the choir and wear a surplice. Afterwards we all forgathered with Victor for a drink and Eric slapped me on the shoulder and said 'Peter, I can imagine you in every kind of disguise, but never thought of you as a cherub'.

Victor Mallet's even closer friendship with the brilliant banker, Marcus Wallenberg, reinforced Foreign Office suspicions that he was too much in the pocket of the Swedes. Wallenberg was often used by the Swedish government to put across arguments which they did not wish to be attributed to themselves. Marcus was the younger of the two brothers who ran the bank, a free enterprise power factor in a country committed to social democracy. The Swedish government rarely made a move in foreign affairs or domestic economic policy without consulting Wallenberg's Enskilda Bank, using its credit and influence abroad or with private industry to achieve its ends. Marcus played the role of the pro-English man of influence, appearing frequently in Stockholm and London in negotiations over the war trade agreement. He was a keen and competent sportsman, yachtsman and tennis player, an amusing and sophisticated addition to any social gathering. We called him Charles Hambro's brother-in-law by divorce. Charles had married Marcus's enchanting divorced English wife.

The elder brother, Jakob, was altogether different, looking after the German interests of the bank and the government. He was a quiet, thoughtful, intelligent man of great integrity. He knew Germany well and abominated the Nazis. Close to opponents to Hitler, in particular Goerdeler, he never gave an over optimistic account of what the resistance might achieve in its brave efforts to overthrow the régime. He did not forget Germany had a record going back many centuries of failed plots and conspiracies, but this did not mean that he liked the policy of unconditional surrender which gave so little hope to those Germans who still believed in the future of a better Germany.

One other personality of great importance to the defence of Sweden against German threats was Gunnar Hägglöf, an official of the Swedish Foreign Office. One of a family of outstanding public servants, he was the man who did probably more than many by seeing to it that Sweden's defences were not starved of fuel and material. He made certain her economy could function with the import of the necessary raw materials and fuel so that the population and its livestock could be fed. He negotiated the war trade agreements with the belligerents and spent much of his time in England. On one occasion with Admiral Tamm, he spent hours with Goering, who was ranting, drugged and reeking with scent, bejewelled like a dowager and made-up like an old whore. They successfully refused the concessions the Germans demanded to relieve their troops in Narvik. There were many other officials of extremely high quality with whom we had to deal in less prominent positions but it was Boheman, the Wallenberg brothers and Gunnar Hägglöf who carried the main burden of responsibility for fighting for their country's interests against the conflicting demands of the Germans and the allies. We may not have liked what they did but there is no denying that they did more than most to maintain the integrity of Sweden in her isolation.

In the early stages of my service in Sweden I spent some time calling on pro-German, pro-Nazi and anti-British Swedes in order to help me assess the problem I faced of influencing Swedish opinion and the opinion formers.

German cultural influence was strong in the academic world, in medicine, the sciences in general and in engineering and engineering standards. Britain's earlier lead in the industrial revolution, in trades unionism, the co-operative movement and in socialism and the rights of women, all played their part in a general appreciation, if not understanding, of Britain's place in the world. In World War I the Swedes had been committed to the Germans and a German victory until the government fell at the time of the Zimmerman telegram and America's entry into the war.

The situation changed in the twenties and thirties and the

arrival of the Nazis faced pro-German Swedes with a serious dilemma, particularly those who had cared for German 'war children'. Many of those who had been saved from starvation and disease by their kind Swedish and Norwegian hosts had now become convinced Nazis and were visiting Scandinavian families again to spread the new gospel and spy out the land. Later in the war the role played by German war children in preparing for the invasion of Norway was a terrible shock to the old guard of German sympathisers.

Many of our strongest supporters in World War II were Swedes who, in World War I, had been wholly committed to Germany. Most of the daily press was anti-Nazi, except for Torsten Kreuger's papers, including *Stockholms Tidningen* whose editor, Börje Brilioth, was totally committed. But the average Swede, however much his education may have been based on German standards, reacted against the Nazis.

Sven Hedin was an exception. He was a great public figure, honoured as an explorer and geographer at home and abroad, in particular in Germany. He had been decorated by the Kaiser and flattered with honorary doctorates and other academic distinctions by German universities and learned societies. The Nazis continued the flattery and he was much courted by Goering.

At 8.15 on the evening of 17 October 1939 I visited Sven Hedin in his flat. His two sisters were there and served coffee while we talked. A pear-shaped man with a little moustache and pince-nez, he was more like a village schoolmaster or vicar than an explorer. I explained that I was puzzled that a man of his eminence could support the Nazi régime which ran counter to the best traditions of German civilisation. In particular I asked him how he, as a Jew, could condone their anti-semitism. He immediately countered by saying there was no truth in the stories of Nazi anti-semitism and I asked him how he could reconcile this statement with the fact that his own country and others in the west had given refuge to thousands of Jews who had escaped from the Nazis. He simply replied that they had been frightened by the stories in the British and American press which was of course mainly owned by Jews. I asked him if he had heard of the Kristallnacht, which he dismissed as spontaneous hooliganism by wild young people. He told me that, in fact, Goering was very pro-Jewish and was anxious to work out with Sven Hedin a plan for a Jewish national home. He then got out his maps and pointed out the empty quarter of Arabia which he and Goering had generously selected. I asked him if he really was serious and he assured me he was. I asked him about water and the prospects for agriculture in this arid desert and, last but not least, what were the likely attitudes of the Arabs themselves whose nomad tribes inhabited these areas. He assured me it was all being looked after and I would be surprised to find how near they were to a solution. Then he asked me if I had not really come to ask him to mediate between Germany and the allies, since Hitler was so anxious not to continue with such a senseless war. I assured him that nothing was further from my mind and suggested that it did Sweden very little good to use people like Birger Dahlerus and their King to bring about the capitulation of the allies. I asked him if he would take a bet with me on the outcome of the war. He thought this very British and amusing and said he would be happy to collect £5 off me when the Germans had won. That was the last I saw of him. I had already left Sweden for France before the German capitulation, so I was unable to collect my winnings. But Hedin, to do him justice, did not swing round as so many did when an allied victory seemed certain. He supported his Nazis to the end and was one of the few Swedes with the courage to stand up and be counted when he publicly said farewell on the quayside to the German Minister, Thomsen, when the latter was repatriated to Germany.

One of the dark horses as an agent of influence for the Germans in Sweden was Thorsten Kreuger, the brother of the late Ivar Kreuger and owner of Sweden's two largest newspapers, *Stockholms Tidningen* (circulation approximately 200,000) and the evening paper *Aftonbladet* (circulation frequently reaching 400,000). At a press conference in the German propaganda Ministry early in the war, Swedish journalists overheard an official who said: 'Thorsten Kreuger has been commissioned to deal with the Swedish press'. It is not certain what his actual connections were, but it is thought that in return for preferential treatment regarding his financial interests in Germany and in the Swedish Match Company in Poland, he had allowed the Germans certain facilities in his press. His crypto-Nazi tendencies however were apparent long before the war broke out and were connected largely with the hope that National Socialism might rehabilitate him after the scandal of his brother's forgeries and his own conviction in the Högbrofors case. Every time Kreuger's papers launched a campaign for rescinding the verdict in this case, they simultaneously launched a pro-German campaign. *Stockholms Tidningen* was a minor offender compared with *Aftonbladet* though the former's editor, Dr Börje Brilioth, never concealed his pro-Nazi sympathies and was once famous for his open flirtation with National Socialism. In 1936 he was one of the founders of the Swedish Nazi Party which then was called Sveriges Nationella Socialister.

*Aftonbladet* was a paper mainly devoted to sensation. Its editor was a vulgar little man, P. G. Petterson, whose one consuming interest was France. The foreign editor, Lönnegren, was a vicious little fellow who maintained a consistently pro-German line against both the British and the Swedish governments. The King of Sweden was the only person who was spared his insults and insinuations. Two anonymous writers, Kettil and Observator, contributed sinister fabrications headed 'Aktuellt utifrån' (Stop Press from abroad). The latter was a certain Major Almkvist on the Swedish General Staff and he followed in the steps of 'Survey' or Valentin Sjöberg, in about 1942. He mainly wrote under the *nom de plume* 'Observator' and his Nazi affiliations went back to the early thirties when he was the leader of Svenska Folkpartiet, and called himself Sweden's Führer. He received his material directly from Germany and his translations were so inept that he left traces of German syntax, even German words, in his text. Kettil was rather more independent. *Aftonbladet* also took a special news service telephoned daily by the *Berliner Börsenzeitung*. These items were all headed AB and date-lined according to taste. There were numbers of provincial papers which were mouthpieces of German propaganda, such as *Norrbottens Kuriren*, *Helsingborgs Dagblad*, *Göteborgs Morgonpost*, and the Nazi papers *Den Svenska Folksocialisten*, *Sverige Fritt*, *Nationell Tidning*, *Nationell Krönika*, *Dagens Eko*, *ABC*, *Adam* and *Dagsposten*. German penetration also occurred even in the most liberal papers, such as *Dagens Nyheter*, where the naval expert was a professed pro-German and the chief editor, Kommendör-Kapten Sten Dehlgren, himself a retired naval officer, tried to free himself from the control of the Jewish Bonnier family and form a consortium under himself with German interests.

While the Swedish co-operative news agency, Tidningarnas Telegrambyrå, was owned collectively by the Swedish press and took Reuter telegrams regularly for which it was persistently criticised by the German press and government, the Germans countered by setting up their own news agencies camouflaged as Swedish. This was useful for them from the point of view of propaganda, as their correspondents in Stockholm could then quote from the Swedish news agencies instead of from the official German DNB telegrams to Berlin as samples of Swedish opinion. The chief offenders among the news agencies were Bulls Presstjänst, founded in Oslo in 1922, which was managed by Bjarne Steinsvik, a Norwegian by birth but a naturalised Swede. He was controlled by the German Legation and his sister-in-law was employed in the German agency, Europa-Press, with which Bulls Presstjänst collaborated. It took King Feature Services which was formerly a Hearst press selling organisation and had a turnover of some 150,000 kr per year. Bulls Presstjänst was quoted sedulously by German journalists in Sweden as an apparently American agency. Another agency was Skandinaviska Telegrambyrån, a subsidiary of the large German agency Europa-Press, with offices in Copenhagen and Stockholm. Its office in Amsterdam gave away its character by being the only neutral so-called news agency able to function after the German occupation. The Copenhagen office was run by the German, Major Ernst Gilbert, for whom Jane Horney allegedly acted as courier to the Russians in Stockholm with German proposals for a separate peace. It is worthy of note that almost any organisation in Sweden or Scandinavia which called itself Scandinavian, National, Swedish, Hansa, Nordic or neutral, was almost bound to be Nazi. The cover was so obvious that it ceased to be a cover. The manager of this agency was Dr Consul John Lönnegren who was no relation to the foreign editor of *Aftonbladet.* He was press officer of the Brazilian Legation and his agency supplied the press with news at cheap rates and was subsidized from Germany. Its news sources were Berlin and Zurich, but it had no compunction in falsifying date-lines from London or New York whenever convenient. Skandia Press was another agency run by Captain Nils von Bahr. Von Bahr was a minor peace huckster and in contact with one of Goering's agents in Båstad. He was also secretary of the International Anti-Komintern Association in Berlin. The agency was originally founded by E. C. Bredberg of the old *Stockholms Dagblad* who later distributed photographs to the press for the German Press Attaché, Dr Grassmann. Bredberg moved to South America as a correspondent for the German press. Other German organisations concerned with propaganda and support for

Swedish Nazi organisations were the German Tourist Bureau which used its window in Kungsgatan exclusively for propaganda purposes and German business firms with whom it collaborated in the distribution of pamphlets and brochures. The Germans ran a Swedish broadcasting service from Königsberg and appointed a radio attaché in their Legation in 1943. The Germans also set up a cultural bureau in the Legation in 1943. There was also the Deutsche Akademie, the Deutscher Akademischer Austauschdienst, the Wissenschaffliches Institut, the German school and the Information Centre.

German films swept the Swedish market in 1941, backed by very crude newsreels. Before the invasion of Norway and Denmark the film of the Polish war *Feuertaufe* was sent to the Legations in Stockholm, Copenhagen and Oslo with instructions that it must be shown to as large a public as possible before 8 April. This was done in all the capitals and suitable key persons were invited to be present and make their deductions. As far as books and publications were concerned, the Germans had at least two publishing houses in Stockholm, Svea Rikes Förlag and Neutrala Förlaget. They produced a harvest of books and pamphlets against Britain on such subjects as Ireland, India, Egypt, Palestine, the Empire, the British concentration camps in South Africa, emigrants and warmongers and France's guilt. From December 1941 they published *Tyska Röster*, initially a successful periodical, but gradually its title faded away and all that was left were the letters *T.R. Signal*, the special monthly number of the *Berliner Illustrierte*, swamped the market and was distributed free or sold at 50 öre. It had a larger circulation in Sweden than any corresponding Swedish paper, but it never exceeded a circulation of 50,000 and by the Spring of 1943 they had to cut it down. By February 1944 the figure was down to 25,000 copies and it ended the war with 13,000, a very different fate to our *Nyheter från Storbritannien* which finished with some 500,000 copies. *Der Deutsche in Schweden*, was the organ of the German colony and appeared every month. The Fichtebund sent over large quantities of propaganda material to Sweden which, however, was confiscated by the Swedish authorities. Later the Germans resorted to printing in Sweden, or made arrangements for German printing material to be despatched to the German Legation for distribution through them in Sweden rather than by post from Germany.

For a time when Sweden was completely cut off from the

west, the bookshops filled up with German books and there were no English books to act as a counterweight. Hans Fallada became the writer of the day; before, it had been A.J. Cronin and James Hilton. The same applied in other spheres such as gramophone records. Telefunken records began to replace those of HMV, which had always been regarded as the best. As the war progressed and communications were re-established, so the balance changed, and while it was impossible to import any large numbers of English books, we managed to set up new publishing enterprises with existing Swedish publishers who printed and sold English books in English. This was a great success and continued for some time after the war.

In the field of church affairs, while there were considerable clandestine contacts between the Swedes and the German resistance, particularly in the case of Bonhoeffer, the Nazis nevertheless made good use of their contacts in the Lutheran church, also in the free church communities of methodists, baptists, adventists and various teetotal organisations, such as the Good Templars and Blue Ribbon sects. *Göteborgs Stiftstidning* was a national socialist organ and the editor, Domprost Rhedin, was severely reprimanded by the consistory court for his unorthodox effusions. He made a violent attack on the Dean of St. Paul's during the latter's visit to Sweden. The Oxford Group, which was deeply penetrated by the Nazis and of which Heinrich Himmler was a member, attracted the most undesirable characters and innocents in Sweden who did not know what they were doing and wallowed in the feeling of uplift promoted by the moral rearmament movement, an excellent weapon of military defeatism. The movement stimulated the same sense of cosy one-upmanship as one found in the Nazi Party, with their bosses enjoying their castles and aeroplanes and fleets of cars, and indulging in their penchant for first class hotels, special trains, luxury liners and male and female lovers. They were an advertisement for the benefits bestowed on those who understood the business value of the deity. The Nazis stimulated a great deal of anti-Semitic activity and published an edition of *Welt-Dienst* in Swedish.

German propaganda made full use of the traditional German military training of the Swedish officer. While the Swedish Air Force had close relations with the RAF and remained untainted by the Nazis, there was a strong German tradition in the army, but the Navy turned out in the end to be more penetrated by the Nazis than any of the armed forces. This was also the case with the Swedish Security and Intelligence Services. There had been very close association with the German navy after its defeat in World War I. The first German fleet visit abroad after that war was made to Sweden and the Swedes are alleged to have been responsible for the clandestine training of German U-boat crews in the years when the German navy had no U-boat arm. Admiral Canaris, the head of the Abwehr, had very good relations with Swedish defence intelligence. The Germans were at great pains to influence the Commander-in-Chief, General Thörnell, who was a simple vain little man responding easily to flattery and attention. He was bracketed with the Romanian Dictator, Antonescu, as a recipient of the Order of the German Eagle, and was greatly impressed at being invited to meals by the German Commander-in-Chief in Norway, General von Falkenhorst, in his private railway carriage when they met on the Swedish/Norwegian frontier. On one occasion when the German government was pressing demands on the Swedish government which were being steadfastly refused, a telephone conversation was tapped in which the Berlin voice said to the German Legation 'Well, if the Swedish Foreign Office will not give in, then try General Thörnell, he is malleable (mürbe)'. Thörnell also rented the flat belonging to his son, who died in the winter of 1940, to a member of the German Military Attaché's staff and turned out a young Norwegian to get him in. But while Nazi activity in the Swedish navy was rife, this was not so in the army.

In the world of music and the theatre the Germans were very active but failed to make any impact with their propaganda among artists who were almost one hundred per cent anti-Nazi. The great German orchestras, such as the Berlin Philharmonic and the Leipzig Gewandhaus, toured Sweden and numerous conductors performed, such as Furtwängler, Carl Schuricht, Franz von Hoesslin and the Dutch collaborator Willem Mengelberg. The jazz pianist, Peter Kreuder, was also extremely popular. One Swedish singer however became the darling of the German troops and especially of Hitler and the other Nazi leaders, in the person of Zara Leander.

Turning to the records of Swedish/Nazi organisations and individual Nazis, it is difficult to pick out the most significant. The main organisations promoting Nazi activities were: Fosterländsk Enad Ungdom (Patriotic United Youth) an organisation founded in September 1941 by Rolf Clarkson in collaboration with Per Engdahl.

The latter was also founder and Chairman of Svensk Opposition (Swedish Opposition). He was one of Sweden's leading Nazis. Already in 1943 he was saying that his party's struggle was almost hopeless and national socialism in Sweden was doomed to become an insignificant sect. Försvarsfrämjandet (defence promotion) was founded in August 1939 under the chairmanship of Major General von der Lancken. He was already in his sixties when the war broke out, had spent 1916 in Germany and had been chief of eastern command in Sweden in 1938. He had always been a leading member of the Swedish-German association, which had existed before Nazi times and had progressively succumbed to Nazi penetration. Nordisk Ungdom was a sub-organisation of Svensk Socialistisk Samling, the principle Nazi organisation in Sweden, led by Sven Olov Lindholm. Their official organ was *Den Svenske*. Lindholm was a Sergeant-Major in the Swedish army, who was released on leave when the press revealed his activities. He began to be active in 1926 when he was Quartermaster Sergeant and became a member of a fascist organisation.

He visited a Nazi conference in Nuremberg in 1929 as representative of the Swedish Nazis and was extremely active as a leading member of Svenska Nationalsocialistiska Partiet in 1931. Both he and Furugård claimed leadership of this party in 1932 but Furugård obtained control during Lindholm's two months absence in Germany. He left the party to form the Nationalsocialistiska Arbetarpartiet in January 1933, after which a three-year battle for power between Lindholm and Furugård developed. He actively co-operated with national socialist parties in Norway and Denmark during 1939 and appeared together with Quisling and Clausen at a big meeting in Copengagen on 13 November 1939. He was greeted with Nazi salutes and cries of 'Heil Lindholm' on his appearances at meetings. He had received regular financial help from a certain Herr Lange since 1930 and was reported to have been paid a thousand kronor a month from Germany in 1937. He was received in audience by the King on 20 November 1942 and explained the aims of the movement and specified why the SSS admired German national socialism. He said that if the government left the country owing to foreign invasion, he would no longer consider himself as owing allegiance to that government. He was fined for provocative behaviour at Skansen in 1943 when he hired a pleasure steamer from

Stockholm to Sandhamn, his Nordic youth in full uniform, blue shirts, shoulder straps and badges. The ship was decorated with flags but the Swedish flag was conspicuous by its absence. This was on Whit Monday, 1943. Lindholm's rival, Birger Furugård, was a veterinary surgeon and one of Sweden's foremost Nazis. He was the editor of *Vår kamp* and was disqualified by magistrates from writing prescriptions for spirits in December 1942. In fact, however, he obtained spirits for his own use by declaring that they were intended for sick cows. In January 1943 he issued an appeal to all Swedish Nazis and Nazi parties to unite under one banner, Svensk Opposition. One of the leading members of the Oxford Movement was Dr Malte Welin. He had been editor of *Rikstidningen* since 1933 and was associated with Nordisk Pressbyrå. In 1933 he was the founder of a society called Tysklands Vänner. He was a docent at Berlin University in 1933 and paid a visit to Quisling on 17 May 1943, Norway's National day, without a German visa to enter Norway. He frequently visited Germany and met Goering in 1940.

Riksföreningen Sverige-Tyskland was a Swedish-German association which later became deeply penetrated by the Nazis.

Samfundet Manhem, was founded in 1934 and devoted to propaganda by lectures and pamphlets on behalf of the Nazis and against the British.

Svensk Opposition was Per Engdahl's party. Svenska Socialistiska Partiet, formerly known as Socialistiska Partiet, was the party of the late Nils Flyg. Its official organ was *Folkets Dagblad.*

Sveriges Nationella Förbund was led by Doctor Rütger Essén and numbered many influential people among its members. It published *Dagsposten* and *Nationell Tidning*. Essén appears elsewhere in the chapter on the Italian navy as one of Walter's contacts. He was the foreign editor and a director of the paper *Dagsposten* and wrote articles in *Der Norden*. An historian, he was author of a book *Sverige upplever världen*. He was connected with *Nationell Tidning* and had a particular interest in Russia and the east. He spoke frequently at Manhem meetings and was a political commentator in several Nazi dailies. He was a committee member of the Svensk-Tyska Föreningen and helped to finance *Folkets Dagblad*. He gave a series of anti-Russian lectures during his visit to Finland in January 1943.

Svenska Aktiva Studentförbundet was a Nazi student

organisation founded in the spring of 1942.

Sveriges Nationalsocialistiska Parti was founded in January 1942 by Bertil Anzén. Membership records of these and other societies, address books and other sources give a picture of a cross section of a not very distinguished middle-class Sweden. There are the occasional members of aristocratic families, academics and public servants with very few members of the working class. They ranged from businessmen and officers to hairdressers and vets, country parsons, frustrated politicians and poets, except when it came to thuggery when they hired villains they found on building sites and on the docks.

# VIII

# Propaganda

My office as Press Attaché started in a modest way and built up in size as the war continued and our work increased. The Press Attaché posts in the other Scandinavian capitals were manned in Oslo by Rowland Kenney, who had been the head of the Foreign Office News Department at the beginning of the war and Press Attaché in Oslo in the First World War. He was married to a Norwegian and had very useful contacts in Norway. His son Kit had been in my post in Stockholm and was moved to the job in Helsinki. Copenhagen was taken over by an old friend of mine, Ronnie Turnbull, who had been a great supporter of my Scandinavian Society in Cambridge. He was a Danish speaker, and an experienced journalist on the *Evening Standard*. My number two who succeeded me after I left was Jasper Leadbitter. He came to Stockholm from Hamburg where he had been training as an opera singer. He married an amusing and intelligent Swedish girl, Anna Lisa, and the two of them continued a successful career in the diplomatic service until Jasper's retirement. Side by side with him was Charlie Montague Evans. We had known him in England as a modern language master at Eton, who had taught mainly Spanish. He introduced me to Lionel Fortescue, another Eton master, who was an expert on Iceland and took me there in 1938. Charlie had been staying with us in Sweden during the summer of 1939 and when I went home to join up at the end of August that year, he stayed behind and offered his services to the Legation where I found him on my return. He remained for two years concerning himself with the press and films and then went home to do a job in the Ministry of Information. After the war he came back to Sweden, married a Swede, started a family and there he died in 1990.

Jim Knapp-Fisher, the chairman of Sidgwick & Jackson, the publishers, who had many close friends in Germany, came out to handle films and books. Also, as a sideline, he was allocated the job of talking to members of the German resistance with Roger Hinks. It was a matter of deep sadness to him that these fine men, Moltke and von Trott, with whom he was in touch, could not be helped and were executed by Hitler for their complicity in the Stauffenberg plot. As Sweden became more isolated so it became more difficult to get hold of British books. It was thanks to Jim Knapp-Fisher that two Swedish publishing houses started to publish English books in English, an enterprise which continued for a few years after the war and helped us out in those days of paper shortages.

George Alexander was a local businessman who was the head of HMV. The company was dependent on imported records, but George was not to be daunted and set up his own local workshop in what had previously been a cheese factory. With a small five-piece band he started recording the latest American and British tunes. On one occasion he was short of sheet music for one tune and had just seen a preview of Robert Taylor and Vivien Leigh in *Waterloo Bridge*, which began with a dinner in the Candlelight Club where they danced the night out to the tune of Auld Lang Syne, played as a waltz. His band had never heard of the tune, so he whistled it to them. They scored it, played it and the recording became the best selling Swedish recording of war years under the title 'Godnattvalsen' or 'The Goodnight Waltz'. He joined us in the course of 1941 to handle the distribution of British films which were beginning to come through on the special courier flights from Leuchars. George had very good contacts in the film world and with the help of Walter Fuchs of MGM and Carl York of Paramount, the films got into the circuits.

Films were a medium much used by the Germans to woo or terrorise the Swedes and we gradually counter-attacked as best we could. Carl and Walter helped us to dent and finally overwhelm the Germans with private showings of censored films and public successes, such as *Mrs Miniver* which ran for months at the Rigoletto.

Von Gossler, the head of the German Tourist Bureau, described to his masters in desperation this film's box office success, its run and his inability to intervene with the Swedes to have it withdrawn. About a film called *The Night Express* he described how the audience burst out laughing every time there was a Hitler salute. He complained of another film which showed German fighters being shot out of the sky. The film, *Foreign Correspondent*, played to ninety percent full houses and *A Yankee Flies to London* with Tyrone Power, he described as excellent in every way in spite of being pure enemy propaganda, as was also *Dangerous Moonlight* and the *International Division*. *Casablanca* took some time to get through the Swedish censor, but when it did it was an unqualified success. We had very successful private showings of Charlie Chaplin's *The Great Dictator* and Noel Coward's *In Which We Serve*. I do not think either of the films was shown publicly until after the war.

The German effort, however, was massive and had been in place before the war. It was reinforced during the war but the Germans complained that they never really established themselves. The Swedish Trade Unions had maintained a blockade against German goods since 1933, but in September 1940 it was lifted and the German film offensive began. At that time Sweden was cut off from the West and British and American films were in short supply. But as soon as our air service was established, our films were flown in and began to dominate the market again. The Germans planned and failed with projects for German-Swedish joint productions and the purchase of cinemas. They tried to stop allied films being copied on imported German raw film, but failed.

They were more successful with newsreels and promoted sixteen and eight millimeter amateur films for private propaganda showings. But their propaganda was too crass. The film on the Polish campaign was shown in all the Scandinavian capitals to selected audiences before 8 April 1940, the day before the invasion of Norway and Denmark, in order to terrorise the audiences. This was also the case with *Sieg im Westen* from February 1941 onwards in public cinemas. Private showings to officers and journalists were made of the early months of the Russian campaign, but then the fortunes of war turned against them and German films ceased to attract attention either publicly or privately. They did not enjoy our practical joke of inviting leading Swedish Nazis to a showing of *Sieg im Westen* at the German Legation after the victories in Normandy and the liberation of Paris. They must have spent fortunes on their film offensive, which was of little avail.

We had a visit from Ewan Rabagliati from the Ministry of Information. He and George got together about the possibility of George taking over the job as Radio Officer for the BBC. He joined the Legation staff and abandoned films which were handed over to Jim Knapp-Fisher. He took over as Radio Officer and BBC representative for the rest of the war. Other colleagues were Börje Nordin who did press reading for us and ended up with a very distinguished medical career and Denis Frean, who had been a fire brigade volunteer in Finland and later moved over to the British Council, which he represented in Finland, Iraq and other places with great distinction. He married the daughter of Len Eyre, a leading businessman in the business community who also joined our staff. One of our translators, a Swede, called Kurt Fröderström, was a tremendous standby as was Norman Lamming as correspondent for *Reynolds News* and liaison man with the Swedish Co-operative and Trades Union movement. Mr Bell, a haggard skeleton of a man, kept us in order as our accountant, and we were helped by numerous others including John Hamilton, an Egyptologist refugee.

A Mr Perschke joined us and another refugee from Finland Mr Foden-Pattinson, who started our photographic and printing department in the basement. He became, among other things, a very competent forger. Mrs Thompson, the wife of the head of Price Waterhouse in Stockholm, had been my first secretary and organised the office. She was succeeded by the diminutive and charming Mrs Virke who looked after me for the whole of the war. Her little brother Harry Carter was an office boy and runner. He is now head of the Foreign Department of the Skandinaviska Enskilda Banken. Last but not least was Gösta Sandström who was found by Charlie Montague Evans as editor of our weekly newspaper. Gösta was not a member of the Press Department but acted independently as the responsible publisher and editor of the paper. He did this with great competence throughout the war, moving up to a remarkably high circulation of 500,000. Charlie got to know him through sailing. He was an expert at exhibitions and communications and had been responsible for part of the Swedish Exhibition at the New York World Trade Fair in 1939. When I made the arrangement with Barbara Ward to print *The Economist* in Sweden, he was the natural choice as the local representative and editor. Many years after *The Economist* ceased to print in Sweden he still continued as their representative. He was a keen sailor. Charlie Montague Evans and I shared a small boat called *Undra*, a clinker-built cockleshell, and Gösta asked us if we would like to buy his yacht *Valkyrian*, a 34 square metre (sail area) archipelago cruiser. We took this on and after Charlie left for England I made arrangements for the boat to be taken over by SOE, leaving me to sail her when I wanted, to maintain her with my SOE colleague, Wilfred Latham, and to use her for briefing our SOE contacts operating in other countries.

The Press Department was well-equipped with radio receivers which provided the main material for our weekly newspaper and for the daily press service we sent out in English with full texts of articles in the British daily press of the day before. Our receiver was intended for Beirut but arrived in Stockholm by mistake. Another sudden bonus came with the German occupation of Hungary when the whole Hungarian Press Department defected to us with all their personnel and equipment including their Hellschreiber provided by the German Ministry of Propaganda. It was an instant source of all German and Axis news releases and propaganda material.

I arrived in Sweden to take up my job as Press Attaché without any brief and was told to work out my own destiny. In addition to my responsibilities to the Ministry of Information and the Foreign Office, the British Council asked me to hold a watching brief for them. In return they provided me for the first few months with photographs and press material, films and gramophone records, none of which was available initially from the Ministry of Information. I had had my contacts with MI6 during my training in Broadway buildings on cipher breaking, and although I had no official connection with them, I was asked to give a hand when I could in the course of my ordinary work. This I did as discreetly as possible, particularly on matters inside Germany.

In 1940 Sir Charles Hambro asked me to help in the setting up of a new organisation to replace 'D' section which had been in charge of subversive activity and sabotage in the early days of the war. Since it was all part of the war effort, I agreed to do what I could and knocked together the beginnings of SOE with Malcolm Munthe. He was the son of the famous Swedish doctor and author, Axel Munthe, and had worked with Andrew Croft, the arctic explorer, in ferrying military supplies across Norway and Sweden to Finland. He had escaped to Sweden after the German occupation of Norway and was appointed assistant Military Attaché in the Legation. I was only too well aware of the potential conflict of interests between SOE, the Ministry of Information and the Foreign Office, as also to some extent, with MI6 and it was important for me to reconcile these conflicts in my own activities. I had never met any of the previous Ministers of Information though I got to know Reith and Duff Cooper later. I explained my dilemma to Charles Hambro and asked if he would introduce me to Bracken whom I knew as a very effective man and close friend of Churchill. I wanted to clear my yardarm with him and met this affable, redheaded giant in his office, pacing up and down in front of the fireplace and stopping to thump me on the back and saying 'good show, my boy, you have my blessing. But don't get your lines crossed and trip yourself up.' With some relief at this mixed metaphor, I returned to Sweden and did my best to pursue my multiple activities without suffering from a split personality.

My first task in Sweden was to be clear about our war aims as they must be the framework of my activity. My few weeks in the infant Ministry of Information, or misinformation as it was nicknamed by many of its employees, left me with the depressing feeling that people were more interested in setting up a new wartime bureaucracy and securing a position in it, than in defining what the war was about and fighting it.

There were formidable disadvantages in that the Germans had already established their own organisations for propaganda and subversion. They were supported by local Nazi groups whose activities ranged from propaganda, papers, news agencies, pamphlets and window displays, to armed gangs, thuggery and preparation for sabotage. While public opinion was generally anti-Nazi, there was a strong pro-German tradition in the older generation with active pro-Nazi groups in the navy and secret police.

By the end of September 1939, German victories in Poland had shattered Swedish morale. Our failure to help our Polish ally, our ineffective leaflet raids on Germany and our arguments about whether we were at war with Nazism or with Germany, made the Swedes wonder whether we were taking the war seriously. The long period of the phoney war reinforced their doubts, which were increased by German and Swedish peace feelers. Hopes of allied intervention to help Finland in the first winter war against Russia were extinguished by the armistice of 12 March 1940. The disastrous failures of our Norwegian campaign and the collapse of France bred the defeatism which led to the agreement for the transit of German troops on Swedish railways and waters to and from Norway and later Finland. 2,100,000 German soldiers moved to and fro, safe from allied air attack in neutral Sweden. This height of Swedish ignominy was coupled with a disbelief that any war aims we had would affect the Nazi war machine. The Swedish government also feared that Britain might be ready to come to terms with Hitler. Then when we stood alone, led by the indomitable Churchill, winning the Battle of Britain, defeating German invasion plans, and finally turning the tide with El Alamein, followed by the Russian victory at Stalingrad, the Swedes recovered their courage.

The Casablanca Declaration of Unconditional Surrender was considered a psychological mistake which prolonged the war, but it finally convinced the Swedes that our war aims were the total defeat of Germany. In spite of the apparent confusion in our war aims, our peace aims displaced the argument on war. There was more interest in the sort of Britain which would emerge from the implementation of the Beveridge Report, the sort of world order that might replace the old one and the part to be allotted to our defeated enemies. In spite of the effort of German propaganda and subversion, we had an asset the Germans could not match in the basic commonsense of a well-educated Swedish population with an intellectual elite mostly opposed to a Nazi dictatorship.

From the start this made it possible for us to avoid brash propaganda as far as we could, concentrating on information instead. We avoided as far as possible interference in Swedish internal affairs and never camouflaged our activities as being anything other than British or allied. We were well supplied with material from London in due course and this was backed by the very excellent services of the BBC, which included the Swedish one. But the following exchange of minutes between the then D.G. of the Ministry of Information, Mr Frank Pick, to Mr Lee Ashton, who later on took over the Victoria and Albert Museum, is evidence of the kind of obfuscation one encountered in the early stages of the war.

30.11.1940

I have been noticing in our recent Foreign Office telegrams that your Press Attaché in Sweden is going madder and madder. I think we must have an immediate review of this gentleman's activities and expenditure. I think he seems to have the notion that he represents British cultural activity and not mere press and propaganda for I see he wants to supply dance music, English books and all kinds of things free to the Swedes. It is no part of our business. We must therefore have a report as to the gentleman's activities in the last six months and his prospective activities, if not for Tuesday next (as I originally intended) at any rate for Tuesday the 10th December. The sooner we bring him in to order, the better.

Reply from Mr Lee Ashton to the D.G. 1.12.1940

I think Mr. Tennant's request for gramophone records is simply a desire to stimulate ordinary commercial channels as he feels cut off from every source, except Germany. The same may be said for his attempt to get the American booksellers to send as much as possible. We are not expected to pay, but he uses us as a channel for the request as well as Mr. Hambro, who represents the black side. I have asked Mr. Kenny to be prepared for tomorrow week and in the meanwhile attach a report we received in September from Mr. Tennant. At the special request of the F.O. this was circulated to all European posts.

The Swedish correspondents in London were splendid allies, in particular Alf Martin with his face of a burly Eskimo and his sailor's gait which betrayed his early life before the mast. In peacetime he used his own transport to and from Sweden in the shape of a splendid Swedish west coast Koster fishing boat. He had been many years in London when suddenly he was called back to Sweden by his editor, Professor Torgny Segerstedt, to become foreign editor of *Göteborgs Handels- och Sjöfartstidning*; but in March 1940 he was told to return to England as his replacement had fallen ill. There he remained for the rest of the war and for the rest of his active life. His cheerful face brightened the press room of the Ministry of Information, his articles in *GHT* were sturdy accounts of courage in the devastation of war and his regular anonymous commentaries on the Swedish service of the BBC gained a wider and wider listening public in Sweden. One day when he was telephoning *GHT*'s shipping editor, Sven Rinman, to give him details of the latest British minefields, the telephone was suddenly cut off and from that time on, there was no longer a telephone link with Sweden for the rest of the war. He suddenly realised England was isolated and this was the title of two volumes of essays published in July and December 1940 *The Isolated Island Kingdom (Det isolerade öriket)*. While we stood alone at that time we were not as isolated as the Swedes, surrounded on all sides by the Germans in Norway and Denmark who were, by then, also surreptitiously building up their forces in Finland. The Baltic was a German lake, but whether it was Sweden or Britain which was isolated, these essays were well-informed views of Britain's contribution to western civilisation and they covered parliamentary government, economics, education, science, sport, literature and art, the army, the Royal Navy, the Merchant Navy and the church. Some of these authors' names recur frequently in these pages and are remembered among those who stood by us when we stood alone. Gustav Hellström, the novelist and journalist, who had been a correspondent in London for many years. Bo Enander, the historian, broadcaster and journalist. The two Heckschers father and son. The economist, Gunnar Westin-Silverstolpe, Emil Boldt-Christmas, former Naval Attaché in London. Asta Kihlbom who, after the war ran the Swedish Institute in London and Greta Hedin on education. Torsten Tegnér, the sports journalist, wrote on sport, Frans G. Bengtsson, the historical novelist and essayist, on English literature, and Gustaf Stridsberg on the benefits Britain had conferred on the world as a world power. Harry Martinson, the sailor writer, wrote of the British seaman and there was Anton Fridrichsen on religion. Wettergren on the theatre. Liljestrand on medical research in England and Axel Romdahl on painting from Hogarth to Bonnington.

Whether they were Swedish correspondents in London or Swedish writers in Sweden, it was far more valuable to us for them to record their views and the news as they saw it than for us to concentrate on communicating direct. For this reason we arranged, as soon as transport was available, for Swedish journalists and writers such as Harald Wigforss, the future editor of *GHT*, Asta Kihlbom and Maj Lorents who had been in England earlier, to visit our isolated island and write their articles and books about us. Gullers, who later became a world-famous photographer, did a remarkable job with his series of photographs of war-time England. One day I was asked if I would make arrangements for a politician called Tage Erlander to visit England on a secret mission at the special request of the Prime Minister, Per Albin Hansson. This quiet, amiable giant called on me and explained his plans to spend two months in England to be briefed on Air Raid Precautions. I never suspected then that he would be the future Prime Minister of Sweden.

Alf Martin's discretion and kindness involved him in a curious Anglo-Swedish diplomatic incident. In the late Autumn of 1941 the Swedish Minister, Björn Prytz, asked him he needed an assistant. Without further ado he produced a tall, slim, young Swede called Lars Lind with a perfect command of English. Lars had been a volunteer in the Finnish coastal artillery. He assumed, wrongly, that the Swedish government would be as enthusiastic about supporting Norway as it had been about Finland. In his Swedish military service he had made Norwegian friends who promised he could be got over to England to join the Norwegian forces and he waited for a message. He was posted to an island far out at sea on the Baltic coast opposite Åland watching German troop transports and planes. Here he received the expected message in the Autumn of 1941. He got leave to return to Stockholm, then went absent without leave and hid underground. He was smuggled to Gothenburg where he was hidden waiting for the opportunity to join one of George Binney's convoys. This failed and he returned to Stockholm where he was hidden in one of our Legation cellars. Our Minister, Victor Mallet, was faced with a rather special problem. The young man turned out to be the nephew of Christian Günther, the Swedish Foreign Minister. Mallet went round to see Günther 'I have come to see you about your nephew', he said. 'Oh dear, poor boy, I understand, however, he is safely away in England', replied Günther. 'No', said Mallet, 'he is actually in my cellar.'

Recovering from the shock, Günther asked if we could help

spirit him away and avoid all the unpleasantness that would ensue if the truth were revealed. We had his hair dyed and carried out other small facial alterations and, with the help of a forged British passport he was slipped past the watchful security guards at Bromma airport and whisked over to London for interrogation by the security authorities. He was then handed over to the Swedish Minister, Björn Prytz, who passed him on to Martin. He achieved his ambition of fighting the Nazis by joining the Norwegian Navy. After the war, he was first with UNESCO under Julian Huxley in Paris, then with the Food and Agricultural Organisation in Rome, then head of information in the new International Atomic Energy Agency in Vienna. After this he joined the World Bank as a director under Robert MacNanamara. Alf Martin's paper *GHT*, of course, never lost an opportunity to attack poor Günther's neutrality policy. Martin was a staunch friend and ally and his booming sailor's voice was heard clearly above the din of war. The unsentimental humour and humanity of his talks were in the best tradition of radio journalism.

People were more important than paper and I spent more and more of my time on people rather than printed matter. I lectured a lot and visited universities and people's high schools and the Workers Education Association. A Swedish initiative in this field was important in getting more balance into our political reporting. This tended to be coloured by Swedish official attitudes and took too little account of the views of leading opinion formers who were not government stooges. The initiative was taken by Doctor Ragnar Svanström, the historian, publisher and current affairs expert, resulting in our monthly ABS dinners (American British Swedish). These were held in private in well-known restaurants, such as Hasselbacken and Gyldene Freden and ranged from small groups of about fifteen to larger ones of forty or more. The British and American Ministers were nearly always present and so were other senior members of the two Legations, whose Swedish contacts tended to be more official than unofficial. No ministers or government officials were ever invited. Sometimes leading visitors from Britain or America joined us. Not only was it a good opportunity for our two Legations to get to know important people, other than those with whom they had official contacts, but for the Swedes it was of great interest as they were able to discuss current problems with British and American representatives who were handling these matters on a day-to-day basis.

While I always gave priority to our personal relationships with a growing number of Swedish and allied friends, we naturally had to make the best use of the media to keep as wide a section of the public as possible informed. We made good use of photographs with the professional help of Martin Martelius of Text Och Bilder, the main suppliers to the press. He also ran display windows which were a great success, in particular when the Swedish censorship had one taken down and a number of our weekly newspaper *Nyheter från Storbritannien* confiscated. Harold Nicolson was impressed by the crowds round our display window on Vasagatan by contrast with the German window which had no viewers other than armed police to prevent vandalism.

We translated and printed many of the white papers and war documents in Swedish and also went in for some more popular illustrated brochures on the war covering the armed forces and the home front. I had much help from Ernest Biggs, an Englishman who was advertising manager of the department store Paul U Bergström. He lost a leg in the First War and settled in Sweden which he knew well. He was an expert at publicity and printing and helped me launch many publications. He later became implicated with the Rickman affair and served a year's prison sentence for subversive activity. He survived this with amazing good humour. He introduced me to that excellent character, Ture Nerman, author and publicist and unashamed opponent of Nazism. He was the editor of the anti-Nazi paper *Trots Allt* which was always getting into trouble with the authorities and he himself served a prison sentence of three months for insulting Hitler.

We ran a duplicated daily press service of excerpts in English from the British Press which had ceased to reach Sweden after the occupation of Norway and Denmark. Our excellent wireless receiver we used for monitoring voice and morse transmissions. This press service was circulated to a restricted list of editors and important opinion formers. The main vehicle for our printed efforts became our weekly newspaper *Nyheter från Storbritannien*, or *News from Britain*, or as we cynically called it, *Storheter från Nybritannien*, or *Great things from new Britain*.

I had begun my own weekly newsletter which I wrote in Swedish, but wound it up by the end of 1939 as it claimed far too

One of many propaganda shop windows, Vasagatan, Stockholm, 1941

much of my time and reached far too few people. So the Ministry of Information, through our mentors and allies Chester Purvis and Grace Thornton, took a quantum leap and authorised me to publish a weekly newspaper to be distributed free. It was a frankly British enterprise and in no way emulated the German technique of masquerading as a patriotic Swedish publication. Gösta Sandström became editor and responsible publisher, designations which were all required by Swedish law, and he turned out to be a firm anchor of our efforts throughout the war. To start with the copies were sent with my compliments from the Legation, but gradually it became a much more businesslike undertaking and when Gösta took over the printing and distribution of *The Economist* after Barbara Ward's visit, we formed a publishing company Förlags Aktiebolaget Britannia which was responsible for the printing and distribution and promotion of both the publications.

For the first half of 1940 the printing was done in Stockholm, but from August onwards it was printed in Västerås by *Västmanlands Läns Tidning*. The first numbers were 47 centimetres x 32.5 on very heavy glossy paper, but from our move to Västerås in August 1940 we enlarged our format to 45 centimetres x 55 centimetres using cheaper newsprint. We started with four page numbers but the size often fluctuated between four, six and eight pages.

It was difficult to find any enterprise in the darkest days of the war which would dare risk being openly identified with the British as printer and distributor of our newspaper. Our first printer, Kihlström, was a small book printing business and was unable to produce more than 30,000/35,000 copies a week. We searched in vain for a printer with greater capacity, first in Stockholm, and then in the provinces. Quite by chance however the Stockholm printer, Karl Rehnskog, met an advertising man, Sven Rygaard, who suggested Anders Pers in Västerås. He was sure he would not hesitate to print. Rehnskog immediately went to Västerås and started negotiations with the splendid old provincial paper with its half dozen associated weeklies and dailies. It was agreed to leave the editorial office in Stockholm where the type could be set and matrices pressed. The final decision however had to be made by Anders Pers (1860-1951), the revered octogenarian Chairman of the firm, who was still doing a few hours in his office every afternoon. The old man and his son took only a couple of minutes to say yes. They gave us an estimate within four days, which we accepted without demur. After some delay about supplying paper, which was entirely our fault, the newspaper procured the newsprint and our paper was launched in its new format on 5 August 1940. This was in the middle of the Battle of Britain and just after Dunkirk, our withdrawal from Norway, the defeat of France and the transit of German troops through Sweden to Norway. We began with 50,000/55,000 copies, and reached 500,000 by the end of the war. Our friends in Västerås were threatened with anonymous letters and barricaded the windows of their printing hall that faced the street. They were threatened with the withdrawal of advertising, but refused to compromise in any way. The price they quoted was very reasonable with no extras to cover their risks. They were faithful friends when very few people were prepared to stand up and be counted. We owe them a deep debt of gratitude.

From 29 January 1940 we printed the BBC news and commentary programmes in English and German to which was added Finnish from 23 March 1940, after the Armistice. Norwegian and Danish were added from 14 April 1940. We also warned against the German service in English called the New British Broadcasting Station while advertising the 'totalitarian interpretation of the news from Königsberg and Moscow'. On 1 July 1940 we devoted a whole page to BBC's European and World services in English, Czech, German, Norwegian, Italian, Polish, French, Portuguese, Spanish, Turkish, Dutch, Arabic, Greek, Finnish, Hungarian, Serbo-Croat and Danish, with instructions as to how best to choose wavelengths. The importance of the BBC can hardly be exaggerated and while we helped to provide material for many of the services, making local recordings in Sweden for some of them, we were particularly close to the Swedish service so ably run by Margaret Sampson and Halvor William Olsen. Margaret visited Sweden and George Alexander finally took over the representation of the BBC in Stockholm and did a useful tour of briefing in England. The Swedish radio Radiotjänst adopted a neutral stance, but was understandably antipathetic to German propaganda. The head of the Service, Yngve Hugo, was a good friend and as the war progressed many of the Swedish correspondents in London, in particular Alf Martin, became familiar voices on the service which was finally served by an accredited representative of the Swedish Radio in London.

*Nyheter från Storbritannien* produced special numbers on

South Africa, New Zealand and the RAF. It is interesting to dig into the 260 numbers over the five years and see how we presented the events and issues of the war as seen on the touchline of Sweden, how we avoided some and overplayed others, but how on the whole we presented a balanced picture. During the whole Finnish war we equated the Russians with the Germans as the villains of the piece, but slowly we began to show that there were cracks in the Russo-German alliance. We moved over with some difficulty to accepting the Russians as our allies, did so wholeheartedly for as long as the war lasted and were thanked most warmly by the Russian Ambassador, Alexandra Kollontay, and their Press Attaché, Mrs Jartseva.

With our mining of Norwegian waters and the German invasion of Norway and Denmark, we deluded ourselves sufficiently to produce banner headlines that Hitler had stuck his neck out. We had given full publicity to the *Altmark* affair and Britain's victory in the battle of the River Plate with the sinking of the *Graf Spee*. On 16 March, three days after the Finnish armistice, we wrote a sad leader surrounded with a black border pointing out that the real culprit in the fate of Finland was the Germans who in the Ribbentrop/Molotov pact had given a free hand to Russia in the Baltic States and Finland.

Our defeats and withdrawal from Norway began the series of disasters that beset us with the invasion of Holland, Belgium and the fall of France. We presented the allied leaders, particularly Winston Churchill. Above all it was the Battle of Britain that sustained us and increased more and more the demand for our newspaper. But not a word was said about the Swedish capitulation to German demands for the transit of troops to and from Norway on Swedish railways. Conflicts of interest between Russia and Germany began to be underlined in the paper from August 1940 onwards. On Wednesday the 12th of November 1941, *Nyheter från Storbritannien* received a message from our Prime Minister in the following terms:

> I have received the hundredth number of *Nyheter från Storbritannien*. I warmly congratulate the editorial staff and all those who assist in the preparation of this excellent newspaper. I am especially pleased to learn that it has so large a circulation, but I am not surprised. Continue to present the truth about the

struggle of this Empire and its allies for the preservation of freedom, democracy and enlightenment and you will naturally find ready acceptance among Swedes who cherish the same ideals. The day will come when we can pursue these ideals in peace. Signed, Churchill.

*Nyheter* always carried details of BBC programmes for overseas. The Norwegian and Danish programmes and their changes were important, as copies of the paper were smuggled to our occupied friends who were well able to read Swedish. The Swedish service started on short-wave only, first once, and later three times daily, and lastly using medium-wave in December 1943. With a full-time BBC officer in George Alexander, he not only promoted and lectured on the BBC round the country, but also got a considerable fan mail by advertising in *Nyheter* free copies of a brochure called *En världsmakt i etern* (*A World Power in the Ether*) and later in 1944 one called *Här är London* (*Here is London*). Although atmospheric conditions sometimes made it difficult to tune into the stations, on the whole the BBC broadcasts got through well and increased the readership of *Nyheter,* which in turn increased the BBC listening public.

Apart from the BBC programmes, *Nyheter* gradually became a useful vehicle for advertising. First, in June 1943, it advertised the re-appearance of British weeklies on the bookstalls, flown in regularly through the German blockade by the splendid BOAC pilots who built up a more regular service. By 29 September 1943 daily and weekly copies of *The Times* were available as well as the miniature weekly copies on thin bible paper. On 2 February 1944 *The Economist*, printed in Sweden under an agreement with Barbara Ward, was published at a price of 26 kr. a quarter. By November 1944 all English papers and periodicals were available. Then came the English books, first in translation and then in English by Ljus Förlag and Zephyr. They were a mixture of well-selected classics and recently published titles. Numerous books by Swedish writers about England, such as Maj Lorents and Harald Wigforss, were advertised, as was also Willy Brandt's book on the world after the war.

The paper carried regular articles on British and allied leaders with texts of the most important speeches and broadcasts by

British publications and weekly newspaper, December 1939

Churchill, Beaverbrook, Bracken, Duff Cooper, Reith, Ernest Bevin, Eden, Smuts, Wavell, Monty, Hugh Dalton, etc., with more and more American material as they had no comparable paper. Among other rarities, it carried Churchill's speech to the Althing in Iceland on 27 August 1941. The Royal family and the talks to the nation by the King, the Queen and Princess Elizabeth featured regularly. The Americans were joined by our other allies, the French, the Norwegians and Danes, with frequent quotes from personalities such as de Gaulle, Trygve Lie and Christmas Møller.

The contributors to the paper included British and allied journalists in Stockholm, such as Ossian Goulding of the *Telegraph*, Edmond Demaitre of the *Express*, Oliver Urch of *The Times* and Denis Weaver of the *News Chronicle*, but most of the material was either lifted from BBC broadcasts or specially commissioned articles supplied by the Ministry of Information. The range of contributions was enormous and very representative of the voices we heard on the BBC and the articles we read in the dailies and weeklies throughout the war.

Each number was well illustrated with excellent photographs, line drawings and cartoons. There was the revelation of the Whittle jet engine in 1944, kept under wraps since 1941; of the V2 in November 1944, a prototype of which had landed in Sweden that summer and been transferred to Farnborough for examination in great secrecy. Air photographs of Taranto, Genoa and Italian yards, the end of the *Tirpitz* in Tromsöfjord and endless photographs of the war at sea and in the air, of the desert war and the liberation of western Europe. Then there was the aerial photograph of *Gay Viking* on 2 August 1944, one of our five motor coasters from George Binney's blockade busting expeditions between Grimsby and Lysekil, news of which had first been released in July. While people in Gothenburg and along the west coast were in the know as far as these expeditions were concerned, they were not generally known to the Swedish public.

The paper gave as faithful a record of events as our own censorship permitted and not much was distorted or omitted. The dissolution of the Komintern was, alas, heralded on 2 June 1943 as a sign of Russia's renunciation of a policy of world domination by subversion and sabotage. It is sad to think how wrong we were. In August 1943 there was the German takeover in Denmark and the rescue of the Danish Jews who escaped to Sweden. Then there was the appointment of Eisenhower and Monty for 'Overlord' and finally the elation of D-Day at 0300 hrs on 6 June which was recorded in our number of 7 June. On 26 July we gave our first news of the Stauffenberg plot of 20 July, to be followed on 2 August with rumours of Rommel's death. On 13 December came a thank you from Churchill to the Swedes for their good wishes on his 70th birthday. We had to try and stem the flood of presents of cigars as the Prime Minister was clocking up a considerable bill with customs on import duties. In spite of the inevitable inaccuracies due to censorship, these numbers still represent a creditable record of the war as we saw it or wished it to be seen from London and Stockholm and great credit must be given to the editorial team.

Themes covered by the paper were firstly our war aims, culminating in the Casablanca Declaration of Unconditional Surrender and then the various arguments about the future of Germany. All this was gradually overlapped by a growing discussion on peace aims both domestically - in particular the Beveridge Report - and internationally with what finally emerged as the United Nations Organisation, the World Bank and the Bretton Woods Agreements. We were well aware in Sweden of the horrors of the concentration camps. We gave them little publicity until September 1944 with the revelations of Maidanek, publishing thousands of copies of these ghastly crimes, and giving publicity to Eden's statement in Parliament in the middle of the war.

1944 ended with a balance sheet of the British war effort and the incomparable contribution British men and women had made to the defence of the country and the liberation of Europe. The last number ended with a wishful dream of the British lead in post-war civil aviation, a jet-propelled Brabazon crossing the Atlantic in fifteen hours. This dream could never compete with the reality of US aircraft production which easily converted bombers to airliners.

The paper omitted most of those matters which were of a sensitive nature for the Swedes. We were frank in our disappointment at the refusal of the Norwegians and Swedes to allow the British and French to transit their troops across northern Norway and Sweden to come to the aid of the Finns. We were too preoccupied by the fall of France and our own retreat from Norway to express publicly what we felt about the Swedish concession in June 1940 to the German demands for troop transit to and from Norway. This concession allowed German soldiers to cross Sweden to and from Norway out of reach of allied attack. The same applied to the German use of Swedish territorial waters and the Falsterbo canal to move their troops to Finland out of reach of our mine-laying aircraft. No mention was made of the transit of the German Engelbrecht Division from Norway to Finland and the crisis this caused when the King was thought to be threatening abdication unless the Germans were allowed to cross the country.

The paper did not reflect our conflicts with the Swedes over iron-ore and ball-bearing shipments to Germany and the measures the Swedes took to try and frustrate George Binney's blockade-breaking expeditions. Finally we did break this tactful silence in April 1944 when we let it be known in *Nyheter* that the British and American governments were not satisfied with the Swedish reply to their joint note about stopping ball-bearing shipments to Germany. The troop transit traffic came to an end with the same lack of mention as it began. There were exceptions to this silence in our reprint of Lord Semphill's lecture to the Royal Empire Society on Sweden in the war and Oliver Urch's article in *The Times* on Sweden which weighed up the pros and cons of Swedish neutrality policy.

From the beginning *Nyheter* had a column or more on English poetry and prose and essays on literature and the arts. We printed extracts in Swedish of descriptions of English life in the nineteenth century by Swedish visitors such as the historian Geijer and the writer Fredrika Bremer. Prizes were given of 25 kr. for the best translation of an English poem. Poems and prose by Tennyson, Masefield, Eric Gill, Arthur Bryant, Thomas Hardy and Dickens, Kipling, E.M. Forster and Robert Bridges, were supplemented by poetry from allies such as Nordahl Grieg with his Norwegian poem 'Eidsvold og Norge'. On 14 May 1941 we printed a facsimile of the letter from Roosevelt to Churchill introducing Wendell Willkie with the quotation from Longfellow's 'Old Ironside' (Sail on oh ship of State) and Winston's reply with a quotation from Arthur Hugh Clough's 'but westward look the land is bright'.

By the end of 1941 I was able to hand over my British Council activities to my Cambridge poet friend, Ronald Bottrall. From then on *Nyheter* carried accounts of Council activities such as an exhibition of English painting in January 1942 and summer schools for English teachers in June, July and August in Sigtuna, Lundsberg and St. Sigfrids. We also advertised a monthly periodical called *Things English* for secondary schools and, in April 1942, a volume of translations of T.S. Eliot edited by Ronald Bottrall and Gunnar Ekelöf with the help of Erik Mesterton, who, with Karin Boye, had first introduced Eliot to Sweden with their translation of 'The Waste Land'. The translations were all by leading Swedish poets including Eric Blomberg, Karin Boye, Johannes Edfelt, Gunnar Ekelöf, Fehrman, Eric Lundgren, Artur Lundkvist, Mesterton himself, Vennberg and Anders Österling, the Secretary of the Swedish Academy.

*Nyheter* certainly provided a good read every week for Swedes interested in England, past, present and future. One likes to think that this weekly paper with its wide circulation made some contribution to maintaining morale in a country which was profoundly demoralised in the early years of the war.

On 21 February 1945 *Göteborgs Handels- och Sjöfartstidning* printed a letter to me in English from Prince Ferdinand of Liechtenstein as a farewell to me and our *British Press Review* which I had just stopped publishing because British daily papers were now available. The following extract is a kindly comment on our efforts to help keep the Swedish and foreign public in Sweden informed of the British war effort:

> Whilst we were breathlessly watching your fight for survival, we could not help but gaze with morbid curiosity first and then with ever growing admiration, into your homes, torn wide open by bombs, and through the pale resolution of your faces, into your hearts. Not with wig and gown but wrapped in a cloak of flame history presided over your trial; we observed your witnesses take the stand; housewives from your burning cities, sailors from the seven seas adrift on rafts for weeks and signing on anew, the ground rescue workers, elderly matrons cheerfully looking after scores of evacuated children, the ghost parade of 300 young men who had died in your skies to help with the Battle of Britain and preserve freedom in this world. We have seen the British people suffer

and their suffering has endeared them to us; we have seen a great nation, freely determined to resist aggression at whatever price, successfully resisting it, and her example has inspired the world . . .. Then when almost every neutral editor had resigned himself, his paper and his country's future to the unavoidability of a New Europe, when even the faithful voice of the BBC seemed to succumb to the all present cacophony of Sieg Heil's and triumphant marches, your Press Review gave us what we needed most, some of your courage and that infallible stimulus; hope. Speaking for myself I can truthfully say that more than once your Press Review alone has helped me over moments of utter despondency and gloom. This statement may make you smile, but I know I have shared this experience with many of your readers.

**Footnote**

My weekly reports on the situation in Sweden are held in P.R.O. files F.O. 371/24858. FO 371/24859 of 21 September 1940 contains my memorandum on the manning and activities of the Press Department at that date.

# IX
# The Rickman Affair

My friend Ernest Biggs, the advertising manager of PUB, gave me invaluable help with printing, layout and the production of brochures in my first few months in Sweden. He was arrested on 19 April 1940, together with Freddie Rickman, shortly after the German invasion of Norway and Denmark. They were suspected of covert propaganda operations but the police discovered stocks of detonators and plastic. At the trial they were convicted of an attempt to disrupt German iron-ore shipments by demolishing two ore loading cranes at the port of Oxelösund. Biggs got one year and Rickman eight, but the latter was released before the end of his sentence. He lunched with me in my home on his way back to England, the only time I ever met him. However I knew Biggs well and my diaries record six meetings with him up till 30 March 1940.

The incident caused consternation in the Legation and the British Colony as nobody knew who might be implicated. My old friend Harry Söderman of the Swedish Criminal Technical Institute got in touch to say he could no longer see me as my name figured prominently in the papers that had been found. I had no idea what it was all about. Relations were re-established some six months later and we continued to work closely together for the rest of the war.

I was blissfully ignorant of this conspiracy. It took some time before I was able to piece things together. My Minister, Victor Mallet, told me that Erik Boheman, the Secretary General of the Swedish Ministry of Foreign Affairs, was contemplating declaring me *persona non grata.* I was amazed and indignant and promptly contacted the Ministry of Foreign Affairs to see Oscar Thorsing, the Head of the Press Department and later Boheman himself, to assure them they had been making a grave mistake. I suspected I was the victim of the Swedish Security Police and their friends in the German Abwehr who would be only too glad to get rid of me.

My researches revealed more and more involved conspiracies. It was however not until 1985 that I learnt the whole story from my friend Craig Graham McKay of Uppsala University, who has a detailed knowledge of the relevant Swedish archives. Charles Cruickshank's book *S.O.E. in Scandinavia* (the official history, Oxford University Press 1986) is based on government documents which have been denied to me. He reveals on page 41 that the head of our Passport Control Office, Commander J. Martin R.N., the representative of MI6, known to us in the Legation as Pincher for short, had been aware for eighteen months that a German refugee journalist Kurt Singer, who was helpful to me and Ernest Biggs, was a double agent. He was passing information to the Swedish police (Torsten Söderström according to Singer) on our printing activities and our association with Ture Nerman the publisher of *Trots Allt*, the organ of his anti-nazi group the Fighting Democrats (Kämpande Demokrater). Martin warned Rickman of the leaks but did not tell him that the source was Singer. Neither did it occur to him to warn me as a colleague in the Legation. The Germans were naturally fully informed. Craig Graham McKay (*The Historical Journal* 29 April 1986, page 977) also quotes a Swedish document recording a Swedish police delegation visit to Heydrich in Berlin in March 1941 when 'various details relating to the case plus photographs of the sabotage material were handed over'. Kurt Singer passed himself off to me as an anti-nazi, but all the time was persuading the Swedish Security Police that I was the leading figure in a major sabotage operation. Presumably this was in order to cover up Martin's involvement as paymaster of the whole exercise. One curious result was that all this enhanced my spurious reputation as the Head of the Secret Service in Sweden, which was a useful screen for those really involved. The long and the short of the story was as follows.

Bill Stevenson, later famous as Intrepid, the remarkable Canadian, Churchill's personal contact man with Roosevelt on subversive warfare and head of the British Security Co-ordination

Organisation, had visited Sweden in the late thirties. He had persuaded 'D' section and Desmond Morton that Swedish iron ore was the Achilles' heel of the German armament industry. He and others believed that by denying the supply the German war machine would collapse. His arguments were reinforced by frantic Swedish efforts to prove that Germany could dispense with Swedish ore supplies. Apart from plans to neutralise the mines in the north, the ports were also listed as targets and Oxelösund was selected as the main one.

He took on Alfred Frederick (Freddie) Rickman (1902-86) as his agent. Rickman made a tour of Sweden with introductions from the Grängesberg Ore Company in 1938 to study the main ore fields and ports. He was the so-called author of a book *Swedish Iron Ore* published by Faber and Faber in 1939 under contract with Laurence Grand of section 'D'. Rickman came out again to Sweden in the summer of 1939 with commercial cover dealing in dental equipment and tinned goods.

George Binney, who came to Sweden as a representative of the British steel industry (see Chapter XIV), met Rickman at dinner with Reggie Sutton-Pratt, the Military Attaché. He had the greatest difficulty in returning to Sweden on his steel business after a short visit to London because the security services accused him of having compromised Rickman by meeting him. Binney was only too glad not to be compromised by Rickman in return. Rickman rented part of a cellar from the Windsor Tea Company of which Biggs was a director and this was where the sabotage material was stored. This consisted of gelignite, hexogen, limpet-mines, detonators and timing devices. The Military Attaché was the intermediary with London and Martin the paymaster.

He seems to have got the go-ahead about 24 January 1940. In spite of tentative visits to Oxelösund with a rather nervous German refugee fearing the project would trigger off a German invasion of Sweden, no action was taken. Things then became hot as the Germans invaded Norway and Denmark and Rickman decided to move the equipment to the country. But before they could move, Rickman and his secretary, Elsa Johansson (later his wife), and Biggs were arrested.

In London Rickman had been introduced to Ingram Fraser of J. Walter Thompson. He gave him an introduction to Biggs and subsequently visited Sweden as the representative of Electra House. He gave instructions on sabotage and black propaganda in inadequate German to three German refugees who were to carry out the deed and distribute the black propaganda in Germany. Fraser, who carried out his work under the cover name of Foster, finally continued his good work as a right-hand man to Bill Stevenson in New York. He had managed to get out of Sweden just before the German invasion of Norway, returning home via Denmark. He stayed very ostentatiously at the Grand Hotel, altering his identity from Ingram Anthony Fraser to Ingram Orazio Clement Fraser and giving his birthday dates as either 5, 6 or 8 April 1905.

The Military Attaché Reggie Sutton-Pratt and his splendid Sergeant Major Wright were deeply involved, but Henry Kellgren, of the Swedish General Staff, and Erik Boheman, of the Swedish Ministry of Foreign Affairs, took the matter lightly and he was not asked to leave. On 19 April, the day of the arrests, I had an appeal from Gerry Holdsworth, who later became famous in SOE with small boats and subsequently as a documentary film maker. He said he had arrived mysteriously via Russia and Finland escaping from the abortive 'D' section attempt to sabotage the Iron Gates of the Danube in Rumania. In fact he had flown in from London just before the invasion of Norway. He urgently needed protection from the Swedish Police and assistance home, if possible by boat from Petsamo. I rapidly printed notepaper for him headed King Haakon's Fund for Norwegian Refugees and set him up in a room in the Grand Hotel until we got the necessary papers. This was sufficient to protect him from arrest which I could have exposed in the press as an unfriendly act by the Swedes against the Norwegians.

The whole affair had bewildered me with names of organisations and people of whom I had never heard, such as Electra House and 'D' section. I was approached later by Charles Hambro, who was marooned in Sweden owing to the invasion of Norway and Denmark, to be asked if I would be prepared to help with a new organisation. This was how I was recruited into SOE to start it off. I was involved with it throughout the war, though there were never any clear lines of demarcation between my overt information work and covert activities, whether SOE or PWE, or the sort of intelligence work that was a normal activity for any member of the Legation staff.

The documents relating to Rickman's trial examined by Craig

Graham McKay contain some startling revelations about my alleged activities. They are all in Swedish or are translations from English. The papers refer to somebody's instructions to me and Rickman. The author may possibly have been Fraser. They allude to support for the daily papers (we never did anything of the kind), the extension of our weekly paper *Nyheter* to eight pages (this was absolutely nothing to do with anybody else but me), the BBC's news bulletins (this was a matter between me and the BBC), better newsreels (this was my business anyhow), the white book on the Anglo-Russian negotiations, a perfectly straightforward task for me and nothing to do with Rickman. These are described as matters put before Sir John Reith, then Minister of Information. That week, 16 February 1940, there is reference to pamphlets to be spread *sub rosa*, the purchase of Polish photographs, instructions to me to print an edition of the pamphlet *Hitler's Concentration Camps* and *Nazi Lies*. These, as far as I can remember, appeared perfectly overtly. There is also an authorisation to spend 11,500 kr. on a 50,000 edition of English war speeches of which I have no record, nor either a proposal for one million copies of something called *The Front* which is a complete mystery.

Then there is a section on propaganda for Sweden and the objectives to be attained.

The aims of this propaganda were to encourage greater Swedish participation in the Finnish war, to agitate for the transit of large contingents of allied troops and resistance to German aggression. Available means were a brochure *Sweden Awake* with £16,600 allocated for overt and covert propaganda. Existing organisations were to be used, such as Finnish volunteers, trade unions, consumer co-operatives industrial associations, while stickers, posters, graffiti and slogans were to be plastered at night on buildings and pavements. It was in the interest of Sweden to urge the allies to help the Finns and themselves to provide 100,000 men to fight the Russians. With the allies in Sweden a German invasion could be fought off. There were to be protest meetings outside the Russian and German Legations and the German Tourist Bureau. Choruses were to intervene in cinemas when newsreels of the Finnish war were shown. Suggestions for brochures, posters and slogans were:

> 'Finland was beaten by her friends, not by her enemies'; 'Russian threats made heroes of the Finns.

German threats made cowards of the Swedes'; 'Sweden's frontier is the Mannerheim line'; 'Germany insists on iron-ore exports being increased to 12 million tons. Let the Finns have weapons of Swedish iron ore not the Germans to suppress the Czechs, Poles and help the Russians against the Finns'.

There was material for Germany, address lists for Essen, Breslau and Dresden of carpenters, butchers, bakers, hairdressers and innkeepers with twelve pfennig stamps and 3000 addressed envelopes. There was a brochure printing a letter from a wife to her husband at the front indicating that she might qualify for the mother's cross of honour third class for a child fathered by the kind S.S. man on the ground floor. There were warnings to U-boat crews and exhortations to the workers by the Social Democrat Front to use their strength to overthrow Nazi terror.

There was the nine-fold amulet for all the plagues of war, a chain letter containing an illustration with two concentric circles the space between divided into nine fields with the words, famine, air raids, influenza, treachery and denunciation, Polish spotted typhus, shells, inflation, gas attack, bullets.

This letter with the nine-fold ring had to be copied three times exactly and the copies sent within three days to people known at the front or at home. In this way one will be protected from all dangers provided no-one breaks the chain.

This is material the police found in Rickman's cellar. If I had known of it, some parts could have been turned to good account. Similar products were made good use of by the SOE German section. The subversive attacks on the Swedish government were clumsy and unnecessary. The Swedes themselves were far more capable than we were of doing the job without any prompting from us. Organisations like Ture Nerman's Kämpande Demokrati and his paper, *Trots Allt*, Amelie Posse's Tuesday Club and the important opposition group Föreningen Norden with its paper *Nordens Frihet* could attack the Swedish government far more effectively than we could.

As far as the Press was concerned, Torgny Segerstedt's 'I Dag' articles in the *Göteborgs Handels- och Sjöfartstidning* could never be rivalled by anything we undertook either covertly or overtly, so we stuck to overt propaganda in our own name for Sweden. When it came to SOE activity Sweden was not a target only a base from which activities were organised in Germany or the occupied countries. For Sweden we made plans with others for stay-behind operations in the event of a German invasion, the most important of which was the construction of radio transmitters, the training of operators and the placing of sets in numerous locations.

These plans were called off before the end of the war as the likelihood of an invasion was minimal and the capacity of the Swedes to defend themselves, both physically and morally, became convincing. The Rickman affair was a sadly bungled operation which did not impress either neutrals, allies or enemies with our war-winning ability.

# X
## Grey and Black Propaganda, SOE, Intelligence and all that

Sir Charles Hambro had recruited me into SOE before it was started in July 1940. Malcolm Munthe, who escaped from Norway through the German lines into Sweden, was appointed assistant Military Attaché and took over SOE Norway. I was asked to handle Sweden, Denmark and Germany until other arrangements were made.

My confusion about the multiplicity of secret organisations operating autonomously was understandable. The rivalry between the KGB and GRU in Russia was typical. Conflict between SOE and MI6 during the last war depended on the scene of operations. In Spain, Sam Hoare made use of Hillgarth as his Naval Attaché for the first half of the war to coordinate all secret activities. The OSS faced rivalry with the FBI. Throughout the war we had very close relations with the OSS representatives, George Brewer, the intelligent and humorous playwright, and Margit Kingston, the very amusing and sparkling representative of *Vogue*. Professor Hopper, the Head of OSS, spent more time on his academic cover than on active operations and we saw very little of him.

In our case, in addition to MI6 before July 1940, first Electra House was responsible for subversive propaganda under the wing of the Foreign Office. Second Section D, again with Foreign Office cover, was responsible for attacking the enemy by means other than conventional warfare. Third, there was the War Office branch Military Intelligence Research (MIR), formerly General Staff

Research (GSR), developing methods of guerilla warfare. They had a small R & D section researching into silent killing which, among other things, developed a very deadly crossbow. Representatives of MIR were our friends Andrew Croft and Malcolm Munthe, whom we saw a lot of in the early part of the war when they were ferrying weapons to Finland from Norwegian ports through Sweden, thinly disguised as agricultural machinery, etc.

It was now suggested all these bodies should be merged under the DMI with ministerial responsibility being shared between the Foreign Secretary, the Secretary of State for War and the Minister of Information. On sabotage in enemy countries, the DMI would be responsible to the Minister of Economic Warfare and the Secretary of State for War. Dalton, as Minister of Economic Warfare, disagreed, insisting that regular soldiers must have nothing to do with irregular activities, which should be run by civilians not subject to bureaucratic military discipline. On 19 July 1940 Neville Chamberlain, as Lord President, recorded that the Prime Minister, Winston Churchill, who had succeeded him, had decided that the sabotage and subversive activities under Section D, MIR and Electra House should be amalgamated to form SOE (Special Operations Executive) under the Minister of Economic Warfare.

On 22 July 1940 the War Cabinet formally approved the arrangements and SOE was formed in Churchill's words 'to set Europe ablaze'. SOE was divided into SO1 (Propaganda) and SO2 (Subversion and sabotage). SO1 became PWE (Political or later Psychological Warfare Executive and finally on the battlefield PWB) while SOE was concerned with subversion and sabotage. When Selborne succeeded Dalton he insisted on the continued civilian direction of SOE, but in the end it was militarised. Sir Frank Nelson, a former member of Parliament, and until recently British Consul in Berne, was the first head of SOE from August 1940 to May 1942 when he was succeeded by Charles Hambro (later Sir Charles). A year later in September 1943, Hambro was succeeded by Major General Colin Gubbins (later Sir Colin) a regular soldier with a special knowledge of underground activities. He was much loved and respected by SOE but militarisation, as we experienced it in Stockholm, was not an unqualified success. Lt. Col. George Larden was put in charge with his tall blonde Danish FANY assistant, Nora Coggin, whom I had known well in Cambridge as the wife of the family where I first met my Swedish wife as a paying guest on her eighteenth birthday. His efforts to subject local SOE personnel to military discipline did not appeal to the undisciplined individualists he found under his command.

Our SOE staff underwent training at Beaulieu and other locations and were familiar with the array of toys, some of which had regrettably been revealed by the Rickman affair. There were supplies of light weapons, hand grenades, sten guns, welrods, plastic and detonators and limpet-mines. Some of the latter came in handy when fitted as scuttling charges by Andrew Croft on George Binney's second convoy. There were also radio transmitters which were initially too heavy and clumsy. A friend of Amelie Posse's and his wife built radio transmitters for us which were much lighter. He devised metal rods on which the dots and dashes were threaded as metal rings separated by bakelite insulators. These could be pulled through the set at speed and transmit a message in a few seconds and thereby evade detection by enemy D/F equipment. One of our useful toys for SOE Norway was the altimeter switch, the size of a pencil, attached to aircraft and set to explode at chosen altitudes. Once, at Leuchars, I was handed a diplomatic bag at the last minute as I boarded the aircraft. I asked what it contained. 'Oh, altimeter switches, chum.' 'Are they cocked?' 'Don't know, but I don't suppose they'll go off.' Well they didn't. And also there was later Ewan Butler's supply of stink bomb liquid for application to German overcoats and caps in cloakrooms. We also developed a good photographic unit which I had started for white propaganda purposes and this achieved some forgeries which were, on the whole, most artistic.

The distinction between PWE and SOE did not matter to us. But it was not until Charles Cruickshank's book on *S.O.E. in Scandinavia* when I realised that apparently Roger Hinks, the delightful art historian, had been sent to join us to supervise both operations under the authority of our Counsellor, Bill Montagu Pollock (later Sir William). The Press Reading Bureau was run by Joe (later Sir Cecil) Parrott with its thirty or so refugees from Germany and occupied countries reading 400 newspapers and interviewing travellers. The daily summaries were telegraphed home or sent by air with the papers for the use of PWE in London and Woburn. Here they provided invaluable background for Dick

Crossman and Hugh Carleton Greene of the BBC German service and their colleague and rival, Tom Sefton Delmer, who had begun his 'black' radio programmes in 1941 just after Hess's arrival in Britain.

There were some eighty 'black' radio transmitters or research units as they were called in the course of the war. Far the most important was the shortwave 'Gustav Siegfried Eins' which purported to be anti-Nazi, patriotic, anti-British, anti-Russian, followed years later by the very powerful medium and long wave transmitter at Crowborough (Aspidistra). This ran the extremely effective 'Soldatensender Calais' (which became 'Soldatensender West' after our recapture of Calais) and Radio Atlantik which was directed to the German U-boat crews. The technical brains behind all these operations were Harold Robin and Gambier Parry who was responsible to C (Stewart Menzies), the head of MI6, for all clandestine radio communications. The headquarters for Delmer's activities was his Gasthaus at the Rookery at Aspley Guise.

'Gustav Siegfried Eins' came on the air first on 23 May 1941 on thirty metres at seven minutes to the hour 'sieben Minuten vor Voll'. The boss, der Chef, was introduced by his adjutant who started with a few easily deciphered code messages to set some false trails for the Gestapo and then Peter Seckleman, known as Paul Saunders or the Corporal at Aspley Guise, would impersonate the anti-Nazi junker officer and with a cynical, aristocratic drawl, spill out his venom against the corrupt and lecherous party bosses who were sabotaging the prosecution of the war against that flat-footed jew Churchill, etc., etc. Peter had been born in Berlin in 1902, came as a refugee to England in 1937 and enlisted in the pioneer corps. He served in France, undertook dangerous bomb disposal work in London and volunteered to be dropped behind the German lines with an SOE sabotage group. But he was a writer by trade, was picked out by Leonard Ingrams and sent to Woburn where he wrote and acted the part of Gustav Siegfried Eins. I met him first after the war when he served with me for two years in Berlin and we have been close friends ever since.

I visited Woburn at dead of night, transported in an official car by Charles Hambro and met Tom Delmer for the first time. He was a cheerful, rotund Rabelaisian dynamo of a man who never seemed to need sleep and whose intelligence and imagination became the motive force of all the 'black' radio and other 'black' activities.

He often courted the disapproval of the 'white' propagandists and such straight-laced socialists as Stafford Cripps. Tom was born in Berlin in 1904 of Australian parents, his father teaching at the university. After school in Germany, he went to St. Pauls in London winning a scholarship for Lincoln College, Oxford. In 1928 he became the *Daily Express* correspondent in Berlin and in the next few years he met all the leading Nazis, including Hitler. He was moved to Paris and, as chief European correspondent, covered the Spanish civil war. Then he was in and out of Germany till the outbreak of war. He was in Poland on 3 September 1930, escaped from Warsaw and via Roumania got back to France becoming a war correspondent again, escaped once more through Bordeaux and back to England. Here he was recruited by his old friend Leonard Ingrams, (the father of the founder of *Private Eye*) the flying banker, who broke down endless security obstacles and got him into Woburn to run a secret right-wing subversive German broadcasting station which, in 1941, emerged as 'Gustav Siegfried Eins'.

We established a good working relationship between Stockholm and Woburn and while they had access to all the Parrott House material, we also kept them supplied with up-to-date German gramophone records and any gossip we picked up. One useful source was Max Hodann, a pupil of the great sexual psychologist, Magnus Hirschfeld. Delmer's relations with the services were excellent, in particular the Air Ministry and the Admiralty, where Donald McLachlan was a faithful ally. The subversive effect of Radio Atlantik broadcasts on U-boat crews was considerable. In Stockholm we were recipients and users of PWE material, in particular 'SIBS' or rumours (sibilare), and these we spread, we hoped to some effect. We were never able, however hard we tried, to avoid some of our rumours being sent home unwittingly as intelligence by others. A problem with good deception is not to deceive your own side. A very useful channel into France was through our friend Robert Rieffel, who had been the *Havas* correspondent but joined De Gaulle and worked for the Free French newsagency in London. He still kept his links with *Havas* through which he was able to funnel truth and rumour to France to be circulated to all in responsible positions in the Vichy régime through the *Cahiers des Interdits* or dossiers of information not to be published.

We had the satisfaction of getting reactions to one very

elaborate 'SIB' about the switch of a consignment of sardines from Portugal to Germany instead of England. This story was planted in bits and pieces in Lisbon and Madrid, Berne and Istanbul and had to be pieced together by the Germans. The consignment had by mistake been delivered to Germany. Why did it matter? It mattered a great deal because each tin had platinum welded in the bottom. It took us a month to plant the separate pieces of the jigsaw. Then the Parrott House began to note in its press reading that orders were being issued by the Nazi authorities to all patriotic Germans to collect and deliver sardine tins to melt down for the war effort. We hoped that this 'SIB' succeeded in wasting much time which might otherwise have been turned to a more war-like purpose. We received regular weekly directives from PWE which combined appreciations of the situation with instructions as to how they were to be handled. By the beginning of 1944 these were becoming something of a weekly yawn. So I perpetrated the following directive which was sent home and for circulation round our Legation on 1 April 1944. Apparently it took some time in London before the hoax was noticed.

PWD/CD/44/1/44

**POLITICAL WARFARE EXECUTIVE**

SECRET
COPY NO.

**CENTRAL DIRECTIVE** 392

Week beginning Saturday, April 1st, 1944.

NOTE: This directive is personal to the individual whose number it bears and he or she is responsible for its safe custody. It must not be shown to anyone else without permission of the Security Officer.

**GENERAL INSTRUCTIONS**

I. **BALKAN SITUATION.**
   **APPRECIATION.**

Prominence is being given to the Roumanian-Hungarian alliance, to the common interests of the two countries in the protection of Transylvania and to the justice of the arbitration of Vienna though care is being taken not to allude to Ciano's subsequent execution and the recent resumption of diplomatic relations between Italy and the Soviet Union. Prince Barbu Stirbey's recent plea for the maintenance of a standing army in Hungary, his support for historical Hungarian claims to Transylvania, for Admiral Horthy's inalienable right to an Italian battleship and the offer of the crown of Hungary to King Peter of Yugoslavia are considered to have been made in good faith. Hungarian pleas on behalf of Roumania, understood to have been advanced by Dr. Antal Ullein-Reviczky, the head of the free Hungarian movement in Stockholm, should probably be discounted. It is understood that he appealed through Dr. Nikolaev, the Bulgarian Minister in Stockholm, whom he met in the Finnish bastu in Sportpalatset. The appeal is understood to have been forwarded to a high Soviet dignitary in the same capital, probably the Soviet Naval Attaché's chauffeur who has the rank of admiral. The latter was apparently under the influence of drink at the time and telegraphed it to Moscow as a Finnish appeal for the autonomy of all Ugrian language groups in the U.S.S.R. This resulted in the appointment of a joint Votiak-Samojed commissar for Foreign Affairs and the matter has since been dropped.

**DIRECTIVE**

Care should be taken to overestimate resistance to the Germans in Hungary and to encourage the Hungarians and Roumanians by promising a Hungarian occupation of Roumania and a Roumanian occupation of Hungary after the armistice. We should play down Roumanian atrocities against Jews, no allusion should be made to hanging them on meat hooks in slaughter houses and Roumania should be treated as an old ally, letting bygones be bygones. Hungary should, however, be singled out for special recriminations. For the time being it is advisable to ignore rumours to the effect that Stalin is supporting Professor Varga's candidature to the throne of Hungary. It should be stressed that the Atlantic Charter applies to Roumania and not to Hungary which will be required to surrender its fleet to Roumania and to subscribe to point 7 regarding free passage on the high seas.

## II. THE MAIN ENEMY.
### APPRECIATION.

Hitler's appearance as Lohengrin at his wedding with Corinne Luchaire at Strassburg Cathedral on Annunciation Day was no surprise to the initiated. His subsequent honeymoon on his yacht the *Grille*, now converted to a hospital ship, appears to have taken place on the Rhine in the same Wagnerian style under the supervision of Dönitz who was costumed as the Flying Dutchman. A considerable impression seems to have been made by Göring as Hans Sachs, Göbbels as Tristan and von Papen as Parsifal. An escort of minesweepers assisted the party to negotiate a successful passage past the Lorelei rock. Dr. Morell and Dr. Brandt were subsequently decorated with the Ritterkreuz first class embellished with crossed hormones in diamonds and platinum, Reichsbischof Müller preached a sermon on the virgin birth in the light of popular German folklore and the Berlin Academy of Sciences published a *Festschrift zur Beleuchtung der neueren Deutschen Chromosomenkunde*. Although Marshal Pétain presented l'Aiglon's christening robe to the happy parents it is not believed that young Siegfried's opportune birth will as was hoped decrease Darnand's troubles with the Maquis or assist Laval in his latest attempt to enlist French workers for Germany.

### DIRECTIVE.

Psychoanalytical arguments should be employed to demonstrate Hitler's nuptials as a Freudian compensation for the failure of the German rocket gun. If the latter should, however, in the interval prove to be a success the acoustic torpedo can be taken as a substitute.

## III. SATELLITES

As it is unknown at the time of writing which of Germany's allies can still be considered as such when this directive comes into operation last weeks appreciation and directive stand. Broadcasts to Finland should speak of Germany as Finland's satellite. If the war should be concluded in the interval and Finland, as is probable, should still be at war with Russia, it is believed that Finland will declare war on Germany, Slovakia and Sweden. Care should be taken in this eventuality not to interpret this move as automatically ranging Finland on the side of the United Nations. A special directive is being prepared for this contingency.

## IV. BATTLE FRONTS.

### Eastern Front.

The significant event of the week is Marshal Shukov's capture of Dresden. With the fall of Stettin this is thought to constitute a serious threat to Berlin.

### Southern Front.

The Allied capture of the Cassino station ticket office and of the commissionaire of the Hotel Continental amount to a considerable tactical advantage.

### Far East.

The announcement that the Mikado has decided to devote the remainder of his life to plant biology is considered to indicate serious Japanese concern for their future in the post-war gardening business.

### Air War.

The ability of the R.A.F. and U.S.A.A.F. to land on and service German airfields is considered to indicate that German air opposition is weakening.

### Second Front.

If it has begun a special directive will be issued. If not, as before.

### Sea War.

The sale of the German high seas fleet to the Argentine is considered to be an infringement of the Monroe doctrine.

### General directive.

Play up coordinated Allied strength in air, on land and sea. Stress particularly the contribution of our Italian and Roumanian allies.

### V. OCCUPIED COUNTRIES

As before, except insofar as they may have been liberated by the time this directive is issued. If liberated, special directives must be awaited as our propaganda will depend on whether any population remains and if so whether the population is friendly or hostile.

### VI. ITALY

Stalin's public repudiation of the offer of the throne of Italy for him and for his heirs gives us a good opportunity to present Soviet policy in the Mediterranean in a favourable light.

APPROVED BY THE DIRECTOR GENERAL, P.W.E.
1st April, 1944.

We were well supplied with subversive print and forgeries from Ellic Howe's outfit in Woburn. We had our own printing establishment in the Legation and became quite adept at producing material for the occupied countries and Germany or for Germans in the occupied countries and in Sweden or passing through. Among these were numerous stickers which we designed for easy reproduction, particularly in Norway, without any text at all.

On one visit home I raised the question of the use of astrology in our propaganda and intelligence. By then we were exploiting the German fondness for the prophecies of Nostradamus by using a good forgery of a Nostradamus booklet as a cover for instructions to German troops about malingering in order to escape being sent to the Russian front. The booklet seems to have been a success and it went into detail on how to simulate complaints such as typhoid, typhus, dysentery, diphtheria, jaundice, partial paralysis, amnesia and tuberculosis. It should have been sufficient to exempt one from the fate of cannon fodder on the eastern front. These booklets were mainly reproductions of the very professional printing and forging unit run by Ellic Howe for Tom Delmer's black propaganda outfit. Gradually we achieved some creditable original productions in our own printing plant in the Legation cellar.

The German transit traffic on the Swedish railways was a useful vehicle for the distribution of such malingering material. Other booklets were seed catalogues and pocket books of traditional songs. We believed at that time that Hitler himself was much influenced by astrology and in particular by Nostradamus. It seems, however, that his interest was not so much to guide his own action as to guess the importance of astrology in the policies and plans of the British. Some believe that Hess's flight to Scotland may have been stimulated by astrologers who thought that conditions were propitious for a peace bid. Hitler's revenge on the astrologers after this incident may have been his punishment for their incompetence.

In London I asked to see one of our leading astrologers, Mr Lyndo, whose writings were very popular at the time. My intention was to discuss with him ways in which his predictions might be geared in with Hitler's believed dependence on astrology and how he might help to mislead him in his decisions. I had a long talk with him. He came all the way from Wales, a dapper person with the determined features of a serious professional man. He put me in my place immediately and told me that astrology was an independent science not to be perverted in the cause of propaganda. Whilst he was convinced that the forces of good would triumph over evil, he did not in any way minimise the cost. He conceded that Hitler might benefit from reading him as he doubted whether Hitler's own astrologers would dare to reveal what they saw in the stars. He then launched into a rigmarole of discreet hints at the importance of his views to those in positions of authority in the land, indicating that he was regularly consulted by senior ministers, churchmen and military commanders. I was firmly given to understand that he was not prepared to be recruited and was made to appreciate the professionalism of his work and to realise that it was not to be debased by becoming a handmaid of the propaganda machine. I felt like a small boy being punished for bending the truth.

Ewan Butler, who took over the German section of SOE in Stockholm, describes in his book *Amateur Agent* how he and Janet Gow had the satisfaction of issuing 3,000 tickets from the German Legation to specially invited Swedish Nazis to attend a German play in Borgarskolan which resulted in the fury and confusion of overcrowding that was intended. My press department developed a very useful card index of many thousands of Swedish Nazis, and Riga, our contact in the German Legation, was most helpful in producing invitation lists and specimen invitation cards which were easily reproduced in our printing establishment. There were many occasions when enthusiastic supporters of the Nazi cause turned up to receptions and dinner parties which never took place, such as an invitation to a viewing of the German propaganda film from 1940, *Sieg im Westen*, after the allied victories in Normandy in 1944.

For us it was always difficult to tell whether we were operating on behalf of SOE or PWE. The one merged into the other in varying shades of grey and black. Major and minor irritants and deceptions grew into strategic operations like 'Fortitude 2' or 'Graffham' to keep the inflated number of German divisions in Norway in position as long as possible by hints of landings on the coast, joint operations with the Russians in the north or evidence that we were negotiating with the Swedes for their support of the allies; but these were 'soft' psychological operations to be distinguished from the 'hard' SOE activities of supporting resistance groups and organising sabotage. While SOE took off in Norway at an early stage, it took much longer in Denmark.

The temporary holding operation for SOE in the Autumn of 1940 was divided between Malcolm Munthe and myself. Malcolm took over Norway and I was supposed to see what could be done to prepare the ground in Denmark and Sweden and in Germany itself. Denmark was in an anomalous situation. Unlike Norway it had not continued to fight the Germans but had surrendered and the Germans left them a semblance of some independence with a government in Copenhagen, an army confined to barracks and their splendid King free to maintain the morale of his people in their sense of disgrace by his daily rides on horseback round Copenhagen. We were fortunate in Sweden in the personality of the leading Danish journalist and arctic explorer, Ebbe Munck, who became the leader and representative of the Danish resistance in Stockholm. We were able to prepare the ground and set up communications with London, waiting for the arrival of Ronnie Turnbull. There was, however, a hitch in his appointment caused by the incompetence of MI5. I was approached by Martin, the head of the MI6 in Stockholm, and asked if I realised that Ronnie was a dangerous enemy agent having close associations not only with the Germans, but with the Russians. It took a long time for me to persuade them that they had made a serious mistake and must have confused him with somebody else of the same name. I asked why if this was so had he been appointed and served as Press Attaché in Copenhagen up till April 1940. It turned out in the end that my suspicion of MI5's filing system was correct and Ronnie and his Brazilian wife, Theresa, accompanied by Pamela Tower as secretary, set off on the long trail to Sweden via the Cape and Cairo, Istanbul, Moscow and finally Stockholm. Ronnie arrived first, followed some time later by Pamela and his wife who had stayed in Turkey for the birth of their first baby. Ronnie arrived and took charge, gradually assuming the whole administrative and financial responsibility for SOE until, later on, London attempted to militarise the organisation by the appointment of Lt. Col. George Larden.

The Rickman affair had convinced us that SOE operations in Sweden itself must be put on ice, ready for activating in the event of a German invasion when we might well be working with the Swedes and not against them. So we prepared for W/T communications by training operators and locating transmitters to be kept for a rainy day. George Binney's blockade-busting operations were ultimately taken over by SOE and Andrew Croft, who succeeded Malcolm Munthe as Assistant Military Attaché, devoted much of his time to it. In particular his expertise was invaluable in the arming of the second convoy and equipping the ships with scuttling charges to prevent them being captured by the Germans.

One of our most useful SOE recruits was Wilfred Latham, an ex-volunteer from the first Finno/Russian winter war. He was a rubber planter from Malaya, a thin, wiry man with black hair and eyebrows and a very quiet sense of humour combined with a readiness to try his hand at anything. This he did with energy and expertise, helping me to maintain and run our yacht, and organising the production of wireless transmitters and the training of operators. He improvised such hilarious happenings as photographing the Svestapo or the Swedish Security Police who watched our Legation.

His success in Sweden led to his transfer, with his Malayan background, to Force 136 which he found dull, bureaucratic and remote from the scene of action.

SOE was catholic in its recruitment of experts ranging from safe-breakers, forgers and other splendid representatives of the criminal classes, to lawyers, merchant bankers and dons. One day we were paid a visit by Ronald Thornley, who had an intimate knowledge of Germany as the export manager of The Ideal Boiler Company, which among other products manufactured water closets. His specialist expertise was invaluable. It happened that he knew Sweden well and had cornered some regular business as a supplier of lavatories to prisons. The secret in the Swedish case was to supply a double u-joint which his firm made specially. This was a Swedish security precaution to prevent the prisoners syphoning the water out of a single u-joint and using the drainpipes as an intercom.

In preparation for activity in Germany we sent agents to explore the ground by gathering the necessary intelligence. I have in my possession a Kodak Retina II (a) camera. It was bought by SOE in Stockholm and is the property of the War Office. They refused to allow me to buy it at the end of the war, but let me have it on loan in perpetuity. I kept it as a memento of a very successful operation by one of six young Swedish anarcho-syndicalists. They had fought in the Spanish Civil War and been introduced to me by the author Eyvind Johnson, a close friend and one of the most outstanding proletarian authors of the time. His autobiographical novel *Nu var det 1914* had placed him in the top rank of Scandinavian writers. These young men were keen to undertake direct action, one of the tenets of anarcho-syndicalism. But I asked them to lie low for the time being and quietly penetrate the enemy camp until such time as action was required. They were however all good observers and one of them had himself hired as a deck hand on a Swedish ship plying with German Baltic ports. I provided him with this camera and one day he came to me crestfallen and handed it over soaking wet. His ship had been boarded in the Kiel Canal by the Gestapo. He had quickly hidden the camera in the u-joint of one of the lavatories. I told him I would do my best to dry it out and see if the film could be developed. The news was good and our photographic department dried out and developed the film which turned out to record some very useful information. This borrowed camera is still in my possession and works perfectly.

At times, inevitably, our activities spread over into intelligence in preparation for SOE or PWE work. Typical examples were the cases of RP and Riga.

Early in the war I was approached by a very verbose Norwegian, a philosopher and psychologist who knew me as an expert on Henrik Ibsen.

His name was Egil Rønne-Petersen and it was hinted that he was the grandson of Ibsen through the illegitimate daughter he fathered at the age of eighteen with a twenty-eight year old girl employee of the apothecary Reimann in Grimstad. The story was faulted by the fact that the child was a boy. He was a man who enjoyed creating an air of mystery about himself and there were some who considered him a charlatan. But such accusations were not uncommon in the Norwegian refugee community.

He had some remarkable connections and was well thought of by leading Norwegian refugees in Stockholm. These included Knut Kavli, the cheese magnate and husband of the actress Karin, Hans Jacob Ustvedt the brilliant doctor, also famous as a speaker and violinist, Harald Gram and Thorvald Udahl. I had my official relations with the Norwegian Legation and their Press Attaché, Jens Schive, who later became Norwegian Ambassador in Sweden. R-P however tended to avoid the official side of life because he regarded the Legation and many of the resistance groups as security risks.

He used to visit me regularly. I often thought that his philosophical musings and speculations as a social psychologist were of little value to the furtherance of the war effort. His talk ranged from G.C. Jung to the Vatican, psychotherapy, test tube reproduction, Niels Bohr and the Atom bomb, Eugen Bleuler, the deep psychology of foreign affairs and man's place in evolution, but he did produce some real nuggets of intelligence which were invaluable. During the interim period when I was nominally in charge of SOE, Germany, I got very little response from the earlier MI6 set-up under Pincher Martin. I made what use I could of the information R-P provided, till Peter Falk, a master from Rugby, came out to handle such matters. I was able to pass R-P on to him and he turned out to be of unique value.

At the same time I passed on a person whom we code-named Riga, who worked in the German Legation and was introduced as an anti-Nazi volunteer in 1939. Riga had good reasons to be anti-Nazi and offered to serve the British for no remuneration other than the promise of a British passport at the end of the war, if still alive. I was in Paris at the end and received a tetchy message from MI6 to the effect that I had promised this person a British passport in return for services rendered. They remonstrated that I had no authority to make such promises and demanded to know how I could justify such an irregularity. I explained that I had no authority to make these promises, but, in view of the remarkable services rendered, I insisted that my promise be honoured, and it was. Peter Falk and his wife, Biddie, took our friend to England and helped Riga with great kindness and sensitivity to adjust to life as a British citizen.

I never met Riga in person till 1951 in Berlin when this brave person paid me a visit and we were able to spend a day recapping the experiences of the war. Through Riga it had been possible to penetrate the German Legation, obtaining valuable intelligence on the activities of the diplomatic and service attaché staff. This latter included details of the work of Doctor Karl Heinz Krämer of the Abwehr. He had contacts with the girls in the Swedish General Staff who slipped him copies of reports from the Swedish Naval Attaché in London, Commander J.G. Oxenstierna. Oxenstierna was innocent but forbidden by us to return to London after leave in Sweden. We continued however to intercept Krämer's so-called Josephine messages to Berlin long after Oxenstierna's departure. The mystery was finally clarified when Peter Falk managed to get Riga to take an impression of Krämer's key which R.P. had copied and future access to his papers was assured. This was only one of Riga's achievements which ranged from frequent visits to Berlin to the planting of misinformation on the German Legation.

Craig Graham McKay has researched the Swedish wartime archives and has given me a copy of a Swedish decrypt of a secret telegram of 7 May 1942 from Doctor Wagner, the head of the Abwehr in Stockholm to the Abwehr Division of the Oberkommando der Wehrmacht in Berlin. This disinformation I had planted on him through Riga. He reported my return on 4 May 1942 from London with full instructions for British propaganda in film and press for the Spring of 1943 in order to prepare for a British invasion of Norway.

One of the little local irritants we developed for our enemies in Sweden and among the German occupation forces in Norway and

Denmark or in transit through Sweden, was itch powder. Ewan Butler obtained a supply in England and we later supplemented this with supplies from joke shops in Stockholm. It was a complicated operation. Our target was visiting German dignitaries who mostly stayed at the Grand Hotel. Discreet relations were developed with the laundry and bedroom staff so that underclothes and bedclothes and lavatory seats were sprinkled with the powder while our SOE ladies helped to package powdered condoms in German army issue envelopes for distribution on the trains and among troops in Norway.

Sabotaging German iron-ore shipments from Sweden was not a very promising undertaking. The failure of the incompetent Rickman attempt in April 1940 and other minor efforts led us to look for other ways of achieving the same end. The 'SIB' technique of planting rumours and false evidence had scored some sterling successes.

I wondered whether it would not be possible to do something of the kind with Swedish iron ore so that dumps, ships' holds and rail cars would have to be searched and much time and effort wasted. We discovered, after much trial and error, that a project for inserting time-fused detonators into lumps of iron ore was an unlikely runner. Instead we decided to persuade the Germans that we had such a device by attributing to it the sinking of ore ships which, in fact, had been mined or torpedoed. This involved selling to the Germans part of the prototype of a detonator and a blueprint for its construction in separate sheets to be paid for in advance. We were never able to assess whether the rumours caused the anxiety and delays we hoped, but they paid off handsomely for the coffers of SOE.

When flights were resumed after Sweden had been cut off by the German occupation of Norway and Denmark, I reported to SOE headquarters in Baker Street and made my number with those in charge of Scandinavia and Germany. Charles Hambro gave me an excellent dinner at the Great Western Hotel as a director of the railway, when there was a chance to meet a number of old friends. He very kindly arranged for me to have some clothing coupons to save me the expense of having suits built in Sweden. I reported to the appropriate section of SOE to draw my ration and found myself in a crowded, second-hand, clothing store. I was promptly taken in hand by a tailor and measured. Then, somewhat to my surprise, they started to make me try on rather incongruous clothes, ripping out identification tapes and labels and sewing in old ones. I looked at one of these and noted that it was in French. My security training had taught me never to ask the reason why, so I allowed myself to be kitted out. After being scrutinised with approval and given a pair of uncouth shoes, I was finally topped with a seedy beret and declared a good Frenchman. My tailor then shook me warmly by the hand and said 'I am not asking any questions, but I wish you luck for tonight'. Then I was equipped with false French identification papers and just as I was to be whisked away in a plain van, I asked if I could be put in touch with Sir Charles. This was frowned on as a gross breach of security, but since Charles at that time was the head of SOE, I was put through to him on the 'phone. 'I am not quite sure, Charles, what the plan is and I am asking no questions, but your clothing coupons are, I gather, a one-way ticket to France. I wonder if steps could be taken to explain to my wife in Sweden that my return may be delayed.' 'What the hell' and much to the discomfiture of my kind despatchers, I was taken to another office where I was issued with coupons instead of fancy dress. I was somewhat relieved, but always felt that this sartorial solecism could have been the beginning of a very good story.

My own contribution to SOE was extremely modest but I have never ceased to admire the courageous characters who were dropped into Norway and Denmark or crossed in and out of Sweden during those years, often facing death, ghastly privations and torture. The value of their activities was out of all proportion to the numbers involved, tying down whole enemy divisions, keeping massive forces on their toes to protect their communications against sabotage and undermining the morale of the enemy.

'All the business of war and indeed all the business of life is', in the words of the Duke of Wellington 'to endeavour to find out what you don't know by what you do; that's what I called guessing what was at the other side of the hill.' The whole business of collecting, assessing and circulating information to those who can turn it to operational use is central to all human activity, whether it be in diplomacy, the defence forces, or business. All diplomatic missions are concerned with intelligence and our Legation in Stockholm was one of our government's valuable sources. Short of persuading the Swedes to become belligerents on the allied side, which was what we tried to do at the beginning and the end of the war, we watched their somewhat flexible interpretation of neutrality according to the fortunes of war. We endeavoured to limit the damage they did to the allies by the transit traffic and their iron-ore and ball-bearing exports to Germany.

These were finally terminated as the war drew towards its close. The amount of overt and covert intelligence on Sweden itself was far outweighed by our intelligence on Germany. Our service attachés scored some remarkable intelligence successes throughout the war. In general we were able to warn London well in advance of the German attack on Norway and Denmark in April 1940 but without any of our warnings being believed. We provided information on the German build-up for the invasion of Russia many months before it took place. The Germans were spying on us all the time and the Swedes were not unhelpful to them in the services, in particular the navy and the security police.

Slowly, however, the mood changed. The old Commander-in-Chief Thörnell gave way to General Jung and Ehrensvärd became Chief of the General Staff. The Swedish intelligence organisations became more open with us about what they knew, motivated to some extent by their dilemma as to what action to take in the event of the war ending with large numbers of German troops still left in Norway. They feared that their discipline might break down and face them with mass atrocities against the Norwegian civilian population or mass desertions across the Swedish frontier. All of this we had to watch and assess and report.

How effective Swedish intelligence was we never knew until Carlgren's study appeared in 1985. But we knew they were tapping our telephones and bugging our flats and houses and shadowing our movements. From hints dropped by Boheman, the Secretary General of the Swedish Ministry of Foreign Affairs, we gathered they were decrypting our telegrams. Carlgren's study says nothing of Swedish operations against the British and Americans and other allies. It was evident however the Swedes were intercepting and reading German communications and had high grade sources.

Many of us in the Legation had watchers or minders supplied by Swedish intelligence, whose job was to see what we were up to and report us to their masters. One singularly inappropriate selection was Lt. Commander Pedro Ahlmark who was one of those allocated to me. We very soon became close friends. He stayed with us out at Viksberg and saw a good deal of us in Stockholm. With a Chilean mother he had a lively, Latin American temperament, was a furious supporter of the allies, even in the worst times of the war, and finally lost his job and was put in charge of the Swedish naval film unit. We kept in touch in the years after the war and he stayed with me in Paris and Berlin. He had the unnerving Latin American generosity of giving one anything of his which one admired, with the words 'take it, it's yours'. One such memento hangs outside my front door in the shape of an old ship's lantern from the Swedish warship *Thule*.

Our friends in the MI6 Passport Control Office lived a life apart, except for Harry Carr and Rex Bosley who came to us from the Legation in Helsinki when we went to war with Finland; these two never hinted at what they were up to but they were by no means treated as pariahs. One of the MI6 assets was a very charming homosexual who acted as a magnet for German homosexuals sent over to see the King whose weaknesses were well known. I acted as a cut-out between Martin and some of his friends, but I never had the remotest idea of the business transacted. Perhaps my greatest value to our intelligence friends was that I was wrongly believed by many Swedes to be the head of the secret service in Sweden and this provided valuable cover for the genuine article. We were not like the Russians who, as allies, expected us to help them with the order of battle of the Swedish armed forces. We never regarded the Swedish armed forces as a serious threat, but the Russians were obsessed with their disposition, equipment and training.

Sweden in one way or another was a good source of intelligence and in retrospect her neutrality was more of an advantage than if she had been invaded either by us or the Germans and we had been deprived of this window on the Nazi chamber of horrors.

# XI
## Cops and Robbers

Cops and robbers became a regular game with the British Legation. Sweden suffered from spy hysteria, a natural ailment in a country so near to such a giant neighbour as Russia. Pro-German feelings in high places still remained very largely regulated by the fear of Russia.

With the outbreak of World War II spy mania spread mainly to the detriment of the allies. I myself was arrested in the summer before the war sketching the church at Nynäshamn which, unknown to me, had that very day become a restricted area.

Sweden was flooded with foreign journalists to cover the first Finnish/Russian war and later the invasion of Norway and Denmark and finally the German attack on Russia. Stockholm became one of the world news centres, much of it spurious. As Swedish law stood at the time any collection and passing on of information could be interpreted as spying. Ralph Hewins of the *Daily Mail* disappeared for a fortnight until we discovered he had been jailed for spying in Falun and we were able to have him released. Water Taub, a Czech refugee, who wrote for the *Observer*, was arrested and held for thirteen weeks for no other reason than a denunciation by the Germans.

Edmond Demaitre, a refugee Hungarian journalist who wrote as Edmond Masterman for the *Daily Express*, caused panic among the Secret Police when he visited a number of chemist shops asking for cyanide to poison the German Minister, the Prinz zu Wied. On another occasion he was surrounded in a telephone booth on the street by armed soldiers and arrested under suspicion of being a saboteur because he was talking French to a girlfriend he was inviting to dinner. On another occasion he was seized by the police for talking to a Swedish chess champion about his impressions of Germany where he had participated in a tournament. Ossian Goulding of the *Daily Telegraph*, although a neutral Irishman, was also put inside.

My dear friend Countess Amelie Posse was frequently interrogated. But largely because of her close connections in the court and with the Royal Family they never arrested her. On one occasion she rang me to come to her flat urgently. I drove round immediately and found her in bed. Prince Eugen, the King's painter brother and an old friend, was sitting at the foot of her bed while two embarrassed policemen twiddled their thumbs on the window-seat. She roared with laughter and introduced me as the English spy, telling the policemen to mind their own business about the wireless transmitters she was having made for the Norwegian resistance. The Norwegians were our brothers and the Prince's brother, King Gustav, would be very upset if any action were taken to prevent help to them. She asked Prince Eugen what he thought and he affirmed that the King would be most displeased. The policemen were totally nonplussed and she then told them they were dismissed. With proper deference to Royalty they stumbled out of the room backwards. I shut the door and the Prince burst out laughing at Amelie's insolence. Under her bed were stuffed the latest transmitters made by our electrician friend Percy.

The ordinary traffic and criminal police were our protectors rather than the opposite and we had little argument with them except on one occasion in Gothenburg when there was a riot round one of our ships in the harbour and a policeman drew his sword and cut off the ear of a woman who had taken sides with the British and Norwegian seamen. The police were armed with swords and revolvers but did not menace law-abiding citizens and foreigners. Our arguments were, however, with the Swedish Security Police, or the Svestapo as they became known. While the uniformed police protected us, the Security Police in various disguises spied on us, tapped our telephones, intercepted letters, lip-read conversations they observed in our flats, intercepted radio transmissions and bugged our fireplaces. Microphones were retrieved in the chimneys of the Naval Attaché's flat in Stockholm and the flat in Gothenburg used by

Christian Günther, drawing by the author

George Binney and Bill Waring for their blockade-running activities.

On 10 June 1938 a Government decree set up a Civilian Security Service to be responsible for counter-espionage in the event of war or risk of war. This was in addition to the Armed Services Security and counter-espionage organisations. Many of us had security service officers keeping an eye on us. But the existence of the Svestapo was unknown to the Swedish public until January 1943 when I blew their identity in the Stockholm Press. The head of the Service was Eric Salomon Hallgren, a policeman with international experience who became Chief of Police in Stockholm in 1930 and Deputy Governor in 1937, from which post he had leave of absence while Head of the Security Service until 1943. The country was divided into seven regions each with its Security Supervisor, the most important being Stockholm itself where Martin Lundquist was in command. Of some 250 men engaged in the Service about 150 were stationed in Stockholm.

The presence of the Security Police watching the Legation became a joke and a nuisance. They concealed themselves behind rocks and in a barn on the opposite side of the road to the Legation offices. They photographed visitors and took a close look, disguised as nursemaids pushing prams, but easily identified by their standard police-issue boots. One day Wilfred Latham crept up on the men concealed on the other side of the road, photographed the lot, fought off their attempts to seize his camera and knock him down, and dashed over to the Legation with his prize. We immediately developed the photographs, which were excellent. I alerted the evening Press which came out with a sensational story: 'German Gestapo spies watch British Legation'. I then waited for the reaction, which was not slow to come.

When I was strolling back to the office from visiting the Press in the centre of the town and walking along Strandvägen, I suddenly saw a familiar figure driving erratically towards me in the French Military Attaché's Citroen. It was my Minister, Victor Mallett, purple in the face and in a towering rage. 'What the devil have you done now, Peter. Günther (the Foreign Minister) has asked me urgently to see him about something in the evening Press about German spies watching the Legation. Go back to your office and wait till I get back.' He drove off and I walked on and waited. After an hour the Military Attaché, Reggie Sutton-Pratt, rang me up. 'Peter, we're having a drink with Victor who would like you to join us.' I went round to find Victor roaring with laughter. He slapped me on the back. 'Well done, Peter, sorry I lost my temper, but I met a red-faced Günther who expressed his abject apologies and explained that the alleged Gestapo agents were not Gestapo at all but Swedish Security police.' Hallgren had been to see him in much distress as his men had now been blown. He gave instructions to stop surveillance immediately.

Henry Denham, our Naval Attaché, had Erik Boheman, the Secretary General of the Ministry of Foreign Affairs, to lunch and faced him with the spying to which he had been subjected. Apologies were proferred and the more obvious activities were called off. But this did not of course stop more sophisticated spying. We enjoyed playing our cops and robbers games of using the telephone to pass misleading messages and make appointments which never took place but wasted the scarce resources of the Service.

Together with a number of Swedish friends, with Doctor Ragnar Svanström, the historian and publisher, as the leading spirit, we formed a dining club called the ABS (American British Swedish). The purpose was to get members of our Legation and the American Legation together with leading figures in Swedish public life - writers, journalists, academics, politicians and professional men who were not usually on the diplomatic cocktail circuit. We occasionally got someone to lead a discussion, or brought in a visitor from Britain to talk of their experiences in wartime. One leading character in these gatherings was Ryttmästare Frank Martin, a retired cavalry captain who was a freelance writer and an unusually well-informed and witty purveyor of political gossip. He had been a member of the Swedish equestrian team at the 1920 Olympics in Antwerp and had been attached to the Cadre Noir in Saumur. He was a leading figure in the Jockey Club and in horse racing circles, an expert on horse breeding and training about which he wrote with great authority. As a rider he won one competition after another. He was also a political writer and journalist in papers such as *Svenska Dagbladet*, *Göteborgs Handels- och Sjöfartstidning*, *Eskilstuna Kuriren* and *Nu*. After the war he wrote regularly in *Dagens Nyheter* and *Expressen*. On 9 December 1939 he helped found the Föreningen Norden society, wrote for its paper *Nordens Frihet* and was a member of its editorial committee. He had been adjutant to the Swedish Volunteer Corps in the winter war in Finland in 1939-40 and had distinguished himself as Head of the Press Department of the Second Army Corps on the west coast during the invasion of Norway and Denmark, under his friend General Ehrensvärd who had been his commanding officer in Finland. He had been specially praised by all the local editors for the intelligent way in which he had handled defence information which had very much contributed to maintaining the morale of the troops and the local population.

On 24 April 1941, we had one of our usual dinners in the cellar restaurant Gyldene Freden in the old town. Victor Mallet and Mr Sterling, the American Minister, were present. Joe Parrott, who was running our press reading bureau and had been tutor to King Peter of Yugoslavia, started a discussion on the implications of the German invasion of Yugoslavia. We had an interesting evening.

Four days later, on 28 April 1941, at 15.00 hours, Frank Martin was called on in his office in Stureplan by a man from the Security Police. Martin accompanied him into the street where they were met by two other men. They took him in a taxi to his home in Djursholm followed by a police car. They then went through all his papers and refused to allow him to ring up his friend Gustav Möller, the Minister of the Interior. He asked them what they were after, but they refused to reply. Martin's wife arrived to find the police rifling his papers and told them they would not find anything, but they took no notice. They examined his writing desk, book shelves, boxes and papers in a wardrobe next to his study. They showed interest in a book by Professor Böök on Germans and Swedes and in Martin's notes. They took a copy of the Swedish Nazi paper *Dagens Eko* with attacks on anti-Nazi Swedes, such as General Rappe, Colonel Ehrensvärd and Rickard Sandler, the former Foreign Minister and now Provincial Governor, who ironically enough headed the Commission after the war which examined the activities of the Swedish Security Police. The paper was full of praise for the Swedish Commander-in-Chief, General Thörnell, who was an old-fashioned pro-German, though not pro-Nazi, soldier. They went through the papers left by Frank's son Roland, who had been killed as a cadet in a night exercise in the Swedish Airforce. They refused to believe that they did not contain secret defence information. They took away some twenty five papers, private letters, quotations from Böök dating from 1912 and a soiled blank sheet of paper to examine for secret ink.

Martin was then driven back to the police station and interrogated until 22.40 hours. He repeatedly asked the police why he had been arrested and they refused to answer. He was again refused permission to ring Gustav Möller. He was questioned about the organisation Nordens Frihet which had mobilised intellectuals to resist German aggression in Sweden and the other Nordic countries. He was interrogated at length about the dinner on 24 April at Gyldene Freden, why the dinner had taken place, who were present, what did they discuss, what were his plans to travel abroad as war correspondent, about Professor Segerstedt, the Editor of the anti-Nazi *Göteborgs Handels- och Sjöfartstidning* and about Director Lilliehöök of the KAK, the Royal Automobile Club. They seemed satisfied that Nordens Frihet was not a conspiracy and were interested to learn that the British and American Ministers, Mallet and Sterling, had been present at the dinner.

In addition to Martin, the police arrested Malcolm Lilliehöök who had not been at the dinner, stripped him to the buff and locked him in a cell. They also arrested the journalist Helge Lindberg of Segerstedt's paper, who was so shocked that later on he committed suicide on 10 November 1941. Martin sued Hallgren for 5,000 kr. damages, Lilliehöök for 10,000 kr. As a consequence Lilliehöök had not accepted an offer of the post of Assistant Military Attaché in the USA. He had already been arrested in January 1940 for talking to Philip Noel-Baker on his return from a visit to Finland, but the police had at least apologised on that occasion. The Executors of Lindberg's estate sued Hallgren for 15,000 kr.

The cause of these arrests was an anonymous letter sent to Christian Günther by someone who may have been a waiter at the dinner at Gyldene Freden. Günther was naive enough to swallow the bait, passed the letter to Hallgren who without further ado undertook the arrests. The letter was illiterate and ill-informed. This should have been recognised by any normal person, but it is indicative of the unbalanced minds of the Swedish authorities of the time that they allowed themselves to be carried away by their spy mania.

It is difficult to give the full flavour of the letter in translation, allegedly written by 'a Swedish patriot'. It could have been written by a Finn or a German. The envelope bore the address of the Hotel Regina in Stockholm, but the letterhead was that of the Torni Hotel in

Helsinki, dated 25 April 1941, and addressed to the Foreign Minister Günther, whose name was misspelt Gynter. In fact Günther's name was often pronounced with a soft g. It read:

> In anger as a Swede at what I have experienced I write this to you so that you may investigate what is happening, but I must remain anonymous as I do not wish to be involved. Yesterday, Thursday, we had an exclusive party for dinner which lasted quite late for the Ministers of England and America, together with Consuls and other Legation personnel and others. The host at the dinner was Professor Segersten from Gothenburg, but he himself did not come, it was said he had no occasion to. You see I understand the English language well and am not stupid, but listened well to the course of the conversation, since as a Swedish patriot it aroused my anger. The party talked of an English expeditionary force against Scandinavia. Those present were the Ministers and a Mr. Martin called Ryttmästare (Cavalry Captain). He was called something like Franc and later took a taxi to Djursholm and also a Mr. Lindgren, or possibly Lindberg, addressed as Doctor, who later took a taxi to Ålsten and he seemed to be instead of Professor Segersten, but because of my poor eyesight I could not see the sums on the cheques they exchanged and it was said that Mr. Martin, the fellow from Djursholm, was going to England together with others to lead the expeditionary force. They talked of getting passport visas from Russia and Japan. Another person present was a Mr. Bonnier, one of the younger ones, and a Mr. Pennand and a Mr. Howards, together with a Mr. with a long name. I must be excused for my indignation about the Corps against Scandinavia, besides it turned out that Professor S. from G-Borg had been with HM the King in a private secret conversation if this really can be true and then Mr. Martin told how HM only believed we will defend ourselves against a great power at most for a few weeks, together with several

military secrets and matters of state which made a sorry impression on me, so I cannot believe it to be true what a Swedish King says to a Swedish man is surely not to be overheard by foreigners. Should one as a Swede surrender one's country and pass on HM's private confidences to a foreigner?

I now remember that Doctor from Ålsten was called Helge and in my eyes he was a stooge to watch developments and further there was an older gentleman called Liljeköck who was something at the Royal Automobile Club. They also talked of a German aeroplane factory in Sweden and troops in north Norway, but no-one was drunk so they must have known what they were talking about. All this made my blood boil and I use this opportunity to pass this on whatever truth there may be in it, but it is terrible if it is true and treacherous to betray one's King's confidence.

I am compelled to be anonymous and sign one of the staff.

This absurd letter was taken seriously by the Foreign Minister, Günther and passed on to Hallgren who had a free hand to take whatever action he pleased. The Sandler Commission after the war reported on this disgraceful incident and considered that such a letter did not justify police action on such flimsy grounds. Although Hallgren was acquitted by the lower Court of Appeal, the Supreme Court sentenced him to a fine and damages because his conduct showed ignorance of his official responsibilities.

The Sandler Commission revealed some interesting facts about the Security Police. Censorship of letters, telegrams and telephone conversations covered all countries outside Sweden. About half a million postal communications were examined each week and of these 360 letters, 180 postcards and 2,000 pieces of printed matter were stopped. The weekly examination of telegrams rose to 32,000 of which 30,000 were to and from foreign countries. 6,000 people had their telephones tapped during the war. The results of censorship were regularly reported to Government departments, the Ministry of Foreign Affairs, the Ministry of Social Affairs, the Information

Directorate and the Defence Staff. The Security Services cost Sweden 32 million kr. The Service appears to have operated without adequate control and the Commission pointed out the dangers of a Secret Service becoming a Police State within a State.

The Segerstedt story was well-known at the time. On 11 October 1940 Segerstedt was summoned to an audience with the King. His paper had been confiscated, without trial, by the Minister of Justice for his persistent attacks on the Germans, his staunch support of the British and Norwegians and his criticism of the Swedish Government. Segerstedt's reaction was to attack the Ministers of Justice, K.G. Westman and Günther, the Minister of Foreign Affairs. Gunther, who had worked with Segerstedt on a pro-allied periodical *Forum* in World War I, tried to persuade him to come to Stockholm. He refused. The same occurred with the Prime Minister, Per Albin Hansson. On 7 October Segerstedt attacked the Swedish Commander-in-Chief, General Thörnell, for accepting the order of the German Eagle from the Germans. This issue of the paper was confiscated. The King then took the matter in his own hands and invited Segerstedt to come and see him. The King received him affably and the audience concluded to the satisfaction of both parties, according to whose story you believed. The King pointed out that the consequence of Segerstedt continuing to write as he did might not only risk the King losing his throne, but Segerstedt losing his own as well. 'You might even see me' said the King, 'running through the woods being shot at like my cousin Haakon of Norway.' 'Your Majesty' Segerstedt is alleged to have replied, 'I trust that I would bear the loss of my throne with as much dignity as yourself and I am convinced that your Majesty's athletic prowess would enable you to bear the hardships of life in the forests better than any of your subjects'.

The Security Police became a laughing stock over this incident and although Günther assured Martin that he saw through the anonymous letter and was upset at the action taken by Hallgren, it did not do much to enhance the Government's reputation for good judgement.

When I left Sweden in February 1945, the same friends who had been present at the dinner gave me a delightful farewell send-off at Gyldene Freden and Frank Martin presented me with a fake farewell letter to the British Secret Service from the Swedish Security

Police apologising for not having understood that the waiter's letter was a forgery as well as the cheque. They explained that after El Alamein and Stalingrad it became evident that they had been on the wrong track and the forgeries had been designed by an unfriendly power to undermine the good name and reputation of the Secret Service. Accompanying the letter was a copy of the anonymous missive and the so-called 'cheque' drawn on the Britische Bank and made out to Riding Master Martin by Victor Mallet on behalf of the Secret Service for the sum of 1,000 pfund. It had, according to the police, been taken from Martin's wallet in the cloakroom and proved impossible to cash. I was wished better luck and bid farewell with a comradely police greeting and wishes for closer co-operation in the future.

The activities of the Secret Police were, however, not wholly one-sided. Their supervision of the Communists was very much in the interests of the Swedish State at the time of the first Finnish/Russian war, but also of the Nazis who egged on their Swedish colleagues to pay particular attention to the Czechs such as Vaňek, the Counsellor of the former Czech Legation. His case was doggedly pursued by Countess Amelie Posse who fought so bravely for her Czech refugees. The supervision and registration of Nazis did not begin till after the invasion of Norway and Denmark in 1940. In addition, there was an unauthorised persecution of syndicalists, presumably because so many had fought in the Spanish Civil War and of the Fighting Democrats who were the first openly declared anti-Nazis and in no way a danger to the State.

To balance the comic opera activities of the Security Police, who were not so comic when they drove people to suicide and deprived them of their liberty, there was however another side to the picture. Captain Ivar Blücker, of the Gothenburg Harbour Police, a stalwart protector of our interests during all our blockade-running activities, lost his job in the process and then became Marine Superintendent for the 'Performance' operation and Chief Navigation Officer on 'Cabaret'.

Another person was Doctor Harry Söderman, the Head of the Criminal Technical Institute. He was throughout the war a friend and ally for whose solid support we were most grateful. I had known him before the war through my brother-in-law Fille Fellenius who had switched from literature and philosophy to psychology and was working with Professor Katz, the German refugee Professor, in Stockholm's Technical High School (later to become a university). They co-operated with Söderman on criminal psychology. He became a close friend, a sailing companion on my boat *Valkyrian* and an eating, drinking and singing gastronome introducing me to the delicacies of *surströmming*, fermented Baltic herring which stank so pungently that it had to be eaten in a sealed room. He was also an expert on reindeer meat, especially tongues and spare ribs at the time of the autumn slaughter, quite apart from his love of French food and wine, as he had lived in Lyon for many years.

Many of my academic friends found it difficult to understand our compatibility. First because some Swedish academic snobs regarded his Lyon doctorate in ballistics as of doubtful value and second because as a criminologist he had investigated the Reichstag fire. He had been misquoted by the Press as promoting the Nazi thesis that it was a communist plot. I discussed it with him at the time and he was in no doubt that van der Lubbe was alone responsible though motivated by his burning hatred of Nazism. Recent investigations in the Federal Republic have confirmed Söderman's findings which were based on his own meeting with van der Lubbe and the conclusions reached by the German criminal police at the time.[1] His reputation in fact provided good cover for his pro-allied activities and this cheerful, burly, eccentric adventurer with his pock-marked face and cloth cap, stood by us through thick and thin.

Harry Söderman was born in 1902 in Stockholm, studied chemistry in Malmö, went into industry and between 1921 and 1924 studied in the chemical industry in Germany. He became fascinated by the application of science to criminology and carried out a long study-journey from Turkey through Asia to China to investigate police methods. He finally returned to Lyons to work under the renowned criminologist Edmond Locard, who appointed him his assistant. He returned to Sweden to publish the first of his many books and then went back to Locard's police laboratory in Lyon, taking his Doctorate in 1928 with a thesis on small arms entitled 'Expertise des Armes à Feu Courtes'. He then lectured for a year in Lyon and in 1930 was appointed to lead a government course in Sweden on criminology. He became a lecturer at what later became Stockholm University (Docent) and from 1939 to 1953 he was head of the State Criminological Institute. He became well-known internationally in police circles, acted as rapporteur general for Interpol during the war and, in 1934, organised and ran New York's Police Laboratory. He had close contacts with Scotland Yard and was a friend of Sir Ronald Howe in CID. We flew him in 1942 for discussions with Sir Ronald in London and they seemed to have spent a riotous fortnight together, fitting in racing at Newmarket and wartime nightlife in between work.

My amateur pre-war training had at least taught me the elements of security which were singularly lacking in our Legation at the beginning of the war. No-one would listen to me so one night, to prove my point, I climbed into the building through a top-floor window and called in on our Naval Attaché, at that time Commander John Poland. He was working at his desk with a glass of whisky in one hand and a revolver in the other. He pursued me till I surrendered and had caused sufficient commotion to make my point. London was told of our deplorable state of insecurity and at my suggestion it was proposed to ask New Scotland Yard if we might approach Söderman to help us locally if they could not provide the necessary equipment. This was agreed and it was evidence of our Government's regard for Söderman that he was called in to advise. He was horrified when he saw the state of our defences, provided us with devices which, at that time, were far advanced and added the urgent recommendation that we should employ a full-time trained security officer. After some months, much to Söderman's amusement, Scotland Yard sent us a fingerprint expert whom Söderman knew well and did not rate very highly. We all got to like the giant Mr Battley with his tiny head and his Anthony Eden hat a size too small. He kept us in order and set us a splendid example by tip-toeing into our offices to catch us napping and travelling with diplomatic bags as a King's messenger to Gothenburg like a pantomime clown, with his string of sausages of diplomatic bags all attached with chains and handcuffs and leg-irons which were then locked to his sleeping-car bunk.

Having seen to our Legation's security, Harry remained in touch throughout the war, except for six months in 1940 when he told me he could not see me until the Rickman affair had been cleared up. We then resumed our sailing weekends at my father-in-law's house Viksberg, near Södertälje. Here we fished and shot and bathed and walked and collected mushrooms and talked. As an Interpol official, he travelled in and out of Germany and Switzerland and ran a training

Bill Waring, drawing by the author

programme in Finland while we were technically at war with them. One useful by-product of his Finnish activities was an enormous supply of out-of-bond angostura bitters which I bought off him for the Legation. The Finns who were to be hosts at the Olympic Games when the war broke out had been left with excessive supplies of various kinds, including drink to satisfy all tastes. They were not familiar with angostura bitters but had bought it in quantities which they imagined would meet foreign demand. They then tried to drink it neat and discovered that in spite of their galvanised stomachs they would be unable to consume the quantities required for many years. So I bought a supply off Harry which lasted the whole of the war for the needs of our Legation.

One day I got his help over a strange German refugee who had allegedly been one of Otto Strasser's men. He came to Sweden with the Jewish exodus from Denmark in 1943 and called on me with plans for him to broadcast on the BBC to subvert German morale. I suspected the man was a German agent and told Harry of my suspicions. I asked him if he could be watched but not arrested, as I had plans if possible to get him over to England. Harry established that the man was in regular contact with the German Legation and that he was making radio transmissions at irregular intervals. They had not been able to decipher them, nor were they able to find the transmitter, but suspected he was using a converter on an ordinary high-powered radio receiver. He continued to visit me and press for a chance to fly to England and broadcast for the BBC. I suggested to Harry that the Swedes might now be glad to be rid of him and we might be able to find some use for him. So finally he was flown over, well received, installed in a flat and given a radio receiver.

He recorded some tapes and was watched. He began transmitting immediately, but it was impossible to find the transmitter. He was followed round London and in the course of a short time no less than twenty contacts were identified until one day, their patience exhausted, the Special Branch broke into his flat too soon while he was transmitting. But he was too quick for them and they never found the device he used to convert his receiver. He was subjected to lengthy interrogation and finally sat out the rest of the war in Dartmoor. But that was not the end of the story. After a few months we received a message from Buckingham Palace saying His Majesty was being plagued by letters from a prisoner in Dartmoor declaring he was a refugee from Hitler and had been kidnapped by a man called Tennant in Stockholm, who had sent him to London on a spurious invitation from the BBC and that he had been unjustly imprisoned as a spy. The matter was explained to His Majesty who continued to be his host for the rest of the war.

A very interesting approach was made to Harry by his old friend the SS General Arthur Nebe, the head of the German Criminal Police, whom Harry knew well and trusted. But in the end the matter was not pursued. Poor Nebe threw his hand in with Stauffenburg and ended with torture and a lingering death (see p. 184).

But Harry's most enterprising exploit was what we knew as revolver Harry's private army. In the 30s some 200 Norwegian police officers had been trained in criminology at his Institute. In the spring of 1942 when he was in London, he renewed his close relationships with CID, dating back to 1934 when he lectured at Hendon Police College. He had known Sir Norman Kendall, the head of CID, for many years. As a police official he met Terje Vold, the refugee Norwegian Minister of Justice, who asked him about training Norwegian policemen in Sweden to take over Norway after the war. This was followed up in Sweden early in 1943 by Olav Svendsen, the Norwegian Police Officer in charge of the Legal Office of the Norwegian Legation, who had the responsibility for sorting out the sheep and goats among the swarms of Norwegian refugees. Over dinner one night they drew up a plan for training fifty Norwegian policemen to replace the Nazi police officers after the German defeat. The Norwegian government in London took a long time to make up its mind but by May, Svendsen had 20,000 kr available to help with training.

Harry then approached Gustav Möller, the Minister of the Interior, with his colleague Thorwald Bergquist. They gave their blessing. Harry then got the help of Stockholm's Police Chief, Eric Ros and G. Biörklund, the head of the State Police College, who provided accommodation and teachers and started with a course of twenty for criminal police officers for three months. The aim was to re-establish law and order in Norway, bring the criminals to justice and avoid the degradation of lynch law. Eight such courses were held and two hundred officers were trained.

The next stage was to find a site for the Norwegian Police College and this was discovered in a country house at Gottröra, a deserted and unpopulated area very suitable for exercises and manoeuvres for some fifty men without attracting attention. The whole scheme had to be kept secret and the secret was well kept from everybody, I think, but the Germans, in spite of the fact that the enterprise in the end encompassed some 15,000 men from very different establishments and large quantities of weaponry and motor vehicles. He scraped together furniture and bedding with the help of Zeta Höglund of the Stockholm Town Council who never failed to give practical help. The first instructor was Ewert Trofelt, a senior Police Officer doing military service as a Captain in the Military Police. This giant figure, six foot seven inches tall, was Harry's righthand man up to the end of the war and followed him on his dramatic entry into Oslo at the time of the capitulation. He was very popular with the Norwegians and stayed in Norway after the war to organise crash training in police methods for members of the Resistance.

The Norwegians were, on the whole, raw recruits with no sense of discipline so they were given military as well as police training. They were equipped with Swedish army weapons by the middle of the summer of 1943. Captain Helge Gleditch, the Norwegian officer in charge, had responsibility for recruitment. The courses included the Norwegian language, criminal law, report writing, police work, criminal police work, exercises, tactics and medical services. The 20,000 kr. provided by the Norwegians soon ran out, even though all Swedish services and manpower and material were provided free.

The next stage was to train a force of some 1,200 men and the Swedish authorities provided the expanded requirements, while the Norwegian Government in London produced $7^1/_2$ million kr. to fund the project. Harry's Norwegians were officially called 'The State Police Corps' responsible to the Norwegian Ministry of Justice. They consisted of eight companies, the men were fully armed with pistols, sub-machine guns, and mausers and each company had a heavy machine gun, two light mortars and twelve light machine guns. There were six dogs per company and each company was fully motorised with twelve lorries and one staff car and six motorcycles. Gottröra was expanded with new barrack buildings and in 1944 a new camp was built at Axvall, another at a place known as Torpet and a further location called Stora Fors, which was a dog and dog handler's training camp.

Then came another sudden expansion of the Norwegian force together with a new Danish one. Harry was put in command of some 10,000 men, with permission to expand to 12,000. He had been given leave of absence from his official post but kept his offices in the Institute which became the headquarters of the organisation.

This expansion started with him and the Norwegian Military Attaché, Ole Berg. Berg later became a General and Commander-in-Chief of the Norwegian Army. They devised a scheme for an additional force to cope with all the possible emergencies arising from a German capitulation and the need to protect the civilian population.

There was also the remarkable Norwegian lung surgeon, Dr Carl Semb, one of many Norwegian doctors in the resistance, who set up numerous 'health camps' all over Sweden to examine the refugees and get them into first class physical condition. These camps were combined with the others until there were some fourteen new camps to accommodate five hundred men each.

First of all these camps was the 17th century country house of Mälsåker near Mariefred on Lake Mälar, which alas was burnt down early in 1945. I visited it with Harry before the disaster and was impressed by the troops who were shortly due to move to Lapland to enter northern Norway when the time came. The worst constraint on the expansion of Norwegian police troops was the lack of trained officers, most of whom had been caught by the Germans and shipped off to concentration camps in Germany. Officers' training therefore had to be carried out in Sweden, much of it with the help of Norwegian officers flown over from England who were fully trained in commando tactics. A late addition to all this was a naval unit started at Mauritzberg Castle where finally nearly 500 sailors and fishermen were trained as harbour police. Another specialised group was trained by SOE-trained Norwegian Officers in sabotage and the handling of the latest allied weaponry.

This huge organisation with all its complicated components had to remain as secret as possible in spite of the tendency of Norwegians to chatter. Security on the whole was remarkably good though some weapons were smuggled over to the resistance in Norway. Swedish insistence on security was not popular with the Norwegians and this was perhaps the worst area of touchy relations between the Norwegian troops and their Swedish hosts. Morale on the whole was high and the desertion figure of about 1,000 over two years was not too depressing out of a body of over 10,000 men, about a quarter of the Norwegian refugees who escaped to Sweden. Many of these were undesirable characters and Quisling spies. Apart from moments of tension between the Norwegians and Swedes, there was also a certain animosity among the Norwegians against their own Legation, which on one occasion led to a serious crisis when the cooks went on strike. Punishment for indiscipline was difficult but culprits were sent to punishment camps far away from towns and with only heavy work in the woods as relaxation. Much trouble was taken to provide entertainment, films, travelling theatre troupes, concert parties and so forth.

As a result of the total German takeover of Denmark on 29 August 1943, the Danish Commander-in-Chief took the initiative to ask the Swedes to do the same for them as for the Norwegians.

The Danes on the whole were a different proposition from the Norwegians as the groups were smaller, amounting only to about 3,000 men, and very much better trained and disciplined since they had their own officers who had escaped from the Germans. General Knudtzon was sent to Sweden by the Danish Freedom Council to organise a Danish Brigade and purchase arms. Their camp was in Sofielund in Småland, where they housed five hundred men. This was followed by other camps to accommodate in the end 3,000 men. The training was more rapid than with the Norwegians as there were many more officers available. In consequence discipline was better and they concentrated more on allied commando military training rather than police work.

With the German capitulation the Danish Brigade crossed over from Hälsingborg to Helsingør, escorted by Swedish destroyers to be met with no German resistance and a warm welcome by the population. But while street fighting broke out in Copenhagen, the Brigade was held back until the following day when it went into action for the loss of only two men and four dead among the Danish Nazi Hipo men. There was no further resistance and the Brigade was given guard duty on the German frontier in Jutland and elsewhere. The Danes were very popular in Sweden and sorely missed when they left.

The Swedish army, in particular General C. A. Ehrensvärd, who as a Colonel had set up the Swedish Volunteer Corps in the first Finnish war, was wholly supportive of Harry's enterprise and made a generous contribution of weapons and manpower for the training of the Norwegian officers. In December 1944, 4,800 Norwegians were taken on manoeuvres in Dalarna with the help of the Swedish Army and among the umpires was no less a person than Prince Gustaf Adolf. The new Swedish C-in-C, General Jung, was also present as an observer. The Norwegians were very popular with the local people and as they marched past the schools the children sang the Norwegian National Anthem, 'Ja vi elsker'. The manoeuvres revealed weaknesses in the staff work of the Norwegians in handling large units and the Swedish army set up a series of staff courses to give them more experience. In April 1945 an even bigger exercise took place with some 6,000 men at Järvsö in Hälsingland. The Minister of the Interior, Gustav Möller, and the future Prime Minister, Tage Erlander, were present. I had just sent the latter over to London for a period of months on a course in air raid precautions. Prince Gustaf Adolf again took part in these manoeuvres.

The German retreat in Finland southwards through northern Norway was marked by a vicious destruction of everything that lay in their path in the winter of 1944/5. The Swedes co-operated with Bernt Balchen, the famous Norwegian/American airman, to bring relief to the local population. In December 1944, Balchen arrived with ten Dakotas first at Västerås, where they loaded a field hospital and Norwegian personnel and then flew on to the airfield at Kallax near Luleå, where Harry's Norwegian policemen joined the American airmen. After bureaucratic delays by the Russians who by now were in Kirkenes in northern Norway, Harry got permission to send in his men. From 12 January 1945, and in the following weeks, 968 Norwegian police and 917,342 kilogrammes of material were flown by Balchen to northern Norway from Sweden. Another base was built at Karesuando, the most northerly inhabited spot on Sweden. Roads were built through the snow and ice before the early spring thaw and some of the Norwegian police troops managed to enter Norway; but the thaw made motorised transport impossible and they had to resort to walking, riding horses or driving in reindeer sledges. Harry staked out an airstrip on a lake at Karesuando which Balchen immediately made use of. By the time of the German capitulation on 8 May all was ready for the Norwegian troops to march in.

Söderman had entered Norway alone by 8 May but the Allies refused to allow his police troops to cross into Norway till two days

Harry Söderman, drawing by the author

later, much to their disgust. The final figures were 1,310 men into Kirkenes in March 1945; then in May, after the capitulation, 3,915 into Narvik, 2,570 to Trondhjem and 4,975 to Oslo, a total of 12,770 men, 792 horses and 600 motor vehicles.

The Norwegians were disappointed that they had no chance to fight, but it was a mercy that the German army behaved in a disciplined manner and that the Quisling Norwegians did not attempt to put up a last stand. Allied fears of a final campaign in a Norwegian redoubt were not realised, largely by the demoralisation of the German troops who all wanted to go home. The final bill for Harry's operation is interesting; all the training provided by the Swedish army and police was a gift, while Sweden wrote off a loan of 50 million kr. to Denmark and 150 million kr. to Norway.

Harry was not content with his own private army; he had to get into Norway ahead of everybody in order to save the prisoners in the concentration camp of Grini and the jails of Oslo from reprisals by the Germans or the Quislings. Through his position in Interpol he got in touch with the head of the Gestapo in Norway, Oberführer Fehlis, to negotiate the liberation of the Norwegians in Grini and Møllergaten No.19 and the 100,000 Russian prisoners of war being used as slave labour in the north. With the agreement of the Prime Minister, the Foreign Minister and the Norwegian legation and with the clearance of our Military Attaché Reggie Sutton-Pratt, whom he discovered in a yard getting his boat ready for the summer, Harry took the train to the Norwegian frontier at Charlottenberg on 21 April 1945 and met the Gestapo Chief, Fehlis. They had a picnic and discussed the whole question of liberating the Norwegians in Oslo and the Russian prisoners of war in the north. Fehlis did not know that Himmler had already allowed the Swedes to liberate Norwegians in the concentration camps in Germany and take them to Sweden and he promised he would get in touch with Himmler to see what could be done. He kept in touch by telephone and then with no answer coming from Himmler, Harry had a message that Terboven, the Reichskommisar in Norway, wished to discuss the matter with him in Oslo. So he left for Oslo on 6 May with the agreement of the Swedish Prime Minister, Foreign Minister and the Norwegians but to the annoyance of certain circles in Britain who did not wish to share credit for liberation with an unauthorised civilian neutral.

He was met by the Gestapo at the frontier, driven to Oslo and accommodated by them in a requisitioned Norwegian shipowner's house where he met Fehlis for discussions. Terboven kept on putting him off until just as he was going to see him on Monday the 7th at 15.50 hours, the radio announced the capitulation of Germany. Harry drove to Grini with his faithful Trofelt and a German official detailed to open up the prisons for him. He called the 5,000 prisoners together, handed over the command of Grini to the Norwegians under Gowart-Olsen, made a stirring speech, and asked the inmates to remain in Grini till further notice. They all sang the Norwegian National Anthem, and then he repeated the same exercise with the 500 women in the camp. He then went to Møllergaten No.19, all cells were opened, he made them a speech, told them to stay there till he could transport them to Grini where they would all be concentrated for feeding and medical inspection. He released five poor wretches who were condemned to death, then to the Gestapo headquarters at Viktoria Terassse, where there were thirty prisoners whom he freed and had transported to Grini. He used these headquarters as his own and with the agreement of the Norwegians took over responsibility for the police. He got the Red Cross to transport all prisoners to Grini and supply rations and medicines. He stopped all sale of alcoholic liquor, occupied the radio station, lifted the blackout and finally the home front underground emerged and asked him to continue in command. They disarmed the Quisling guard at the Castle and fought off a threat of attack at Møllergaten No.19 with another harangue by Harry to the crowd. In the meantime Fehlis disappeared and was later found to have committed suicide with the double security of a cyanide pill and a shot in the head with his revolver. On the Wednesday Harry handed over to the Norwegians and drove back to Sweden.

The next day, hoping for a short rest, he was asked to go immediately to Saltfjord in Northern Norway to look after the Russian prisoners of war. Together with Balchen he filled seven Dakotas with supplies of cigarettes, food and medicine and flew to Bodø which was still occupied by the Germans. A Norwegian underground committee had been formed to look after the Russians and he then proceeded to visit all the camps spread from Mo i Rana to Narvik as forced labour for Hitler's northern Norway railway. The loss of life had been horrific in this brutal Todt organisation operation. He was stunned by the starvation and illness that prevailed in the camps and by the brutality of the Wehrmacht which had always been so proud of its honour and its discipline. He then had a victory parade in Bodø with his police troops, the Americans and a mixed bag of Ostarbeiter mainly Russians and Yugoslavs. The Swedish Red Cross came in and nurses took charge of the sick with medicine and food.

This was the last of his wartime efforts after which he returned to his Institution with the new title of Director General. He remained there till 1953 when he left for the United States. After the war he became one of the leading lights of Interpol; when it was reorganised he was made Chairman of its European Narcotics Committee. In 1951 he spent seven months in West Germany to help with the organisation of the German Federal Police. Then in 1952 he acted as an adviser to the Israeli Government on police matters. In 1955 he suddenly moved to an international police appointment in Tangier and sold up his delightful country house Berga near Södertälje, which he had bought off a mutual friend who was a neighbour to my wife's family at Viksberg. He died unexpectedly of a heart attack in Tangier on 16 March 1956, aged only 54. He had married for the third time and left a young family of four children in addition to his son Pehr by an earlier marriage. His loss was felt very deeply by his friends around the world, not only in police circles. He had had too much experience of the abuse of power by the Secret Police in Nazi Germany and in occupied Norway and Denmark to have any sympathy for the lack of political control of Sweden's own Security Police. He was a brave and extrovert adventurer with intelligence and expert knowledge of his profession, together with a love of humanity which endeared him to people in many countries, especially in Scandinavia and Finland.

**Footnote**

1. See three articles on the Reichstag Fire by Harry Söderman in *Dagens Nyheter* 23, 25 and 28 October, 1933.

# XII

# Germany

Our view of the German scene was a very fragmented one. I never had any direct dealings with Bonhoeffer, Moltke, von Trott or von Cramm, though some of my colleagues were closely involved. We had many contacts with German refugees from the Nazis, employing some of them in our Press Reading Bureau. The bulk of these refugees were social democrats who gave us little information of what was happening in the resistance. However the German Officer Corps, public servants, churchmen, businessmen and academics were active in using Stockholm and other neutral capitals as means of communicating with the allies, giving us some idea of more conservative upper middle-class opinion and that of some of the aristocracy.

Up to the time of Munich there had been direct contact with London and for a while afterwards but all chances of a *coup d'état* were eliminated by Munich. Once the war had started it was left to a few peripatetic peacemakers like Birger Dahlerus to bring the war to an end through the spurious good offices of Goering. Representatives of resistance groups themselves passed messages to and through neutral countries, the foremost of them in the beginning of course being the USA, which itself became embroiled in the ill-timed initiative of Sumner Welles's visit to Berlin and London. Meetings became more and more rare after the Venlo incident. One of my contacts, Walter Jacobsen, (see pp. 176 and 194) appreciated the confusion that must have been caused by the proliferation of resistance groups. Some of these were provocations to sow suspicion about negotiations for a separate peace in the first phase of the war to split the Anglo-French entente and in the last phase to undermine the alliance with Russia. Some questioned whether we were concentrating on the annihilation of the Nazi régime and not of Germany and others on whether we should not treat with the Nazis themselves. Questions were raised as to whether the Germans should restore the whole of Poland and Czechoslovakia and the independence of Austria and whether the injustice of Versailles might be mitigated by the return of colonies to the Volk ohne Raum, combined with the decentralisation of Germany and a move of the centre of gravity from Prussia to the south. Finally these issues were simplified by events, first by the Atlantic Charter, then by the Casablanca Declaration of Unconditional Surrender which left little or no hope for the German resistance of any help from outside. With the mystery of the Hess defection, the Russians suspected us, or pretended to suspect us, of negotiating for a separate peace till Casablanca stopped the pot simmering for a while.

It appears that for the early part of the war, Canaris had such faith in his Swedish friends doing his job for him, as he had trained one of them himself, that he only began to instal his own men in the second year after the invasion of Norway and Denmark. Canaris's man in the German Naval Attaché's office in Oslo sent us warnings about German agents in the Admiralty. Most of these could be attributed to German ability to read our naval ciphers at the time. In one case they gave us the exact location of the British minefields to be laid in Norwegian waters in April 1940 long before we laid them. But this again may well have been a success in cryptography rather than proof of a mole in the Admiralty. These events were marginal indications of resistance to Nazism. Canaris and his men were certainly, at that time, not identified by us with the German resistance.

In the autumn of 1939 I got to know Ivar Andersson, the editor of *Svenska Dagbladet*, and his foreign editor, Otto Järte, and spent many evenings in Järte's house and on walks in Djurgården when he passed me information they had received from General Beck and Goerdeler, von Bock, Halder and Oster with warnings of the invasion of the Netherlands and Belgium. These attacks were called off so frequently that in the end when the Dutch were given the actual date and time, no-one believed them and they were taken unawares.

One of these warnings came to me through a Dr Walter Jacobsen[1] in Sweden who was a friend of Dr Robinsohn, a Jewish refugee, in Denmark. The latter sent us a message in November 1939 he had received from a Dr Fritz Elsas, in whose house Reichenau had met Goerdeler, to tell him of Hitler's plan to invade Holland. This message reached Jacobsen in Sweden and was the precursor of many others.

Dr Walter Jacobsen invited me on 18 January 1940 to meet an emissary of what he described as his, i.e. Jacobsen's, opposition group. The Foreign Office had given us assurances of the bona fides of Jacobsen's friend, Dr Hans Robinsohn. He had handed over a document to O'Leary in Copenhagen who had forwarded it to London. My visitor asked for a meeting in Stockholm with some senior Foreign Office official with a prominent member of the German Group whose name would be revealed when a meeting had been agreed. The matter was urgent in order to frustrate the German spring offensive in the west. My visitor said he understood the extreme caution of the British government in view of the Venlo affair and 'of the fact that they are probably receiving independent proposals from some twenty-five other similar opposition groups offering similar peace terms'.

He said his own group was now ready to take over the country through the army chiefs in twenty-four hours. They could occupy all key points and arrest all the Nazi chiefs; the SS would be the only serious opposition and they could be mastered by the army. The people would be wholly on the side of the opposition. The Luftwaffe was the only service entering the war with any enthusiasm. The Polish campaign had opened the eyes of the Officer Corps to the horrendous behaviour of the SS and Gestapo. The allies must not exploit the temporary weakness of Germany during such a coup to their military advantage. Poland would be reconstituted as a small and independent state and so would Czechoslovakia, frontiers to be determined by international agreement. Austria was to remain in the Reich. They were prepared for a crusade against Russia and the overthrow of the Stalin régime as 'Russia must be Europeanised and not excluded from western civilisation'. European frontiers could be determined by international agreement and the transfer of populations. Customs barriers would have to be abolished and raw materials of the world would be made accessible to all countries - a hint of the return of the German colonies. Young people were to be given the opportunity of early responsibility and German agriculture must be modernised. It was all much of what one must have seen in London of the same nature with, variations, on the fate of Poland, Czechoslovakia, Austria and Russia. Nothing came of these approaches and they joined the files of intelligence which piled high year after year. These terms were repeated and elaborated as the war continued and hardened, and the more reasonable and elaborate they became the more unlikely they seemed capable of implementation.

Stockholm like all neutral capitals was a flypaper for peace feelers. As the number of neutrals diminished so this activity was more concentrated in Stockholm, Berne, Madrid, Lisbon and Ankara. British intelligence had since 1917 concentrated its activity on Soviet Russia and was badly equipped to analyse and counter the Nazi menace. Churchill in his wilderness years kept a close eye on developments and so did Vansittart. Both were considered unreliable by Chamberlain and Horace Wilson. The same was the fate of journalists and politicians. Their warnings were discounted and their knowledge of the anti-Nazi forces in the German army, civilian and church circles was not appreciated until too late after the Munich Agreement had put paid to any hope of Hitler being overthrown before the war.

Sweden produced many peacemakers. After the Venlo incident we were cautious about the risk of provocation and kidnapping. It is an irony of history that Walter Schellenberg, who set up the Venlo kidnapping, made a final appearance on the scene as a peace emissary of Himmler to trade the lives of Jews, Scandinavians and other concentration camp victims to Count Folke Bernadotte in return for the overthrow of Hitler and the saving of his own life. We knew something of Himmler's plan through his masseur, Dr Felix Kersten, who lived in Stockholm but treated Himmler in Germany every month. On his return he told our US colleague, George Brewer of the OSS, what his patient had confided to him.

Himmler knew something about the penetration of peace movements along the lines laid down by Willi Münzenburg with his communist 'innocents clubs'. Before the war he made it known that he was a fervent Buchmanite, supporter of moral rearmament and the Oxford Group movement, a lover of children, a chicken farmer, a protector of animals, etc. But after the horrors for which he had been responsible, it was a little difficult to accept the plausibility of his opposition to Nazism. Our 'black' transmitter, Radio Atlantik, blew the story of his defection on 28 April 1945, which resulted in Himmler's dismissal, Dönitz being appointed as head of state after Hitler's suicide to sue for peace within a few days.

Apart from direct approaches from Germans, whether genuine or spurious, there were numerous self-appointed peacemakers and Sweden had its full complement. One such person was the pretentious and garrulous Birger Dahlerus, a cousin of Goering's first Swedish wife. He endeavoured to dupe Chamberlain, Horace Wilson and Halifax into believing that Goering was ready to depose Hitler and make peace with Britain. He was an assiduous visitor before the war and after the outbreak continued his visitations. On 29 September he saw the Foreign Secretary who firmly told him that nobody believed a word Hitler said. On 11 October he made further peace proposals to Nevile Bland, our Ambassador at the Hague, who was instructed to refer him to the Prime Minister's speech of 12 October inviting Germany to make proposals for establishing her sincerity. Dahlerus then visited Berlin and in late October made detailed proposals to our Legation in Stockholm, showing us a copy of a letter from Goering thanking him for his activities on behalf of peace. On 16 November Dahlerus again met Goering and on 20 November suggested to our Legation in Stockholm that a secret meeting should be arranged between British, German and French representatives. Early in December Dahlerus saw Goering again and on 11 December repeated his former suggestion of a meeting between the three belligerents. On 15 December he was politely discouraged by the Legation from a visit to London. However, he saw Goering again on the 18th and told him there was no prospect of a secret meeting. But he visited London again in spite of our warnings on the 28th and saw Sir Alexander Cadogan. He said he had nothing to add to our previous statements and that the disappearance of Hitler was essential as was also evidence that the new régime was of a different nature from the present one. But Dahlerus never tired and in February 1940 was in Moscow pursuing Finnish peace proposals. Early in January 1940 Erik Palmstierna, the former Swedish Minister in London, had a private talk with a friend he had known at No. 10, asking him to warn the British Government that Dahlerus was unreliable, though this could not be said officially by Prytz, his successor as Minister.

Another Swedish peace pedlar was Baron Knut Bonde who had married a niece of Lord Rennel twenty-eight years previously. He had been approached by von Cramm who frequently stayed with his tennis partner, King Gustav, and was a personal friend of Goering who again wished us to know he was prepared to head a new German government. Bonde saw Halifax in great secrecy at the Dorchester on 13 December 1939 and handed over a memorandum which had been seen by Count von Rosen, who was married to the sister of Goering's first wife. Von Rosen had visited Goering who had seen the memorandum and von Rosen reported to the Swedish King 'that Goering is absolutely loyal to Hitler until the moment comes to lock him up'. Halifax was suspicious of Bonde's approach insisting that action against Hitler must be effective and not a second Elba.

In all the confusions of peace initiatives by the Pope, Roosevelt, Sumner Welles, the King of the Belgians, the Queen of Holland and Group Captain Christie's secret meetings with Goerdeler, it was difficult to identify any resistance group which seemed capable of overthrowing the régime and replacing it with one acceptable to the western allies. The attempt on Hitler's life by Georg Elser in the Burgerbräu Keller on 8 November 1939 was impossible for us to assess. So were also almost simultaneous warnings from the German army which were the first of many about an offensive in the west. With all the brave attempts on Hitler's life culminating in the plot of 20 July 1944, the British took the irrevocable decision to consider no terms other than unconditional surrender. We based our plans on high grade intelligence provided by the decrypting of German communications or other well-corroborated sources. We thought in Sweden that insistence on unconditional surrender prolonged the war, but we were in no position to view the whole picture as seen from London. It is sad to read the words in Beck's memorandum of 21 January 1940 that the result of a world war, unless it could be prevented by the overthrow of the Nazi régime, would be 'a Germany bled white, doomed to surrender unconditionally'. His own bungled suicide spared him the tragic fulfilment of his prophecy.

It was only on rare occasions that I actually met Germans and they were usually not of great interest. I remember a long talk with a German who was staying with the King and was the Swedish Consul General in Stuttgart. Great precautions were taken to see I was not kidnapped, but an hour or so with him produced nothing except greetings to his friend Lord Reith and assurances that our bombing of Stuttgart was brutal and ineffective. But there were other serious people with whom I was in touch indirectly through Ivar Andersson, and Otto Järte. They had good contacts with the generals and Goerdeler, also with Moltke and Adam von Trott. I never met either of these but they regularly saw my colleagues, Roger Hinks and Jim Knapp-Fisher, while von Cramm, who was another frequent visitor, was seen by David McEwan. None of us, as far as I know, ever met Peter Kleist or his mysterious intermediary, Edgar Klaus. Other valuable sources were the remarkable banker, Jakob Wallenberg, and through my press friends the Swedish Minister in Berlin, the appeaser Arvid Richert, and his outstanding military attaché, Curt Juhlin-Dannfelt, who, at the end of the war, became head of Swedish intelligence.

The Bonhoeffer-Bishop Bell meeting in May 1942 took place in the strictest secrecy. The memorandum of the German proposals handed over by Bonnhöfer and prepared by von Trott is a tragic testimony to one of the might-have-beens of history if the allies had declared their readiness to treat with such a new German government. But the Atlantic Charter committed us to total victory to be followed later by the Casablanca Declaration of Unconditional Surrender.

On 22 January 1940 I met the Reverend Forell, the Swedish Pastor in Berlin, and we met often later. He talked about Goerdeler who was described as an adviser to Rundstedt. He spoke of the views of German officers serving on the western front and their readiness for peace if just terms were offered. My note reads:

> The general impression his description left was one of the utter listlessness and hopelessness of the German people in face of what is for them a meaningless war, together with a certain mystical desire in some quarters to put an end to it and to Hitler's whole régime without the willpower or the initiative to put such pious resolutions into effect.

Our contacts with Germans were essentially with refugees and most of these were social democrats and trades unionists. One of them purported to be an Otto Strasser man who turned out to be a Nazi agent. I saw a good deal of Bruno Kreisky and Willy Brandt.

Both for a short while helped us in Joe Parrott's (Sir Cecil Parrott) press reading bureau. This covered hundreds of papers daily from Germany and occupied Europe. Kreisky was always insistent that Austrians, Germans, and Czechs would never again trust a British government unless it was a Labour one. The trades unionists included a mysterious character called Knüfken whom the Swedes protected in prison on a spurious charge as he was wanted, as was also the sinister Wollweber, by the Nazis, the latter also by the Russians. Knüfken represented the international transport workers and my contact with him was at arm's length through the veteran Swedish trades unionist, Charlie Lindley. He visited him regularly and brought messages and presents from his friends in England. He was released before the end of the war and flown to London after a celebratory meal with me and Charlie.

The Parrott House teemed with refugees from Europe. Some of them turned themselves into shadow governments, addressed one another with imposing titles such as President, Prime Minister, etc., and deposed one another at regular intervals. While these teams gave us a good insight into much of what was happening in Germany and its neighbours, all this work was essentially overt intelligence using largely published material. Little of it was concerned with talking to groups in Germany who had plans for the overthrow of the régime.

One was very much aware of the despair and frustration felt by the representatives of the resistance groups at being used by us for nothing more than intelligence purposes. This became more and more the case as the war progressed and war aims hardened, particularly after the entry of Russia with their incurable suspicion that we and the Americans were preparing for a separate peace and not pressing on with the second front. While peace feelers from Germany were a regular feature of these years, there was one occasion when the Germans apparently thought the British were ready to throw in the sponge. On 18 June 1940, with France capitulating and our troops withdrawn from Norway, the Swedes were under extreme pressure to give way to demands for troop transit through Sweden to Norway. I happened to meet two Swedish politicians, the social democrats, Alan Vougt, and Rickard Lindström, the editor of *Social Demokraten*, leaving a meeting of the Foreign Affairs Committee. They appealed to me with urgency for assurances that Britain was not going to do a deal with Hitler since the Swedish government was giving way to German demands as the result of a telegram from Prytz, the Swedish Minister in London, which indicated readiness for a compromise peace. The telegram tipped the balance which was already so heavily weighted in Germany's favour. The Swedes feared a conflict between Germany and Russia which had already occupied the Baltic States, a move which they thought might be followed by a fresh attack on Finland. With assurances to my friends that there was no truth in Prytz's assumptions, I reported the contents of the telegram in the Legation, but the Swedes were not allowed by the British to publish its text for many years.

Prytz's telegram reported a conversation with Butler in the Foreign Office assuring him that the war must continue but 'begged me to be assured that no chance would be missed to reach a compromise peace if opportunity were offered for reasonable terms and that no die-hards would stand in the way. He considered that Great Britain had greater opportunities for negotiations than it might have later on and that Russia might play a greater part than the United States of America if conversations were started. During our talk Butler was called in to Halifax, who sent me a message that commonsense not bravado would dictate the British Government's policy by which Halifax understood that such a message would be welcomed by the Swedish Minister but that it should not be interpreted as peace at any price. In conversation with other members of Parliament, it seems to be expected that if and when negotiations begin, possibly after 28 June, Halifax might succeed Churchill'. Butler later offered his resignation, but Churchill refused to accept it.[2] Churchill made his famous fighting speech on 18 June and the British Minister in Stockholm, Victor Mallet, in reply to the Swedish Minister for Foreign Affairs, Günther's question about Prytz's telegram, referred him to Churchill's speech. No explanation of the situation in London ever reached us in Stockholm, but Mallet was commended for his sturdy reply to Günther and the Swedes were reprimanded for their weak-kneed behaviour. Halifax also made the British position clear in his public speech in reply to Hitler's of 19 July.

In Stockholm Halifax's message was interpreted as a message for Berlin. Prytz had already, in January, indicated that Swedish mediation with the Germans was under consideration, but when asked, he replied that the opinions expressed in his telegram were not

Sir Victor Mallet, drawing by the author

those of the British Government but the private views of Halifax and Butler. The *News Chronicle* correspondent in Stockholm, Eric Dancy, with whom I had been lunching after hearing the news, reported the story but it was suppressed by the censorship in London and the Foreign Office informed Stockholm that Prytz had assured Butler he had misunderstood him.

However, on 19 June the Swedish Minister in Berlin, Richert, had seen Weizsäcker in the Auswärtiges Amt and told him, without the authority of the Swedish Government, of the Prytz telegram which he had seen in the Swedish Foreign Office the previous day. On 22 June Wiezsäcker spoke to Richert again, referring to a newspaper cutting about Lloyd George forming a government in London to make peace. He speculated on which member of the British cabinet might be acceptable to the Germans as a negotiator. He ruled out Churchill, Chamberlain, Eden, Simon and Duff Cooper but not Halifax; he added that the Germans saw no signs of a British wish to negotiate and that Richert's report was the first they had heard. Richert reported the conversation to the Swedish Ministry of Foreign Affairs and on 25 June the Swedes reported to Mallet, through the medium of Marcus Wallenberg, that the Auswärtiges Amt was interested to know if the British were ready to negotiate and that Halifax was acceptable as a negotiator. Mallet replied that he saw no inclination by the British government to negotiate but reported the message home.

Dahlerus then came into the act again in a meeting with Goering on 26 and 28 July, who stressed the need for peace and suggested that the only person who had the necessary prestige in Germany and England to get negotiations going was the King of Sweden. King Gustav had previously expressed a desire to mediate and did not miss this opportunity. The Swedish Government then instructed their Ministers in Berlin and London to inform the respective governments of the King's readiness to proffer his good offices, with the assurance that this was his own personal initiative and not prompted by any other party. The replies from Hitler and George VI were firm refusals. A serious rebuff for the old King. Churchill suspected the initiative had been inspired by the Germans. This incident further lowered the standing of King Gustav in England and added to the accumulation of peace feelers. It did nothing to persuade the British government that there was a serious resistance movement in Germany which could eliminate Hitler and his régime and establish a government acceptable to the allies. On 3 August Churchill wrote a minute to Halifax commenting 'I might add that intrusion of the ignominious King of Sweden as a peacemaker, after his desertion of all Finland and Norway and while he is absolutely in the German grip, though not without its encouraging aspects, is singularly distasteful'.

Another interesting approach which I have not seen recorded anywhere[3] from a member of the resistance, came to us through my friend Dr Harry Söderman. Söderman was respected in police circles internationally. He had worked in France, Germany and the United States and was well-known to Sir Norman Kendal and Sir Ronald (Ronnie) Howe of Scotland Yard and to the Hendon Police College.

Among other responsibilities, Söderman acted as a representative of Interpol which gave him access to the police authorities in the belligerent countries as well as in other neutral ones, In the spring of 1942, he travelled to Switzerland and Vichy France and on his way back called in on Arthur Nebe, the head of the German criminal police. He had known him for years, as had also Scotland Yard, and had a high regard for him both professionally and as a person. In fact he considered him to be the best of the Germans he knew in the Third Reich and he had to meet some loathsome characters officially in the course of his work. Nebe had been an army officer in World War I, joined the Berlin police under the Weimar Republic and was rapidly promoted, particularly after he had joined the Nazi Party in 1933. His excuse for joining was the policeman's hope that the Nazis stood for law and order against chaos, a not unnatural attitude at the time. He became head of the Prussian Landeskriminalpolizeiamt. Just before the war, when the regional police forces had been abolished, he became director of the Reichskriminalpolizeiamt. As such he was head of the whole criminal police and in parallel to the Gestapo directly under Heydrich as head of the Reichssicherheitshauptamt. As a member of the SS he had reached the top when Söderman met him in 1942 as SS Obergruppenführer und Generalleutnant der Polizei. He had been commander of Einsatzkommando B in Russia much to his own disgust. He had not resigned his post as he was able in some degree to counter the loathsome activities of this organisation and also to prevent some Nazi sadist taking over command.

Söderman liked Nebe and trusted him. He described him as tall and good looking, he was married and had a daughter and, unlike other top people in the Nazi régime, still lived in the same modest villa on the Wannsee as he did in the days before the Nazis. He was a great reader, a hard worker and a man of moderate habits. He was liked in other countries and during the war, when Söderman visited England, he was always being asked about Nebe.

Nebe genuinely hated Himmler, Heydrich and the whole Gestapo organisation. He would unburden himself very freely to Söderman of his feelings about the rogues and villains who surrounded him. He commanded the undivided loyalty of the civil police who did not identify him with the political secret police. When Söderman called on Nebe, on his way back from Switzerland, he found him very pessimistic. He had just returned from camping for several months outside Moscow with a large police staff in preparation for becoming Chief of Police in Moscow after its capture. Nebe was sarcastic about the régime and reported a considerable amount of discontent. He had been involved in the opposition to Hitler from the very beginning before the war and in particular the coup prepared by the army officers and civilians before the Munich Agreement put the lid on it.

In the autumn of 1942 when Söderman visited him again, he was even more frank. He saw a collapse of Germany fast approaching. Shortage of oil was making itself felt at the front. He arranged some meetings in the attic of his house on the Wannsee with Graf Helldorf, whom Söderman described as a repulsive homosexual. He was police president of Berlin, also a conspirator and they discussed ways of overthrowing the régime. Since the two men considered Germany ready for collapse, they suggested that an Allied airborne landing in the heart of Germany would be enough to precipitate it. With the support of the Wehrmacht they would be able to paralyse the SS panzer units near Pasewalk and Weimar which were held in readiness to quell civil disturbances. Nebe would then have the civil criminal police arrest all leading Nazis. It could be done in the night and he himself would arrest Hitler and Himmler. Helldorf would surround Berlin and the civil police (the Schutzpolizei or Schupos) would occupy all key points. The transformation of

Helldorf from a sadistic Nazi to an opponent of the régime was explained by Nebe as being the result of Helldorf's revulsion against the orgies of cruelty he had seen committed in Russia. He did not believe he could be absolved from his sins by this conversion, but intended to hand himself over to the allies as a war criminal for the judgement of a military court.

Söderman saw me on his return to Sweden. The plan by then had become somewhat more realistic in that the airborne landing was suggested for the Hamburg area to be backed up by a seaborne one on the German coast. Söderman had gone into considerable detail and was prepared to use his own police transmitter under cover of Interpol to communicate with Nebe by special code. We then flew him over to London to see his friend, Sir Ronald Howe. At that time Howe was Chief Constable C.I.D. succeeding Sir Norman Kendal as Assistant Commissioner C.I.D. in 1945. The proposals were looked at with interest but rejected. Söderman duly informed Nebe that his plan had been turned down.[3]

Our reasons were mixed. The British did not trust Nebe and regarded the scheme as hare-brained. At no time either was there any discussion of what was to follow such a coup, what kind of military or civilian government and German frontiers could be acceptable. One assumed it was a matter of a coup with allied intervention to be followed by an armistice and then the occupation of Germany by the allies. We had not the capacity to carry out any such operation of this magnitude at that time, nor did we either see any opening for a deception operation. We also suspected a possible Russian provocation to blackmail us into a second front, or a provocation by the Germans to make the Russians believe we were prepared for a separate peace. There was also an absence of any recognition of the need to deal with the Russians as well as the western allies. Nebe and Helldorf, as we know, continued their good work which came to an end with the July plot of 1944 and the execution of both of them. Nebe had been active till the end and had been instrumental in procuring the explosive for Stauffenberg. He escaped, went into hiding and dyed his hair but was finally captured and executed.

It is fit that these men and women of the German resistance should be honoured for the stand they took in face of hopeless odds in their opposition to Hitler and lack of support from the allies. It took the courage of Stauffenberg to overcome the haunting fear of breaking the Hitler oath which had so often been the excuse for army officers doing nothing. That he failed was a stark and gruesome tragedy for himself, for his brave friends who suffered with him and for his country. Their physical and moral courage and dreams for the future will always remain a shining example of human endeavour in an otherwise black and shameful period of German history.

This note I made in December 1943.

I wish to report the following items of information regarding certain aspects of German export trade and scientific relations with this and probably other enemy or neutral countries. The lengths to which the Germans are prepared to go in acquiring foreign currency are indicative of possible shortages of foreign exchange and of a remarkable lack of moral principle.

Scientific experiments in hormones and endocrinology have been advanced by the mass execution of victims in concentration camps. A by-product of this mass incarceration and execution of victims has been the export of human hair shorn from the heads of women for the benefit of the hairdressing trade of this and probably other countries where the exigencies of fashion have demanded large supplies of false hair for the return to the more exuberant female coiffures characteristic of the years preceding and during the last war. It is not improbable that the Germans have been instrumental in stimulating this change of fashion to further their export trade.

The German experiments on human guinea pigs have, however, resulted in a surplus of the main product of this assassination industry in the form of ductless glands. I have evidence that German scientists are seeking the aid of their colleagues in this country to assist them in their researches in this field, as the material available is greater than the capacity of the staff detailed for this special work. One Swedish doctor of pro-German persuasion has, to my knowledge, received through the intermediary of the diplomatic bag of the German Legation and by the good offices of the 'German Scientific Institute' in Stockholm, fresh specimens of these tragic human remains in order to pursue this research for the furtherance of science.

The specimens provided are documented in each case and

details are provided of the scientifically supervised torture and privations to which the victims are subjected before execution and the extraction of the glands for the examination of the resulting physiological and chemical reactions. One German doctor was recently lecturing here on interesting experiments carried out on arrested menstruation in the case of women condemned to death, who were periodically subjected to the strain of being brought to execution and reprieved before finally being executed. In another case I have the evidence of a medical doctor's published thesis on the pituitary gland, furnished, with the thoroughness characteristic of such German publications, with a voluminous bibliography which included the names, sex, age, and date of execution of Poles from whose decapitated heads the fresh pituitary glands had been extracted for examination.

While these sidelights on German mentality are perhaps not surprising, it is additional evidence of incorrigible perversity that they should show so little reserve in publicising such accomplishments, which can scarcely be calculated to increase their prestige as a master race and the leaders of Western civilisation.

I wrote this minute on 4 July 1944.

I have had an opportunity of a long conversation with a Swedish industrialist who has just returned from a three weeks' visit to Germany, during which time he had the exceptional experience of discussing future plans with a member of the inner circle in the Reich Chancellery. He would not reveal the identity of his source, but assured me that he was a man of considerable importance in the present régime. He is not a party member but a person of substance who has always played a leading role behind the scenes as a financier. He appears convinced that in the event of a change of régime, a compromise peace with the Russians or with us, or even of total defeat, he holds sufficient trump cards to remain in the saddle.

The man in question seems to be closely associated with Schnurre, the political scarecrow who is regularly used by the German government to intimidate the Swedes whenever there are economic negotiations afoot. He is also connected in some way with a certain Finke who appears to be a mysterious Gestapo agent in Sweden. The latter is said to be playing a double game and to be feathering his nest for himself and his friends in this country against the possibility of disaster befalling his Fatherland.

The gist of his information was the following. Germany might by a miracle still win the war. Even, however, if she lost it, were ravaged and laid waste and occupied, she might still be in a position to win the peace and thereby the next war. Germany's great mistake had been to rely too much on military, political, economic and propaganda tactics instead of the wider aspects of strategy. Her leaders had so pinned their faith on the theory of the Blitzkrieg, on quick returns, on winning battles instead of campaigns, that they had ignored the wider issues and were now frantically endeavouring to stem the tide that had turned against them by resorting to the production of new and unconventional weapons. If time were on their side it was possible that present research and experiment might result in a weapon of such destructive force that not only would disaster be averted for the present but it was highly probable that the Allies would be forced to come to terms. The weapon to which he alluded would throw rockets and flying bombs into the shade, would be almost infinite in range and unimaginably destructive in effect.

He was, however, himself not interested in such emergency measures and was instead devoting his attention to long term planning regardless of the outcome of the present war. Together with a select group of colleagues he was preparing a secret organisation which would continue after defeat and occupation. This would have so many manifestations that it would be practically impossible for the occupying powers to suppress it. The directing force of this organisation would not in any way be connected with the Nazi party, as it would be safe to assume that the Allies after the occupation would devote their main attention to the suppression of the Nazis and those who had in any way assisted them into power. The organisation would, however, make use of a smoke screen of Nazis who would be trained in traditional terrorist methods on the lines of the Fehme. Such training was already in progress in the schools, the Hitlerjugendschulen and Ordensburgen. Boys were trained in shadowing suspects and in silent killing. After they had completed their courses they were formally expelled from school, their parents would be stigmatised, and then opportunities would be offered to the boys to find work in other parts of Germany where they were not known, on the pretext of sparing them the social censure of their own localities. The boys themselves, fully conscious of what they were doing, were trained to iron discipline, and organised in cells of five with a sixth anonymous and unknown leader whose orders they obeyed implicitly. They were taught to accept orders unconditionally as emanating from the Führer himself, whatever might appear to happen to the Führer or to Germany, even if the Führer were announced as dead, a democratic *coup d'état* were carried out, Germany capitulated, etc. They were to work closely with the Allied authorities and denounce persons to them if so ordered.

All this and other organisations of men and boys and girls which were being formed were, however, merely intended as a red herring for the Allied occupying authorities, who would be kept busy all this time in their hunt for war criminals and Nazis, suppressing terrorism and sabotage, detecting clandestine radio stations, coping with refugees, transport, housing, feeding and public hygiene, together with the almost hopeless task of identifying individuals and property in a country in which bombing had destroyed a large portion of the available records and people were easily able to change identity. In the midst of this chaos it would be possible for the few conscious and many unconscious agents of the real organisation to work unseen and unhindered, contributing to the state of confusion necessary to their plan by dividing the Allies amongst themselves and gradually reversing the roles of victor and vanquished by making the Allies compete with one another for the favours of their former enemies.

The organisation had carefully studied the proclaimed war aims of the different powers and was prepared to exploit them in so far as they differed from one another. Inherent fear of Russia would not, however, prevent the organisation using the Communists to create tension between Russia and the Western powers by carrying out Soviet propaganda in the Western zones of occupation. Similarly Conservatives, Socialists, Catholics and Protestants would succeed in confusing the ideological and religious issues between the powers, while the fearful living conditions of large sections of the population and particularly the fate of children and old persons would be made use of to kindle the humanitarian sentimentality of the British and Americans.

In this propitious atmosphere of international dissension the work of the organisation would proceed on the long term reconstitution of Germany as the dominating world power. This war had begun as a conflict between militarist nationalism and peace-loving democracy. Force of circumstances had compelled the democracies to combat their enemies by gradually approximating to their methods, not only by hailing the totalitarian U.S.S.R. as a 'democratic' ally, but by themselves indulging in total warfare which transformed their whole military, economic, political and propaganda machine into the expression of a nationalistic totalitarian society. While the Allies proclaimed that they were democratic and fighting for democracy, they had wrongly assumed that they all meant the same thing by democracy. For the Russians it meant the dictatorship of the proletariat, for the Americans it was confused with the identity of one great political party and a vague equation between liberty and licence, while for the British it meant the stability of parliamentary and local government, the rule of law and the sanctity of the throne and the aristocracy in the eyes of the working classes. Aristotle had indeed justly defined democracy as an 'Aristocracy of orators, sometimes interrupted by the monarchy of a single orator'. The development of wireless as a political medium had strongly enforced Aristotle's dictum. The peace-loving, international minded democracies would find themselves at the end of the war transformed imperceptibly into militaristic, nationalistic, totalitarian states. They would find it a painful and perhaps impossible process to return to the free social order they had left at the starting post. Germany, on the other hand, if she enjoyed the inestimable advantage of total defeat, would be able to start afresh.

It was the object of the organisation to educate the German people to an understanding of the strength of democracy as a means to dominate the world, while their enemies had unconsciously succumbed to the political fallacies which had been the bane of German history since the days of the Great Elector and Frederick the Great. Defeated Germany would leave the victorious 'democracies' armed to the teeth with the outmoded weapons of this war, a prey to mutual rivalries and suspicions, burdened with debt and responsibilities towards restive, undernourished, impoverished populations in their own and other countries. Germany would have no responsibilities and could rewrite her history on a clean slate.

The Germans would firstly more than satisfy all claims advanced by the Allies. War criminals would not only be surrendered to the Allies and judged, but the Germans themselves would go further and try thousands of their nationals who had been responsible for their servitude under Nazism. Not only would they pay all reparations demanded, but they would offer more in goods and services to the countries which had suffered from their aggression. This would have the beneficial effect of forcing the Allies to interest themselves in the re-establishment of the German economy on a sound basis. They would agree to the dismembering of Germany and the transfer of populations to any extent, as the future of the German people as an entity was not in any way dependent on artificial ethnological, geographical or economic frontiers that might be imposed on them. They would indulge in the most complete demilitarisation ever known in the history of nations, disarm the police and forbid the use of any firearms by all civilians because such weapons were out of date and the next war would not be won with them.

They would devote their energies and their wealth to the reconstruction of their cities, public services and industries on the most modern lines and in the spirit of convinced pacifism. Education would be remodelled far beyond any plans the Allies might have in store, so that the team of nursery governesses preparing now to pounce on German youth and mould their minds will probably find themselves among the pupils rather than with the teachers. Music, art and letters would be revived to an unprecedented degree, and the jaded intellectuals of the still regimented Allied countries would soon find themselves on pilgrimages to Germany as a haven of peace and progressive thinking. Sociologists and architects from all over the world would soon be coming to Germany to study the solution of housing problems and social security, which in their own countries were still mouldering in dusty blue prints. Germany would lead the way in town and country planning, books by Allied experts would be written about the new Utopia with its modern drainage, pre-natal care, its green belts, garden cities, its 'Health through Joy' movement, much as books were written about Sweden before the war. Zionists, after the Arab pogroms in Palestine, would accept the generous

German offer of Prussia as their national home, while the good German people would expel or enslave all Prussians not already eliminated by the Russians, sterilise them and stigmatise them for the rest of their lives by compelling them to wear a Swastika arm band and the letters S.P. (Saupreusse) embroidered across their shoulders. Germany would become the centre of the ecumenical movement, a new Christian theology would flourish, the Boy Scout movement, the Salvation Army, the R.S.P.C.A., the Oxford Group, and all oppressed minorities would find a welcome refuge in this haven of liberalism. A tourist industry of unforeseen dimensions would bring visitors from all over the world to see this promised land.

Gradually in this new pacifist society learning would be revived, the universities would become famous again throughout the world and attract the best brains from all countries. Within the universities and in specially founded institutes scientific research would be developed. All the resources of the State or States would be devoted to this end in the same proportion as previously to the armed forces. The Kaiser Wilhelm Institut would be renamed the Ossietsky Institut, the Germans would outdo Carnegie and Rockefeller in providing funds for advanced research by foreign scientists whose contributions would swell the volume of German scientific knowledge.

And then one day while the Allies, if not already at war with one another, were still standing by armed to the teeth with tanks, guns, ships, aeroplanes and other weapons of the last war, the pacifist German State or States which by then had won the admiration of the world for solving the problems of a free human society, where such things as state control, force and the death penalty were unknown, this new Germany would make a last irresistible bid for world domination. An ultimatum would be sent, for instance, to the United States, protesting in the name of peace and humanity against the existence of its navy which should within the space of fourteen days proceed in separate units to specified ports and hand itself over for scuttling. Unless this ultimatum were complied with, the peace-loving German people would regret that in the name of peace and humanity it would be necessary for a certain engaging, pink-cheeked, old professor with large spectacles and a long white beard to press certain buttons on an instrument board which would mean the instantaneous destruction of New York, Washington, Chicago and San Francisco. If after this the ultimatum were not complied with, etc., etc. And so the next and the last war would begin.

My informant added ironically that perhaps the safest guarantee against the revival of Germany's struggle for world domination would be not to waste so much time in planning how to make Germany democratic but to force Germany to remain in a state of fossilised Nazism under Allied control for fifty years. *Auribus tenemus lupum.* She could thus be preserved for this period as a fictitious common enemy in the interests of world peace and international collaboration.

He fears that unless we maintain this fictitious state of war against a common enemy after his defeat we shall find it difficult to discover a similar common foundation on which to build the peace. Unity against a common enemy is the surest guarantee of peace. The destruction of Germany as a world menace is the surest prelude to universal anarchy.

## Footnotes

1.  Dr Walter Jacobsen was a psychologist who had been introduced to me by Professor Katz, a German Jewish professor of psychology at Stockholm High School whom I had known before the war. He was born in Hamburg in 1895 and died there in 1986. Before 1933 he was a member of the Deutsche Demokratische Partei and the Deutsche Staatspartei. He was dismissed from his employment in 1933 and in 1934 joined the resistance. He emigrated to Sweden in 1937.

2.  A private letter from Winston Churchill to Halifax dated 26 June 26 1940 from 10 Downing Street (PRO FO - 800/322 ST 290) stated that 'Butler held odd language to the Swedish Minister and certainly the Swedes derived a strong impression of defeatism'. He suggests Halifax should find out from Butler what he said referring to his own statement in the Secret session of the House of Commons that 'present government and all its members were resolved to fight on to the death and I did so, taking personal responsibility for the resolve of all'.

3.  There is in Riksarkivet a letter dated 19 February 1943 from Sir Norman Kendall to Söderman expressing regret at not being able to arrange

another visit for him to London but asking whether he wished to talk about N (Nebe), wondering whether he was as strong-willed as ever and whether there was any change 'in the hierarchy in the South'? The interest in Nebe was obviously still alive in 1943 but only from an intelligence point of view. I can find no record in the UK. It may be possible to discover material in Germany. Söderman's personal archives reveal nothing. There is, however, a mass of secret material concerning Söderman in the Swedish State archives which still has to be examined.

# XIII

# The Invasion of Britain

This is one of many notes I wrote on German invasion plans.

27th October 1940

    I have previously referred to the plan for the invasion by a three-pronged tunnel beneath the Channel and to the Swedish Professor Pallin's elaborate project for a pontoon bridge across the same stretch of water. It is understandable if the German General Staff abandon these projects after our recent bombardments of the occupied coast. Their invasion barges have proved unfit for the task and in particular their method of sawing off bow and stern of two barges and fitting them together seems to have produced a more than usually unseaworthy vessel which breaks its back in the slightest swell, especially when loaded with heavy gun turrets fore and aft and with men and equipment aboard. Their recent experiences at sea, whether on an exercise or, in fact, assembling for attempted invasion, must have proved very distasteful. Reports have reached me of thousands of German wounded being evacuated from this engagement to convalescent camps in Norway and Denmark to recover from severe burns contracted from the oil and phosphorous bombs dropped by our aircraft, which transformed wide stretches of sea into pools of fire.

    Whatever their military projects may be, they are certain to be delayed some time for want of suitable seagoing invasion craft as sea transport will be absolutely necessary for the support of any bridgeheads won by parachute troops, More interesting, perhaps, are their plans for psychological warfare once on British soil. It appears that before the war, secret missions were despatched to the British Isles to study two elements of our defence in depth, which were believed to offer us considerable opportunities for baffling our enemies. These were British humour and sport.

It appears that the quixotic humorist, Heinrich Himmler, whose civil status is described in the Who's Who of the Nazi party as that of a chicken farmer, netted the British Isles with teams of studious humorists before the war. They plotted the permutations and variations of jokes on elaborate graphs from Cockney London to Hull, Glasgow, Inverness, Manchester, Wigan, Swansea, Belfast and Dublin. They compiled an exhaustive bibliography of comic literature in English which has been published as an official document for confidential circulation. They assembled incomparable libraries of the same literature, and by subscriptions in neutral countries to the comic press of the British Isles they are able to supply a team of press readers who continue to classify and record every aspect of British humour. Their attendance at music halls, political meetings, public houses and religious gatherings gave them incomparable experience which has since been recorded in dossiers on the lives and mannerisms of comic artists past and present. Their press reading is assisted by the monitoring of comic transmissions on the B.B.C. I am told that Mr. Vic Oliver and Mr. Thomas Handley have a considerable vogue in these select circles.

The purpose of this research is to disarm the British with what is believed to be their exclusive secret weapon. Training camps are in being for the instruction of Service and civilian personnel in the history and practice of British humour. The persons concerned are divided in special camps according to the areas in which they are to be posted, and everything is done to give these establishments appropriate local colour, Bavarians mainly being selected for Scotland, Prussians for the Midlands and Berliners for the East End of London. They are taught not only to study and report jokes, but to repeat them and even to make original ones for which prizes and scholarships are awarded. Competitions are arranged for understatement, club and mess stories, lavatory humour, practical jokes, proper and prim jokes, kind and unkind jokes, self-deprecating jokes, licentious jokes, witty jokes and boring jokes. It is widely believed that the British Secret Service is not only maintaining the morale of Britain and her Allies and undermining that of her enemies by a studied campaign of humorous frivolity, but that this same body expends large sums on the secret vote in maintaining a Government joke factory and a training school for humorist agents. The German counter-agents will undertake the task of searching out and eliminating these dangerous men and women while their propagandists will maintain a ceaseless flow of humour and wit for the benefit of the general public which will be unconsciously disarmed and become favourably disposed towards their masters.

In the realm of sport similar investigations were made which in one case resulted in a formidable thesis for the University of Kiel entitled 'Ein Grundriss der Philosophie des 'Fair-Play'. The author devotes two-thirds of the closely printed 600 page work to an exhaustive bibliography of sources with scale diagrams of fields, pitches and the armament of sport with balls of all calibres, weights and materials, wooden and metal implements and furniture, and the sartorial requirements with their social implications. He makes many strange deductions from his observations, one of which is that the chastity and continence of Englishmen and women, and their consequent reserves of mental and physical energy, are due to a sublimation of their sexual urges in sport of various kinds. He tends to oversimplify our games into derivations of early Celtic phallic cults to be found in such surviving emblems as bats and balls and billiard cues, stumps, fishing rods and hockey sticks. In the realm of manners and morals he sees in the British sporting spirit a survival of Roman stoicism, mediaeval chivalry, and masochistic protestant conscience.

Training schools have again been established in this subject, and young German men and women are put through intensive courses of our main games and field sports, divided this time into subjects according to age and aptitude. The older ones train at hunting, shooting, fishing and golf in the English and Scottish manner, correctly dressed in tweeds which are manufactured specially for the purpose in mills controlled by the party. Some would appear to have undergone rather sketchy courses, as, for instance, with the invasion of Norway when the Norwegians were amused to find German officers and women making a run on the outfitters and sports shops of Oslo to buy every English article they could find. After this they set forth dressed in the most outrageous checked tweeds and outsize plus fourteens, with yellow brogues or co-respondent shoes, their headgear ranging from deerstalkers and costermongers' caps to bookmakers' beige bowlers, loaded with creels and gaffs and landing nets, to fish with floats and worms with fly rods.

Their thoroughness is, however, not to be underestimated. Not only did the Germans before the war import from Britain specimens of the paraphernalia of British sport, but they have since manufactured these articles for the equipment of their specialists on a large scale. They have been specially interested in the fact that Britain as the home of sport never achieves any great distinction in international sporting events, partly owing to incorrigible amateurishness and a dislike of professionalism, partly, it is believed, owing to a delight in the exquisite pleasure of losing. The Englishman for the German is envied as the good loser who can morally never be beaten. In this light they have made a careful study of cricket, and in particular of village cricket. They are training with great assiduity numerous teams of bad cricketers, in Hitler's Ordensburgen, the stud farms for the breeding of Nordic Nazis which are the Fuhrer's answer to the British public school. The tasks of these cricketers will be to follow in the wake of the shock troops on British soil, to make friends with the local population, produce scratch cricket teams to be beaten, and thereby gain moral ascendancy over their victors. It is not uninteresting that cricket has been selected, as it would indicate that they envisage the invasion taking place during the cricket season. More precisely it looks like a landing on a Thursday, challenging the local village on the Friday and consolidating their bridgehead by losing the match on the Saturday. There is, of course, always the risk that the Germans might win but their study of the philosophy of the good loser is dangerous because if they lose the war they will at least stand a chance of winning the peace against a nation of cricketers. Fortunately, however, not all Englishmen and none of the Allies like cricket or apply the M.C.C. or Queensberry rules in political practice.

# XIV
## Blockade Running

Our Minister, Victor Mallet's, briefing in London left him in no doubt about British intentions to deny Swedish iron ore to the Germans. In spite of this he was successful throughout the vicissitudes of the war in maintaining good relations with the Swedish Government.

His success in relations with the Swedes led him frequently to be accused by London of being in their pocket. His support for unconventional activity under diplomatic cover was not wholehearted. This was perhaps understandable since his first priority was to maintain good relations with the Swedes and that often clashed with the undiplomatic activities of some of his staff. Apart from a few established members of the Service, the overwhelming majority were irregulars fighting their own war in their own corner. One he clashed with was George Binney (1900-1972), although they maintained a friendly relationship with one another throughout the war in spite of recurring disagreements.

George came out in December 1939 representing the British Iron and Steel Control. His objective was placing orders, shipping special steels, machine tools, and ball bearings, which were essential for the war effort. George was 39, the second of four sons of the Vicar of Richmond, educating himself by scholarships to Eton and Merton. He became famous as an Arctic explorer on three Arctic expeditions from Oxford, two of which he led. He recorded his experiences in a book *With Seaplane and Sledge in the Arctic* (1935) and joined the Hudson's Bay Company during which time he wrote

Sir George Binney

*The Eskimo Book of Knowledge* to educate his beloved Eskimos. After this he joined the United Steel Companies for whom, apart from the war, he roamed the world as Export Director. He was a man of discriminating taste and his house at 17 Porchester Terrace - which was managed by his faithful servant, Lucas, who was butler, cook, valet and handyman - was a storehouse of antique silver, china and glass, furniture, carpets, incunabula and a collection of musical boxes I remember very well. Many of these pieces were prizes he gave himself when he pulled off some successful venture. He bought a turquoise egg in Tehran to celebrate a gigantic rail contract before the war with the Persians, and when Sir Andrew Duncan - who later became the Minister of Supply - offered him the job of representing Iron and Steel Control in Scandinavia, he marked the event with the purchase of a fine William and Mary silver tankard.

George had missed World War I by one day, getting his Commission in the Scots Guards on Armistice Day 1918. He dreaded the prospect of a chair-borne war in Whitehall and this posting gave him the freedom and responsibility which suited his initiative. Cyril Alington, his Headmaster at Eton, called him the ingenious and ingenuous Binney, a good description of this stocky, jovial buccaneer, with his keen blue eyes and ruddy complexion. He kept himself fit with squash and skiing. He continued in Stockholm, as in London, not to stint himself on the good things of life, entertaining his friends, after going to the market with his housekeeper, with the most delicious luncheons and dinners.

In London he was briefed by Charles Hambro, Harry Sporborg and Mike Wheeler of Steel Control. In their varying capacities in what was later SOE and the Ministry of Economic Warfare, they backed his dare-devil operations throughout the war against the obfuscation and obduracy of the official machine. He used to tell how his nurse would complain that 'Master George is so obstinate' and it was this obstinacy and determination which helped him win through - 'I spend 75% of my war effort' he wrote, 'stopping other people from stopping me from doing what has to be done'.

He flew from Perth to Kristiansand on 9 December 1939, arriving in Stockholm on 13 December. He moved from the Grand Hotel, which was crawling with enemy agents to the Strand where they were more sparse and he installed himself in the Penthouse suite with a beautiful view of the harbour. I met him here as the result of an introduction from my cousin, Ernest Tennant. They had been at Eton together and were both involved with the steel trade, Ernest, through C Tennant Sons & Company, being major suppliers of ferrosilicon to the British Steel industry from their works at Bjølvefossen in Norway. George appointed Carl Setterwall & Company AB, who were Tennant's agents in Sweden, to represent the British Steelmakers; their Chairman, Adolf Fagerlund, remained a staunch ally throughout the war. He made his number with the Legation, with Jernkontoret, the opposite number to the Iron and Steel Federation and with Axel Axelsson Johnson, with his huge shipping and steel empire. George then decided to reconnoitre the northern iron-ore mines of Sweden. He got himself invited to Luleå and by Mr Waldenström, the Chairman of Grängesberg, to Kiruna on the railway between Luleå and Narvik. He read Rickman's book on Swedish iron ore but having met him earlier at lunch with our Military Attaché, Col. Reggie Sutton-Pratt, he decided very wisely to have nothing to do with him. This was fortunate as Rickman was later arrested by the Swedish police with a warehouse full of explosives and detonators and demolition materials provided by Section D for the destruction of Swedish ore loading facilities.

From Kiruna George took the train to Narvik, the iron-ore port in Norway. Here he met a motley crowd of Norwegians, Germans and English, including four Naval Control officers. These masqueraded as civilians but received their correspondence from the Admiralty openly addressed to them with their Service rank. Through them he got a telegram to return to London immediately. He doubled back to Stockholm where he was sharing an office with the Head of the French Purchasing Commission, Rolf Nordling, who went with him to London via Copenhagen. Nordling was the brother of Raoul who had been personally appointed by the King of Sweden as Swedish Consul General in Paris. He played a part later on in the war in the negotiations for the evacuation of Paris without a battle.

In London he was approached by a shadowy figure from the Secret Service who explained that he had been recalled and must never return to Sweden because he had met, and possibly compromised, Rickman. George was furious and explained that it was the Legation that had introduced him and he himself had decided he would have nothing to do with him. As on many other occasions George ignored the order and continued his discussions with his steel bosses together with Nordling. There was much talk of intervention in the Russo-Finnish war and the seizure of the railway and the Swedish ore fields if the Germans occupied the south of Norway and Sweden. Circumstances fortunately frustrated these plans and preserved us from finding ourselves at war with Russia and at the mercy of the Germans with their much shorter lines of communication.

On 13 March 1940 George took off again for Sweden. The Secret Service relented to the extent of allowing him to go and clear up his affairs for a month. In fact, he remained there for ten. Ironically, George who was regarded as a security risk, likely to compromise the Secret Service protégé Rickman, survived their efforts to undermine his enterprise while Rickman was caught red-handed by the Swedish police. After much delay, George arrived in Malmö via Amsterdam and took the night train to Oslo. There was now no longer any question of Allied intervention in north Norway and Sweden to help the Finns.

The Finns had negotiated an armistice. In Oslo George met up with my cousin Ernest who discovered that his German agent, Eugen Lehnkering and his frumpy wife, were staying in the hotel. Lehnkering prided himself on being the twenty-first member of the Nazi Party. He was waiting in Oslo with other Nazis for the German invasion. They exchanged strained pleasantries and Lehnkering put a watch on George's movements. The atmosphere was full of menace but the naive Norwegian Government refused to pay any attention to Swedish and British warnings of German invasion. A few nights later he was in Stockholm and back on the night train to Oslo only to find himself booked in a double compartment with Rickman. He agreed with him to exchange banalities for the benefit of the Swedish secret police tape machines. George went on a skiing holiday with friends in the mountains and then back in Oslo was once more confronted by Lehnkering, who sarcastically asked him how his business was in Norway. George went on negotiating with his ferro-alloy suppliers and continued in Trondhjem, where, for fun, he bought a third-class ticket to the station of Hell. He went up-country to the works at Meraker and in the middle of his talks got a call from Oslo to say the German Fleet was proceeding up Oslo Fjord and they were to be expected in Trondhjem at any time. He must quickly make for the frontier. He took the train to the Swedish border from where he sent a telegram 'Urgent Lehnkering Grand Hotel Oslo. Should you require new currency for Norway suggest you call it the Altmark. Binney'.

He went to Stockholm and on 10 April reported to the Legation where he met Charles Hambro, who was now stuck in Sweden after completing trade negotiations. Charles took him to see Mitcheson, the Commercial Counsellor, and the new Minister, Victor Mallet with whom he was to work and argue throughout the war. He said of him very fairly

> If . . . . . I sound a little impatient with him I acknowledge freely that as Minister plenipotentiary he had a difficult balancing act to perform in maintaining good relations with the Swedish Government while at the same time doing his utmost to persuade them to interpret Sweden's neutrality to our maximum advantage. The aims which I was pursuing were more pragmatic and demanded a finesse of a different kind.

Kicking his heels for the moment he put up a plan to Victor for organising a refugee camp for British refugees from Norway and Finland. Mallet agreed and George got busy with the Consul, Ken White, and his Vice Consul, Bill Aird. They found a location at Hälsingmo near Järvsö. This camp, curiously enough, played a major part in providing George with manpower for subsequent operations.

George then went to Namsos with Rolf Nordling and his brother, Raoul, the Consul General in Paris, to see whether any supplies from Sweden could be shipped home via this part of Norway. This turned out to be abortive so he returned to Stockholm. On 1 May he dined with Mallet to meet Admiral Evans of the *Broke* who had come over to liaise with the King of Norway. He was finally forbidden to carry out his plan for the recapture of Trondhjem. Then came an urgent directive from Sir Andrew Duncan, now Minister of Supply, 'It is of paramount importance that we receive all the war stores on order in Sweden (ball bearings, machine tools, special steels, Swedish iron, etc., etc.). You must repeat must at all costs get them to England'. George immediately started to explore the possibilities of the Artic highway from Rovaniemi to Petsamo. He went with a M. Bonnet of the French Purchasing Mission and a Finnish speaker to Helsinki to negotiate with General Talvela. The prospect seemed good but on his return to Stockholm on 9 June he heard the news of our withdrawal from Norway the day before.

The next day he got out a chart of the Skagerrak and studied it with Adolf Fagerlund at Carl Setterwalls. The Skagerrak was the only outlet to the North Sea. The north side, or the so-called Norwegian Channel, was very deep, 2,400 to 4,200 feet, and, in fact, impossible to mine although both belligerents had declared that they had mined the area. He saw Mallet about breaking the blockade, but he and his Service attachés were against it. He then called on William Kjellberg and his assistant, Alva Henriksen of the Ellerman Wilson line in Gothenburg. They discussed the British and German minefields and decided that they might well be a diplomatic *ruse de guerre*. There was obviously a risk from surface vessels and aircraft but it was worth taking. After discussion with the Consul General, Freddie Coultas, and his assistant, Peter Coleridge, the latter was sent to find out what Norwegian ships and crews were laid up in Gothenburg.

In the end they decided to test the route by chartering a small Finnish ship. Then, following our withdrawal from Norway, came the ghastly news of the fall of France. This was a moment which tested the friendship and courage of those in Sweden who supported us. Among the faint-hearted, however, was Marcus Wallenberg of Enskilda Banken, who proposed to Mallet that the British should pay for Swedish orders as soon as they were completed, not when the goods were loaded on the ships. This proposal was accepted by Whitehall but Binney reacted violently against it and had what he says was the only hostile interview of the war with Wallenberg himself. He started by hectoring and telling him that Britain was finished and her credit was rotten. Binney told him exactly what he thought of him and that, as a free man and not a diplomat, he would personally sign an agreement with Jernkontoret between them and the British Steel industry, to the effect that goods would be paid for when delivered over the side in Gothenburg. George telegraphed back to London and Whitehall immediately agreed with his proposal. This resulted in the signing of an agreement in the Swedish Foreign Office between George and Wiking Johnson, the Chairman of Jernkontoret. The Legation agreed to give him all co-operation and provide means of communication but insisted on vetting his telegrams. While he had access to theirs, he was debarred from having any to the Minister's communications with London on the subject.

George had one of his many turbulent discussions with Mallet on 21 June. The interview culminated in remarks by Mallet to the effect 'You don't seem to realise Mr Binney that the war may be over in four or five weeks, at least that is what is being said by some of my friends at the Foreign Office'. George countered with an indignant outburst and said that even if England were overrun, hostilities would never cease. Mallet was obviously somewhat abashed at Binney's counterblast and said 'Well, that's what I am told unofficially'. Mallet, alas, was well informed as he had knowledge of a telegram sent by the Swedish Minister in London, Björn Prytz, recounting an interview with R.A. Butler, which he interpreted as an indication that Britain was ready to come to terms with the Nazis. George's reaction was to become even more determined to get his supplies through the German blockade of the Skagerrak. Churchill's defiant tone put all doubts at rest and George set to with zest to win a battle with all the odds against him.

If the enterprise was to run efficiently, George must have an assistant to help him with the logistics and the legal and accountancy problems. The Legation produced a string of unsuitable candidates and then, by chance, I introduced George to my old friend, Bill Waring, who with his wife Anne and little boy Patrick, had managed to escape to Sweden from Norway where, from the outbreak of war, he had been attached to the British Consulate in Oslo. Bill and his wife had been taken on in the cipher department at the Legation but when George asked him if he would like to join him, he immediately applied for his release. This, however, took them till August. Bill Waring (1906-1962) whose father was in the Indian Police, was a chartered accountant with Whinney, Murray & Co. in Berlin and Hamburg. I had met him in Oslo in the early 30's when I was doing post-graduate research and Bill was at work on the liquidation of Kreuger interests after Ivar Kreuger's suicide and the collapse of his match empire. We met regularly at weekends, skiing together in the evenings in the dark with torches on our heads. That autumn they came to share a house with us, Bergshyddan in Djurgården outside Stockholm, but not far from the Legation. Bill, who was left-handed and suffered from a stutter, expressed himself happily on paper and was fluent in German and Norwegian. He wrote verse and fairy stories which we intended to bring out together with my illustrations.

We were deflected from this excellent enterprise by other events but kept in touch.

Bill was caught in Norway on 9 April. Anne got away first to Sweden with Patrick. Bill was summoned to the Legation in the night to burn documents and in the morning took off on his own towards Trondhjem, first on foot and then on a bicycle he bought off a workman in a bicycle factory. That evening he got to Hamar and the next day to Elverum, which was destroyed by the Luftwaffe. He finally crossed the Swedish frontier and made his way to Stockholm from where he was sent to reconnoitre a trade route through Finland via the Artic highway to Petsamo. This was the only remaining outlet to America and the West, the Germans having blockaded the outlets through the Kattegat and the Skagerrak to the North Sea and Atlantic. He crossed into Norway but had to return when we evacuated Narvik. He doubled back into Finland, was arrested and had a pleasant fortnight as the guest of the local Finnish General in a hotel on Lake Inari. His guard was a charming Finnish officer who, however, had the awkward habit of drinking a mixture of brandy and Swedish punch all night. When he had drunk the last bottle he insisted on shooting the rapids down the river in a rickety boat into Lake Inari. After this enforced holiday Bill returned to Sweden. Now early in July 1940, he wondered how he could get back to England. The only routes then open were through Russia, either by the Trans-Siberian Railway to Vladivostok, Japan and the USA, or southwards across the Caspian and round the Cape of Good Hope.

It was now that he met George Binney. The two men were perfectly matched, each complementing the other. Bill was dark haired with a black moustache, dark eyes behind heavy hornrimmed spectacles, thickset, a good rugger player going back to his days at Christ's Hospital, a lover of open air life, a good shot, keen fisherman, yachtsman, a voracious reader and writer, blessed with the same sort of sense of humour as George. George with his laughing blue eyes, ruddy complexion, grey hair and stocky physique which he had hardened with Arctic exploration and intensive games of squash, was less of a games player than Bill but far more travelled and experienced. As son of a Vicar he retained a simple Christian faith throughout his life, while Bill was more of a sceptic, much more numerate and a tough manager. George was, however, an instinctive leader and adventurer with a profound understanding of human nature. He was a taker of calculated risks, Bill was much more cautious. They both made friends easily and George kept his friendships in constant repair whether they were from his schooldays or Oxford, post managers in the Canadian Arctic, trappers, ordinary or extraordinary seamen, Norwegian sealers, Eskimos, dons, domestics, businessmen, Civil Servants or Ministers of the Crown. George, like Bill, had a love of the English language and he was meticulous in its use. In later life he was so careful that he, regrettably, never achieved the book he should have written on his wartime exploits, distilled from the voluminous notes he left for other writers. When Bill and I in the 50's started to write a filmscript of his exploits, George begged us to desist as he was on the point of completing his own book. Alas, this never came about. Later in life he found writing a burden, but in the war he was at his peak and his telegrams and letters and messages to his crews were a model of lucidity which often took long to compose.

George and Bill began working together in the summer of 1940 when our fortunes were at their lowest, with Germany occupying the whole European coastline from the North Cape to the Spanish frontier. But George found nothing so stimulating as frustration and was determined to ship his precious cargoes to embattled Britain. Some shipments were tried through Petsamo but this was soon stopped. A small amount of material was sent by rail through Russia but it was a slow and exhausting business. One fairly large shipment of ball bearings arrived in England intact after more than a year crossing Russia, the Caspian, Iran, the Persian Gulf, India and round the Cape to Britain.

There were a number of Norwegian ships in Swedish ports immobilised by the German blockade. Also there were the masters and men of four British iron-ore ships captured by the Germans in Narvik and then released and evacuated to Sweden when we recaptured the town. A pilot exercise was carried out in July with a small Finnish merchantman, the *Lahti*, loaded with 500 tons of war material. Her Master was a rogue and we knew it, and probably in the pay of the Germans. She was intercepted by a German air patrol after negotiating the whole Skagerrak. This proved to our satisfaction that the deep channel was too deep for mines. If one were to follow this course with fast ships in bad weather and on long nights, the chances of escape were not as bad as supposed.

The difficulties faced were formidable. The jittery nerves of the Norwegian authorities, initial lack of confidence in the prospect of success in our own Legation in Stockholm, lack of fuel and shortage of crews for ships, non-co-operation by many of the big Swedes and the tapping of telephones by the Swedish secret police. There were the swarms of German agents, cops and robbers scenes of Swedish secret police and German Abwehr men following in Stockholm and Gothenburg, watching our flats and offices and, above all, trying to get access to the ships. George decided not to bother about the lack of security in Gothenburg as he never intended to make a dash for it from the harbour but to go up the coast and lie up until a propitious moment arrived. There he would be well away from German observation if he could get the co-operation of the Swedish harbour police. This he did. None of the Norwegian captains of ships in Gothenburg nor the British captains from Narvik were prepared to sail and the vessels in all cases were captained by mates. All the ships had diesel engines and all our engineers were trained on steam, so we had great difficulty in finding engineers, many of whom were Swedes. The Swedish members of the crew were under German pressure and some were imprisoned by their own authorities for passing information to the Abwehr. However, George had considerable experience in handling crews of different nationalities from his time in the Canadian Arctic and his chartering of Norwegian sealers for his expeditions.

This was the beginning of the operation code named 'Rubble', one of the most daring and successful enterprises of World War II, to be succeeded by 'Performance', 'Bridford' and 'Moonshine', under the aegis first of MEW and then of SOE. The ships were unloaded of their old cargoes and reloaded with the new ones in November and December 1940. All Norwegian ships in Swedish waters had been requisitioned by the Norwegian Government and the Swedes resisted all German attempts to transfer them to their ownership.

After overcoming the hesitations of the Foreign Office, the Admiralty and our Legation, George was given the official diplomatic status of Assistant to the Commercial Counsellor and Bill Waring was co-opted with similar diplomatic cover. With the help of Adolf Fagerlund of Setterwalls in Stockholm, and William Kjellberg and his assistant, Alva Henricksson of Ellerman Wilson in Gothenburg, preparations went ahead. Anne Waring, Sally Ladell and others in Gothenburg and Stockholm were the back-up team together with the charming and efficient girls in our Legation known as the cypherenes. The Consulate General in Gothenburg gave whole-hearted backing to the operation, first under Freddie Coultas as Consul General and then under his successor Graham Sebastian, with Peter Coleridge, his assistant, playing an indispensable part. Sebastian was stone deaf to all but good music and wit, but had an alarming facility for hearing what he should not in between bouts of his absorbing hobby of *petit point*. He was an excellent cook and a generous host and looked after his team with loving care.

The fleet of ships for Rubble consisted of five Norwegian freighters chartered from the Norwegian Government's Shipping Board, by the Ministry of Shipping. The five ships were all diesel engined, the *Elizabeth Bakke* 5,450 tons doing 17 to 18 knots, *John Bakke* 4,718 tons 13 knots, *Tai Shan* 6,962 tons with 14 to 15 knots, *Taurus* 4,767 tons 14 to 15 knots and *Dicto* 5,263 tons and 14 to 15 knots. While their departure from Gothenburg could not be concealed from the Germans, they could move up the coast and hide in a fjord till they slipped out unobserved. Brofjord, near Lysekil, was selected. The recruitment of crews was a problem but Binney's determination to accompany them on this dangerous enterprise was largely responsible for getting some of the refugees from the ore ships in Narvik in the camp at Hälsingmo, together with Norwegians, to volunteer. One Norwegian second engineer was unhappy in his job because his Belgian wife could not bear to be parted from him, so George recruited her as chief engineer to supervise her husband - to the delight of both of them. *Dicto* had to leave the party due to litigation by her Norwegian owner and was replaced by the 12,000 ton tanker *Ranja*. George as Commodore of the fleet was to hoist a recognition flag for the Royal Navy force sent to meet him in the North Sea. It was a white flag 6' by 4' with the blue letters GB in the centre which our Naval Attaché, Captain Henry Denham, suggested to the Admiralty 'indicates not only the destination of the convoy but also the initials of the Commodore'. This flag was the altar cloth at George's memorial service at St. Martin's in the Fields on 2 November 1972.

The ships had all been fitted with scuttling valves invented by Mr Townsend, the Lloyds surveyor. They assembled at the end of

December 1940 in Brofjord. George always drove himself very hard and demanded the same from others but he was also able to relax. During these weeks of waiting in Brofjord, he would play patience or backgammon in his cabin, or enjoy camouflage painting his ship in the sub-zero temperatures. 'I always enjoy this kind of work' he wrote, 'manual and semi-automatic like weeding and hoeing it relieves your thoughts from the immediate tasks ahead.' They waited these three anxious weeks in intense cold and thickening ice for suitable weather and then at 11.30 on the morning of 23 January 1941, he decided to go to sea as a result of a message from Bill Waring brought to him by Ivar Blücker. This indicated Henry Denham's fears that the Admiralty was getting impatient about immobilising the warships detailed to make the escort rendezvous in the North Sea (58.45N 03.30E). 'There was slight snow falling' he recorded, 'at least we had this much encouragement to believe that things were on our side.' He shaved, put on a clean shirt and hard collar and his best blue suit. 'So that no one should accuse me of mourning my own personal fate in advance, I scrubbed my nails until they positively glistened.' These were his recollections as he pondered the reasons for the success of his operation. Careful planning, luck or destiny, the combination of invisibility at the start in the light snowfall with the mysterious breakdown of telecommunications along the Swedish coast arranged by Ivar Blücker so as to paralyse the Nazi intelligence network. This combined with the surprise emergence of the *Scharnhorst* and *Gneisenau* which must have been the main preoccupation of the German defence forces that night.

The first ship to sail was the 12,000 ton *Ranja*, the slowest of the convoy and carrying only salt water ballast. Then *John Bakke*, with its lady chief engineer, *Taurus* and *Elizabeth Bakke*, and lastly the flagship *Tai Shan* with Binney accompanied by Ivar Blucker, who left at 17.45 hours with the pilot.

The weather lifted in the night and with clear skies at dawn they were well within sight of the Norwegian coast. Eventually at 12.10 *Tai Shan* sighted the escorting warships and just as the recognition signal was run up to the masthead, a Blohm and Voss 138 reconnaissance 'plane appeared and *Naiad* opened fire. Binney recorded his emotion at seeing his GB signal at the masthead, 'such a moment would never come again in my life and I was deeply moved by it, but not, I hope, visibly'. The escort accompanied them to Kirkwall from where they sailed to Glasgow to unload. There was nearly a disaster when one of the vessels ran aground in a particularly dangerous place, but she was refloated.

The result of the operation was five vessels adding 43,000 tons to the Allied merchant fleets and 25,000 tons of war material to a value of over £1 million. No ships were lost but the Swedish first officer of the tanker, *Ranja*, Nils Rydberg, was shot through the stomach by a German 'plane and died three days later in Kirkwall. Apart from this sad incident, all the crews came through safe and sound, 147 men and 1 woman, the Belgian wife of the second engineer. They consisted of 58 Englishmen, 57 Norwegians, 31 Swedes and 1 Latvian. Willy Siberg, the Managing Director of SKF at Luton, could hardly believe his eyes when the railway trucks rolled in with the material they needed so desperately. The cargoes represented something like a year's import of steel products from Sweden under the war trade agreement.

When George spent his first night ashore in Kirkwall, he recalled how 'I switched off the lights and lay in the flickering firelight deeply beholden to my Maker'. His puckish sense of humour, courage and pig-headed determination, meticulous planning and integrity, lifted him over obstacles which would have defeated more mundane and less imaginative personalities.

George was rewarded with a Knighthood, the Masters of the ships with OBE's and awards for members of each crew. Rydberg was presented with a posthumous MBE and a pension for his widow. George was anxious to recognise Ivar Blücker, who had played such a key role in the success of the operation but could not be mentioned officially as his action was not strictly regular. When King George heard the story, he asked George Binney if Blücker would accept a pair of cufflinks with the Royal cypher. He took off the ones he was wearing hoping he would not mind a second-hand pair.

Binney was offered a cushy job with the British Supply Mission in Washington. He refused and insisted on returning to Sweden to repeat the operation before the nights shortened after the New Year of 1942. Hitler had had a fit of carpet biting over the whole Rubble affair. The Swedes were put under intense pressure not to allow a repetition and more units of the German navy were immobilised by being put on the alert to prevent it.

Recovering from an attack of jaundice, Binney flew back to Stockholm in April 1941 and preparations were made for a second expedition. Instructions were received to place orders for about 20,000 tons of material of vital necessity to the war effort. There were many who argued against tempting fate in this way, whether Foreign Office or Swedes. Finally it was agreed that if, as Binney believed, there was a 50/50 chance of getting through, the risk was one which had to be taken. Very small quantities of supplies were beginning to go by air and there was strict rationing of freight but we overruled the restrictions when sending home the ashes of one of our ships Master's to his widow. Months later a futile enquiry was set afoot in the Legation because the widow wrote to Victor Mallett thanking him for the welcome side of smoked salmon. We never discovered who got the ashes.

Bill and George continued to operate from their little office at the kitchen entrance of the Minister's residence. They were offered more prestigious accommodation in the Legation itself but refused as they had got used to their little cubbyhole. The new operation, codenamed 'Performance', was conducted partly by SOE and this resulted occasionally in unexpected visitors. One evening some Norwegians delivered a large parcel which they asked George to keep overnight. The little office was used to the delivery of parcels, but this one seemed too light for steel and it was discovered to be a corpse. Fortunately it was fetched in the very early morning and Victor and Peggy remained unaware of how their hospitality had been abused.

In June, Bill flew to England to sort out problems over some of the material that had been delivered and to prepare details for new orders. He started some leave but was suddenly told to return to Sweden. He and George plunged into preparations to fit out, man and load, ten large Norwegian vessels with a total (gross) tonnage of 65,000 tons. The fleet comprised the tankers *BP Newton* 10,324 tons, *Rigmor*, *Buccaneer* and *Storsten*, about 5,000 tons each, and the little *Lind* of 461 tons. Then there were two merchant ships of about 5,000 tons each, *Dicto*, *Lionel*, 2 coal burners of less than 1,000 tons, and a 12,000 ton pelagian whaler, *Skytteren*. Orders were placed for materials which could not at that time be obtained in the USA and special arrangements were made to accommodate orders for the Russians and Dominion Governments. By comparison with 'Rubble', there was no lack of volunteers for crews, mostly Norwegian. Some of the British who had not volunteered before were anxious to join. Another source was the British volunteers from the Finnish war. Some 500 had arrived before the Armistice on 13 March and for the time being they remained in Finland. When the Finns had become co-belligerents with the Germans against Russia in June 1941, most had been evacuated to Sweden. A few joined the Legation in Stockholm while others volunteered as crews for George Binney's ships. He needed good reliable men with experience of discipline and with arms training to help protect the ships with whatever armament it was possible to smuggle on board.

One of these volunteers was Brian Reynolds. He had made several unsuccessful attempts to escape home via Petsamo and ended up in a Finnish jail. He was finally extradited to Sweden where he immediately became popular with the Legation, undertook odd jobs and broke the hearts of many of the girls. They called him 'The Lion' because of his red hair and beard and took it in turn to curl his moustache with an old fashioned moustache curler. He had a background of horses and racing at J.V. Rank's stables and was a daring and enterprising adventurer. George and Bill recruited him to join them in the 'Performance' operation. While Bill could not be spared from his responsibilities ashore in running the business administration, Brian was made George's second in command afloat. He had special responsibility for the secret work of getting scuttling charges and Lewis guns on board the ships, and selecting and training the crews in their use. The operation of moving these armaments into and across Sweden was carried out without the knowledge of Victor Mallett and the career diplomats, but with the conscious and unconscious help of many volunteers. One unconscious helper was Malcolm Sargent, on a visit to conduct orchestras in Stockholm and Gothenburg, who willingly took a couple of extra suitcases with his luggage on the night train from Stockholm to Gothenburg and delivered them to the Consulate General. He had no knowledge of their contents but would undoubtedly have been delighted if he had done so.

Meanwhile, the Germans exerted every possible pressure on the Swedes to prevent these ships from leaving. They threatened to stop the safe conduct traffic if a single Anglo-Norwegian blockade runner slipped through. The Germans also indulged in legal harrassment to prevent the ships from sailing. They began by jailing

Brian Reynolds (alias Bingham) in command of his flotilla of motor cruisers

the original Norwegian owners, demanding from them powers of attorney to dispose of the vessels in October 1941. On the strength of these documents they requested the arrest of the ships in Gothenburg harbour. They instituted proceedings in the Swedish courts against the British Government for damages and against the Captains to eject them from their ships. This had been foreseen by us and the ships had been made the subject of a 'demise charter' given by the Norwegian Shipping and Trade Mission to the Ministry of War Transport. We claimed immunity for them, contending that the courts had no jurisdiction. This resulted in a legal wrangle lasting many months in which many international lawyers were involved. We won the case in the lower court in Gothenburg but the Swedish Navy put every obstacle in our way to frustrate the clearance of the ships. Then, within twenty four hours, the Swedish Government rushed special legislation through Parliament to the effect that in the event of the ownership of an object being in dispute, it could not be removed from Sweden until the matter had been through all the courts. The ships were re-arrested and blocked in the river by Swedish naval vessels.

More delay followed and in the middle of December we lost our case in the Appeal Court and did not finally receive the favourable verdict of the Supreme Court until 17 March 1942. Everything was done by our opponents to delay matters until it was too late for the ships to sail. The nights were, in the meantime, getting light and the weather less favourable for a successful attempt.

Our cargoes had already been loaded. Suddenly, in December, our new Russian allies accepted our invitation to carry 5,500 tons of cargo for them. Trucks from all over Sweden converged on Gothenburg with Russian orders. Then they asked about insurance but were told that this was an uninsurable risk. The Russian Commercial Counsellor, Nikitin, and Alexandra Kollontay's engineer son, arrived in Gothenburg to say they had no authority to load without insurance and it must all be off-loaded. They agreed to pay the cost and off-loading was carried out. Then, with a congestion of Russian material piling up in the docks, they changed their minds and re-loaded without insurance.

By now the ships were fully manned with some 430 Norwegians, British, a few Dutch and Poles. Security of the operation was very flimsy as the Norwegians were infiltrated with some traitors. They talked freely in public places so the real plans were kept completely secret between George, Bill and Peter Coleridge. They were spied on all the time. One evening when the fireplace started smoking they found a microphone in the chimney, as had happened in the Naval Attaché's flat in Stockholm. Before destroying it they recorded their distress at the instructions they pretended to have received for calling off the whole operation.

The winter was one of the coldest on record and the long wait was very frustrating for the crews. Although the ships were now technically free the weather was abominable - 40 degrees of frost and clear. Our Naval officer who made up our weather maps from Admiralty cypher reports gave little hope of suitable warmer, foggy weather to compensate for the longer days and shortening nights.

The Swedish authorities refused to allow us to move the ships up the coast and hide them in a fjord from which they could escape undetected. We were forced to leave Gothenburg in full view of the Germans. On 30 March the weather seemed to be shaping favourably. The captains were briefed and given secret sailing instructions. The Royal Navy was unable to promise the close support we had before due to new minefields and a much reinforced sea and air blockade. At 4 p.m. a final meeting was held on board the flagship *Dicto*. There was a promise of fog and heavy weather so it was decided to leave that evening and follow the Swedish coast till the fog came down. Each Master had to use his own initiative on leaving the coast and no one was to allow his ship to be captured. Before leaving, everyone received a copy of the order of the day signed by George and addressed to Masters, Officers, crews and other volunteers aboard *Buccaneer, Charente, Dicto, Gudvang, Lind, Lionel, BP Newton, Rigmor, Skytteren* and *Storsten*. It read as follows:

> To-day at long last we are going to England determined come what may to render a staunch account of our voyage as befits Norwegian and British seamen. Indeed we run a risk, but what of it. If we succeed these splendid ships will serve the Allied cause and with their cargoes we shall aid the task of war supplies. To sink our ships and cargoes rather than see them captured by the enemy is, of course, our duty and on your behalf I have taken such measures as

you would wish. Should we encounter misfortune at sea remember that in our homes and among our countrymen it will be said with simple truth that we have done our best for the honour and freedom of Norway and Britain. But I for one have never held with this blockade and look once more to our success, believing that before two days have passed your laughter will resound within a British port. So let us merchant seamen, 400 strong, shape a westerly course in good heart counting it an excellent privilege that we have been chosen by providence to man these ships in the immortal cause of freedom. God speed our ships upon this venture. Long live King George, long live King Haakon. MS *Dicto*, Gothenburg, George Binney.

Many Norwegians were wanted by the Gestapo. None had any illusions about the fate that awaited them if they fell into German hands. The ships all carried the identification mark LN for the air escort standing by - 'Leve Norge'. The first ship slipped down the river at 8 p.m. The bank of fog and cloud could be seen approaching. The pack ice lay thick almost to the edge of territorial waters and the ships were unable to sneak up the coast unobserved. In addition they were marked by Swedish escort vessels with full lights on.

The weather then disintegrated, meeting the cold air over the Swedish coast and cover became minimal. The captains took their own decisions to head for the North Sea. George on board *Dicto* broke wireless silence at 6 a.m. on 1 April with the message 'Weather now unfavourable and likely to remain so for some days'. The message was never received by the other vessels, possibly due to sabotage of the transmitter by German agents, or to faulty assembly in the dark by the ships own two operators. *Dicto* with George on board and *Lionel* turned to port. The tanker *BP Newton*, the largest, and *Lind*, the smallest in the convoy, arrived safely. The remaining six scuttled themselves and the crews were captured except for those of the *Rigmor*, a tanker of 6,305 tons, which got close to the British coast, was disabled by German aircraft and finally sunk by our own gunfire. The crew was saved and taken to the UK.

S.H. Gibson, describing himself as ex AB RNVR, wrote to the

*Daily Telegraph* on 12 October 1976 referring to a review of Ralph Barker's book *Blockade Busters*. He told how, as a crew member of the destroyer HMS *Wallace*, one of an escort of six - a veteran of 1918 - they raised steam at Rosyth, rolled and pitched on an easterly course until they met ships from the home fleet coming south from Scapa Flow. At about 6.30 a.m. on Thursday 2 April 1942, they were passed by a merchantman and then found another, the *Rigmor*, hardly making way as she had been disabled by German aircraft. The destroyer escort stood by but soon came under attack and were left with no alternative but to take off the crew and sink the disabled ship. The gunnery control officer on *Wallace* was HRH The Prince Philip of Greece and Denmark, who made pertinent remarks about the rate at which we were using up ammunition trying to shoot down aircraft from a heaving ship.

The Swedish Navy played an inglorious part in these operations forcing the British ships out on to the guns of the German armed trawlers, making it impossible for them to take refuge again in territorial waters. Two of the warships were the *Puke* and *Psilander*, the former Italian destroyers still smarting from the humiliation of the Faroe Islands incident. The German Naval Attaché, von Wahlert, noted in his diary in connection with preparations for a conference between the German High Command and the Swedish Chief of Staff,

> The Swedish Navy felt most distressed because it was possible that the German Navy might feel that the Swedish Navy had failed to uphold Swedish neutrality through the whole affair. This would be even more disappointing for the Swedish Navy since it had been felt that the Navy's behaviour throughout had favoured the interest of Germany predominantly.

Except for a handful who got to Norway by lifeboat and were flown to England to join the Norwegian forces, all the crews of the six ships which were scuttled were captured by the Germans except for three who were killed. Finally in 1943 about one hundred and fifty were sentenced to Nacht und Nebel detention in the notorious Sonnenburg concentration camp, where forty three died before the end of the war. The survivors have all borne the marks of the unspeakable cruelty of this camp for the rest of their lives, both physically and mentally. 'Performance' was an unmitigated disaster from a human point of view.

Two vessels reached the UK, one a very fine large one. A great deal of material arrived in our factories. 27% of the total sterling value of the cargoes, excluding material for the Russians which we did not know the value of, reached England; 25.5% was lost by enemy action; 47.5% returned to Gothenburg for later shipment. Total value of the tonnage loaded, excluding Russian material, was £1,280,000.

This, however, was not the end of the affair. On 7 April 1942 a Reuter telegram quoted a Norwegian member of one of the crews, on his return to England, stating that the German planes had been kept at bay with Lewis guns. This did not square with British assurances that the ships were unarmed in conformity with Swedish neutrality. On 10 April the Swedes received a lengthy protest from the Germans accusing them of a breach in their neutrality by allowing the British ships to leave Swedish waters exporting arms to a belligerent, permitting them to be armed. They also had taken offensive action against German naval units. These were exercising their international right to intercept these ships. A few days later the German Legation submitted a new memorandum to the Swedish Ministry of Foreign Affairs. The interrogation of captured crews had established that all the ships had been armed and weapons and scuttling charges placed on board by Sir George Binney. Boheman asked to see Mallet and Binney for an explanation. Mallet was placed in an embarrassing situation as he had in all innocence assured Boheman that the ships were unarmed. George made a clean breast of his actions which he justified as being his duty to protect his crews in so dangerous an enterprise. Mallet noted, 'I must say I admired the honesty with which Binney admitted what he had done but I felt uncomfortable at having unwittingly had to make an earlier statement to Boheman which I had indeed made in all innocence'.

Boheman admired Binney for the frankness with which he explained the whole business and confessed that in Binney's position he would have acted in the same way. Official protests were lodged with the Foreign Office, Binney was recalled as *persona non grata* and flew home on 18 April. The Swedes rejected the German note but informed them that *Dicto* and *Lionel* would not be allowed to leave again. Brian Reynolds was welcomed back to Sweden and the Swedes demanded the recall of Bill Waring and Peter Coleridge. But the

Foreign Office stood firm and Bill stayed to process further operations while Peter Coleridge ultimately went home.

That was not the end of the operation. *Dicto* and *Lionel* became an obsession for Erik Boheman, waking and sleeping. He was to say to his wife that if they ever had twins they would have to be christened *Dicto* and *Lionel*.

The two ships turned themselves into another operation, codenamed 'Cabaret' and under the direction of Bill Waring. The Swedish Foreign Minister having promised the German Minister personally that they would never be allowed to leave, had to eat his words. He found that with the entry of the Americans into the war a much tougher attitude was adopted by the Allies towards Sweden. Boheman went over to the USA via the UK in the autumn with Nils Ståhle to negotiate with the Americans on the safe conduct traffic. In spite of a personal introduction to Roosevelt by Winston, who thought highly of Boheman who had met him in No. 10 and spent the weekend at Chequers, Roosevelt gave him short shrift. He was preoccupied with the landings in Africa which had taken place the previous day. He subjected him to the Chinese torture of American bureaucracy with a high level committee of seven politicians and officials including Dean Acheson, Dexter White - later found to be a Russian agent - McCloy, Patterson, Jim Forrestal and Bill Donovan of OSS, as well as Sumner Welles. All but Dexter White agreed to allow the imports requested by Sweden. Finally with the help of Harry Hopkins who was in bed in the White House with influenza, the President gave his approval to the majority recommendation but with certain conditions. One was that *Dicto* and *Lionel* should be allowed to leave Gothenburg harbour. The Swedes managed to get two tankers through the blockade before the Germans stopped the safe conduct traffic as a reprisal for this breach of faith.

*Dicto* and *Lionel* were forced into a corner of Gothenburg harbour by a ship of 20,000 tons placed alongside with chains across the bow to prevent escape. The post-Alamein and post-Stalingrad period, however, had begun and the Swedes trimmed their sails to the changed fortunes of war. After endless pressure the ships were released on 11 January 1943 and proceeded down the river to the sea on 17 January. They anchored out of sight of land, still in Swedish waters, waiting for Admiralty orders. They were to be met by fast motor gunboats with George Binney on one of them to transfer guns,

*Dicto* steaming down Göta Älv

ammunition and gun crews to the two vessels to protect them on the crossing. The project was again frustrated by the Swedes who ordered them back to port where they waited till 2 February. Then they were allowed to leave in full view of German agents, unable to conceal themselves up the coast. After a day and a half messages came to the effect that the MGBs had had to return owing to a gale in the North Sea. After further waiting the operation was called off but the exercise had had good nuisance value. It had tied up no less than thirty-four German naval vessels and aircraft waiting to prevent their escape and forced the Swedish Government to see on which side their bread was buttered.

Bill Waring was still under threat of expulsion but this was lifted so that in May he could fly home to plan new operations with George Binney. The air lift was expanding but it could not cope with the volume and weight of materials required. Beginning with slow Hudson's and Whitley's, graduating to Lockheed Lodestars, Dakotas, Liberators and Mosquitoes, the latter did the journey in between two and three hours, as opposed to the six, eight or twelve for the larger planes. The tonnage carried by air from November 1943 to March 1944 spanning the next operation codenamed 'Bridford', was 88 tons to a value of some £1.5m. The pilots did a heroic job in very difficult circumstances. As a passenger one was parcelled up in a flying suit and parachute pack with an oxygen mask, Mae West, whistle and red light to attract the attention of passing rescuers if one landed in the drink. It was very cold and even more so when once the door of a Whitley started to flap open and we were covered with frost. The Mosquitoes were the most comfortable. One wedged ones feet against the bulkhead in the bomb bay and the bomb doors closed beneath one. It was cosy enough and insulated from cold and noise by the laminated wooden fuselage. One communicated by intercom with the pilot, particularly to close bomb doors which tended sometimes to open in the slipstream and pulled at ones rugs and boots.

One needed the patience of an ox and the waiting for wind, cloud, moon and forecast of aircraft movements resulted in long delays.

I once spent three weeks at St. Andrews, going out to Leuchars airport every evening, dressing up, briefing, then sometimes embarking, sometimes not, sometimes taking off, sometimes returning. It was a tedious business and if it was trying for the passengers it was far worse for the crews. From 1941 when the air service began, there were 1,200 flights, 490 of which took place in 1944.

Bill got down to planning with George what became known as Operation 'Bridford'. *Dicto* and *Lionel* were used as base ships in Brofjord off Lysekil and a fleet of five 149 ton motor gunboats was converted for carrying cargo. Originally built for the Turkish Navy, they were transformed into fast freighters capable of lifting some fifty tons. Powered by three diesels they proved to be somewhat unreliable. As an SOE operation with Charles Hambro in the background, it was an advantage that as a director of the Bank of England he was able to purloin spares from the diesels which powered the air conditioning system of the Old Lady of Threadneedle Street. Ellerman Wilson of Hull were the obvious choice to act as agents as the ships were to fly the red duster. They helped in recruiting local crews. George took pains to find appropriate names for the little Grey ladies. *Nonsuch,* the first ship to sail for his old Hudson's Bay Company, *Hopewell, Gay Viking* and *Gay Corsair* with finally *Master Standfast,* all of them representing traditions, aspirations, light-heartedness and Bunyan's firmness of purpose.

Brian Reynolds had fought his way over in 'Performance', was *persona non grata* in Sweden and left his Commando unit to join George. He grew a beard and changed his name to Bingham. He nearly got into trouble, being reported by security officers for using an assumed name, wearing a Naval uniform to which he was not entitled and decorations which he had not earned. These he had won as a captain in the Commandos. George was appointed Commodore of the flotilla and Brian his vice-commodore, with Bill as deputy head of the operation for the Gothenburg end.

The Swedes turned a blind eye to George and Brian in their Naval reincarnations and they both went ashore without trouble. Once I dined with George in his full regalia as a guest of Professor Torgny Segerstedt in Gothenburg. There were more non-Naval chief officers such as Lord Fitzwilliam, a Guards officer who had served with Brian in the Commandos. He kept the ship supplied with game from his estate and travelled to Sweden as Peter Lawrence. The ships were completed by the end of August 1943 and training began.

In June Bill flew back to Sweden to place urgent orders for ball bearings before the Germans blocked us with pre-emptive purchases of which we had secret intelligence. After delays at Leuchars, he and Willy Siberg, the head of SKF at Luton, were flown in the first two Mosquito flights and Mallet sent a telegram from Sweden, 'Waring and Siberg arrived alive'.

Bill had tough arguments with Erik Boheman but convinced him that a vessel 110 feet long was defensively armed when carrying eight Vickers and four Oerlikon guns provided these were hidden away when in Swedish waters. He reconnoitred the coast for a good landfall and seems to have started rumours that the British Army was preparing to begin the invasion of Europe by landing in Sweden.

The little port of Lysekil was selected as a suitable base. Cargo was transported there, cranes erected, accommodation ashore arranged and all the administrative details settled with the Naval authorities who still continued to be unhelpful. The five vessels left Hull on 27 October 1943 as a flotilla but only one arrived in Lysekil the next day. It had not heard the order to return because of the breakdown of one of their number. Regular runs were made till March 1944 with the loss of one ship and its crew, the *Master Standfast*, which was captured by a German Naval vessel carrying Swedish colours. Although *Dicto* and *Lionel* never moved until the war was over, they remained at anchor up the fjord guarded by Swedish warships and keeping the Germans guessing as to their intentions.

The motor coasters crossed the North Sea in daytime, arriving at the entrance to the Skagerrak by nightfall, putting on speed and making the Swedish coast in the early dawn.

I visited George and Bill and Sally Ladell in Lysekil on 15 March 1944 and discussed the pros and cons of various forms of publicity when 'Bridford' had been completed. It was the last sailing of the season. I saw them off in a snowstorm making a foggy photographic record and sketching with numbed fingers. Publicity was important so as to scotch wild rumours of piratical adventures and help the captured crew of *Master Standfast* by making it clear that it was a merchant navy operation. The Swedes, we hoped, would also find it more difficult to withdraw facilities for the coming winter and publicity would boost the morale of the crews. It would also, we believed, raise the morale of our growing number of Swedish supporters, a fact that had always been in George's mind from the beginning. We coped with the security angle by exaggerating the speed of the ships. It took several drafts and censors' blue pencils before at last, in July, a statement was issued. This covered all the points we wished to make together with the local interest in Hull, the home port of the masters who were named with the majority of the crew. The release ended with the words, 'It is perhaps worth adding the *Hopewell* took her name from a Hull whaler which was famous in the early whaling history of that port. The name was conferred on the present Hopewell as a compliment to Hull which was the home of the majority of the crew'.

This was George's last of four round trips. He suffered a serious heart attack and was invalided out of the operation to his disgust but with the consolation of a DSO, a befitting acknowledgement of his heroic performance.

The crews were put up in a third rate hotel for the night. We hired the local baths for the occasion and then took over the local cinema for the evening. The next day, they embarked after loading and repairs had been completed. The German Consul would see us arrive under his windows on the quayside and it was well-known on the west coast that this traffic was taking place. Security was complete as no one ever knew we were coming until we arrived. When we left we moved off north to *Dicto* and *Lionel* which were well out of sight and waited there till ordered to leave. Some had to wait a long time and one of them was there from 28 December 1943 till 18 February 1944.

On 2 December 1943 *Hopewell* arrived with a broken main gear box. A spare was flown over from Scotland to Gothenburg and *Hopewell* was taken there for fitting. She passed through the inner leads between the small islands flying the red ensign, the first vessel to fly it entering port since 9 April 1940. Bill Waring wrote, 'As she came up the river the workers from the shipyard (Götaverken) were going home and she received a tremendous reception as she went to her berth. Whatever the opinion of the Swedish authorities, the great majority of Swedes were extremely pro-British'. The Swedish naval, as opposed to civilian authorities, continued their harrassment of our vessels. One serious incident developed when the Swedish Navy tried to spy out the secret of Radar. Two men disguised as Post Office engineers accompanied one of the boats to Brofjord under the pretext of deciding the best way of sealing the radar tubes so that they could not be used for radio transmission. They were discovered to be employees of a Swedish subsidiary of the German firm AEG.

Although the Germans already had the information about this early type of radar, we lodged a strong protest and got apologies from Erik Boheman and the Prime Minister himself. The incident was a useful bargaining counter in resisting repeated Swedish demands for the recall of our Naval Attaché, Henry Denham. His help with George Binney's operations and steady flow of intelligence on the German Navy, made him a cornerstone of the Allied war effort in Sweden.

'Bridford' was a remarkable success, having together with the air service exceeded the target of 400 tons of valuable freight in the course of the winter months, 347 tons by motor coaster and 88 tons by Mosquito and Lodestar. The air service lost 2 Lodestars, 2 Mosquitoes and 23 lives. The Grey Ladies lost 1 of their number, *Master Standfast*, the life of Captain Holdsworth and 19 prisoners. The value of the freight was incalculable to the war effort. Ralph Barker quotes the estimate of the Ministry of Aircraft Production that 100 tons of ballbearings covered 75% of the airframe work for 1,200 Lancasters and 60% of the airframe work for 1,600 Mosquitoes, the remainder being available from stock. George had set a target for 400 tons and more than achieved it by sea and air. In addition 67 Norwegian volunteers took passage on the motor coasters.

Bill then got involved in the Anglo-American negotiations to stop Swedish ball-bearing exports to Germany. This issue exploded into print in the American press as a result of the horrendous American losses in the raids on the German ball-bearing factories at Schweinfurt, where the damage was alleged to be being made good by SKF in Sweden. Albert Speer in his memoirs says that the Germans were able to make up these losses themselves and were back in full production within a fortnight. If the Allied raids had continued he thought the war might have been ended much earlier. Bill's American opposite number, Stanton Griffis, a president of Paramount Films, was a hard nut if there was one. I remember taking them both out to lunch at Sällskapet, one of the two men's clubs in Stockholm, surrounded by civil servants, politicians and editors. Mr Griffis shouted his intention of bombing the SKF works at Gothenberg unless the damned Swedes stopped trading with the enemy.

The Germans did everything to intensify the import of Swedish iron ore and exceeded their quota for 1943. The Allies reacted violently, demanding not only a cut-back in exports to Germany but a total cessation regardless of War Trade Agreements.

On 13 April 1944 an American note supported by the British insisted on a total cessation of the export of ball bearings, roller bearings, all machine tools and special steels for the manufacture of such bearings. The note was rejected by the Swedes on 22 April. On 9 May, Bill arrived back in Sweden with Stanton Griffis to exert pressure on SKF together. An interim agreement was reached on 27 May but was rejected by the British and US Governments. Discussion was resumed on 5 June, on the eve of D-Day which clinched the deal. An agreement was reached with Harald Hamberg of SKF on 12 June to reduce their exports to Germany by 60% for the next four months. Bill flew to England with the signed agreement on 14 July. The intricate financial obligations took long to work out. They were finally scribbled on a damp piece of paper in the turkish baths one evening where Bill and Mike Wheeler and Ted Senior, the ball-bearing controller, were recuperating after interminable conferences.

Following 'Bridford', a final operation with three of the small boats, codenamed 'Moonshine' was undertaken under the command of Brian Reynolds, as George's heart attack had put him out of commission. Brian retained his 'Bridford' alias as Bingham. He shaved off his beard and was given the temporary rank of Lt. Commander RNR, partly to make it easier for the Swedes not to recognise him as the *persona non grata* gunrunner of 'Performance', partly to smooth his path with the Germans in the event of capture. On this occasion there was less emphasis on the special cargoes from Sweden than on the cargoes of arms and warlike material which, with full co-operation of the Swedes, were off-loaded on to lighters for the Danish resistance. The three ships were *Hopewell*, *Nonsuch* and *Gay Viking*. From September 1944 to January 1945 weather made the passage impossible. Finally they moved their base from Hull to Aberdeen and made the only successful voyage on 13 January 1945. They transferred their camouflaged cargo and moved south from Lysekil to Gothenburg to service the vessels during a full moon period. This was an occasion for showing the red duster again and the officers and men enjoyed the most warm hospitality.

Eventually the ships sailed from Hunnebostrand, a new departure point, on 5 February. *Nonsuch* had an uneventful return voyage but *Gay Viking* was rammed in bad weather by *Hopewell* and was abandoned. The Chief Officer only got away after setting the demolition charges by leaving his lifejacket which got entangled. He

*Gay Viking* under repair in Gothenburg

had to swim 200 yards in water just above freezing point. One of the dinghies pushed away without paddles and was found being propelled by two frying pans and a large Swedish sausage. *Hopewell*, with both crews on board, limped back to Gothenburg for repair and Commander Bingham found a message waiting from the Chief of Staff of the Swedish Navy promising every assistance.

*Gay Viking* seems to have been salvaged and turned into a passenger boat. I traced her soon after the war in Denmark running between Copenhagen and Aalborg, and Ralph Barker reported her operating in 1970 in the Bahamas. *Hopewell* was repaired in a yachtbuilders yard as the shipyards were on strike. A good job was done and she returned safely to the UK. Operation 'Moonshine' ended on 12 March 1945.

Brian Reynolds had distinguished himself throughout as a brave and gallant officer. Two days after VE Day tragedy overtook him. He set out in a Naval MGB from Aberdeen to retrieve *Dicto* and *Lionel* and was never seen again. The boat must have struck a floating mine, a peril he had avoided throughout all his expeditions. He was lost and of his crew of 32 only 2 were rescued on a raft four days later. George returned to United Steel for whom he roamed the world till his retirement. I kept in touch trying to persuade him to write his book which ended up in a huge pile of drafts out of which he intended to make three books and a film. In fact, it was left to others, in particular Ralph Barker, to write the story of his adventures. I joined him once at the instigation of his great friend, Sir Frank Lee, then the Permanent Secretary to the Board of Trade, on an expedition to Ghana for three weeks to advise Nkrumah on industrialisation and agriculture. The expedition was a comic opera experience and did little to improve the macro or micro economies of that delightful country. George married very happily, Sonja, the widow of Lt. Col. F C Simms, and retired finally to a lovely old house Le Domaine Des Vaux in Jersey where he died on 27 September 1972, still preoccupied with his antiques and designing his beautiful garden. The last I saw of him was with a hoe in his hand, his white hair and blue eyes glinting in the sun. Bill Waring got a CMG for his efforts which were stupendous. He had had responsibility for the administration of the expeditions, purchasing and loading of materials and endless negotiations with Ministers and Government departments in London which he visited some twenty-two times. His papers are impressive in their detail. They had to be detailed as apart from his devoted secretary, Sally Ladell, later Lady Anderson, he had very little staff other than the one or two who could help him in the Gothenburg Consultate General. He had responsibility for negotiating with Dominion Governments and with the Russians who were unbelievably dilatory. They complained that some of the machines and tubes left on *Lionel* and *Dicto* had suffered water damage and insisted on remedial action. Bill began the peace as head of steel control in Germany, then he moved to GKN, left them to become head of the steel division of the Economic Commission for Europe in Geneva and finally went back to GKN on their main board and as director of the firm's steel works at Brymbo near Wrexham. He parted from his wife, Anne, and married Sue Jacob whom he left a widow in 1962 when he was killed in an aircrash in Luxembourg in the GKN plane on his way to a meeting of the European Coal and Steel Community. He knew more about the European and world steel industry than anyone else in Britain and his loss was a grievous one to his family, his friends, his firm and his country.

These remarkable exploits made one realise how the fortunes of war so often depend as much on the few as on the massive weight of the many. George Binney alone was the man who challenged the impossible in breaking the German blockade of Sweden. He conceived his enterprise long before SOE but the final two operations were co-ordinated by SOE. Like so many SOE undertakings these bore out the words of Napoleon - 'À la guerre, les trois quarts sont des affaires morales, la balance des forces réelles n'est que pour un autre quart' . . 'In war three quarters are a matter of morale, the balance of manpower and materials accounts only for the remaining quarter'. George was a leader others would follow to the death. He was not always lucky but he backed luck with caution and careful planning and concern for those who worked with him.

**Note on Sources**

Apart from my own records, the Public Records Office, Bill Waring's papers and Ralph Barker's excellent book *The Blockade Busters*, I am much indebted to the late Lady Binney and her son Marcus for the loan of Sir George Binney's own records.

# XV
# How We Failed to Buy the Italian Navy

Stockholm was a most unlikely place in which to negotiate the defection of the Italian Fleet. Berne or Lisbon would have been more convenient since communications between Italy and Sweden were much more vulnerable to the Abwehr. Couriers had to cross Germany or take the circuitous route through the USSR until June 1941 when the German invasion of Russia took place.

A key figure in this operation was Countess Amelie Posse. She was rescued from the Nazis in Czechoslovakia in 1939 by a burly, jovial Swede named Walter, a courageous adventurer who carried out this daring Scarlet Pimpernel exploit against the Nazis under the cover of his business activities. These ranged from coal imports to the purchase of armaments.

The Swedish Minister in Prague, Malmar, who later helped Walter in Belgrade on his journey to Italy in 1941, delivered her to him at midnight at the main railway station. Only then was Walter told her identity, discovering later that she was a well-known writer, wife of a Czech painter, Brazda, and friend of Beneš and Mazaryk. They arrived safely in Sweden in spite of her indiscretions with smuggled currency. They became firm friends and she called him her brigand Knight-errant. Later with the help of a Swedish diplomat, he smuggled out all her precious notes for a book on her childhood in a bag of dirty washing.

In November 1940 when our fortunes were at a low ebb but the Germans had failed to invade us and we had done deadly damage to the Italian Navy at Taranto (11 November) and their Army in Libya and Abyssinia, the ever buoyant Countess got in touch with me and asked if we would be interested to buy the Italian Navy. I replied 'Snap - subject to the concurrence of my friend and colleague, Captain Henry Denham our Naval Attaché,' who immediately telegraphed the Admiralty for guidance. The suggestion had come from her Scarlet Pimpernel friend, Director J.H. Walter. The Countess gave him the cover name of Karlsson in order to fool the Swedish Secret Police and Intelligence Services who may have been confused but not deluded. She christened me Pilkvist for good measure.

Denham sent a signal on 24 November and the background was filled in over the next few days. Amelie Posse had invited both of us to meet Walter at lunch. An Italian friend of his whom he refused to identify had left Rome on 17 November and was returning on the 27th. He reported that the Italians were under pressure to give way to the occupation of Italy by the Germans and surrender their Fleet. Anti-war feeling was growing and senior Italian Naval Officers would be unable to resist the Germans unless presented with an alternative. The alternative suggested was the surrender of the Italian Fleet to Great Britain. The families were to proceed to Portugal or an Allied country and to be certain of no reprisals by the Italian Fascists or Germans. The signal to the Admiralty had been sent on 24 November. The Foreign Office rather unfairly accused the Admiralty of dilatoriness in not replying in time to catch the Italian emissary before he returned. He was not identified, but described as a high-ranking Fascist who Walter understood represented the views of two Admirals. One was in command of a sea-going squadron. There were a certain number of other Naval Officers. The Admiralty agreed to give the necessary assurances and guarantees to advance to the intermediary the insignificant sum of 50,000 kr. (£3,125 at the going rate of exchange), to ease his cashflow. 15,000 kr. were paid to Walter on 17 December and a receipt obtained on behalf of the intermediary. The Foreign Office in cynical minutes by Bob Dixon, Orme Sargent and Jack Nicholls considered the venture unlikely to succeed but, nevertheless, were ready to try our luck.

Before continuing the story, it may be useful to give some of Walter's background which lent some verisimilitude to what he told us. Born in 1888, the son of a schoolteacher, he had too poor a physique to do military service. After a year studying Marine Engineering at Chalmers in Gothenburg, he took a commercial course and launched on a business career. This was marked with successes and failures. He successfully launched an American tin-opener on the Swedish Army. He made an unsuccessful attempt, with an American, to beat Ivar Kreuger at his match business, and ultimately succeeded with the help of Vernons of Liverpool, in a massive advertising campaign in setting up Tipstjänst or what corresponded to the British football pools. He lost a law suit against a British company in the commodity business. The Swedish pools were nationalised and he was demoted by the Minister of Trade, P.E. Sköld, from his income of 100,000 kr. a year to the rank of Managing Director with a salary of 18,000 kr. instead. This was the beginning of a feud with Sköld who later became Minister of Defence. Walter refused the Managing Director post, accepting instead a handshake of 70,000 kr. which was not enough to pay his tax arrears and the expenses he had incurred in setting up the football pools.

It was in the course of attempting to buy armaments worth 200 million kr. from the Skoda Works that he rescued Amelie Posse. The shipment was stopped by the Germans but he was then attempting to have them shipped via Fiume. On 5 October 1939 he met an old friend, the Member of Parliament Harald Åkerberg, in a restaurant in the old town, who expressed his deep concern at Sweden's poor Naval defences. Walter raised his hopes by assuring him he could purchase surplus warships from Italy. Navies were one of his hobbies and he always carried on him a copy of *Weyers Taschenbuch der Kriegsflotten.* After quick telephone calls to a friend in the Rumanian Legation. he was given introductions to Doctor Basile, the Commercial Attaché in the Italian Legation, and then to another Italian in Oslo by the name of Savabini who represented parastatal armaments concerns. Neither of these gentlemen, however, showed any sign of interest. Finally he rang up a retired Italian General, Sailer, a member of the Fascist Grand Council, whom he had met on a holiday in Yugoslavia. He then activated a young German Jewish refugee called Goldschmidt who had changed his name to Engberg, and was employed in the Swedish Consulate in Milan, to pursue further enquiries. He used an Italian attorney called Naldi and a well-known Naval Engineer, Ricciuti, to help him in Italy. In Sweden he appointed Yngve Schartau as his front man in order to conceal his participation from the Minister of Defence, Sköld, who had his knife in him since the football pool affair. Walter had a positive reaction from Sailer, a friend of Admiral Cavagnari, the Under Secretary of State for the Navy and Chief of the Naval Staff, who reported that he was interested. A series of protracted negotiations began.

This is the starting point of a two-pronged drama with elements that interlocked. One was the purchase of the Italian warships, two destroyers and two torpedo boats, *Puke* and *Psilander*, *Romulus* and *Remus*, with prolonged litigation by Walter against the Swedish Government . They had endeavoured to deprive him of his commission on the purchase of these vessels. He eventually won his case and got 150,000 kr. compensation and 20,000 kr. costs. This case started on 24 May 1940 and ended with the favourable judgement of the Lower Court of Appeal on 19 March 1943. The Swedish Government tried, but failed, to stop a testimony by Italian witnesses before an Italian Court being used by Walter in the Swedish Court. The Court was also greatly influenced in Walter's favour by the misuse of secret police telephone tappings in testimony against him by Sköld, who under more usual circumstances would have had to resign.

The second case may well have been influenced by the first and started in the middle of the first one when Walter was arrested at 18.30 hours on 30 November 1942 for espionage. He was sentenced on 19 March 1943 to one year's hard labour and on appeal on 24 January 1944 to two and a half years. On further appeal to the High Court he was released later that year. When we met him Walter was preparing a visit to Italy early in 1941 to obtain further evidence for his case against the Swedish Government. He had a good record from World War I, when he was involved in transit trade with Britain and America. He was, he said, anxious to resume relations with us as he considered us more reliable and realistic partners than the Swedish Government. We told the Countess we were interested and proceeded to brief Walter. In the meantime, she gave him introductions to her anti-Fascist friends in Italy where she had lived for fifteen years.

Walter did not belong to the same social stratum as his rival, Holger Graffman, who supplanted him as the Government negotiator for the purchase of the warships. Graffman, whose company AB Transfer was backed by the Wallenbergs, was married to the charming daughter of a Dutch Ambassador. He entertained the Stockholm establishment generously and provided Christmas hampers for his friends in the Diplomatic Corps. Walter was denigrated as a rogue and social outcast but after the establishment and secret police had taken their revenge on him with heavy sentences, he was finally rehabilitated and pardoned and, in the meantime, won his case against the Swedish Government.

The four Italian warships were arrested in the Faroes by the Royal Navy on the orders of our Government in spite of the safe conduct provided for them by the Admiralty. This contributed to much of the anti-British feeling in the Swedish Navy. The warships leaving Genoa in convoy accompanied by the supply ship *Patricia* and a slow, small tanker, *Castor*, were held up for a month in Lisbon. In the middle of June they found themselves sailing into a very critical situation. Dunkirk and the fall of France, Italy's entry into the war, the evacuation of Norway and, on 17 June, Sweden's acceptance of German demands for the transit of their troops across Sweden to and from Norway, all combined in an atmosphere of crisis to be a test of strong nerves.

At 07.15 hours on 20 June Captain C. Caslon came with an ultimatum from the British Government to take the destroyers into protective custody. This was a decision taken in the War Cabinet on 19 June on a suggestion by Thomas Inskip, later Viscount Caldecote, Secretary of State for Dominion Affairs. It was not an Admiralty decision but a Government one. Captain Torsten Hagman who commanded the convoy, handled the incident with calm dignity. The crews were transferred to *Patricia* and *Castor*. The destroyers were boarded by British crews and taken to Kirkwall. While Caslon obviously took this action with reluctance, Hagman and his officers agreed that they must comply under protest as any resistance would have been met by force represented by four Tribal class destroyers, three armed trawlers and a number of other vessels. This event did much to fuel the anti-British feeling of the officers and crews, except for Hagman. This was increased when the destroyers were later handed back in Kirkwall and the Swedes had to repair the damage done by the British in ripping out fittings in their search for incriminating objects. It was a humiliation for Hagman. The motives for the British action were hard to swallow. The Swedish acceptance of the German demands for the transit of troops was the last straw.

Churchill's orders were 'Immediate steps should be taken to see that the destroyers did not slip through our fingers and we could consider later what explanation we should offer'. Flimsy explanations were given that Britain was justified in international law by right of Angary of which instances were provided when neutral ships were impounded by belligerents and compensation paid. Eventually one million kr. was paid by the British in compensation. Anyhow, the British changed their minds and the Swedes sailed off to Kristiansand in occupied Norway.

On 10 July the convoy was met by the Swedish warship *Tapperheten*, and made for Gothenburg where there was no ceremonial welcome and Hagman went ashore in a launch on his own. Erik Boheman, the Secretary General of the Swedish Ministry of Foreign Affairs, is alleged to have lost his temper saying Hagman should have been hanged for not standing up to the British. The Chief of the Naval Staff issued an order to the Navy on the day Hagman was acquitted at his Court Martial to the effect that 'I forbid all officers under my command to hand over their ships to a foreign power under whatever pretext. The honour of our Flag is paramount'. Hagman's career was ended by this incident and he was never promoted. George Binney's convoys of merchant ships and motor coasters met as much opposition from the Swedish Navy as from the Germans. Throughout the war the Swedish Ministry of Foreign Affairs was being egged on by the Navy to declare our Naval Attaché, Captain Henry Denham, *persona non grata*. They tried eight times but the British Government refused to take any notice. There were, however, wiser men in Sweden at the helm and the country has to thank Captain Hagman that he kept his cool in the Faroes without bringing Sweden into the war on the wrong side as many of his hysterical young officers would have liked. In a television programme on the Faroes incident in 1972, Mrs Sigrid Hansson, the widow of Per Albin Hansson, the Prime Minister at the time, said that 'Per just before his death said that one of the few things he regretted in his life was that he did not travel down to Gothenburg and, as Prime Minister, welcome Hagman when he arrived there with the destroyers in 1940'. In fact, the only person who did welcome him was our own Naval Attaché. Earlier Per Albin had also said 'One should really strike a special medal to commemorate Torsten Hagman's wise handling of a situation which was so sensitive and risky for our country'. Shortly after the incident, the Swedish Minister in London, Björn Prytz, had an affable conversation with Churchill who commented (translated from the Swedish record),

> If the Swedish Commander had been an English officer in a corresponding situation we would have wished to distinguish him especially with a suitable decoration to express our admiration and the Nation's gratitude for the way in which he handled this difficult and sensitive affair. Exceptionally well done, admirable, he saved both countries a lot of trouble.

With this background to the acquisition of the four destroyers from the Italians, we can return to the proposals put to us by Director J.H. Walter to buy the whole Italian Fleet. His negotiations with the Italians had given him access to inner circles in the Italian Navy but, as an inveterate name dropper, one wonders if he ever reached as high as he hinted. We had several meetings with Walter, (25/28 November, 6 and 11 December). Although the formal assurances from the Admiralty had not reached Stockholm before the Italian intermediary returned to Rome on 27 November, Walter assured him that all would be well and then prepared to go to Italy in January to further his law suits against the Swedish Government. By then Walter was equipped with the five assurances which the Admiralty was prepared to give the Italians. They were as follows:

1. Safe passage to British or Dominion ports and return to Italy after the war.
2. No question of Italian ships or Italians being called upon to fight against Italy.
3. Escort to any merchant ships containing wives and families of any Italian personnel so inclined who could not be accommodated in Italian warships.
4. Asylum on British soil and generous assistance for men and families. Any who wished to continue to fight for freedom against the Germans would be welcomed and for them British rates of pay would be assured.

5. Personnel will be treated with honour and will not be repatriated to Italy without their consent.

In the meantime, in response to a personal request, Mallet, our Minister in Stockholm, sent a despatch on 19 December to Henry Hopkinson in the Foreign Office reporting Walter's poor reputation in Swedish business circles. This was sent without the knowledge of Denham or myself because Mallet had been asked by the Foreign Office to investigate independently and report personally. However discreet he may have been, it is likely that the business circles included Marcus Wallenberg, which meant Walter's rival, Graffman, was alerted and the Swedish secret police put on Walter's tracks, if they hadn't been there already. This almost certainly resulted in a leak to the Abwehr or Sicherheitsdienst. Mallet unwittingly confirmed this in a telegram of 23 January to the effect that German suspicions had been aroused and no channels were now open. Many Italian Naval officers were arrested at this time by the Fascist police. They were not released until the German invasion of Russia in June 1941 when German control in Italy was relaxed and the channels opened again. Walter was determined to leave for Italy and did this through Russia. His transit visa to Italy via Germany had been refused, and he noticed from then on that he was being followed, his telephone tapped, his flat bugged and his correspondence intercepted.

He left on 24 January with the intention of meeting Admiral Cavagnari and Parola (in fact, Angelo Parona, Cavagnari's *chef de cabinet*, who had been decorated by the Swedes for his help over the destroyer purchase) and minor Naval contacts he had made in previous negotiations. On 11 February Mallet telegraphed the Foreign Office asking our Naval Attaché in Belgrade be warned of a possible contact by Karlsson since the German buildup in Bulgaria might frustrate his return through Russia. Cordeaux, the Royal Marine Colonel in the Admiralty who later came out to Sweden, sent the necessary signal to Belgrade on 15 February but the facility was not used. On 4 March Walter returned and reported he had been in touch indirectly with Cavagnari and Riccardi, who assured him there was no risk of the Fleet coming under German control. Cavagnari, though, as one of a possible triumvirate with Badoglio and Grandi, was criticised by the younger officers for the disaster at Taranto for which he shared responsibility. There was no possibility of surrender at that time but it might be dictated by future events. This coincides partly with the mystification of the so-called Franco-Italian letter in the espionage trial which is quoted below. At this point all papers on this matter were shown to Churchill and it was agreed to tell the Italians (Foreign Office telegram 115, 19 March) once more that we would gladly receive any units of the Italian Fleet that might come to us and do our best to escort merchant ships with families. In return for a real effort by their Navy, this would weigh heavily with us when considering peace terms. We would do our best to save Italy from German domination before and after the final peace conference.

Telegram 143 of 14 March from the Naval Attaché Stockholm to DNI reported further details of Walter's visit to Italy. It was not thought feasible to evacuate families of warships' crews *en bloc* as was at first thought. Instead they made two proposals:

A. The families of some prominent officers must be evacuated to certain foreign countries and receive some grant.

B. Officers and crews of surrendered warships would eventually require compensation for their families to start them in new professions later on.

The Italian representatives then proposed the following terms:

The British Admiralty to pay in dollars for ships surrendered -

| Battleship | 300,000 |
| Heavy Cruiser | 60,000 |
| Light Cruiser | 50,000 |
| Destroyer | 30,000 |
| Submarine | 25,000 |
| Torpedo Boat | 15,000 |

If it were found more practical to sabotage warships, half the amount would be paid for the benefit of those who carried out the work. Payments would be made after the war when proof was furnished that warships had been surrendered or disabled. An immediate deposit of $600,000 was to be lodged with a United States bank, up to 15% of which was to be made available then to assist families of senior Naval personnel whose names and destination would be communicated. It was felt that the acceptance of the scheme in principle would enable us to telegraph at once to put it into execution with a chance of it coming off. At most the British Government would only stand to lose 15% of its deposit. Walter was prepared to run the risk of returning to Italy, though he was not blind to his chances of a handsome reward in the event of success.

An independent anti-Fascist intermediary had been handed the terms of the Foreign Office telegram 115 of 9 March and undertook to deliver the message which he predicted would be genuinely appreciated. The response came with the telegram 140 of 19 March stating 'While chances of the scheme succeeding appear slight we accept it in principle. You are authorised to telegraph at once to put it into execution.' - to which Churchill commented in his own hand 'This all seems fantastic. WSC.' The First Lord replied to the Prime Minister on 25 March 'I agree that the chance of success in this venture seems remote but the payments which were necessary to prosecute it were so small compared with the importance of the prizes to be secured that the scheme appears to be worth pursuing'.

Churchill had plans for setting up a Free Italy based on Cyrenaica in February 1941 (War Cabinet meeting 13 February) which in the end were frustrated by Rommel taking command in Tripolitania and driving us out. One of the motives for this plan was to provide the Italian Fleet with its own harbours for the desertion. No harbour in Cyrenaica was, in fact, deep enough for the larger vessels and no suitable leader could be found to match the stature of a General de Gaulle. One candidate 'old electric whiskers', General Annibale Bergonzoli, was too much of a figure of fun. There was also the question of not pre-empting the status of the Italian colonies in relation to the future of the indigenous population.

Then on 28 March 1941 came a further humiliating defeat for the Italian Navy at Cape Matapan. While the channel still remained opened the records reveal nothing and one has to rely on vague recollections of Italian proposals for surrendering half the Fleet to the British while the other half was to be escorted across the South Atlantic to Buenos Aires for internment for the duration. Obviously their Lordships were less than enthusiastic over such suggestions. Plans were also put forward for a signals system to facilitate the surrender and avoid detection by the Germans, but nothing seems to have come of this either.

With the German invasion of Russia in June 1941 the channel of communication revived, but Walter was no longer able to visit Italy via Russia. Certain Italian officers were released from prison and an emissary arrived with assurances that the plan outlined in telegram 143 of 14 March would be put into execution. A telegram of 15 July stated that he would be returning on 19 July and a reply from the Admiralty on 18 July authorised us to confirm that the British side of the bargain still held good. The emissary reported that Admiral Riccardi had been on the point of resigning as a result of German interference. Then with the outbreak of the war with Russia, German control slackened and at the same time several Italian Naval officers had been relieved of their appointments and reprisals taken against them.

In January 1942 Colonel J.K. Cordeaux of the Admiralty again came into the picture and suggested visiting Stockholm in connection with financial aid for the families of senior Italian Naval Officers. He was concerned particularly with the activities of two Italian anglophiles, the Duchess Nina Colonna di Cesaro, and the Marchese Riri Visconti Venosta, who were secretly raising funds for these families. The Duchess was believed to be related to Count Guido Colonna, the Second Secretary of the Italian Legation in Stockholm, who with his charming Russian wife, Tatiana, were known to be pro-British.

In July Cordeaux came out to Sweden and was stuck for two months owing to light nights providing inadequate cover for our courier planes. He met Walter in Denham's flat on or around 12 July. With El Alamein in October 1942, the tide began to turn in our favour and we waited for a positive move by the Italian Navy. But alas, we heard no more. On 30 November Walter received 55,000 kr. in notes as an advance on a promised 100,000 kr., the rest to be paid over when he had returned from Italy. At 18.30 hours that day, the Swedish police put paid to the whole operation by arresting Walter and prosecuting him on a charge of supplying information to a foreign power concerning military and political matters relating to another foreign power.

A certain continuity, however, may have been maintained with the Stockholm operation by Francesco Fransoni, the first Italian

Minister in Stockholm, who was considered an uncommitted Fascist. On 19 June 1941 he was replaced by Giuseppe Renzetti and his German wife from Berlin. Fransoni was posted to Lisbon where he became a channel for the Allies for Italian dissidents, playing a part in the final surrender.

Swedish law on espionage was open to somewhat elastic interpretation. It meant that anyone who, in the interest of a foreign power, pursued activities in Sweden in the field of secret, military or political intelligence aimed either against Sweden or against another foreign power, could be sentenced to a maximum of two years in prison with hard labour. If vital Swedish interests were damaged the penalty was more severe. Poor Walter's activities, which were in no way directed against Sweden, came within the scope of these laws. The Italians with whom he was dealing included many of those with whom the Swedish Government had negotiated the purchase of the four destroyers and who later went over to the Allies in September 1943 and were identified with the new Government for whose interests Walter had worked. On 11 September 1943, eight days after the surrender had secretly been signed by Badoglio and two days after it had become effective, Cunningham signalled the Admiralty 'Be pleased to inform their Lordships that the Italian Battle Fleet now lies at anchor under the guns of the Fortress of Malta'.

The Italians declared war on Germany on 13 October.

As mentioned on p. 232, on 19 March 1943 Walter was sentenced to one year's hard labour for unlawful intelligence activity. But on appeal on 24 January 1944, the Court of Appeal increased his sentence to two and a half year's hard labour due to a change in the law that had taken place in the interval. The court declared forfeit the sum of 55,000 kr. which the police had found on him together with part of the questionnaire. Walter, after an appeal to the King, was shortly afterwards released by unanimous decision of the Supreme Court. He was in the anomalous situation of serving a sentence for communicating between one co-belligerent and another. The Italians having changed sides, there could no longer be any question of Walter working against a foreign power. The war had now reached a stage where the Abwehr was actively attempting to ingratiate itself with the Allies, particularly through the Swedes, so that the secret police adopted a low profile. However, Walter never got back his 55,000 kr. nor did he receive any compensation for damage to his name and reputation. But he had won his case against the Swedish Government for payment of his commission and expenses incurred originally in negotiating the purchase of the Italian warships.

The Swedish police files do not reveal as much as one would hope from their letter censorship, telephone tapping, microphone bugging, lipreading and other activities. Countess Posse visited Walter in prison and was herself interrogated at length. She was amazed at the mass of information the police had collected, much of it irrelevant.

A study of the records of the two trials and accompanying police reports reveals a Walter much more colourful than the garrulous Walter Mitty we got to know. Even the biased State Prosecutor, Eugen Glas, and the caricature spy hunter, Inspector Danielsson, admitted he was a man of intelligence, ability and knowledge in many fields with an interesting record of success and failure in a multiplicity of enterprises. Thanks to crossing swords with P.E. Sköld, when he was Minister of Trade, over the football pools and being deprived of his income, Walter was in serious financial straits when we got to know him, though we were not aware of this. His only assets seem to have been a stamp collection and his wife's jewellery which he pawned. He attempted but failed to raise a loan on the security of the Court judgement in the destroyer case since the money had been withheld by the Government. His bank account looked somewhat dicky but his friends lent him money and he paid them back. All agreed that he was a man of honour. He was temperamental, suffered from bouts of depression and explosions of indignation but always bounced back with impertinent courage.

His impudence even went to the length of entering the enemy camp, asking the lawyer and Swedish Nazi editor of *Dagsposten*, Dr Rutger Essén, to help him get a transit visa through Germany for his second journey to Italy and even possibly go there on his behalf to help him over Italian witnesses. He may have been boasting but said that he had baffled the Germans by asking them if, on crossing Germany on his way back from Italy, he might call in on the Abwehr headquarters in Berlin to see their telephone tappings of his calls to Italy because he knew they had been so helpful to the Swedish police in this regard. Also he used the services of the lawyer, Schartau, as his front man with Sköld in his destroyer negotiations. He knew that he was intimate with Grassmann, the German Press Attaché, and von Grolman, a Counsellor in the German Legation, and that he acted as adviser to the Germans in the case of the impounded Norwegian ships in Gothenburg which had been demise chartered to the British. He had catholic tastes but all agreed that he was openly pro-British and pro-American and despised the Nazis. Countess Posse was biased in his favour but the record of her interrogation by the police is a very fair assessment of the man. 'He is a little pushing, rather chatty and boastful but is kind and full of goodwill'. She relates how delighted he was to have rescued her manuscript of childhood memories and smuggled them out of Czechoslovakia.

> Adventures of this kind were very characteristic of him. When I travelled with him from Prague he distributed to all and sundry worthless cheques, 100 crown notes and confided to the guards under an oath of secrecy that I was a member of the Swedish Royal Family travelling incognito. It was most important not to be found out, etc., etc. In the same way he seemed amused to appear as Mr Karlsson. Even if he is childishly delighted and bluffing a bit, I would not imagine this man capable of doing anything wrong. He doesn't appear to me to be in any way politically motivated but he is a good patriot and a convinced anti-Nazi, which for me are synonymous concepts as they are for the majority of decent democratic Swedes. I could never believe he is the sort of person who could be bought and he would never do anything against his convictions however large a sum was laid on the table in front of him. All this in spite of the fact that he is interested in lotteries and betting and has somewhat of a gambler's temperament. Poul Bjerre has been his doctor. I spoke with him about him once and he confirmed my appreciation of him, but at the same time he said he was somewhat worried that Walter's nerves would not be able to hold out under the great stress of the anxieties of his trial. I remember I once said to Denham 'Please do not compromise Walter. He is a naive and credulous person'. Denham smiled and

said they were friends and he would certainly not attempt to harm him. The reason why I said this to Denham was because Walter chatted so openly on the telephone with me and I was a little afraid he could do the same with Denham from pure absentmindedness. I certainly think I could swear that Walter never betrayed anything about Swedish affairs to foreigners or even wished to do anything which could damage our country. In some ways he is an old-fashioned Swedish imperialist, a little boastful, fond of adventure, possibly not all that reliable but still somehow or other a pleasant and sturdy person and not at all a spy type. As far as indiscretions on the telephone are concerned he is the most indiscreet and impulsive person I have ever met in my life. He is certainly not suited for conspiracy and it is most unlikely that he is indulging in anything of the kind, even if it amuses him to surround himself with an atmosphere of secrecy and self-importance and he likes to seem to be remarkably well-informed. Tennant and he were good friends even if Tennant always laughed at him a little and never took him very seriously. He called him the adventurous knight-errant and thought he had rather romantic and exaggerated ideas. I did not meet Denham as often but I can understand that Walter and he became real friends. I know once when someone in Denham's presence laughed about Walter, Denham said 'Don't say that, there is a lot of good in that man. He has been unjustly treated and needs to get on his feet again'. I understood that they were close friends which I don't think was the case with Tennant.

So much for Walter's character. When he was arrested, he had 55,000 kr. in notes on his person, a notebook, some of the thirteen questions - most of which was found in his flat, a copy of what came to be called the Franco-Italian letter in Swedish translation, his bank statements and cheque stubs, etc. There were intercepts of his correspondence and telephone calls. One of the most incriminating items was known as the Japp letter. The curious thing about the whole affair is that the central issue of the Italian Navy was more or less successfully treated by Walter as a matter he had heard of secondhand, but in which he was in no way involved. He spoke of Denham's preoccupation with what he called the Italian Navy Liquidation Company and the Mafia against the Fascist regime of the royal house, Badoglio and Cavagnari which he pretended not to take seriously himself. The interrogations concentrated on Walter's relations with Denham whom Walter described as a close friend introduced by Amelie Posse. He first got to know him when briefing himself on the Faroe incident. Denham had been helpful in providing information about the sale of warships in the past twenty years so that he could work out the rate of commission by comparison with brokerage fees for merchant ships. He insisted that the 55,000 kr. was a personal loan from Denham as an advance on a promised total of 100,000 kr. and demanded its return.

Though the Court did not believe him, they seemed to consider Cordeaux the arch-villain in the plot. Denham knew nothing of the questionnaire but received so-called 'security' for his 'personal loan' in the shape of a post-dated and uncovered cheque and bill of exchange for 30,000 kr. and 25,000 kr. respectively. These were subsequently shown to the Court by Walter's lawyer, Georg Stjernstedt, as evidence of a perfectly innocent transaction, however curious the 'security'. Denham was described as a close personal friend which he was not, a frequent host to Walter on his yacht which he never was, and offering an open invitation, which was never given, to come cruising with him on his new yacht in the Mediterranean after the war. There were frequent allusions to personal loans from Denham, exchanges of cognac, whisky and tobacco. He spoke of the loan of illustrated English weeklies with the photographs of naval and air actions and discussions on the progress of the war at sea. He told the Court quite truthfully that Denham had called on him one day when he was staying at Skälderviken in the summer of 1942 when he had taken him to see a German transit train passing through. He visited Denham frequently in his flat at Riddargatan 46 in Stockholm for no obvious reason, though it would appear from the evidence that he did this in order to build up a picture of a close friendship.

There is no direct evidence in the trial documents of the identity of the Italian intermediary. He never told us who he was but indicated on various occasions that he was a high-ranking Fascist or a bank courier. To the police he said he thought the person might well have been a Swede. On one occasion he alluded to a high-ranking Fascist, and after prompting by the police, said he thought the conductor, Vittorio Gui, a close friend of Amelie Posse, who visited Sweden twice during the war, might have been involved. This seems unlikely but Gui did leave a message to the effect that an Italian Admiral, whom he did not name, had described Italy's situation as involving inevitable defeat whoever won the war. If England won, Italy would lose least. To make this possible, Italy should contribute by seeking an understanding between the English and Italian Navies so that the Italian Fleet could hand itself over to the British.

It was also to Gui that the so-called Franco-Italian letter was attributed. A copy of this letter was found in Swedish in Walter's flat. Denham had never seen such a letter but Walter told the police that Denham had shown him an extract written in French and interspersed with Italian which had been written to someone in the Italian Legation and passed on to him. He asked Walter to translate it on the spot as he would not let him keep it. So Walter did a quick one into Swedish which he took home when he turned it into English and dropped it into Denham's letter box the following day. The whole story is unconvincing since there was no need for an Italian to write to Italians partly in French and partly in Italian unless it was thought that French was better understood by the English. Nor was it likely that Denham would ask Walter to translate it when he had admirable and secure facilities for doing this in the Legation. Walter was proud of his command of languages, of his library of eight hundred French books and could have invented the incident to show off his prowess and his status as Denham's confidant. The letter vaguely matches two of the messages Denham telegraphed to London on 8 March and 14 March 1941. The letter itself is not dated and Walter told the police that it must have been in the Autumn of 1941, half a year later. Translated from Swedish it reads as follows:

> Would you be kind enough to tell your Swedish friend that his account and proposals have been the object of careful examination. If things are as his account makes clear, then the joint project must be dropped. At an early stage your friend was told clearly and specifically that financial support from him was a

necessary condition. This he understood and promised guarantees which are valueless at the present time. However, it has been explained that the timing and execution of the project must be according to Italian decisions and judgements and not at the bidding of your friend, or as a result of a conference between your friend and interested parties close to him. The difficulties have been very great and have not been reduced, particularly as the war has brought with it restrictions and increased pressures in many respects, conditions which your friend must find difficult to understand in a land at peace. I regret that too much reliance has been placed on your friend's various expectations which did not correspond in any concrete form to Italian conditions and wishes. As I have already said, would you be so good as to tell him that all plans must, unfortunately, be dropped, not from any lack of will or interest on our side but exclusively because of lack of understanding by your friend.

Although this provides no hard evidence, its general air of mystification must have added to police suspicions gathered from Walter's indiscretions on the telephone and as a result of intense bugging. The writer of the letter used the second person plural in French and not the intimate 'tu'. Police suspicions were intensified by Amelie Posse's cops and robbers joke of giving Walter the cover name of Karlsson and me the name of Pilkvist, the discovery in his pocket book of instructions about the use of secret ink and the reading of such letters by wiping a blank page with cottonwool dipped in ammonia. All this added to their suspicions which were not allayed by the true explanation that this was to facilitate communication with the Czech painter, Professor Obrovsky, for whom the painter and close friend of Amelie Posse, Prince Eugen, was endeavouring to find refuge in Sweden.

Another count on which he was found guilty was the so-called Japp letter. Japp was a German businessman living in Paris whom two of Walter's daughters knew before the war when learning French. He was on holiday in Sweden when the war broke out, but not being in sympathy with the Nazis he stayed on for a few months and did not report for military service. He returned to Paris and continued his business. Walter hinted that he was well-informed and on 2 July 1942 wrote a letter to Amelie Posse which quoted Japp as writing 'Mr W-D (Max Weygand) is in the best of health and belongs to the true Christians. The evils of our time mean that he must wait and be patient and so it is for him. Assuming that events as a whole, in particular in the East, develop according to certain aspects we can count on surprising things from Mr W-D and his faithful'. He then appealed to Amelie to convert me from my scepticism about Weygand which was backed by an article in the *Manchester Guardian* which I had circulated in my press bulletin. The police thought the Weygand letter of first class importance to the Allies and accused Walter of passing it to me. I never saw it, and tried to point out in a letter I wrote to Amelie which was shown to the Court, that if I had seen it it could not have had the slightest value as intelligence. This seems to have confirmed the State prosecutor in his conviction that it was a matter of prime importance and only made matters worse for Walter.

Another mistake was the case of a poor, innocent Swedish Merchant Navy captain, John Erik Axel Ericsson, who, arrested on 14 December 1942, was sentenced for espionage because Walter had arranged for him to meet Henry Denham on behalf of an old friend, Gustafsson. Ericsson, like many Swedish Merchant Navy officers, wanted to volunteer for the British Merchant Navy in which he had served before. By giving his particulars of past and present experiences, he was accused of providing intelligence for the British, which he never did. If Walter had not been so indiscreet and mysterious, Ericsson could well have been recruited quite openly without any sinister implications provided we could have found transport for him.

Finally, there was the mystery of the thirteen questions which the Swedes suspected emanated from Denham. It was thought that the 55,000 kr. were an advance payment for his answers to these questions for which he was preparing a second visit to Italy, possibly via the UK and Portugal, as transit through Germany was barred to him. Denham never saw the questions and their origin remains a mystery. The police thought the money was an advance on a total of 100,000 kr. promised on his return. Why the questions were divided into eleven on one page and then two more marked 1. and 3. on another, we shall never know. The text of the first set of questions was as follows:

1. What are the three cruisers at Navarino?
2. State of Roma and Augusta aircraft carriers.
3. Where is cruiser Cadorna?
4. How many Italian SMs are operating in the Atlantic?
5. How many submarines have been sunk up to January 1st 1942?
6. How many submarines are there capable of carrying human torpedoes?
7. What German personnel are carried in Italian warships?
8. Where and in what condition is cruiser Trieste?
9. Where is Impero and in what state of construction?
10. How many new Regolo cruisers are building and how many in all?
11. What damage was suffered by Axis forces in the recent Malta convoy operations?

The text of the other two questions read:

1. What damage was caused to Ansaldo in recent air attack on Genoa?
3. Report state of morale in any individual ships of Italian Navy and morale of any individual Naval officers.

T. H. Lindquist gave the Court on 26 January 1943 the Swedish Defence Staff's assessment of the value of the questionnaire. They found it difficult to date the longer one but the shorter one would seem to date from the Autumn of 1942 with its reference to the bombing of the Ansaldo Works. It may be that the longer list was given him when he first met Cordeaux. The questions were considered far from innocent and accurate answers would have been of value to the Allies in their air and naval offensive against Italy.

Walter told the Court that Cordeaux was a kind of inspector whose task was to check up on Naval Attachés' offices. He thought Cordeaux's interest in him was to assess the reliability of his information. He produced an unconvincing explanation of the questionnaire as being part of a routine circular to all Naval Attachés who might be able to piece together answers from people they met. Walter's task, as far as the Naval Attaché was concerned, was operational, acting as an intermediary in the defection of the whole or part of the Italian Fleet. Cordeaux's interest was in Intelligence and while poor Walter was probably rightly convicted for preparing to carry out illegal intelligence activity, he was not qualified to produce any results. His contacts in Italy would not be of much use as informants or intermediaries. None were allowed to leave Italy to testify in a Swedish Court in favour of Walter in the destroyer case, and had instead to swear affidavits before an Italian Court. He won his case against the Swedish Government for compensation for loss of his brokerage fee with the testimony of a very old and ill Fascist ex-General Sailer, his anti-Fascist son-in-law Naldi, who was Legal Adviser to the Swedish Consulate in Milan, his own lawyer Serrao and the Naval architect, Dr Carlo Ricciuti. None of these would seem to be likely conspirators and Amelie Posse's friends would not have achieved much against the omnipresence of the Abwehr agents, nor would Vittorio Gui who visited Sweden twice. Walter spoke of his contact in Italy with one Italian officer who represented twenty other dissident colleagues but did not specify who he was.

One must assume that, from a fairly early stage, Walter's chatty indiscretions on the telephone and in Denham's flat, which was bugged as were many others, had provided the Swedish police with a wealth of material to arouse their suspicions. And since it was well-known that Wagner, the Head of the Abwehr in Stockholm, was regularly informed by the Swedish security authorities, the Germans must have known enough to suspect the loyalty of their allies. They could, of course, also have suspected that much of the story was a plant in the great game of deception. I have referred to the fact that Walter thought the whole operation might have been taken over by the Americans who had concealed this from the British, but there is no evidence in Washington that this was the case.

I was told casually after the war that a party of three British Naval officers from NID, probably led by Commander Patrick Barrow Green, visited Italy to check up on the whole story. They were met with indignation by Italian officers who demanded compensation for their losses and the indignity they had suffered as a result of their participation in the plot. Although a report was written there is no trace in Foreign Office or Admiralty archives. There is intense interest in Italy in certain circles in protecting the honour of the Italian Navy and the reputation of individual officers suspected of treacherous intent. This school of thought has accused the British of a monstrous deception to shake the faith of the Germans in their Italian allies. There is some plausibility in this interpretation but there is no way in which we could have known whether Cordeaux had decided to make his contribution to the subversion of the Axis in this way. For security reasons we all worked in watertight compartments and had little or no idea of what others in our Legation were up to. SOE, with which I was involved, was not concerned with this operation. The lines of communication were between the Naval Attaché and the Admiralty and through the Minister to the Foreign Office. Cordeaux and his men worked on their own and now that he is dead we will be unlikely to know the truth.

As a postscript it is interesting to note that one of the black radios operated under the direction of Tom Sefton Delmer was Radio Livorno, which posed as representing the Italian Resistance broadcasting from the radio cabin of an Italian warship in Livorno harbour. Its programmes were closely co-ordinated with the Admiralty. It transmitted every night to the Italian Navy in the north Italian ports making it clearer and clearer that it was negotiating with the Allies for the liberation of the Italian Navy from the Germans. Randolf Imozzi, the Maltese/Italian speaker on the station, was convinced that it was his instructions that achieved the surrender of the Fleet to Cunningham. On the day the surrender was announced, he put on his best uniform and reported to Delmer that the Italian Navy had complied with his orders. There is no evidence that the Italian Navy ever heard the station but it may well have been monitored by the German and Italian Intelligence Services and contributed in some small way to what happened. Eden evidently thought it had played its part and sent a warm message of congratulation to Delmer.

We were convinced of Walter's honesty and courage. It may be that, with hindsight, we trusted him too much and that Cordeaux's attempt to check on his bona fides was a sensible move. The questionnaire was asking more than a most efficient master spy could possibly achieve in one short visit. One wonders whether it was not turned into a plot to disturb the special relationship between the Axis Powers. Finally, the Italian Fleet took refuge with the British but poor

Walter, who did his bit to bring this about, had to wait until the following year to have his sentence quashed. We heard no more of him except indirectly through Graffman who complained to our Legation in Stockholm after the war that Walter had been in Rome and been helped by the British in continuing to build up his case against him and the Swedish Government. He died on 27 August 1960 mourned by his widow and three married daughters, never having had any more contact with the British in Sweden.

One asks oneself sometimes whether, in fact, we were not being taken for a ride by Walter, the Italians or our own masters of deception who were using this operation to subvert the Fascist regime or enhance the nervousness of the Germans about their Italian allies. While Walter stood to gain if the operation succeeded, we judged him to be a courageous adventurer with a genuine commitment to the defeat of the Nazis and with a standard of business ethics no worse than that of most of his countrymen.

It would appear on the other hand that the operation might not have been a hoax, at least in the beginning. This is supported by the intense interest shown in the Public Record Office papers by past and present officers of the Italian Navy, politicians and others involved in the writing and re-writing of the history of this period, in the making and breaking of reputations of those involved. There may be evidence in Italy or Germany or the USA which has not yet been revealed.

## Footnote

For much of my information I am indebted to Captain Henry Denham, who was our Naval Attaché in Stockholm at the time, to the Public Records Office, to the Swedish State and Stockholm City Archives, and above all to Professor Alberto Santoni in Rome who has assiduously researched this story. (See his articles in *Storia Illustrata*, Mondadori, Milano, numbers 297 and 298 in August and September 1982.)

# XVI

## The Russians

The first Finnish war was not a time for getting to know the Russians. While at the beginning of the war Swedish opinion was split between sympathy and antipathy as far as Germany and the Nazis were concerned, their antipathy to the Russians was a national tradition having little to do with Communism. This antipathy was stimulated by the Russian attack on Finland, the earlier partition of Poland with the Nazis and Russia's swallowing up of the Baltic States. The statue of Charles XII on Kungsträdgården in Stockholm, pointed to Russia as the traditional enemy. It also pointed at the German legation a few hundred yards away behind the Grand Hotel. The Swedes were proud of the fact that their east Viking raids across Russia to Constantinople and the settlement of Novgorod had given birth to European Russia. The very name 'Russia' comes possibly from the Swedish eastern province of Roslagen which is perpetuated also in the Finnish word for Sweden 'Ruotsi'. There was even a Swedish tsar Carl Filip at one time for a short period. Centuries of trading and raiding ended with the disastrous wars of Charles XII and his successors with their loss of Finland and other territories. After the Napoleonic wars the Russian bogey was ever present. Before the First World War there was a widespread spy hysteria which was centred on the so-called Russian saw sharpeners. Mostly these probably were innocent journeymen, but were believed to have much more sinister intentions.

Spy mania was general in the years before and during the last war. Neutral patriotism was manifested in a suspicion of foreigners in general, which was not only reserved for Russians. The Finnish war dragged on without any sign of the country receiving effective help from the British and French in spite of numerous volunteers to add to the numbers of Swedes who joined up. The Swedish volunteer division amounted to some 12,000 men including about 700 Norwegians. Alexandra Kollontay, the Russian Ambassador who had a special relationship with Finland, played a leading part in bringing about the armistice on 13 March 1940. The Swedes helped to start the negotiations which had been blocked by the Russians' refusal to deal with any one except their own puppet Finnish government under Kuusinen.

Germany and Russia remained near allies up till 21 June 1941. Throughout this period there was an increasing buildup of German troops in Finland, a not unwelcome situation for the Finns who owed much of their independence from Russia in the 1917 Revolution to the intervention of the German trained Jägerbattalion.

The buildup of German forces on the Russian frontier continued throughout 1941 and intelligence on the German order of battle became more and more ample. So as not to blow our remarkable ultra sources, of which we were completely ignorant in Sweden, and presumably the same was the case with our Embassy in Moscow, the only messages passed to the Russians were from other first and secondhand sources in Sweden, Finland and Poland. None seemed to convince Stalin that the Germans were preparing an attack.

Early in June Sir Stafford Cripps, our Ambassador in Moscow, passed through Sweden with his wife and daughter on their way to London. I looked after Lady Cripps and the daughter by showing them round the Swedish co-operatives while Sir Stafford was subjected by our Minister, Victor Mallet, to an intensive programme of briefing on the intelligence picture as he saw it. Erik Boheman, Head of the Swedish Foreign Office, was also helpful in providing information. The Swedes at that time, until the Finnish Military Attaché blew the gaff to the Germans in 1942, were intercepting and decrypting German telecommunications with Norway, and Boheman gave Cripps the date of the German attack in June. He wrote to thank Boheman for this tip off. The Swedes had been decrypting the German Geheimschreiber messages since the autumn of 1940 thanks to the brilliant work of an Uppsala mathematician, Arne Beurling. Cripps believed till then that the

German buildup might be no more than blackmail to negotiate transit facilities to the Middle East in a pincer movement to meet Rommel. We hoped Cripps got a clear picture of reality as we saw it, but he alarmed us by showing extreme scepticism, assuring us he had seen Molotov a few days earlier who convinced him relations with the Germans were most cordial and rumours of an imminent attack were quite unfounded. We all believed that Cripps in fact was going to be replaced for having been ineffective and because Stalin despised his socialist philosophy.

He was sent back to Moscow with a great flurry of publicity as the man who had alerted Stalin to the imminence of a German attack. We were all most grateful for his generous presents of caviare. My tour of the Swedish co-operatives with Lady Cripps ended in disaster. In spite of her protests as a vegetarian, she was taken to see a new slaughterhouse and all the gory details were explained with statistical thoroughness.

The Germans attacked Russia on 22 June 1941 and the Russians became our allies overnight. It was a weird experience compounded by the fact that we then later declared war on Finland. No shots were exchanged and we all met again after the second armistice in 1944. It was hard to feel our Finnish friends were now on the wrong side and we could only meet very rarely by accident.

We met our opposite numbers and others in the Russian legation under the management of Alexandra Kollontay with her personal title of Soviet Ambassador in a country where, at that time, there were only legations with ministers as heads of mission. These meetings took place in our own homes and in crowded diplomatic parties. We made formal contact with our opposite numbers, mine being Madame Jartseva, an ample lady of the dimensions of Hattie Jacques but with straight dark hair parted in the middle with a bun, whose lips occasionally flickered into a smile. Her husband was the Commercial Counsellor, a decorous version of George Formby. We invited them home and tried without much success to mix them with our friends. I explained to Jartseva that our war-time alliance in no way changed my beliefs. These had been fortified by a visit to the Soviet Union in the early 1930's. I thought their form of society was a far cry from the concept of human freedom for which we were fighting. But I equally encouraged her to rely on me and Hellis for honest advice in their personal lives and their attitudes to the Swedes. I pointed out that Communist propaganda would meet with no

## The Russians

sympathy and that any attempt at subversion would be more than counterproductive. I encouraged them simply to put across human stories about the war, trials and tribulations, victories and defeats and matters of human interest which could be appreciated by ordinary people instead of the normal silly, heroic, Marxist claptrap. They gradually understood and we got to know them very well. She even one day took out a family photograph album when she invited Hellis to tea and it became clear that not only was she sad at being parted from her children but perplexed at being outsize by comparison with women in the West. She said she would love to have some pretty Swedish clothes but they were too small. After all she was Russian and Russian men liked big women. We took them sailing which they greatly enjoyed, even if they were hesitant at first. They relaxed over picnics and singing and drinking. Misha Kossov, the *Tass* representative who later had quite an important career, was a highly intelligent and amusing young man with great charm who made many friends in the newspaper world among foreign correspondents. But the Russians could not resist recruiting journalists for the KGB of which the Jartsevas were agents, especially among refugees such as Czechs and Poles. The Jartsevas left in 1944. After we had given them a farewell party, he asked to see me in my office. This he did and seemed so hesitant that I thought he was on the brink of defecting. I turned on my radio at which he smiled and then said very movingly to me 'You have been a good friend. You have been very kind when you need not have been and I am worried on your behalf. Everyone knows you do not like Communism and I fear that one day this may get you into trouble. I am going to be a very important person in the Ukraine and I want you to know that if ever I can help you I will. All you have to do is to mention my name.' I thanked him and he left but so far I have not had any occasion to take him up on his kind offer.

Our Naval Attaché, Henry Denham, contacted his Russian opposite number and found himself involved in a domestic tragedy. The Russian's wife and children were to be shipped out to join him. This involved a complicated journey through Turkey and round the Cape to Scotland where they were to do the last stage by air. Progress reports were shared on the journey. Then suddenly, after a ceremonious farewell from the official Russian Embassy chauffeur at Leuchars, whom we knew was an Admiral, the 'plane was shot down by the Germans. Our Russian colleague was overwhelmed with grief.

We did our best to console him but to no avail until one day he called on Henry in a state of extreme elation. 'Imagine what my people have done. Are they not good and kind.' Henry was puzzled and asked what had happened. 'They are sending me a new one by diplomatic bag. A new wife. Imagine how kind.' This they did duly packaged and labelled. Our colleague assured us that she was a most satisfactory substitute.

Vladimir Semjonov was the political head of the Soviet legation under Madame Kollontay. He played a part as a German expert in the months before the war in bringing about the Ribbentrop/Molotov Pact when he had been serving in the Russian Embassy in Berlin. He spent much time making propaganda for a second front in the West by organising leaks about secret Russo/German talks on a separate peace. Russian fears of Britain doing the same with Germany were enhanced by Stalin's obsessive suspicion that Hess's flight to Scotland on the night of 11-12 May 1941 was part of a British peace plot.

At the same time, with the Russian armies in full retreat in the summer of 1941, Peter Kleist of Ribbentrop's office reported that Kollontay was prepared to desert to the Nazis and buy herself a house in Germany if she could receive the necessary safe conduct. Whether the Germans believed this or not or whether the story had been concocted by their double agent Edgar Klaus, it seems that Canaris was sceptical and certainly anyone who knew Kollontay would have judged such behaviour entirely out of character. German rumours simultaneously directed at the Russians whispered indiscretions about a separate peace with the Western Allies in return for the elimination of Hitler and the Nazi regime. It is said that Edgar Klaus spoke to Peter Kleist on a visit to Stockholm in November 1942 after the German armies had been surrounded at Stalingrad. He let it be known that Semjonov and his chief, Alexandra Kollontay, were prepared to talk of peace on the basis of the Molotov/Ribbentrop frontiers agreed in 1939. These matters were allegedly discussed with three Germans in Stockholm in April 1943 by three Russians, Nikitin, Taradin and my friend Jartsev.

Semjonov has done well and through his Stockholm friendship with Willy Brandt and Bruno Kreisky, also close friends of ours as refugees, he has played his part in detente politics, German Ostpolitik, SALT and MBFR and finally as Ambassador in Bonn, where he played his beloved Beethoven looking out over the moonlit

Rhine. He opposed NATO by further detente manoeuvres and proposals for a reunification of the two Germanies in one neutral buffer state between East and West. He is a soft-spoken, pale, moon-faced man with a deep appreciation of the arts but he feared anything later than the 19th century romantics as decadent, 'entartet' and politically dangerous. I am told that he has now changed and that his flat in Moscow is full of quite good modern pictures from the West.

The outstanding personality in the Russian legation and in the Diplomatic Corps in Stockholm was Alexandra Kollontay (1872 - 1952). She always had a special involvement with Scandinavia, whether as a revolutionary agitator or as Ambassador to Norway and later Sweden. She spoke a fluent, broken mixture of all the Scandinavian languages. Her liberal-minded family in the days before the Revolution had, like many Russians living in Petersburg, a summer holiday house in Finland, then a Grand Duchy of Tsarist Russia. Her family home was at Kuusa which her mother inherited from Alexandra's Finnish grandfather and her close involvement with Finland explained the initiative she took in the two Finnish wars with Russia to bring about peace. But she failed to soften the very hard terms of the final peace treaty. Her father was General Domontovitch, a well-to-do middle class professional man. She was devoted to her family and contracted a very conventional marriage with Vladimir Kollontay, an engineer, with whom she had one son Mischa. He used to visit her in Stockholm with her grandson. Her marriage broke up as a result of her feminist and revolutionary activities. After many passionate love affairs she married a much younger man, a sailor, Dybenko, from the fleet at Helsinki. This marriage finally came to an end as well. Dybenko made a great reputation as a military commander and remained the passion of her life, hurting her by his fierce repression of the Kronstadt rebellion and his death sentence on Tukachevsky in 1937, only himself to be executed in Stalin's last purges.

She always said she became a Communist and revolutionary after visiting a factory where child labour was being exploited and several children died every day. There were many apocryphal stories about her, how she murdered her father and how she ran away with Lenin, none of which were true. Lenin made her his first Minister for Social Welfare. She was active in Russia and in international affairs abroad, ending up as Ambassador to Norway and in 1930 to Sweden. When she presented her credentials to King Gustav V, driving to the

Royal Palace in the seven paned ceremonial coach, she was still under the expulsion order of 1914 which was preceded by her sojourn in Malmö prison. She used to revel in describing the conditions in various countries where she had been shut up. She would regale diplomatic dinner parties with descriptions of vermin infestation, bad sanitation and putrid food, claiming that Sweden, with its passion for clinical cleanliness, was the worst.

King Gustav was awkward in his reception of this revolutionary duchess and for small talk he asked her what King Haakon of Norway said when she called on him. He said 'Madam would you not like to sit down', which she promptly did. The dark head of hair of her youth had turned to pepper and salt, her body shrunk, wrinkled with age and poor health but she was still full of sparkle and humour. She was imperious in her treatment of her legation officials and was used by the Soviet Government as a teacher for Russians who would have to be posted abroad and pass themselves off as civilised and well-mannered pin striped people. One day when Harold Nicolson was on a lecture visit to Stockholm, I took him to lunch with her and below the salt there were a dozen or so trainees. She totally ignored them except when she would interrupt a conversation and shout 'Ivan, you must not eat peas off your knife' or 'Igor, stop making that disgusting noise with your soup' and then would continue talking to us as though the serfs did not exist. She told Harold that she used his book *Diplomacy* as essential reading for her courses in international behaviour. It interested him because Maisky, the Russian Ambassador in London, had asked him for fifty copies and that was all that Harold heard of his book. Alexandra Kollontay said 'Yes, we translated it and printed an edition of 100,000 copies'. 'But what of my royalties?' asked Harold. 'You will have to use them up in roubles in Russia' she said 'and besides you may not have any at all as it is probably classified as educational common property which must not be commercialised.'

I met her first at one of her Diplomatic receptions. She said she had heard of me through Jartseva, that I disliked Communism but was a helpful ally. 'I must see more of you,' she continued, and this she did. I was often invited round to little family lunches with the serfs. She chatted on most amusingly about life in Russia, about her sister and her parrot and their incredible experiences in the German siege of Leningrad.

She was a friend of Zhdanov, Stalin's crown prince whom he later murdered, the commissar in command in Leningrad. He was posted to Finland as Head of the Armistice Commission. I like to think she may have briefed him before he went. He got on very well with the Finns and on arrival said a few words in Finnish to the guard of honour meeting him at Helsinki airport. He would often wander round Helsinki unprotected, visiting workers' homes to see how they lived and was much impressed. He and Field Marshal Mannerheim, who was considered a war criminal by the Russians, became firm friends. They used to sit up late at night while Mannerheim told Zdanov about life at the Court of the Tsars. One evening Zdanov offered him the post of Marshal of the Diplomatic Corps in Moscow with a guarantee of reprieve. He described how Molotov's new year reception of the Diplomatic Corps was unworthy of a great power such as the USSR. The diplomats had been drawn up in two rows, Molotov came in with two Field Marshals loaded like white knights with jeroboams of Caucasian champagne, each with a bouquet of glasses in the other hand. When they had run the gauntlet of the foreign diplomats, the Field Marshals took the bottles between their knees, uncorked them and then shuffled down the rows filling the guests' glasses. Mannerheim laughed and politely declined Zdanov's invitation.

At one of Kollontay's lunches she suddenly dumped two large volumes on the table beside me.

> Send one to your Government and spell your way through the other yourself. It will help you with your Russian. But I want you to do more because it is very important. It is the Soviet Government's official report on education. For many years we have examined educational systems in the world and have come to the conclusion that your private education is the best and that the best of the public schools is Eton. So we want to set up replicas of Eton all over Russia and at the same time not continue with the sentimental nonsense of co-education.

These were wry remarks for a passionate feminist.

> So I want you to get someone in England, someone with a name, to write an informative article about Eton College, Windsor, which you can print in your propaganda paper in Russia *Britanski Soyuznik*. We will let you have a print order of 200,000 copies which we will guarantee to distribute to every schoolteacher in Russia.

I thanked her, knowing the difficulties we always had with the Russian authorities to get any circulation at all, however much self-censorship we imposed on ourselves. I wanted to know why on earth they had come to such a conclusion. She explained

> You have much to learn. You have never been a secret Russian agent outside Russia dependent on couriers and wireless transmissions which are always intercepted. We want to educate people like Pavlov dogs as you do in your public schools so that they know how to act in isolation and without any communication. You have run the biggest Empire in the world with very few people. They are products of the public school conditioned reflex. They can be in the depths of the Sudan or the Punjab, dress for dinner every night, quell riots or administer justice in an endless variety of circumstances without any cumbersome reference to headquarters. I would never have been caught and jailed as many times as I have been if I had been to a British public school. But I suppose in any case it would have been Roedean or Cheltenham. We are going to embark on this great experiment.

I said I found it very interesting and that there was something in what she said, but I pointed out that while the British public schools did produce Pavlov dogs to some extent the result was to teach self-reliance and individual initiative, which did not seem to me to fit in with Communism. 'Oh, you and your Communism,' she replied. 'Just do as I ask you as a friend.'

So I sent off the book and the message and a short while later flew to London. I saw the people in the Ministry of Information who assured me this interesting proposition was in hand and being dealt with. Some weeks later, back in Stockholm, I had a telephone call. It was Kollontay. She seethed with anger. 'What have you done? I thought you were a friend. Come round and see me immediately.' So I faced my grand duchess in trepidation. 'How can you do a thing like that. You have made a fool of me.' I was puzzled and asked what it was. 'Oh, how typically British, careless, insensitive lackadaisical. Don't you really know.' 'No,' I said. 'Well,' she replied, 'you remember the article about Eton I asked you to arrange for your propaganda paper. We cannot possibly print it. It is an insult. It makes fun of Eton and is written by some parlour pink left-winger call Stephen Spender. Your propaganda paper will probably be suppressed as a result and we shall continue to follow through our policy of Etonising our education system without you'. I apologised and thought as I left I saw a slight twinkle of mirth in her furious eyes. What actually happened? I am told that experiments were made in Russia, that some co-educational schools were broken up and the boys were put into something more resembling tsarist cadet schools than Eton while Roedeans and Cheltenhams were planned. These attempts were not followed through as they might have undermined the privileged hierarchy of Communist society. Kollontay was the last of the old Bolsheviks to die a natural death a year before Stalin. Finally, after the strain of the second Finnish Treaty negotiations, she was crippled by the worst of a series of strokes, left Stockholm and lived in a wheelchair till her death in Moscow in 1952. Finland can probably thank her to some extent for the peace terms not being worse than they were.

**Footnote**

The Finnish Jägerbattalion came into being officially in 1917 as the '27th Royal Prussian Jägerbatallion'. It consisted of young Finns, mostly students who had first made contact with the Germans after the outbreak of war in 1914 appealing for weapons and training to help in a war of liberation from Russia. The Germans agreed to help and in February 1915 the first contingent of Finns made their way to Germany. The Jägerbatallion played a useful part in the defeat of the Red Army in Finland.

# XVII
## The British Council

When I went to Sweden at the end of September 1939, the British Council asked if I would handle their cultural business alongside that of the Ministry of Information and the Foreign Office. For a long while they kept me well supplied with photographs and articles which the Ministry of Information failed to do.

My employers agreed I should work for them and I did my best. It was not too difficult and I got the help of a Mr Charlesworth, a lecturer in the Swedish Workers Educational Organisation which covered the whole of Sweden (Arbetarnas Bildningsförbund). I had contacts in Stockholm's Högskola, the predecessor of the present university, and I made my number in the Universities of Uppsala and Lund. We ran a cultural shop window in Stockholm with books and photographs but had no separate office. In due course I found it difficult to combine my information activity with the work of lectures for the Council. In 1941, when I visited London, I asked them to send out a representative. They agreed but suggested I should find one. I put up a friend of mine from Cambridge, Ronald Bottrall, a poet with some experience as a lecturer in Finland. He was languishing from boredom as a Principal in the Ministry of Aircraft Production. He was immediately hired and he and his charming wife Margaret flew out to Sweden. The Swedes found it difficult to accept this giant who looked more like a retired boxer with his broken nose, than an emissary of British culture. They were convinced for a time that he was the Head of the Secret Service just as was the case with the

French Cultural Attaché who represented the Deuxième Bureau. They also confused the British Council with the British Consul. Ronald did a superb job and we all gave him as much support as we could. He worked with Swedish writers and together with Gunnar Ekelöf, one of the foremost Swedish poets of the period, produced a translation of some of T.S. Eliot's poetry.

The cost effectiveness and cost benefits of the British Council are continuously a matter of debate and it has suffered as the whipping boy of the Treasury and of the *Daily Express*, particularly in the days of Lord Beaverbrook. But it has survived. There are ways in which its effectiveness can be measured but they are often not sufficiently convincing for the Treasury or for Parliament who make a virtue of cutting expenditure by measuring the cost and rarely the value of an undertaking. The value of the British Council in projecting the image of British life abroad provides a strong foundation for our policies in many other fields.

In Sweden during the war we had one example of a benefit which must have saved thousands of lives. On 18 July 1944, Victor Mallet, our Minister, drove the Swedish Minister for Foreign Affairs, Christian Günther, to Sigtuna to attend a British Council event at a summer school for teachers where they were having their last night concert and supper. On the way Victor tackled Günther about the V2 rocket which had landed in Southern Sweden. The experts in Farnborough had asked to be allowed to fly it home for a thorough inspection. Mallet pointed out the carnage these ghastly weapons might wreak among the civilian population even though we were over-running at that time the launching sites of the far less formidable V1s. Victor writes in his unpublished memoirs

> Günther said he would have to think about my request but refused to make a decision. At the Summer school Ronald Bottrall laid on an admirable concert of Elizabethan songs and madrigals ending with a very congenial supper. On the way back Günther said he had been much moved by the music and the happy atmosphere of this Anglo-Swedish school. It had made him reflect on the subject of the bomb and he had decided that it would not be right for him to deprive us of the opportunity of counteracting such a

devilish weapon which might be used to destroy thousands of innocent British civilian lives. I might telegraph to the Foreign Office and say that we could take it away as long as this was done with the greatest secrecy. The next day the bomb was collected and flown home.

Victor tells how a few days after the end of the war, Air Marshal Lord Tedder flew from Copenhagan to Stockholm with the object of personally thanking General Nordenskiöld, the Head of the Swedish Airforce, for the great help he had given us in this matter by immediately telling our Air Attaché of the extraordinary find the Swedes had made.

'Years afterwards,' Victor wrote, 'I reminded Mr Günther (they were then both colleagues as Head of their missions in Rome) of our talks on the way back from Sigtuna and of the momentous decision which he had taken then. I said to him "Your decision was something of which you can always be proud". The dear modest man merely answered "Not proud but thankful".'

Many of us felt that Günther was miscast as Foreign Minister, but we have reason to be thankful to him for this decision and to the British Council for its contribution. The cost to Britain would have been incalculable if the decision had not been made.

# XVIII
# Visitors

Up till Sweden's encirclement by the German occupation of Norway and Denmark in April 1940, there were regular air services and we received many visitors, many of them on their way to or from Finland during the Russo/Finnish war. The heroic performance of the Finns attracted great support in Britain and hundreds of volunteers crossed Sweden into Finland in the hope of fighting for them, or offering their services as a fire brigade or the quaker ambulance unit. Philip Noel-Baker came and went and Malcolm Lilliehöök, who was a friend of his and of Lionel Curtis of the Round Table and supporter of the League of Nations Association, was arrested by the Swedish Security Police as a dangerous allied agent. It must not be forgotten that at that time the Germans were the allies of the Russians and the Sicherheitsdienst was active in support of the Swedish Security Services.

A Trade Union delegation passed through and this was my first meeting with Walter Citrine whose friendship and wise counsel I valued for the rest of his long life. Later in the war we got to know many other British Trades Unionists, one of which was Arthur Deakin who was helpful to me in my subsequent incarnations in industry. Another visitor during the Finnish war was Harold MacMillan (Lord Stockton) and I spent some time briefing him on the conflict between Swedish government caution about involvement in hostilities and public opinion which, in many cases, was prepared to enter the lists against their traditional enemy the Russians. The issue was, of course, complicated by the British and French governments seeing the Finnish war as a useful pretext for the transit of troops through northern Norway and Sweden to Finland and thereby giving us the opportunity of incidentally immobilising the vital supply of Swedish iron ore to Germany. The issue came to a head at the time of the Finnish armistice on 12 March 1940 when both governments refused our requests. The armistice eliminated the pretext and prevented us from finding ourselves at war with Russia.

With the invasion of Norway and Denmark the flow of visitors came to an end for a while, but we started up a special service towards the end of 1940, first with very slow aircraft with low capacity, graduating to larger and larger machines, such as Witleys and Liberators which were supplemented by a very fast service of Mosquitos. These did the journey to Leuchars in about two hours with a single passenger sitting in the bomb bay instead of the eight hours or so in cold and discomfort in the larger planes.

We had official visitors such as Charles Hambro (Sir Charles), Harry Sporborg, Mike Wheeler (Sir Charles) and Ted Senior (Sir Edward) from MEW, Steel Control and SOE who came over in connection with George Binney's expeditions and the War Trade Agreement. Then there were our BBC friends such as Margaret Sampson who ran the excellent Swedish Service and our bosses in the Ministry of Information who later moved to SOE, George Wiskeman whose sister, Elizabeth, became famous for her intelligence work in Switzerland and Euan Rabagliati. George was a director of the timber merchants, Price and Pearce, who had considerable interests in Finland, and earlier in Russia. Nearly all the Finnish experts taken on by our Government had been employed by Price and Pearce in Finland where they learned the rare Finnish language working in the forests and sawmills, such as Rex Bosley and Seamus McGill (later Colonel). Ewan Rabagliati was a man of incredible courage who had been in the Royal Flying Corps in the First World War and had taken to motor racing and driving the famous Chichi-Bang-Bang racing car at Brooklands. He had an accident on the banked corner at Brooklands at full speed, his co-driver and mechanic was killed and Ewan was left for dead with his skull cut open. He was found to be alive, was patched up but remained unconscious in hospital for two weeks. Then he suddenly woke up, ordered a bottle of champagne and walked out to continue his adventurous life. The Ministry of

Information was not sufficient challenge though we greatly enjoyed bouncing ideas off him. He moved on to try and clean up the SOE disaster in Holland where the enemy had disposed of some sixty of our agents.

There were other visitors who were kept under wraps, such as the great scientist, Sir William Bragg, who stayed quietly at the Legation for a month and Bishop George Bell of Chichester who, in June 1942, covered his tracks by overt visits to Archbishop Eidem and others. The real purpose of his visit was to meet secretly in Sigtuna, through Dr Manfred Björkquist, the courageous German pastor Bonhoeffer. In collaboration with Adam von Trott he put to Bell the need for the allies to give the German resistance some hope that if they got rid of Hitler the country would not receive the same treatment as a Hitler Germany. Bell got the support of Stafford Cripps who forwarded his memorandum to Eden, but the British government would not countenance any negotiations. Herbert Waddams visited us as a church diplomat with deep insight into world affairs.

Our favourite visitors were those who came to perform publicly. There was Malcolm Sargent who swept the board with his flamboyant conducting and wit. Furtwängler sent a message through Swedish friends asking if they could meet but it was strictly forbidden. There was Sir William Holford, the architect, and Sir Walter Monckton who had only recently read his own obituary in *The Times* when his Russian aircraft got lost on its way from Tehran to Moscow. A very secret meeting was arranged by Ivar Andersson, the Editor of *Svenska Dagbladet* for him to see von Trott but there are no records of what passed. Kenneth Clark (later Lord Clark) did not enjoy Sweden which he regarded as a cultural wasteland but he made some startling discoveries of fake Turners in the Swedish National Gallery and elsewhere in private collections. Harold Nicolson spoke brilliantly on current affairs and was so impressed with the pro-allied sympathies of the Swedes that he congratulated me on having landed a sinecure. There was T.S. Eliot whose *Waste Land* had been translated by my old teacher, Erik Mesterton, the Swedish lector in London.

But perhaps the visitor one remembers most was Barbara Ward. She tripped out of the sky into Stockholm in bandbox condition and charmed all she met by her intelligence, her elegance and her humour. At that time she was writing for *The Economist* and I did a business deal with her to print it in Stockholm every week. Over and above its Swedish sales, copies reached occupied Europe and Germany. Her reputation spread throughout Europe by her writings and broadcasts with their deep humanity, wisdom and lack of any tub-thumping propaganda. We all fell in love with her and were bewitched by the personality of this beautiful young woman and her gentle voice, clear mind and bubbly sense of fun which could switch to a deep mood of tragedy at man's inhumanity to man.

The American film magnate Stanton Griffis visited Sweden to stop Swedish iron-ore and ball-bearing shipments to Germany. In the end, with a mixture of threats and cajolery, the Swedes reluctantly gave way, deeply resenting the un-British behaviour of this brash American. Carl Jensen, the American Press Attaché, once asked me to help two Americans whom we christened Tweedledum and Tweedledee, Messrs Acheson and Lowe of the *Reader's Digest*. They were a mixture of medical missionaries and christian evangelists who believed in the mission of their publication to make a better world and a healthy profit at the same time. They wanted help in publishing in Sweden and preparations for publication in the adjacent occupied countries and Germany after the war. I gave them introductions in the world of printing, publishing and distribution and found them candidates as editorial managers for the enterprise.

There were prisoners of war who escaped, whose courage was humiliating to civilians like us enjoying the fleshpots of Sweden. I will never forget the delightful young Naval Lieutenant Evans whose MTB had been sunk off Ijmuiden. He escaped from his camp with an impressive copperplate letter addressed to the German naval authorities in English from the Royal Bulgarian Navy introducing him as Lieutenant U Buggeroff whose mission was to study the German convoy system in the Baltic. Dressed in his Royal Navy uniform he escaped and then was entertained by one German naval mess after another along the Baltic coast until he reached Stettin and was caught trying to get away on a Swedish freighter. He was returned to camp and punished with solitary confinement, but escaped again and this time made it by clinging on to the bogeys of a railway truck that was crossing on a ferry to Sweden. There were others from Stalag Luft III whose stories have all been told. Of course the bulk of our 'visitors' were refugees from Norway and Denmark with whom we came in touch at all levels, sailors, workmen, peasants, university and school teachers, doctors, writers, clergy, lawyers, musicians and painters. Most of them wanted us to get them to England but we only had capacity for very few either on our aircraft or blockade-busting ships. Perhaps the most distinguished 'visitor' of all was Professor Niels Bohr, the Danish atomic scientist. He was smuggled over from Denmark in great secrecy and finally flown over to England by Mosquito. But his head was too big for the intercom earphones to communicate with the pilot and since the pilot got no response he feared his precious passenger had died from lack of oxygen, until on arrival at Leuchars he was found unconscious but smiling, in spite of the panic his outsize brainbox had caused.

The arrival of the messenger from the outer world has been a dramatic convention for unravelling the plot since ancient times in the theatre. In our isolation in Sweden at that time, these messengers helped to stimulate us into new activity. The Swedes welcomed them as a breath of fresh air in their somewhat claustrophobic isolation.

# XIX
## Epilogue

In December 1944, in the middle of the Ardennes offensive, I was summoned to Paris by our ambassador, Duff Cooper, to look me over as a candidate for the job of Press Attaché - now with the more portentous title of Information Counsellor. He decided to take me on and I left Sweden with my family on 3 March 1945. There was far too little time to say our good-byes to hundreds of kind friends and the days were spent packing and fitting in farewell parties. The press was full of articles about me, mostly friendly, except for one in my old enemy *Aftonbladet* which I treasure as a testimony to the success of my activities.

Hellis and the three children were bundled into flying suits, swaddled in parachute harness and packs, garlanded with Mae Wests and each equipped with the regulation whistle and red light to attract attention if we dropped in the North Sea. Hellis clung on to the little one Suzie who was only two and a half and unlikely to be able to handle the parachute rip-cord on her own. We took off from Bromma at 11 p.m. Swedish time and arrived at Leuchars at 7.15 a.m. English time to begin a new phase of our lives. In a way it was sad not to be in at the kill in Sweden with the defeat of the Nazis together with that select band of old friends who belonged to the pre-Alamein Swedes. They sent me sheaves of telegrams and letters in Paris and made me feel very homesick. The end of the war in France was celebrated with parades but not with the same wild enthusiasm with which they had greeted the liberation.

Never having seen the end of the war in Sweden, I could only rely on personal accounts and the press. The tensions of the war were released in scenes of wild exultation. The motives behind these scenes were various. There was relief at no longer having to be neutral. Neutrality does not make the adrenalin run. Our pre-Alamein friends were relieved as there were times when their confidence in allied victory hung on their faith in the rightness of our cause while all the dice seemed loaded against us. Our old allies were swept aside by new ones who overwhelmed us with their enthusiasm, in spite of years of sullen non-committal or support for the Nazis. A friend of mine sat behind the King at the thanksgiving service to celebrate the end of the war. The old man slept for most of the time with his head on the shoulder of his A.D.C. Suddenly he woke up and exclaimed 'Where is the elk. Give me my gun'. He was already verging on senility but perhaps this incident subconsciously showed how little he appreciated what the war was about. His son the Crown Prince and later King Gustav VI Adolf redeemed all his father's failings, a man of outstanding character and among many attainments a world-renowned archaeologist.

In the years since the war many attempts have been made to draw up a balance sheet. The Sandler Commission did much to clean the stables, to reveal the perversions of justice and the activities of the security services which were heavily biased in favour of the Nazis. But it is not to be forgotten that the Security Services operated under the orders of their masters, the government and the legal department of the Swedish Foreign Office.

The Swedish government issued documents to justify their concessions to the Germans on the transit traffic. It was only after many years that the British government agreed to the Swedes publishing the telegram from their Minister Prytz in London on 17 June 1940, describing his conversation with Rab Butler which led them to believe that we were prepared to do a deal with Hitler and thereby gave them the justification for conceding the German demands for the transit traffic. It was an awkward interlude in our war record.

While the Air Force was pro-allied and the army's morale rose with its readiness to fend off aggression, it took long for the navy to abandon its pro-nazi sympathies. We failed to stop Swedish exports of iron ore and ballbearings to Germany till the last year of the war. These exports were written into the War Trade Agreements endorsed by us at the beginning of the war when we had failed by sabotage and other means to put an end to this strategic trade.

Swedish neutrality was an act of survival carried out successfully by a small cadre of highly competent officials and two merchant banker brothers who resisted every attempt by the belligerents to lure them into the war on their side. Churchill pointed out to Boheman the advantage of joining the allies in the last stage of the war, but Boheman replied that Sweden could play a more important part in helping to repair the ravages of occupation and terror on her Scandinavian neighbours and other occupied countries when the war was over. This part she played in full measure.

Sweden's role was a somewhat inglorious one in World War II but her neutrality was an advantage to both the allies and the Nazis as she provided a backdoor view of what was going on in the other man's kitchen and for us to give what help we could to the resistance to German occupation. Sweden certainly suffered for some time for her wartime policies and took a back seat in international counsels. But for those of us on the allied side who lived in Sweden during the war, a country in which the Germans had a head start with all their preparations for subversion and propaganda well before the war began, it was a matter of great satisfaction to see the defeat of all these evil schemes and the victory of free speech and parliamentary democracy. Our activities played no small part in building up a spirit of resistance to Nazi domination.

# Who's Who

Adlercreutz, Colonel Carlos. Head of Swedish Defence Staff Intelligence.
Åkerberg, Harald. Editor. Member, Foreign Affairs Committee. Approached Walter on purchase of Italian warships for Sweden.
Alexander, George. H.M.V. representative in Stockholm who joined the Press Department of the British Legation and became broadcasting officer.
Andersson, Ivar. Editor of *Svenska Dagbladet*. Conservative Deputy.
Badoglio, Marshal Pietro. Head of first anti-fascist government in Italy.
Balfour, Michael. On planning staff of shadow Ministry of Information, friend of Moltke, joined Political Warfare Executive.
Beck, Colonel-General Ludwig. Arrested with Stauffenberg, attempted suicide and finished off with *coup de grâce*.
Bell, Bishop George of Chichester, who visited Bonhoeffer in Sweden.
Bernadotte, Count Folke. Deputy Chairman, Swedish Red Cross.
Beurling, Professor Arne of Uppsala who, in 1940, constructed a machine to decrypt the German Geheimschreiber.
Biggs, Ernest. Advertising Manager of the department store P.U.B. Gaoled in Rickman affair.
Binney, Sir George. Arctic explorer and representative of the British Steel Industry in Sweden. Broke the German blockade with convoys of merchant ships, motor coasters and aircraft.
Björnstjerna, Colonel Carl. Dismissed from intelligence post on Swedish General Staff for passing information on German naval movements to British Naval Attaché Denham.
Blücker, Captain Ivar. Chief of Gothenburg harbour police, dismissed for helping Binney.
von Bock, Field-Marshal Fedor. Rejected participation in coup against Hitler.
Boheman, Erik. Secretary General, Swedish Ministry of Foreign Affairs.

Bohr, Professor Niels. Danish atomic scientist smuggled out of Denmark and flown to England.
Boldt-Christmas, Captain Emil. Anti-nazi former Swedish Naval Attaché in London.
Bonhoeffer, Pastor Dietrich. Met Bishop Bell of Chichester in Sweden. Executed for his part in Stauffenberg plot.
Bonnier. Jewish Swedish publishing family and owners of *Dagens Nyheter*.
Bottrall, Ronald. Head of British Council, Stockholm.
Brandt, Willy (Karl Frahm). German refugee in Norway and Sweden. Later Chancellor of German Federal Republic.
Brewer, George E. Jnr. Office of Strategic Services American Legation.
Brilioth, Börje. Pro-Nazi editor of *Stockholms Tidningen*.
Bull, Francis. Professor of Literature, Oslo University.
Butler, Major Ewan. Head of Stockholm Special Operations Executive German section.
Butler, R.A. (later Lord). Under-Secretary of State at the Foreign Office under Lord Halifax.
Canaris, Admiral Wilhelm. Head of Abwehr, executed for complicity in plot against Hitler.
Carlgren, Professor Wilhelm. Archivist and historian of Swedish Ministry of Foreign Affairs.
Carlsson, Gunnar. Swedish ship-owner.
Carr, H.L. Passport Control Officer, Helsinki till 1941, British Legation Stockholm 1941-45.
Christian X. King of Denmark.
Coleridge, Peter. Vice-consul Gothenburg involved with blockade-running.
Collier, Sir Laurence. Foreign Office Northern Department, Minister to Norway.
Cordeaux, Colonel J.K. Marine officer first with Admiralty then Foreign Office; visited Stockholm on Italian Navy affair.
Cripps, Sir Stafford. British Ambassador in Moscow and later Chancellor of the Exchequer.
Croft, Colonel Andrew. Arctic explorer and assistant Military Attaché in support of Special Operations Executive.
Cronstedt, Count Otto. Formerly Swedish businessman in London

who headed Ministry of Foreign Affairs Press Bureau in Grand Hotel.

Dahlerus, Birger. Industrialist and peace broker. Cousin of Goering's first wife who was Swedish.

Danielsson, Otto. Police inspector and spycatcher.

Dehlgren, Sten. Editor *Dagens Nyheter*.

Delmer, Tom Sefton. Journalist and head of 'black' radio stations at Woburn.

Demaitre, Edmond (Demeter Ödon, Edward Masterman). Hungarian refugee correspondent of *Daily Express*.

Denham, H.M. Captain R.N., British Naval Attaché.

Denniston, Commander Alastair. One of cipher breakers of Room 40 in World War I; ran training programme for cypher breaking in World War II and set up cypher-breaking operation at Bletchley.

Ehrensvärd, General Carl August. Chief of General Staff in last year of war.

Enander Dr Bo. Historian, broadcaster, journalist, editor of weekly *Nu* and co-founder of Nordens Frihet.

Erlander, Tage. Minister of State and later Prime Minister.

Eugen, Prince. King Gustav's brother. Painter and anti-nazi.

Fagerlund, Adolf. Chairman Karl Setterwall and Company AB. Appointed by Binney to represent British steelmakers.

Falk, Peter. Rugby master who went to Sweden to handle German affairs for Secret Intelligence Service.

von Falkenhorst, General Nikolaus. German C in C Norway.

Fellenius, Emy. My mother-in-law. Walloon family (Janse) from north Sweden.

Fellenius, Hellis. My first wife. Daughter of Professor Wolmar and Emy Fellenius.

Fellenius, Professor Wolmar. My father-in-law. Professor of hydraulic engineering at Stockholms Tekniska Högskola.

Fitzwilliam, Lord, alias Peter Lawrence. One of George Binney's chief officers on the motor coasters.

Fraser, Ingram. Advertising agent (J. Walter Thompson) employed on sabotage by Sir William Stevenson.

Fuchs, Walter. Head of M.G.M. Stockholm.

Gerhard, Karl. Actor, impressario and author of popular revues and of the Trojan Horse sketch in his musical *Gullregn*.

Goerdeler, Karl. Former mayor of Leipzig and opposition leader executed for complicity in Stauffenberg coup.

Goering, Hermann. German Marshal whose first wife was Swedish.

Goulding, Ossian. Correspondent of *Daily Telegraph* with Irish passport. Married to Yasuko Tamm, daughter of Japanese mother and Swedish Naval Attaché in Tokyo.

Gow, Janet. Assistant to Ewan Butler of Special Operations Executive German section.

Graffman, Holger. Chairman of AB Transfer, a company owned by the Wallenbergs. Swedish government negotiator for purchase of Italian warships in competition with J.H. Walter.

Grafström, Sven. Swedish diplomat who ran Swedish Government Press Office in Grand Hotel with Count Otto Cronstedt.

Grassman, Dr Paul. German Press Attaché.

Griffis, Stanton. Film magnate and U.S. negotiator on ball-bearing issue.

Gubbins, General Sir Colin. Head of Special Operations Executive after Hambro.

Günther, Christian. Swedish Foreign Minister from 1939 to end of war.

Gustaf Adolf, Crown Prince, later King of Sweden. Married to Mountbatten's sister, Princess Louise.

Gustav V. King of Sweden.

Haakon VII. King of Norway.

Hägglöf, Gunnar. Head of Foreign Ministry trade department, Minister to Belgian and Dutch governments in London, and later Swedish Ambassador in London.

Hagman, Captain Torsten. Commander of convoy of four Italian destroyers from Italy to Sweden detained by the British in the Faroes.

Halder, General. Deputy Chief of German General Staff who succeeded Beck as Chief of General Staff 1942. Arrested for complicity in Stauffenberg coup.

Hallamaa, Colonel. Head of Finnish G.C.H.Q. who with his staff took refuge in Sweden at the end of the war.

Hallgren, Eric Salomon. Head of security service till 1943. Chief of police Stockholm 1930, deputy governor 1937.

Hamberg, Harald. Director of S.K.F. Swedish negotiator over ball-

bearing exports to Germany.
Hambro, Sir Charles. Banker, trade negotiator, first Head of Special Operations Executive.
Hansson, Johan (Kulturjohan). Anti-nazi owner of publishing house Natur och Kultur.
Hansson, Per Albin. Swedish Prime Minister.
Hedin, Sven. Explorer, pro-nazi jew.
Henriksen, Alva. Assistant to Kjellberg of Ellerman Wilson Line in support of our blockade running.
Hewins, Ralph. *Daily Mail* correspondent.
Himmler, Heinrich. Head of Gestapo and Sicherheitsdienst.
Hinks, Roger. Art historian. Worked for Special Operations Executive and Political Warfare Executive. Contact with von Moltke and von Trott.
Höglund, Zeth. Social democrat editor and politician.
von Horn, Major Carl. Handled exchange of British and German P.O.Ws. Later General commanding U.N. troops in Middle East and Zaire.
Howe, Sir Ronald. Chief Constable C.I.D. 1932. Asst. Commissioner C.I.D. 1945-53.
Hudson Robert. British Trade Minister.
Ironside, Field-Marshal Edmund. C in C Norway. Had commanded allied intervention forces in North Russia in 1919.
Jacobsen, Dr Walter. German refugee psychologist introduced by Professor Katz as contact with German resistance.
Järte, Otto. Foreign editor of *Svenska Dagbladet*.
Jartsev, Boris. Head of commercial department, Soviet legation. K.G.B. (NKVD)
Jartseva, Alexandra. Soviet Press Attaché. Wife of Boris Jartsev. K.G.B. (NKVD)
Jensen, Karl. United States Press Attaché.
Johnson, Herschel. U.S. Minister followed Sterling in Stockholm. Formerly in London.
Juhlin-Dannfelt, Colonel Curt. Swedish Military Attaché Berlin and later head of Swedish intelligence service.
Jung, General Helge. C in C Sweden after Thörnell.
Katz, Professor of Psychology, Stockholms Technical High School. German refugee. Collaborated with Söderman on criminology and

introduced me to Dr Jacobsen of the German resistance.
Kendall, Sir Norman. Assistant Commissioner C.I.D. 1928-45.
Kenney, Rowland. Press attaché Norway in both world wars. In between in Foreign Office Press Department.
Kersten, Dr Felix. Physiotherapist who treated Himmler.
Kimmins, Commander Tony. Visited Sweden for première of *In Which We Serve*.
Kjellberg, William. Head of Ellerman Wilson Line, Gothenburg.
Knapp-Fisher, Jim. Publisher who handled books and films in Press Department. Contact with Moltke and Trott.
Kollontay, Alexandra. Soviet Ambassador, Stockholm.
Krämer, Dr Karl Heinz. Abwehr 'secretary' German Legation. Centre of Josephine affair.
Kreisky, Bruno. Austrian refugee and later Chancellor of Austria.
Kreuger, Torsten. Brother of Ivar the swindler. Pro-German proprietor of *Stockholms-Tidningen* and *Aftonbladet*.
Kuusinen, Otto Wilhelm. Russian stooge intended as head of Finnish puppet government.
Ladell, Sally (later Lady Anderson). Assistant to Bill Waring.
Lamming, Norman. Trade union officer in Press Department. Later Labour Attaché, International Labour Organisation.
Landquist, Commander Daniel. Chief of Swedish combined service intelligence. Succeeded Björnstjerna.
Larden, Lt-Col. George. Assistant Military Attaché. Head of Special Operations Executive Stockholm.
Latham, Wilfrid. Rubber planter from Malaya. Volunteer in Finland. Special Operations Executive Sweden. Later Force 136 Far East.
Leadbitter, Jasper. Assistant Press Attaché, Stockholm.
Lilliehöök, Malcolm. Director of Royal Swedish Automobile Club. Twice wrongly arrested as allied spy.
Lind, Lars. Nephew of Foreign Minister Günther who joined Norwegian forces in England.
Lindley, Charlie. Retired head of Swedish Transport Workers Union.
Lindquist, Major Thorvald. Head of Swedish Military Security service. Close relations with Dr Hans Wagner, head of German Abwehr in Sweden.
MacAdam, Ivison. Head of Chatham House, Royal Institute of International Affairs.

Mallet, Sir Victor. British Minister, Stockholm from 1940.
Mannerheim, Marshal Gustaf. President of Finland.
Manton, L. British railway expert visited Sweden for operation Graffham.
Marett, Bob (Sir Robert). Member of original planning group for shadow Ministry of Information.
Martelius, Martin (Malle). Head of Text och Bilder photographic agency.
Martin, Alf. Swedish correspondent in London.
Martin, Frank. Retired cavalry officer and anti-nazi journalist.
Martin, Commander J (Pincher) RN. Passport Control Officer (MI6) Stockholm.
Maycock, R.B. British Air Attaché (3rd).
McLeod, Enid. Author with deep knowledge of French literature and history. Chaired planning staff of shadow Ministry of Information. Later French desk Ministry of Information and finally head of British Council in Paris.
Menzies, Major General Sir Stewart. 'C' (Head of MI6).
Mesterton, Eric. Swedish lector in London, translator of T.S. Eliot. Introduced me to Karin Boye and Pär Lagerkvist.
Mitcheson, J.M.L. Commercial counsellor British Legation.
Møller, Christmas. Danish resistance leader.
von Moltke, Graf Helmut James. Leader of Kreisauer Kreis and executed for opposition to Hitler.
Monson, Sir Edmond, Bt. British Minister in Stockholm before Mallet.
Montagu-Evans C. Assistant Press Attaché and then Swedish section Ministry of Information.
Montagu-Pollock, William (later Sir). Counsellor, British Legation.
Morton, Desmond. Churchill's adviser on industrial warfare.
Munck, Ebbe. Danish arctic explorer and journalist. Head of Danish resistance in Sweden.
Munthe, Malcolm. Son of Dr Axel Munthe. Worked with Andrew Croft in Finnish war, shipping war materials through Norway and Sweden to Finland. Escaped to Sweden and set up Special Operations Executive, Norwegian section. Expelled by Swedes.
Myrdal, Gunnar and Alva. Swedish economists and politicians.
Nebe, SS General Arthur. Head of German criminal police. Executed

for complicity in Stauffenberg plot.
Nerman, Ture. Anti-nazi writer and journalist. Imprisoned for three months for insulting Hitler in his weekly *Trots Allt*. Founder of anti-nazi organisation Kämpande Demokrater (Fighting Democrats).
Nielsen, E.E.M. (Tommy). Head of Special Operations Executive Norwegian section in Stockholm.
Nikitin, Mikhail. Soviet trade representative in Stockholm.
Noel-Baker, Philip. M.P. Visited Sweden during first Finnish war.
Nordenskiöld, General Bengt. C in C Swedish airforce.
Nordling, Raoul. Swedish Consul General in Paris.
Nordling, Rolf. Head of French purchasing commission in Sweden. Brother of Raoul.
O'Brien, Toby. British Council Press Officer. Later Conservative Research Department and P.R. consultant.
Olav, Crown-Prince, later King, of Norway.
O'Leary. Passport Control Officer, Copenhagen.
O'Neil, Sir Con. Member of planning staff of shadow Ministry of Information. Resigned from Foreign Office over Munich.
Örne, Anders. Chairman of Amelie Posse's Tuesday Club.
Oster, Major General Hans. Executed for complicity in 20 July plot. Deputy Chief of Abwehr under Canaris.
Oxenstierna, Commander Johan Gabriel. Swedish Naval Attaché, London.
Parrott, Joe (Sir Cecil). Member of planning staff of shadow Ministry of Information. Tutor to King Peter of Yugoslavia. Posted to press office in Norway, escaped to Sweden. Head of Press Reading Bureau.
Paués, Anna. Fellow of Girton and Reader in Anglo-Saxon, Cambridge. First woman to hold a professorship in Sweden. Taught me Icelandic and Swedish.
Pers, Anders. Owner of *Västmanlands Läns Tidning* in Västerås and printer of our weekly paper *Nyheter från Storbritannien*.
Posse, Countess Amelie. Writer married to Czech painter Brazda. Escaped from Czechoslovakia and ran an anti-nazi campaign with her Tuesday Club.
Prytz, Björn. Swedish Minister in London.
Quisling, Vidkun. Norwegian traitor and head of Norwegian puppet

government under German occupation.
Rabagliati, Colonel Euan. Pilot and racing driver, Ministry of Information and then Special Operations Executive Netherlands.
Reichenau, General. Met Goerdeler in house of Fritz Elsas on 6 Nov 1939 and sent warning to Allies about Hitler's plan to invade the Netherlands.
Reynolds, Brian (alias Bingham). Finnish volunteer, joined Binney with his convoys and was second-in-command of fast motor coasters. Lost at sea two days after end of war.
Richert, Arvid. Swedish Minister in Berlin.
Rickman, Alfred Frederick (Freddie). Arrested by Swedes for unsuccessful attempt to sabotage ore-loading cranes at Oxelösund.
Rieffel, Robert. Free French journalist formerly with Havas and then B.U.P. and A.F.P.
Riga. Cover name for British agent in German Legation.
Rønne-Petersen, Egil. Norwegian psychologist who provided us with valuable intelligence.
Ross, A.D.M. (Sir Archibald) 2nd Secretary. Ended career as Ambassador to Sweden.
Rushbrook, Commodore. Visited at Admiralty by Landquist, head of Swedish service intelligence.
Sampson, Margaret. Head of B.B.C. Swedish service.
Sandler, Rickard. Swedish Foreign Minister till 1939 before Günther.
Sandström, Gösta. Editor of British weekly *Nyheter från Storbritannien*.
Sargent, Sir Orme. Deputy Under-Secretary of State at the Foreign Office during war under Cadogan.
Schellenberg, Walter. Himmler's No.2 in Gestapo. Responsible for Venlo kidnappings in 1939 and for Himmler's peace feelers to allies via Sweden 1945.
Schive, Jens. Norwegian Press Attaché in Stockholm and later Ambassador.
Schnurre, Karl. German political and trade negotiator with Sweden.
Sebastian, Graham. Consul-General in Gothenburg.
Segerstedt, Professor Torgny. Editor of Goteborgs *Handels- och Sjöfartstidning*.
Selborne, Lord Roundell Cecil. Head of Ministry of Economic Warfare and Special Operations Executive.

Seltman, Charles. Classical archaeologist, fellow of Queens', Cambridge, one of Denniston's trainees in cipher-breaking.
Semjonov, Vladimir. Counsellor Soviet legation. Later ambassador in Bonn.
Senior, Ted (Sir Edward). Steel control and ball and roller bearings.
Siberg, Willy. Head of S.K.F. at Luton.
Singer, Kurt. German refugee writer and journalist.
Sköld, Per Edwin. Minister of Defence.
Söderman, Dr Harry. Head of Criminal Technological Institute. Organised training of Norwegian and Danish police troops in Sweden.
Sporborg, Harry. Solicitor and director of Hambros Bank. Ministry of Economic Warfare 1939. Director and later vice-chief Special Operations Executive 1940-46.
Stauffenberg, Colonel Claus Schenk von. Executed for attempt on Hitler's life 20 July 1944.
Sterling. U.S. Minister who preceded Herschel Johnson.
Stewen, Martin. Finnish Military Attaché Stockholm. Leaked secrets of Swedish code-breakers to Germans.
Stevenson, Sir William (Intrepid). Head of British Security Co-ordination Organisation, New York.
Stridsberg, Gustaf. Former foreign editor *Svenska Dagbladet*, friend of Amelie Posse and anti-nazi activist.
Sutton-Pratt, Colonel Reggie. Military Attaché
Svanström, Dr Ragnar. Historian, publisher and founder of American British Swedish dining club.
Terboven, Josef. German Reich Commissar in Norway.
Thomsen, Dr Hans. German Minister in Sweden after Wied.
Thörnell, General Olof. Swedish C in C.
Thorsing, Oscar. Head of Ministry of Foreign Affairs Press Department.
Thornton, Wing-Commander Bill. Air Attaché (2nd) 1940. Revisited Sweden 1944 as spurious Air Vice Marshal for deception operation Graffham.
Thulstrup, Dr Åke. Historian and co-editor of *Nu* with Enander.
Tower, Pamela. Assistant to R.B. Turnbull, Special Operations Executive Danish section.
von Trott zu Stolz, Adam. Member of German resistance. Visited

Sweden. Executed.
Turnbull, R.B. Head of Special Operations Executive Danish section, Stockholm.
Urch, R.O.G. *The Times* correspondent. Formerly Moscow and Riga.
von Uthmann, Lt General Bruno. German Military Attaché.
Vanek, Dr Vladimir. Counsellor at former Czech legation in Stockholm. Imprisoned by Swedes for cooperation with the Allies. First Czech Ambassador in Rome before the Communist coup.
Vinde, Victor. Swedish correspondent of *Dagens Nyheter* during French defeat of 1940.
Wagner, Dr Hans. Head of Gestapo (Abwehr and later Sicherheitsdienst) in Sweden.
von Wahlert, Commander Paul. German Naval Attaché Stockholm.
Wallenberg, Jacob. Brother of Marcus and co-director of Enskilda Banken. Handled Swedish commercial interests in Germany.
Wallenberg, Marcus. Younger brother of Jacob and co-director of Enskilda Banken. Handled Swedish commercial interests with Allies.
Wallenberg, Raoul. Distant relation of Jacob and Marcus. Young diplomat kidnapped by Russians in Budapest in course of saving lives of thousands of Jews.
Walter, J.H. Swedish businessman gaoled for trying to buy the Italian Navy for the British.
Ward, Barbara. Journalist on *The Economist*, lectured in Sweden and arranged for printing of *The Economist* in Stockholm.
Waring, Anne. Wife of H.W.A. Waring. Norwegian section Special Operations Executive.
Waring, H.W.A. Deputy to George Binney in blockade-running and joined Stanton Griffis in putting an end to Swedish exports of ball bearings to Germany.
Welchman, Gordon. Fellow of Sidney Sussex, Cambridge. Mathematician recruited by Denniston for cipher-breaking and one of Bletchley Enigma team.
Wheeler, Mike (Sir Charles). Director of G.K.N. Expert on ore-purchasing for Steel Control.
White, Ken. British Consul-General, Stockholm.
Wied, Victor zu. German Minister in Stockholm before Thomsen.

Wigforss, Harald. Journalist, editor *Nordens Frihet*, later of *Göteborgs Handels- och Sjöfartstidning*.
Wilhelm, Prince. King's brother. Anti-nazi writer.
Wilson-Wright, Mab. Office of Strategic Services. Representative of *Vogue*.
Wiskeman, George. Ministry of Information and later Special Operations Executive.
York, Carl. Paramount films.
Young, Gordon. Correspondent of Reuters and later *Daily Express*.
Zhdanov, Andrei. Head of Allied Control Commission, Finland. Murdered by Stalin.

# Bibliography and Sources

Personal papers, diaries, scrapbooks, cuttings from Swedish and British newspapers and periodicals, Public Record Office, Imperial War Museum, Swedish archives and official publications.

| | |
|---|---|
| Baden-Powell, D. | *Operation Jupiter. S.O.E.'s Secret War in Norway* (London, 1982). |
| Balfour, Michael | *Withstanding Hitler* (London, 1988). |
| Balfour, Michael and Frisby, J.F. | *Helmut von Moltke* (London, 1972). |
| Barker, Ralph. | *The Blockade Busters* (London, 1976). |
| Beesly, Patrick. | *Room 40. British Naval Intelligence 1914-18* (London, 1982). |
| Beesly, Patrick. | *Very Special Admiral. Life of Admiral J. M. Godfrey, C.B.* (London, 1980). |
| Bennett, J. | *British Broadcasting and the Danish Resistance Movement 1940-45* (Cambridge, 1966). |
| Bernadotte af Wisborg, Folke. | *Folke Bernadotte. Svensken ochevärldsmedborgaren.* Essays on his life (Stockholm, 1949). |
| Bernhardsson, Carl Olof. | *Spoinpolisen på jakt* (Stockholm, 1952). |
| Bertelsen, A. | *October 1943* (London, 1955). |
| Boheman, Erik. | *På vakt* (Stockholm, 1964). |
| Boldt-Christmas, Emil. | *Voro vi neutrala* (Stockholm, 1946). |
| Brandell, Ulf. | Numerous articles especially *Svenska Dagbladet* 20 March 1988 about the Reichstag Fire and 'Sweden versus Great Britain and the Soviet Union during the Second World War', *Contemporary Review* (February 1981). |
| Briggs, Asa. | *The War of Words. The History of Broadcasting in the United Kingdom*, vol III (Oxford, 1970). |

| | |
|---|---|
| Bull, Francis. | *Tretten taler på Grini* (Oslo, 1945). |
| Butler, Ewan. | *Amateur agent* (London, 1963). |
| Butler, R.A.B. | *The Art of the Possible* (London, 1971). |
| Carlgren, Wilhelm M. | *Svensk Utrikespolitik 1939-1945* (Stockholm, 1973). |
| Carlgren, Wilhelm M. | *Svensk underättelsetjänst 1939-1945* (Stockholm, 1985). |
| Carlgren, Wilhelm M. | *Studier tillägnade Wilhelm Carlgren 6 Maj 1987* (Stockholm). |
| Cave-Brown, Anthony. | *Bodyguard of Lies* (London, 1977). |
| Cedercrantz, Bror. | *Berättelse om ett hus på Djurgården* (Stockholm, 1985). |
| Childs, Marquis. | *Sweden, the Middle Way* (London, 1936). |
| Churchill, Winston S. | *The Second World War* 6 vols (London, 1948-1954). |
| Churchill, Winston S. | Biography edited by Martin Gilbert vols VI, VII, VIII (London, 1983-9). |
| Cruickshank, Charles. | *Deception in World War II* (Oxford, 1979). |
| Cruickshank, Charles. | *The Fourth Arm. Psychological Warfare 1938-45* (Oxford, 1981). |
| Cruickshank, Charles. | *S.O.E. in Scandinavia* (Oxford, 1986). |
| Deacon, Richard. | *The Cambridge Apostles* (London, 1985). |
| *Det isolerade öriket*. | 2 vols (Stockholm 1940). Leading Swedes on aspects of British civilisation. Published in English (London, 1942) as *Sweden speaks*. |
| Delmer, Tom Sefton. | *Die Deutschen und ich* (Hamburg, 1963). |
| Delmer, Tom Sefton. | *Trail Sinister* (London, 1961). |
| Delmer, Tom Sefton. | *Black Boomerang* (London, 1962). |
| Demaitre, Edmond. | *Eyewitness* (New York, 1981). |
| Denham, Henry. | *Inside the Nazi Ring* (London, 1984). |
| *Djurgårdsbladet*. | No.3 and no.4 (Stockholm, 1980 and 1984). My account of life at Bergshyddan. |
| Ehrensvärd, Carl August. | *I rikets tjänst* (Stockholm, 1965). |
| Elting, J.R. | *Battles for Scandinavia*. Time Life Books, 1981. |
| Farago, Ladislas. | *The Game of the Foxes* (London, 1972). |
| Flender, H. | *Rescue in Denmark* (London, 1963). |
| Foot, M.R.D. | *S.O.E. The Special Operations Executive* |

| | |
|---|---|
| | *1940-46* (B.B.C., 1984). |
| Fritz, Martin. | *German Steel and Swedish Iron Ore* (Gothenburg, 1974). |
| Gerhard, Karl. | *Om jag inte minns fel* (Stockholm, 1952). |
| Gerhard, Karl. | *Lite Gullregn* (Stockholm, 1961). |
| Gowing, Margaret. | *Britain and Atomic Energy 1939-45* (London, 1964). |
| Griffis, Stanton. | *Lying in State* (New York 1952). |
| Gripenberg, G.A. | *London-Vatikanen-Stockholm. En beskickningschefs minnen* (Stockholm, 1960). |
| Gunther, Christian. | *Tal i en tung tid* (Stockholm, 1945). |
| Hägglöf, Gunnar. | *Samtida vittne* (Stockholm, 1972). |
| Hägglöf, Gunnar. | *Var försiktig i Berlin* (Stockholm, 1986). |
| Hagman, Kommendörkapten. | Report to C in C Swedish Navy on arrest of destroyers in Faroes on board *Patricia*, 23 June 1940. |
| Hammargren, Henning. | *Vapenköp i krig* (Malmö, 1986). |
| Hansson, Per Albin. | *Svensk hållning och handling* (Stockholm, 1945). |
| Hansson, P. | *The Greatest Gamble* (London, 1967). |
| Hicks, Agnes. | Article on Sweden in the war in Arnold Toynbee (ed.) *Survey of International Affairs 1939-46. The War and the Neutrals* (Oxford, 1956). |
| Hinks, Roger. | *The Gymnasium of the Mind* (Salisbury, 1984). |
| Hinsley, Sir F.H. | *British Intelligence in the Second World War* vols I-V, (H.M.S.O., 1979-84). |
| Hoffman, Peter. | *The History of the German Resistance 1933-45* (London, 1977). |
| Hoffman, Peter. | *Widerstand, Staatsstreich, Attentat. Der Kampf der Opposition gegen Hitler* (Munchen, 1970). |
| Howard, Anthony. | *R.A.B. The Life of R.A. Butler* (London, 1987). |
| Howard, Michael. | *British Intelligence in the Second World War vol 5, Strategic Deception* (1990). |
| Howe, Ellic. | *Urania's Children* (London, 1967). |

| | |
|---|---|
| Howe, Ellic. | *The Black Game* (London, 1982). |
| Hyde, H.M. | *The Quiet Canadian* (London, 1962). |
| *Innersidan.* | 150th anniversary of *Västmanlands Läns Tidning* which printed our *Nyheter från Storbritannien* (Västerås, 1981). |
| Leifland, Leif. | (Swedish ambassador in London) Essay on deception operation 'Graffham' in *Historisk Tidskrift.* |
| Ludlow, Peter. | *Britain and Northern Europe 1940-45* (1979). |
| Ludlow, Peter. | Scandinavia between the Great Powers. Attempts at mediation in the first year of the Second World War. *Historisk Tidskrift* (1974). |
| Macmillan, Harold. | *The Blast of War 1939-45* (London, 1967). |
| Maisky, Ivan. | *Journey into the Past* (London, 1980). |
| Mallet, Sir Victor. | Unpublished memoirs deposited at Churchill College, Cambridge. |
| Martin, Alf. | *England trots allt* (Stockholm, 1979). |
| Martin, Alf. | *Och bomberna de föll* (Stockholm, 1980). |
| Masterman, J.C. | *The Double Cross System in the War 1939-45* (New Haven, 1972). |
| Meurling, Per. | *Spionage och sabotage i Sverige* (Kristianstad, 1952). |
| Mommsen, Professor Hans and others. | *Reichstagsbrand. Aufklärung einer historischen Legende* (1987). |
| Munch-Petersen, Thomas. | *The Strategy of Phoney War* (Stockholm, 1981). |
| Munch-Petersen, Thomas. | 'Common Sense not Bravado'. The Butler Prytz interview of 17 June 1940. *Scandia.* Band 52:1 (1986). |
| Munck, Ebbe. | *Svingdør til den frie Verden* (Copenhagen, 1967). The Danish resistance leader's clandestine activities in Sweden 1939-45. |
| Munthe, Malcolm. | *Sweet is War* (London, 1954). |
| Muus, F.B. | *The Spark and the Flame* (London, 1956). |
| McKay, C.G. | Iron Ore and Section D: The Oxelösund operation. *Historical Journal* 29:4 (1986). |

| | |
|---|---|
| McLeod, Enid. | *Living Twice* (London, 1982). |
| *Nyheter från Storbritannien.* | British weekly published in Sweden 1940-45. |
| Perrault, Gilles. | *The Red Orchestra* (New York, 1969). |
| Petrow, R. | *The Bitter Years. The Invasion and Occupation of Denmark and Norway April 1940 - May 1945* (London, 1974). |
| Porter, Cathy. | *Alexandra Kollontay* (London, 1980). |
| Posse, Amelie. | *Åtskilligt kan nu sägas* (Stockholm, 1949). |
| Posse, Amelie. | *Minnenas park* (Stockholm, 1954). These are two of a series of ten volumes of memoirs starting with her childhood in Sweden and covering her internment with her Czech artist husband in Italy during World War I, her life in Czechoslovakia, her escape to Sweden and anti-nazi activities during World War II. |
| Rickman, A.F. | *Swedish Iron Ore* (London, 1939). |
| Rockberger, Nicolaus. | *The Gothenburg Traffic. Swedish Safe Conduct Shipping during the Second World War* (Stockholm, 1974). |
| van Roon, Ger. | *Europäischer Widerstand im Vergleich* (1985). |
| van Roon, Ger. | *Helmut James Graf von Moltke.* Documents. |
| Santoni, Professor Alberto. | *Storia illustrata.* Mondadori. Milano, nos. 197 and 298, Aug - Sept 1982. |
| *Schwedische und Schweizerische Neutralität im Zweiten Weltkrieg* (Basel, 1986). | |
| Singer, Kurt. | *Duel for the Northland* (London, 1945). |
| Singer, Kurt. | *I Spied and Survived* (New York, 1980). |
| Söderman, Dr Harry. | *Skandinaviskt mellanspel* (Stockholm, 1945). |
| Söderman, Dr Harry. | *A Policeman's Lot* (London, 1957). |
| Söderman, Dr Harry. | *Inte bara brott.* Swedish translation of above (Stockholm, 1956). |
| S.O.U. | *1946:36 1946:93 1948:7. Parlementariska undersökningskommissionen angående flyktingsärenden och säkerhetstjänst 1 - 3* (Stockholm, 1946-48). |

Stevenson, W.　　　　　　A Man called Intrepid (London, 1976).
Sweet-Escott, Bickham.　Baker Street Irregular (London, 1965).

Thulstrup, Professor Åke. *Med lock och pock. Tyska försök att påverka svensk opinion 1933-45 Transiteringsfrågor* (Stockholm, 1962).
Thulstrup, Professor Åke. Gustav V's roll under midsommarkrisen 1941. *Historisk tidskrift* (Stockholm, 1972).
*april - juni 1940* (Stockholm, 1947).
*Transiteringsfrågan juni - december 1940* (Stockholm, 1947).
Utrikespolitiska institutet. *Svensk utrikespolitik under andra världskriget* (Stockholm, 1946).
Utrikespolitiska institutet. Chronological card index 1939-45.
Wäsström, Sven. Essay on Swedish intelligence in *Schwedische und Schweizerische Neutralität im Zweiten Weltkrieg* (Basel, 1986).
Woodward, Llewellyn. *British Foreign Policy in the Second World War* I - II (London, 1970-71).
Young, Gordon. *Outposts of Peace* (London, 1945).

# Index

*ABC* (German newspaper), 97
Abdication, threatened, of King Gustav, 91, 123
Aberdeen, 226, 227
ABS (American British Swedish) dining club, 115, 156-60
von Abshagen, Karl, 6
Abwehr, 6, 8, 33, 35, 127, 148, 209, 229, 236, 240, 241, 249
*Adam*, 97
Adlercreutz, Colonel Carlos, 33-4
Admiralty, the, 3, 4, 11, 34, 50, 54, 137, 209, 220, 230, 235, 236, 239, 250; alleged penetration of, 175
*Aftonbladet*, 96, 97, 98, 270
Agents: Allied, 31, 158, 265; German, 31, 165-6, 180; other 31; Russian, 61, 260. *See also*: Arrests, Espionage
Ahnlund, Professor Nils, 78, 82
Aid, Swedish humanitarian, 20, 36, 76, 95, 177, 272
Aird, Bill, 204
Aircraft Production, Ministry of, 8, 225, 262
Air Forces: German, 14, 27, 28, 208, 211, 217-8; RAF, 63, 110, 180, 221-2, 225, 265, 266, 269; Swedish, 35, 52, pro-British attitude of, 100, 271; USAF, 23, 30, 170, 172
Air Lift, from Britain, 23, 120, 149, 221-2, 225, 265, 266, 269
Air Ministry, the, 137
Air raids: on Germany, 23, 63, 110 (leaflets), 180, 225; threatened, on Sweden, 23, 225
Ahlmark, Lt-Commander Pedro, 151-2

Åkerberg, Harald, 231
Åland Islands, 12, 17, 19, 25, 28, 30, 40, 114; 1921 Convention, 24; demilitarisation of, 24, 25; proposed militarisation of, 19
Alexander, George, 106, 108, 118, 120
Alliances, Nordic, 19; proposed Swedish-Finnish, 24
Almkvist, Major, 97
Althing, Churchill's speech to, 121
*Altmark*, 119, 204
*Amateur Agent*, 144
Åndalsnes, 26
Andersson, Ivar, 82, 83, 175, 180, 267
Anglo-German Fellowship, the, 10
AP (Associated Press), 61, 63
Aspley Guise, 136
Armies, British, in Norway, 28, 29, 119, 181; German, in Norway, 70, 148, 151, 171, 172; Swedish: *see* Defence. *See also* Invasion, Volunteers
Armistice, Finnish-Russian, 20, 25, 30, 60, 111, 119, 203, 253, 266; possible German, 186. *See also* Capitulation
Arms: *see* Weapons
Arrests, of Allied agents, 31; of German agents, 31; of journalists, 153-4; proposed, of Nazi leaders, by German resistance, 176; of Norwegians 43; of Norwegian ships, 215; of Russian agents, 61; of pro-British Swedes, 158, 232, 239, 265
Ashton, Lee, 111-2
Astrology, 142-3

Atlantic Charter, the, 175
Atrocities, German, in Norway, 70, 151, 172
Attachés; British, in Belgrade, Naval, 236; in Stockholm, Air, 35; Assistant Air, 52; Military, 52; Naval, 53; Press, 1; Finnish, in Stockholm, Military, 32, 253; French, in Stockholm, Cultural, 263; German, in Oslo, Naval, 175; in Stockholm, Press, 35, 242; Swedish in Berlin, Military, 34; in Helsinki, Military, 34; in London, Naval, 35. *See also* Adlercreutz, Boord, Denham, Fleet, Juhlin-Dannefelt, Oxenstierna, Sutton-Pratt, Tennant, Thornton, Wagner
Austria, 68; German resistance plans for, 175, 176
Axelson, George, 62

Badoglio, Marshal Pietro, 236, 240, 244
von Bahr, Captain Nils, 98
Balchen, Bengt, 170, 172
Balfour, Michael, 6
Balliol College, 56
Ball bearings, 14, 21, 22-4, 31, 123, 151, 223, 225, 268, 271. *See also* Blockade, Exports
Baltic Sea, 24, 28, 40, 113
Baltic States, 24, 33, 65, 119, 182
Barker, Ralph, 225, 227, 228n.
Bases, Russian, 24
Basile, Doctor, 231
Battle of Britain, the, 111, 118, 119, 124
Battley, Mr (Security Officer), 50
BBC, 62, 78, 108, 111, 113, 118, 120, 130, 165; Swedish service, 266
Beck, Colonel-General Ludwig, 175, 179
Belgrade, 236

Bell, Bishop George, of Chichester, 180, 267
Beneš, President Eduard, 75, 229
Bendixson, Harald, 45; Ivar, 45
Berg, (General) Ole, 168
Bergen, 2, 8, 10
Bergman, Ingrid, 46
Bergshyddan: see Tennant, homes
Berlin, 26, 28, 33, 34, 98, 127, 148, 152, 178; Philharmonic Orchestra, 101; University, 82, 103
*Berliner Illustrierte,* 99
*Berlingske Tidende,* 63
Bernadotte, Count Folke, 36; Marshal Jean Baptiste (Carl XIV Johan), 16; Prince Oscar, 91
Beskow, Bo, 39, 47; Zita, 47
Beurling, Professor Arne, 32, 253
Beveridge Report, the, 111, 122
Biggs, Ernest, 116, 126, 127
Binney (Sir) George, 21, 23, 50, 85, 121, 128, 135, 145, 201-28, 266; and Boheman, 92; Knighted, 58; and Lind, 114; and Mallet, 57; and Swedish obstruction of operations, 123, 155, 234; Marcus, 228n., Sonja, 227
Biörklund, G, 166
*Bismarck,* 53
Bjølvefossen, 10, 202
Björkquist, Dr Manfred, 267
Björnstjerna, Colonel Carl, 32, 34, 54
Blackmail (of Swedish King), 92
'Black' radio, 63. *See also* Propaganda, 'SIBS'
Blockade: Allied, of Germany, 18; German, of Sweden, 21, 57, 93, 121, 123; blockade-running, 201-8; Swedish Unions', of German goods, 107
*Blockade Busters, The,* 218, 228n.
Blomberg, Eric, 124
Blucker, Captain Ivar, 162, 211, 212

## Index

Blue Ribbon Sect, the, 100
von Bock, Field Marshal Theodor, 175
Bodø, 173
Boheman, Erik, attitude of, 92-3, 129; and blockade-running, 92, 223; briefs Cripps on German attack on Russia, 253; checks pro-German bias in Swedish Intelligence Service, 35; defends trade contracts, 23; and detention of Swedish warships, 234; hints that Swedes are reading British codes, 32, 151; and Mallet, 57; and Tennant, 126-7, visits UK and USA, 220
Bohr, Professor Niels, 269
Boldt-Christmas, Captain Emil, 79, 113
Bombing: *See* Air Raids
Bonde, Countess Ebba, 76; Baron Knut, 179
Bonhoeffer, Pastor Dietrich, 100, 174, 180, 267
Bonnier family (publishers), 97; Tor, 46
Books: British, 100, 106, 120; German, 99; on etiquette, for Russians, 258-9
Boord, Sir Richard, Bt, 52; Ethel, 52
Bosley, Rex, 55, 152, 266
Bothnia, Gulf of, 24
Bottrall, Ronald, 8, 123-4, 262-3
Boye, Karin, 124
M/S *BP Newton*, 213, 216, 217
Bracken, Rt. Hon. Brendan, 110
Bragg, Sir William, 267
Brandt, Willy (Karl Frahm), 63, 120, 180, 256
Branting, Hjalmar, 18, 19
Brazda, Jan, 75; Oke, 74, 82, 229; Slavo, 75
Bredberg, EC, 98

Brewer, George E Jr, 53, 133, 177
'Bridford', Operation, 221-5
Brilioth, Börje, 95, 97
Brising, Dr Harald, 46
*Britanski Soyuznik,* 260
British Council, the, 6, 8, 55, 108, 109, 123, 262-4
*British Press Review,* the,124
British Legation: *see* Legations
British United Press, 62
Broadcasting (German), 99
Broadway Buildings (MI6) 4, 5, 6, 109
Brofjord, 210, 211, 222, 224
'Buggeroff, Lieutenant U', Royal Bulgarian Navy, 268
'Bugging' *see* Microphones, Telephones
M/S *Buccaneer,* 213, 216
Bull, Professor Francis, 2
Bulls Presstjänst, 98
Butler, Major Ewan, 53, 55, 135, 144
Butler, Rt. Hon. R. A. (Lord), hints at peace, 182-3, 194n., 206, 271

'C' (Chief of Secret Intelligence Service), 136
'Cabaret', Operation, 162, 220-1
Cadogan, Sir Alexander, 178
*Cahiers des Interdits,* 62, 70, 137
Caldecote, Viscount, 233
Cambridge, 1, 3, 6, 7, 8-9, 43, 52
Canaris, Admiral Wilhelm, 11, 33, 101, 175, 256
Capitulation, proposed, of Britain, 96, 111, 182-3; of Denmark, 56; of France, 27, 119, 181; of Germany, 36, 37, of Germans in Denmark, 169, in Norway 170; of Italy, 240, 250
Carl XIV Johan, King, 16
Carlgren, Professor Wilhelm, 151
Carlsson, Gunnar, 56

Carr, Harry, 55, 152
Carter, Harry, 108
*Casablanca,* 107
Casablanca Declaration, the, 111, 122, 175, 180
Caslon, Captain C, RN, 233
*SS Castor,* 233
Cavagnari, Admiral, 232, 236, 244
Cedercrantz, Bror, 45, 48
Cedergren, Elsa, 79
Censorship, 65; British, 9-10, 121, 183; Swedish, 28, 69; Scope of, 160
di Cesaro, Duchess Nina Colonna, 239
Chain-letters, 131
*M/S Charente,* 216
Charles XII, King, 78
Charms, 131
Chatham House (Royal Institute of International Affairs), 4, 5, 78
Cheltenham Ladies' College, 260
*China Revue, the,* 61
Christian X, King of Denmark, 144
Christmas Møller, John, 121
Churchill, (Sir) Winston, 110, 111, 127, 177; and Boheman, 92, 220; and Butler's peace hints, 182-4; and Italian Navy deal, 237; and King Gustav, 91; letter from Roosevelt, 123; sets up SOE, 134; and Swedish destroyers, 234-5; thanks Sweden for birthday wishes, 122
Ciphers, 4, 5, 11, 18, 34, 35, 109, 175, 206. *See also* Decrypts, Intercepts
Circulation, of British publications in Sweden, 108
Citrine, Sir Walter, 265
Clark, Kenneth (Lord) 55, 267
Clarkson, Rolf, 101
Clearing arrangements, between Germany and Sweden, 22
Coal, 15, 18, 21, 229
Coggin, Nora, 2, 134
Coke, 15, 21
Coleridge, Peter, 205, 210, 216, 220
Colleges, Balliol, 56; Cheltenham Ladies', 260; Eton, 200, 205, 259, 260, 261; Lincoln, 137; Magdalen (Cambridge), 53; Marlborough 51; Merton, 200; Newnham, 1; Queens', 2, 4, 43; Sydney Sussex, 4; Trinity (Cambridge), 2; Winchester, 51, 56, 61; *See also* Universities
*Colliers Magazine,* 62
Columbia Broadcasting, 62
Communists, Swedish, 71, 162
Compensation, British, for detention of Swedish warships, 234; denial of, to Walter, 240
Concentration camps, British in Boer War, 99; German, in Norway, 37, 86, 171; Swedish aid to, 20, 36, 177
Concessions, Swedish, to Germany, 14-15, 27, 66, 68
Confiscation, of German propaganda, 99; of Swedish newspapers, 66, 68, 70-1, 86
Consulates, British, in Gothenburg, 210; in Oslo, 206; German, in Gothenburg, 224; Swedish, in Milan, 231, 249; in Prague, 229
Cooper, Duff (Lord Norwich), 183, 270
Co-operation, German-Finnish, 28; Swedish-Finnish, 24, 28. *See also* Volunteers
Co-operative Movement, Swedish, 13, 61, 108, 254
Copenhagen, 2, 7, 19, 34, 53, 55, 98, 102, 169, 176
Cordeaux, Colonel JK, RM, 236, 239,

## Index

248-9, 250
Correspondents, Swedish, in London, 112-4
Coultas, Freddie, 205, 210
Coups, against Hitler, 176, 185-6
Courier flights, German, over Sweden, 14, 28. *See also* Air Forces, Transit traffic
von Cramm, Baron, 174, 179, 180
Cripps, Sir Stafford, 137, 253-4, 267
Croft, (Colonel) Andrew, 20, 52-3, 109-10, 134, 135, 145
Cronstedt, Count Otto, 62
Crossman, Dick (Rt Hon Richard), 136
Cruickshank, Charles, 127, 135
Czechoslovakia, 61, 68, 74, 75, 80, 82, 176, 229, 242
Czech Telegram Bureau, 61

*Dagens Eko*, 97, 157
*Dagens Nyheter*, 79, 83, 97, 156
*Dangerous Moonlight*, 107
*Dagsposten*, 97, 103, 241
Dahlerus, Birger, 96, 174, 178, 183
*Daily Express*, the, 60, 62, 121, 137, 153, 263
*Daily Herald*, the, 60
*Daily Mail*, the, 51, 61, 153
*Daily Telegraph*, the, 51, 62, 121, 154, 218
Dalton, Rt. Hon. Hugh, 134
Dancy, Eric, 183
Danielsson, Inspector Otto, 76, 241
Danish Brigade, the, 169
Danube, River, 129
Deakin, Arthur, 265
Deception operations, 35, 36, 58; possible, 251. *See also* 'Fortitude', 'Graffham'
Decrypts, 31-3, 34, 148, 179, 253. *See also* Ciphers, Intercepts
Defence, of Sweden, 16, 24-7, 28, 30, 75, 100; manoeuvres, 75-6; organisation, 33. *See also* Air Force, Army, Navies
Dehlgren, Kommendör-Kapten Sten, 84, 97
Delmer, Tom Sefton, 63, 136-7, 143, 250
Demaitre, Edmond (Demeter Ödön, Edward Masterman), 62, 121, 153
Denham, Captain Henry RN, 53; and blockade-running, 211; and detention of Swedish warships, 230; given intelligence on German Navy, 32; and Italian Navy, 234, 244, 245, 247; microphone in flat, of, 154, 156; and Russian Naval Attaché, 255-6; threatened with expulsion, 225; Godfather to Susie Tennant, 46
Denmark; Allied liberation of, 36; Austro-German defeat of, 17; German invasion of, 21, 99; German takeover of, 121, 169; loses Norway to Sweden, 16; morale sustained by pro-Allied Swedes, 79, 87-8; resistance movement, 47; Swedish debt waived, 171; troops trained in Sweden, 30, 169; underground press, 87. *See also* SOE
Denniston, Commander Alastair, RN, 4
*Den Svenske Folksocialisten*, 97
*Den Svenske*, 102
Denunciation of pro-British group, 158-60
*Der Deutsche in Schweden*, 99
Deutscher Akademie, 99
Deutscher Akademischer Austauschdienst, 99
Deuxième Bureau, 263

M/S *Dicto*, 210, 213, 216, 217, 219, 220-4, 227, 228. *See also* Blockade
Diplomacy, 258
DNB (German News Agency), 98
Dönitz, Admiral Karl, 178
Duncan, Sir Andrew, 201, 204
Dunkirk, 118

Economic Warfare, Ministry of, 13, 134, 201, 209, 266
*The Economist*, 108, 117; printed in Sweden, 120, 268
Eden, Rt Hon Anthony (Lord Avon), 183, 250, 267
Edfelt, Johannes, 124
Ehrensvärd, General Carl August, 25, 31, 32, 34, 151, 157, 169
Eidem, Archbishop, 267
Ekelöf, Gunnar, 124, 263
El Alamein, Battle of, 20, 30, 71, 86, 111, 162, 220, 239
Electra House, 129, 133
Eliot, T S, 39, 124, 263, 267
Elisofon, Elliot, 63
M/S *Elizabeth Bakke*, 210, 211
Elks, 41, 271
Ellerman Wilson Line, 205, 209, 222
Elser, Georg, 179
Embassies, British, in Paris, 6; in Moscow, 253; German, in London, 6; US, in Moscow, 63, 78
Enander, Dr Bo, 79, 83, 86; Inga, 83
Engdahl, Per, 101, 103
Engelbrecht Division, 14, 91, 123
*En världsmakt i etern* (A World Power in the Ether), 120
'Enigma' (cipher machine), 4, 5
Erlander, Tage, 114, 170
Ericsson, John Erik Axel, 247
*Eskimo Book of Knowledge, The*, 201
*Eskilstuna Kuriren*, 86, 156

Espionage, 80, 90; German, 95; KGB, 61; Swedish, fears of, 252-3; Swedish legal interpretation of, 240; Swedish measures against, 153-60. *See also* Agents, Arrests
Essén, Dr Rütger, 103, 241
Eton College, 200, 205, 259, 260, 261
Eugen, Prince, 14, 74, 82, 90, 91, 154, 246
Europa-Press, 98
Evans, Lieutenant RNVR. (David James MP), 268
*Evening Standard*, the, 105
*Exchange Telegraph*, the, 60
Executions; of German anti-Nazis 106; of Norwegians, 43; of Poles 187-8
Experiments, German, on concentration camp inmates, 187-8
Explosives, 126, 128, 135, 149, 202, 214, 227. *See also* Weapons
Exports, Swedish, 16, 19, 20-4, 225-6
*Expressen*, 156
Eyre, Len, 108

Fagerlund, Adolf, 202, 205, 209
Falk, Peter, 148; Biddie, 148
von Falkenhorst, General Nikolaus, 34, 101
Falsterbo, 14; canal, 123
Faroes, 233, 244
Farr, Walter, 61
Fehlis, Oberführer, 171-2
Fellenius, Emy, 44; Fille, 162; Hellis; *see* Tennant; Professor Wolmar, 41-4. *See also* Viksberg
Ferdinand, Prince, of Liechtenstein, 75, 124
*Feuertaufe*, 99
Fighting Democrats, the, 127
Films, British, 87, 106-7; German, 99, 107-8

# Index

Finland, 71, 83; armistice with Russia, 20, 25, 30, 60, 111, 119, 203, 253, 266; civil war in; 19, 33; frontiers, 24; German retreat through, 170; Independence, 19; peace negotiations, 30, 88; press censorship in, 65; Russian bases in, 24; possible Swedish intervention in, 130; at war with Britain, 55; weapons to, 52, 134. *See also*: Åland Islands, Volunteers
Fitzwilliam, Lord (alias Peter Lawrence), 222
Fleet, Don, 52
Fleisher, Jack, 63
Foden-Pattinson, Mr, 108
Fogelklou, Emilie, 79, 81
Fogelkvist, Torsten, 77
*Folkets Dagblad*, 103
Food, 15, 21, 26
Föreningen Norden, 131
Forgery, 108, 115, 135, 142, 162
*Foreign Correspondent*, 107
Foreign Office, the, 4, 5-6, 8, 9, 11, 54, 58, 93, 109, 110, 133, 176, 183, 209, 213, 230, 236, 250, 262, 264
Foreign Policy Institute, the 78, 80
Förlags Aktiebolaget Britannia, 117
Försvarsfrämjandet, 102
Fortescue, Lionel, 105
'Fortitude 2', Operation, 35, 58, 144
Fosterländsk Enad Ungdom, 101
France, capitulation of, 27; Deuxième Bureau, 263; influence in Sweden, 17, 18; press representation, 62. *See also:* Legations
*France in London*, 62
Fransoni, Francesco, 239
Fraser, Ingram, 128-9, 130
Frean, Denis, 108

Fröderström, Kurt, 108
Fuchs, Walter, 106
Fuel, 15, 16, 18. *See also*: Coal, Coke, Oil
Furugård, Birger, 101, 102, 103

Gambier-Parry (Brigadier), 136
de Gaulle, General Charles, 121
*M/S Gay Corsair*, 222
*M/S Gay Viking*, 121, 222, 227
Geddes, Jack, 63
'Geheimschreiber' (cipher machine), 32, 33, 253. *See also*: Ciphers, Decrypts, 'Enigma'
Gellhorn, Martha, 62
Gerhard, Karl, 87-8
George VI, King, 121, 165, 183, 212
German Tourist Bureau, 98, 106, 130
*Gespräche mit Hitler*, 66, 68
Gestapo, in Germany, 136, 146, 188; in Norway, 86, 171, 217; in Poland, 176; in Sweden, 80. *See also*: Abwehr
Gilbert, Major Ernst, 98
Gleditch, Captain Helge, 167
*Gneisenau*, 211
Goerdeler, Karl, 13, 83, 93, 175, 176, 179, 180
Goering, Field Marshal Hermann, 26, 94, 95, 98, 103, 174, 178, 179, 183
Good Templars, 100
von Gossler, Herr, 106-7
*Göteborgs Handels- och Sjöfartstidning*, 71, 79, 80, 84, 86, 113, 124, 156
*Göteborgs Morgonpost*, 97
*Göteborgs Posten*, 86
*Göteborgs Stiftstidning*, 70, 100
Gothenburg, 8, 86, 114, 121, 205, 216, 220, 224, 234; German agents in, 217; police behaviour in, 155, 162; POW exchange in,

85, attempted sabotage in, 54; US threat to bomb, 23. *See also*: Blockade-running
Gottröra, 166, 167
Goulding, Ossian, 51, 62, 121, 154; Yasuko, 62
Gow, Janet, 55
'Graffham'. Operation, 35, 58, 144
Graffman, Holger, 232-3, 236, 251
*Graf Spee*, 119
Grafström, Sven, 62
Grand Hotel (Stockholm), 7, 62, 63, 129, 149, 201, 252
Grandi, Count, 236
Grassmann, Dr Paul, 98, 242
*Great Dictator, The*, 107
Green, Commander Patrick Barrow, RN, 249-50
Greene, (Sir Hugh Carleton), 136
Grieg, Nordahl, 123
Griffis, Stanton, 23, 225, 268
Grimsby, 121
Grini, 2, 37, 86, 171. *See also:* Concentration camps
Gubbins, Major General Sir Colin, 134
*M/S Gudvang*, 216
du Guerny, Yves, 61
Gui, Vittorio, 75, 245, 249
Gullers, (photographer), 114
*Gullregn* (*Golden Rain* or *Laburnum*) revue, 88
Günther, Christian, appointed Foreign Minister, 19, 25; and anti-Nazi song, 88; defeatist attitude of, 31; and Germans, 26, 28; and anonymous letter, 158, 160; and Mallet, 57, 182, 263-4; and nephew's predicament (Lind). 114; and Segerstedt, 161; and V2 for England, 263-4
Gustav Adolf, Crown Prince, 170; King, 90

Gustav V, King, pro-German sympathies of; 18, 31, 96, 97, 102; tells Hitler that Sweden will resist aggression, 26; rejects Hitler's request for transit rights, 29; homosexuality of, 91, 152; idiosyncrasies of, 90-2, 271; and Kollontay, 257-8; mediation attempts, 18, 19, 91, 183; and Segerstedt, 71, 87, 161; and Walter, 240
'Gustav Siegfried Eins', 63, 136, 137
Gyldene Freden restaurant, 115, 157, 158, 161

Haakon VII, King of Norway 91, 258; Fund for Refugees, 129
Hägglöf, Gunnar, 26, 56, 94
Hagman, Captain Torsten, 233-5
Halder, General Franz, 175
Halifax, Lord, 178, 179, 182-3, 194n.
Hallamaa, Colonel, 32
Hallgren, Eric Salomon, 155, 158, 160
Hälsingmo camp, 204, 210
Hamberg, Harald, 23, 226
Hambro, (Sir) Charles, 13, 136, 149; and blockade-running, 204, 222; role in SOE, 109-10, 129, 133-4
Hamburg, 8, 105
Hamilton, John, 108
Hammarling, Villgot, 10
Hangö, 25
Hansson, Johan, 66, 76-7
Hansson, Per Albin, 12, 28, 88, 91, 114, 161, 234
*Här är London*, 120
Harrie, Ivar, 79
Harris, Air Marshal Arthur ('Bomber'), 63
Harris, Tom, 62
Harstad, 26
*Havas* News Agency, 137

*Index* 299

Heavy water, 47
Heckscher, Professor Eli, 13, 113
Hedin, Greta, 78, 113
Hedin Sven, 78, 95-6
Heidelberg, University of, 86
Hellis (wife): *see* Tennant
*Helsingborgs Dagblad,* 97
Helsinki, 7, 105, 152
Helldorf, Graf, 185, 186
'Hellschreiber' 109. *See also*: Ciphers, Decrypts, 'Enigma'
Hellström, Gustav, 113
Henriksen, Alva, 205, 209
Hess, Rudolf, 175, 256
Hesselgren, Kerstin, 79
Hewins, Ralph, 51, 61-2, 153
Heydrich, SS General Reinhard, 127, 184, 185
Himmler, Reichsführer SS, Heinrich, 36, 100, 171, 177-8, 185
Hinks, Roger, 54-5, 106, 135, 180
*Historical Journal, The,* 127
Hitler, Adolf, 19, 31, 43, 44, 78, 79, 83, 84, 87, 93, 96, 107, 116; attempt on life of, 179; commits suicide, 178; executes German opponents, 106; Swedish delegation to, 26; and Swedish King, 29, 91, 183
*Hitler's Concentration Camps,* 130
Hitler Jugend, 86
Hoddan, Max, 137
Högkvist, Emilie, 45
Holdsworth, Captain RNR, 225
Holdsworth, Gerry (Commander Gerard RNVR), 129
Holford, Sir William, 267
M/S *Hopewell,* 222, 224, 226-7
Hopkins, Harry, 220
Hopkinson, Henry, 236
Hopper, Professor, 133
Horney, Jane, 98
'Horseshoe traffic' *see* Transit

Howe, Ellic, 142, 143
Howe, Sir Ronald, 164, 186
Hugo, Yngve, 118
Hull, 222, 224, 226
Hungary, 37, 65
Hunnebostrand, 226

Ibsen, Henrik, 2, 17, 84
Iceland, 3-4, 105
Icelandic, 2
Industry, Swedish, 15
Information Centre (German), 99
Information, Ministry of, 7, 8, 9, 106, 109, 110, 111-2, 113, 121, 130, 260, 262
Imozzi, Randolf, 250
Imprisonment, 61, 62, 79, 80, 90, 116, 209, 214. *See also*: Arrests
Ingrams, Harold, 136, 137
Inskip, (Sir) Thomas (Viscount Caldecote), 233
Intelligence, British, 25, 53, 129, 151, 202, 225, 249; in Germany, 146-8; brief on Italian Navy, 247-8; on Russia, 177, 253; German, 211; Swedish, 25, 31-6, 54, 151, 230. *See also*: Abwehr, MI6, Security Services
Intercepts, 4-5, 32, 34, 35, 101, 154, 243, 253
International Anti-Komintern Association, 98
Interpol, 164, 184, 186
Interrogations, of Krämer, 36; of Walter, 244
Intervention, possible Allied, in Finland, 110, 203; in Germany, 186; in Sweden, 20; Swedish, requested, in Denmark, 36; in Finland, 19, 28; in Norway, 26, 30, 35, 36, 144, 148, 203. *See also* Volunteers
Invasion, British, of Germany,

proposed by German resistance, 186; German of Belgium, 175-6; threat of, to Britain, 111, 229; note on, 196-9; of Denmark, 21, 25, 43, 77, 88, 107, 119, 128; Intelligence dividend of, 31; warnings of, 34, 151; of Greece, 71; of Netherlands, 175-6; of Norway, 11, 21, 25, 43, 56, 77, 88, 107, 119, 128, 203; Intelligence dividend of, 31; role of German 'War children' in, 95; War Office ignorance, 92; of Poland, 16; of Yugoslavia, 71; of Russia, 27, 28, 34, 61, 71, 239, 254; advance information on, 151; Russian, of Finland, 19, 24, 34; threat of, to Sweden, 24-7, 30, 75, 76, 102, 128, 130, 145, 223
*In Which we Serve,* 87, 107
*S/S Iris,* 10
Iron Gates, the, 129
Iron ore, 14, 15, 16, 18, 19, 31, 52, 57, 123, 126, 128, 151, 200, 225, 268, 271; explosives in, 149; importance to Germans, 20-22; qualities of, 21, 22. See also Exports, Oxelösund, Rickman
*Isolated Island Kingdom, The,* 113
Italy, 65, 74; attempt to buy Italian Navy, 229-51
Itch powder, 149

Jacobsen, Dr Walter, 174, 176, 194n.
Jägerbattalion, 253, 261n.
Janse, Emy (Fru Fellenius), 42
Japan, 62, 71
Japp letter, the, 243, 246-7
Järrel, Stig, 88-9
Järte, Otto, 45, 82-3, 175, 180; Esther, 82-3
Jartseva, Alexandra, 119, 254-5, 258

Jartsev, Boris, 254-5, 256
Jensen, Carl E, 268
Jernkontoret, 205
Jews, 37, 86, 95, 97, 122, 165, 177
*M/S John Bakke,* 210, 211
Johnson, Axel Axelsson, 202
Johnson, Eyvind, 146
Johnson, Herschel, 23, 52
Johnson, Wiking, 205
'Josephine' reports, 35-6
Journalists, foreign, in Sweden, 60-4, 153-4; Swedish, 112-8
Juel, Karin, 88
Juhlin-Dannfelt, Colonel Curt, 34, 180
Jung, General Helge, 31, 33, 151, 170

KAK (Royal Automobile Club), 158
Kalix, 32
Kämpande Demokrati, 131
Karesuando, 170
Karl Johan XIV, King, 16, 45
Kattegat, 207
Katz, Professor, 163
Kavli, Karin, 88, 147; Knut, 147
Kellgren, Henry, 129
*HMS Kelly,* 87
Kendall, Sir Norman, 166, 194n.
Kenney, Rowland, 6, 7, 8, 105; Kit, 105
Kersten, Dr Felix, 36, 177
KGB, 61, 255
Kiel Canal, 146
Kihlbom, Asta, 78, 113, 114
Kimmins, Commander Tony RN, 87
King Feature Services, 98
King, Wallace, 60
Kingston, Margit, 133
Kirkenes, 170, 171
Kirkwall, 212, 233
Kiruna, 202
Kjellberg, William, 205, 209
Klaus, Edgar, 180, 256

## Index

Kleen, Colonel Willy, 79
Kleist, Peter, 180, 256
Knapp-Fisher, Jim, 54, 106, 108, 180
Knudtzon, General, 169
'Knüfken', 89, 181
Koch, Karin, 79
Kollontay, Alexandra, 75, 88, 119, 215, 254, 257-61; and Finnish armistice, 253; praises English education, 259-61; alleged peace feelers with Germany, 256
Königsberg, 99, 118
Kornsjö, 27
Kossov, Misha, 63, 255
Krämer, Dr Karl Heinz, 36-7, 148
Kreisauer Kreis, 6
Kreisky, Bruno, 63, 180, 181, 256
Kreuger, Torsten, 95, 96-7
Kristiansand, 234
Kuusinen, Otto Wilhelm, 253

Labouchere, George, 50; Rachel, 50
Ladell, Sally (Lady Anderson), 210, 223, 228
Lagerkvist, Pär, 46
*SS Lahti*, 208
Lamm, Professor Martin, 2
Lamming, Norman, 61, 89, 108
Landquist, Commander Daniel, 34, 54
von der Lancken, Major General, 102
Landskrona, 26
Languages, 4; Anglo-Saxon, 1, 2; in BBC Services, 118; in censorship, 9; Finnish, 118, 266; French, 1; German, 1; Icelandic, 2; Modern, Fellowship in, 2; Scandinavian, 3; Swedish, 2
Larden, Lieutenant-Colonel George, 134, 145
Latham, Wilfred, 109, 145-6, 155
Laws, Swedish; on espionage, 153, 155, 240; on press, 67-9; on ships, 215
Leadbitter, Jasper, 54, 105
League of Nations, the, 3, 5, 12, 19
Lee, Sir Frank, 227
Leeper, Rex, (Sir) 7
Legations, Brazilian, in Stockholm, 98; British, in Copenhagen, 7, 53, 55, 105, 176; in Helsinki, 7, 152; in Oslo, 7, 105, 207; in Stockholm, 1, 7, 49-59, photographed by Swedish Security, 145; security of, 164; surveillance of, 155; Czech, in Stockholm, 162; Finnish, in Stockholm, 32, 253; French, in Stockholm, 263; German, in Copenhagen, 99; in Oslo, 11, 99, 175; in Stockholm, 33, 35, 98, 99, 101, 165, 242; forged invitations from, 144; penetration of, 148; Hungarian, in Stockholm, 109; Italian, in Stockholm, 231, 239; Norwegian in Stockholm, 147
Lehnkering, Eugen, 203-4
Leipzig Gewandhaus, 101
Leopold, King of the Belgians, 19
Leuchars, 221, 255, 266, 270
Lie, Trygve, 121
Lieven, Prince, 61
Lilliehöök, Malcolm, 158, 265
Lincoln College, 137
*M/S Lind*, 216, 217
Lind, Lars, 114-5
Lindberg, Folke, 78
Lindberg, Helge, 158
Lindberg, Hugo, 79
Lindberg, Pelle, 3
Lindemann, Helmut, 7
Lindhagen, Anna, 79
Lindholm, Sven Olov, 102-3
Lindley, Charlie, 89-90, 181
Lindquist, Thorvald, 248

*M/S Lionel*, 213, 216, 217, 219, 220-1, 224, 227, 228
Lloyd, Lord, 6
Lofoten Islands, 28
London, University of, 3, 9
Lönnegren, Dr Consul John, 98
Lorents, Maj and Yngve, 77, 78, 114, 120
*Lortsverige*, 14
Louise, Crown Princess, 87, 90
Luleå, 170, 202
Lund, University of, 85, 262
Lundgren, Eric, 124
Lundkvist, Artur, 124
Lundquist, Martin, 155
Lysekil, 121, 210, 222, 223, 226
Lyttkens, Alice and Yngve, 84

MacAdam, Ivison, 4
McDonald, Norman, 62
McEwen, David 180
McGill, (Colonel) Seamus, 266
McKay, Craig Graham, 130, 148
McLachlan, Donald, 137
McLeod, Enid, 6
McMillan, Rt Hon Harold (Lord Stockton), 265
Magdalen College (Cambridge), 53
Mälar, Lake, 14, 16, 39
Mallet, Sir Victor, and ABS Club, 157-8; and Binney, 50, 57, 58, 204, 206, 214; and Boheman, 32 (telegram warning), 56-7, 92, 126, 219; and Butler's defeatism, 182-3; and deception, 58; and Günther, 92, 114, 155-6, 263-4 (V2 rocket); and Marcus Wallenberg, 93; and Walter, 236; Peggy, 56, 81
Malmö, 18
Mälsåker, 168
*Manchester Guardian*, the, 81, 247
Mannerheim, Field Marshal Gustav, 30, 33, 259
Mariehamn, 40
Marin, Jean, 47
'Market Garden', Operation, 36
Marlborough College, 51
Marshall, Cyril, 60
Martelius, Martin, 116
Martin, Alf, 112-4, 115, 118
Martin, Ryttmästare Frank, 79, 89, 156-8, 161
Martin, Commander J RN, 55, 127, 145, 147
Martinson, Harry, 113
Mazaryk, Jan, 229
Masterman, Edmond, 153-4
*M/S Master Standfast*, 222, 223, 225
Matapan, Cape, Battle of, 238
Mauritzberg Castle, 168
Maycock, Wing-Commander RB, 52
Merchant Navies, 28; British, 208, 212; Finnish, 208; German, 26; Norwegian, 205, 208, 209, 210, 213, 215, 218-9; Swedish, 21. *See also* Blockade, War Trade Agreements
Mediation, in World War I, 18; in World War II, 18, 19, 91, 183. *See also* Dahlerus
Menzies, Major-General Sir Stewart, 136
Merton College, 200
Mesterton, Eric, 3, 267
MEW: *see* Economic Warfare, Ministry of
MGBs (Motor Gun Boats), 221, 222, 227, 268
MI5, 145
MI6, 4, 55, 59, 109, 110, 127, 133, 136, 145, 147, 148, 152
Microphones, 154-5, 216, 241, 246
Milles, Carl, 14, 46
Mines, iron, 202; sea, 18, 149, 205, 208, 227; British, 11, 15, 113,

119, 123, 175; Swedish, 25. *See also* Blockade, Territorial Waters
Ministries, British, of Propaganda, 5; German, of Propaganda, 109. *See also* Aircraft Production, Economic Warfare, Information
MIR (Military Intelligence Research), 133
*Mrs Miniver*, 106
Mitcheson, J M L, 52, 204
Mobilisation, Swedish, 24, 26, 28, 29, 30, 32. *See also* Armies, Defence
Mo i Rana, 172
Molotov, Vyacheslav, 254, 259
Möller, Gustav, 88, 157, 158, 166, 170
von Moltke, Graf Helmut James, 6, 83, 106, 174, 180
Monson, Sir Edmund, Bt, 11, 56, 91
Montague-Evans, Charlie, 54, 75, 76, 105, 108, 109
Montagu-Pollock, (Sir) William, 11, 38, 50-1, 54, 55, 90, 135
'Moonshine' Operation, 209, 226-7
Morton (Sir) Desmond, 22, 128
Munck, Ebbe, 47, 63, 144
Munich Agreement, 174, 177
Munich, University of, 82
Munthe, Dr Axel, 91
Munthe, Major Malcolm, 20, 52, 55, 75, 76, 109, 133, 134, 144
Music, 100, 101
Myrdal, Alva, 13, 38, 78; Professor Gunnar, 13, 38, 78

*HMS Naiad*, 211
Namsos, 26, 204
Narvik, 22, 26, 27, 94, 171, 172, 202, 207
Nationalsocialistiska Arbetarpartiet, 102
*Nationell Krönika*, 97

*Nationell Tidning*, 97, 103
Natur och Kultur, 66, 77
Navies; British, 56, 210, 211-2, 216; detains Swedish warships, 233-5; German, 27, 29, 32, 54, 101, 203, 212; Italian, possible purchase of, 74, 76, 229-51; Russian, 29; Swedish, 26, 27, 29; buys warships from Italy, 232; ships detained by British, 233-5, Nazi sympathies of, 79, 87, 100, 110, 151, 271; opposition to Binney, 215, 218, 220; tries to investigate British radar, 224
Nazis, German, 3, 67, 79, 85, 94, 100; plan for post-war underground, 188-94; Swedish, 101-4, 107, 144, 162
*Nazi Lies*, 130
Nebe, SS General Arthur, 166, 184-6, 195n.
Nelson, Sir Frank, 134
Nerman, Ture, 79, 86, 116, 127, 131
Neutrality; 14, 66, 74, 80, 92, 115, 123, 204; advantages of, to Allies, 152; assessment of, 271-2; breakdown of, 27; defence of, 24, 26; declarations of, 16, 19; German complaints on, 219; reassertion of, 28-29, Swedish interpretation of, 150-1
*Neue Zürcher Zeitung*, 63
Neutrala Förlaget, 99
New British Broadcasting Station (German), 118
Newnham College, 1
News agencies, German, 97-9
*News Chronicle*, the, 60, 61, 121, 183
News Department, of Foreign Office, 7, 8, 64, 105
*New York Times*, the, 62
Nicolson, Harold, 68, 116, 258, 267
Nicolaysen, Professor Ragnar, 47

NID (Naval Intelligence Division), 53, 249
Nielsen, E E M (Tommy), 55
*Night Express, The*, 107
Nikitin, Michail, 215, 256
Noel-Baker, Philip, 158, 265
*M/S Nonsuch*, 222, 226
Nordens Frihet, 78, 83, 86, 131
Nordenskiöld, General Bengt, 35, 75, 264
Nordin, Börje, 108
Nordisk Pressbyrå, 103
Nordling, Raoul, 37, 202, 204
Nordling, Rolf, 202, 204
Nordström, Ludwig, 14
Normandy, 35, 36, 107
*Norrbottens Kuriren*, 97
North, Herbert, 54
Norway, *Altmark* incident, 119; atrocities, 43, 79, 86; capitulation of Germans in, 170; British Commando raids, 28, 29; concentration camps, 37, 86, 171; Gestapo, 86, 171, 217; King Haakon's flight, 91; British intervention, 119, 181; German fears of, 29; German invasion: *see* Invasion; morale, 79; German plans to recruit Norwegians, 82; police training in Sweden, 166-71; Resistance, 2, 154; Swedish debt waived, 171; underground press, 87; Union with Sweden, 16, 17; weapons to Finland, 52. *See also* Merchant Navies, Söderman
Norwegian Channel, the, 205
Notes, diplomatic: *see* Protests
*Nu*, 79, 83, 86, 156
*Nyheter från Storbritannien*, 39, 70, 99, 116, 130; circulation, 108, 118; message from Churchill, 119; topics covered, 118-9; topics omitted, 122-3

O'Brien, Toby, 6, 8
*Observer*, the, 61, 153
Obrovsky, Professor, 246
Official Secrets Act, 4, 5
Oil, 15, 16, 21, 28. *See also*: Coal, Coke, Fuel
Ohlin, Professor Bertil, 13, 79
*Old Possum's Book of Practical Cats*, 40
Olsen, Halvor William, 118
O'Neil, Sir Con, 6
Operations; *see* Bridford, Cabaret, Fortitude II, Graffham, Market Garden, Performance, Overlord, Rubble, Stella Polaris
Öresund, 15, 18
Örne, Anders, 77-8
Oscar I, King, 17, 90
Oslo, 2, 7, 18, 171; Gestapo in, 171-2; transit traffic through, 27, 29; University of, 2
OSS (US Office of Strategic Services), 53, 133, 177
Oster, Major General Hans, 175
Österling, Anders, 46
'Overlord', Operation, 122
Oxelösund, 52, 57, 126, 128
Oxenstierna, Commander J C , 35-6, 148
Oxford, University of, 51, 61, 137, 177, 208
Oxford Group, the, 100, 103, 177

Parachutists, 47, 76
Palmstierna, Carl-Fredrik, 78
Palmstierna, Erik, 178
Paper, 15, 21
Paris, 6, 37, 55, 107, 148, 152
Parona, Angelo, 236
Parrott, Joe (Sir Cecil), 6, 49, 54, 135, 157, 181

## Index

'Parrott House', the, 61, 137, 138, 181
Passport Control Office, 152
*SS Patricia*, 233
Paués, Professor Anna, 1-2; Wilhelm, 1
Pauli, Ivan, 79
von Paulus, Field Marshal Friedrich, 29
Peace feelers, alleged British, 27, 110; Finnish-Soviet, 30, 88; German, 36, 178; Russo-German, 98, 256. *See also* Mediation
*HMS Penelope*, 53
Penetration, of enemy services, 36, 148. *See also* 'Riga'
'Performance', Operation, 162, 209, 213-20; freight in, 213, 215, 219
Pers, Anders, 117-8
Perth, Lord, 5, 7
Peter, King of Yugoslavia, 6, 157
Petersén, Major Carl, 33, 34
Petersson, Knut, 79, 80
Petrol, 21. *See also*: fuel, oil
Petsamo, 21, 204, 207, 208, 214
Petterson, P G, 97
Pick, Frank, 111-2
'Pilkvist' (author's cover-name), 230, 246
Pineus, Conrad, 88
Photographs, 116, 121; of air raids, 64; of German port, 146; darkroom in Legation, 108, 135; of Swedish security agents, 145-6
Platinum, 38
Poland, 11, 65, 175, 176
Poland, Commander John, RN, 53, 164
Police, Danish, 30, 37, 169, 171; Norwegian, 30, 37, 166-9, 170-1; Swedish, 40, 129, 239. *See also* Security services, Söderman
Political Warfare, 15. *See also* PWE
Pools (gambling), 231, 241
Portugal, 138, 230, 247
Posse, Countess Amelie, 46, 73-81, 90; and Italian Navy deal, 229, 231, 242, 244, 246; and 'Stay behind' preparations, 135; and Swedish Security, 154
*Pow-Wow*, 85
Press, American, 23; German, 85; Swedish, 65-72; banning of, 84; communist, 71; confiscation of, 66, 67, 70; foreign protests about: see Protests; legal controls on, 67-9; Nazi, 71; prosecutions, 70, 71, 88; State Information Board, 70. *See also* Correspondents, Journalists, Public Opinion
Press Council, 87
Press Department of British Legation, 49, 105, 108, 109, 125; of Hungarian Legation, 109; of Swedish Foreign Ministry, 10, 47, 62
Press Reading Bureau, of British Legation, 54, 108, 116, 135, 174
Price, Nancy, 3
Prisoners of war, 31; British, 85, 268; Russian, 31, 172
Propaganda, British, 5, 7, 11, 15, 35, 78, 105-25, 130, 131, 133-49; 'black', 63, 129, 136; German, 77, 96-101, 107, 109, 110, 111
Protests, diplomatic, British, 72, 225; German, 20, 28, 66, 67-8, 71, 88, 219; Iranian, 69
Provocation, feared, of Germans, 32, 186
Prytz, Björn, 10, 114, 115, 178, 235; and telegram about alleged British peace-feelers, 182-3, 206,

271
*Psilander,* 218, 232
Public opinion, Swedish, 17, 19, 20, 25, 31, 94, 110-11, 181
Publishing, British, 100, 106; German, 99. *See also* books
*Puke,* 218, 232
Pulp, 15, 21
PWE (Political Warfare Executive), 129, 134; fake directive, 138-42

Queens' College, 2, 4, 7, 43
Quislings, 169, 171
Quisling, Vidkun, 102, 103
Quotas, 16. *See also* War Trade Agreements

Rabagliati, Ewan, 108, 266-7
Radio, for Italian Navy, 238; traffic, 34, 35; training, 145; transmitters, 135, 136, 154, 178, 217. *See also* Intercepts
Radio Atlantik, 136, 137, 178
Radio Livorno, 250
Radio Officer, in British Legation, 108
*M/S Ranja,* 210, 212
Rationing, 16
Rauschning, Herman, 66, 68
*Reader's Digest,* the, 268
Records (gramophone), 100, 106, 137
Red Cross, Swedish, 172, 173. *See also* Aid
Refugees, British, in Sweden, 204
Regensburger, Dr, 63
Rehabilitation, 20
von Reichenau, Field Marshal Walter, 176
Reichstag fire, 163, 173n.
Reith, Sir John, 130, 180
*Remus,* 232
Rennel of Rodd, Lord, 179
HMS *Renown,* 53

Renzetti, Giuseppe, 240
Repatriation, 31
Reprisals, 37, 66
Resistance Movements, 15; Czech, 81; Danish, 47; German, 25, 93, 100, 106, 174-81, 184-7; Norwegian, 2, 154; Swedish, 76; tribute to, 186-7. *See also* Beck, Bull, Bonhoeffer, Goerdeler, Halder, Moltke, Munck, Nebe, Stauffenberg, Trott
Reuters, 62, 97
Reynolds, Brian (alias Bingham), 214, 219, 222, 226, 227
*Reynolds News,* 61, 108
Rhedin, Domprost, 70, 100
von Ribbentrop, Joachim, 10, 256
Ribbentrop/Molotov Pact, 8, 24, 88, 119, 256
Riccardi, Admiral, 236, 239
Ricciuti, Dr Carlo, 231, 249
Richert, Arvid, 180, 183
Rickman, Alfred Frederick, 52, 57, 93, 116, 126-32, 135, 145, 149, 164, 202, 203
Ridsdale, Sir William, 64
Rieffel, Robert, 62, 137
'Riga' (agent), 144, 147-8
*M/S Rigmor,* 213, 216, 217, 218
Riksföreningen Sverige-Tyskland, 103
*Rikstidningen,* 103
Rinman, Sven, 79, 113
*S/S Rio de Janeiro,* 56
Rjukan, 47
Robin, Harold, 136
Robinsohn, Dr Hans, 176
Roedean School, 260
Rommel, Field Marshal Erwin, 122, 238, 254
*Romulus,* 232
Rønne-Petersen, Egil, 147
Roosevelt, President Franklin D, 92,

123, 179, 220
Ros, Eric, 166
Ross, ADM 'Archie', (Sir Archibald), 50, 51
Rovaniemi, 204
Royal Empire Society, 123
Royal Family, Swedish, 90
Royal Institute of International Affairs (Chatham House),5
Royal Navy (in Crimean War), 17. *See also* Navies
Rubber, 15
'Rubble', Operation, 209; Value of, 212
Rumania, 65, 129
Rumours, 64. *See also* Deception, 'SIBS'
von Rundstedt, Field Marshal Gert, 180
Rushbrook, Commodore RN, 34
Russia (pre-1917), Crimean War, 17; emnity with Sweden, 17, 252-3; takes over Finland, 16. *See also* Åland Islands, Soviet Union
Rydberg, Nils, 212
Rydh, Hanna, 79

Sabotage, 22, 54, 109, 128-9, 149, 168; by Germans, 217; of Italian ships, 237. *See also* SOE
Safe-conduct traffic, 21-2, 214, 220
Sailer, General, 231-2, 249
Sailing, 40, 108, 109, 255
St. Paul's School, 137
Salla, 25
Saltfjord, 172
Samfundet Manhem, 103
Sampson, Margaret, 78, 118, 266
Sandler, Rickard, 3, 5, 12, 19, 24, 25, 92, 157
Sandler Commission (on Swedish Security Services), 160, 271
Sandström, Gösta, 39, 108, 117

Santoni, Professor Alberto, 251n.
Sardines, 3, 138
Sargent, Sir Malcolm, 214, 267
Sargent, Sir Orme, 230
Scandinavian Society, the (at Cambridge), 105
*Scharnhorst*, 211
Schartau, Yngve, 231, 241
Schellenberg, Walter, 36, 177
Schive, Jens, 147
Schleswig, 17, 19
Schnurre, Karl, 188
Schools, 13, 115, 124; Anglo-Swedish, 263; German, 99; St. Paul's, 137
Schweinfurt, 23, 225
'Scorched earth' policy, 30, 170
Scott, John, 63, 78
Seals, 40-1
Sebastian, Graham, 51, 210
Seckleman, Peter (Paul Saunders), 136
Secret Service, 5, 202, 203. *See also* MI6
'Section D', 57, 109, 128, 129, 133, 134, 202. *See also* Rickman, Sabotage, SOE
Security Service, Swedish, 31-6, 50, 57, 76, 80, 127, 154, 156, 230, 236, 240, 265; cost of, 161; pro-German attitude, of, 110, 151
Segerstedt, Professor Torgny, 71, 80, 81, 83, 84-7, 91, 112, 131, 158, 161, 222
Selborne, Lord, 134
Seltman, Charles, 4
Semb, Dr Carl, 168
Semjonov, Vladimir, 256-7
Semphill, Lord, 123
Senior, Ted (Sir Edward), 266
Shanke, Ed, 63
*HMS Sheffield*, 8
Siberg, Willy, 212, 223

'SIBS' (rumours), 137, 149. *See also* Propaganda
Sicherheitsdienst, 265
*Sieg im Westen,* 107, 144
Sigtuna, 124, 263, 267
Singer, Kurt, 127
Sjöberg, Valentin, 97
Skagerrak, 21, 205, 206, 207, 208, 223
Skälvik, 40
Skandia Press, 98
Skandinaviska Telegrambyrån, 98
Skåne, 29
SKF (Svenska Kullager Fabriken), 23, 223, 225. *See also* Ball bearings
Skoda Works, 231
Sköld, Per Edvin, 78, 231, 232, 241
*M/S Skytteren,* 213, 216
Slogans, 130
Smuggling, 40; of arms, 57; of currency, 229; of Lind, 114; of literature to Resistance, 87, 120; of papers from Czechoslovakia, 242-3
Social Democratic Front (German), 131
Social Democratic Party, 83
Söderman, Dr Harry, 37, 44, 126, 162-5, 170-3; and German resistance, 184-6
SOE (Special Operations Executive), 13, 39, 47, 54, 109, 110, 129, 266; controls blockade-running, 209, 213, 222, 228; establishment of, 134-5; Danish Section, 55, 133; German Section, 53, 131, 133, 144, 147; Norwegian Section, 55, 133, 144; Swedish Section, 133
*SOE in Scandinavia,* 127, 135
Sofielund, 169
'Soldatensender West', 136

Solidarity, Nordic, 19
Soviet Union, Chap XVI, 252-61; first armistice with Finland, 20; second armistice, 30; demands bases in Finland, 24; attacks Finland, 19; German invasion of, 34; dissolution of Komintern, 121; peace negotiations with Finland, 30, 88; press in, 65; submarine attacks on Swedish ships, 29. *See also* Åland Islands, Kollontay
Spain, 65, 133; civil war, in, 146, 162
Speer, Albert, 225
Spies, spying: *see* Espionage
Sporborg, Harry, 201, 266
Stagg, Commander, Frank RN, 3, 4
Stålhane, Bertil, 77
Stalin, Josef, 253, 254, 256
Stalingrad, Battle of, 20, 30, 71, 86, 111, 162, 220, 256
State Information Board, 70
von Stauffenberg, Colonel Claus Schenk, 13, 106, 122, 166, 186, 187
Stay-behind organisation, 132
Steel, 15, 22, 52, 128, 226. *See also* Ball bearings, Iron ore
Steinsvik, Bjarne, 98
Stjernstedt, Georg, 244; Marika, 79
'Stella Polaris', Operation, 32
Stevenson, Bill (Sir William), 127-8
Stink bombs, 135
*Stockholms Dagblad,* 98
Stockholms Högskola, 45, 163
Stockholm Plan, the (for Åland), 12
*Stockholms Tidningen,* 95, 96, 97
*Storia Illustrata,* 251n.
Storlien, 27
*M/S Storsten,* 213, 216
Strang, Sir William, 7, 36
Stridsberg, Gustaf, 73, 74, 77, 81-2, 113

# Index

Strindberg, August, 2
Ström, Fredrik, 79
Students, 103, 115, 123. *See also* Schools
Submarines, Polish, 56; Russian, 29. *See also* U-boats
Subversion, British, 109, 250; German, 78, 110, 111
*Sunday Despatch*, the, 61
*Sunday Times*, the, 60
Surveillance, 151-2, 155-6, 209, 236, 241
Sutton-Pratt, Colonel Reggie, 52, 128, 129, 155, 171, 202
Svanström, Dr Ragnar, 79, 115, 156
Svea Rikes Förlag, 99
Svendsen, Olav, 166
Svensk Opposition, 102, 103
Svensk Socialistisk Samling, 102
Svensk-Tyska Föreningen, 103
Svenska Aktiva Studentförbundet, 103
*Svenska Dagbladet*, 45, 82, 156, 175, 267
Svenska Folkpartiet, 97
Svenska Socialistiska Partiet, 103
*Sverige Fritt*, 97
Sveriges National Socialistiska Partiet, 104
Sveriges Nationella Förbund, 103
Sveriges Nationella Socialister, 97
'Svestapo', 145, 155. *See also* Security Service
Sweden, General survey, Chap II, 12-37; British influence in, 90, 94; French influence in, 18, 91; German influence in, 91, 94-5, 110; pre-war image, 12-14; size, 15; trade, 16, 19, 20-4, pro-British writers, 113-4. *See also* Air Forces, Ball bearings, Defence, Intelligence, Iron ore, Navies, Neutrality, Security Service
*Sweden Awake*, 130
Sweden, the Middle Way, 12
Swedish Academy, The, 46
*Swedish Iron Ore*, 128
Swedish Transport Workers Union, 89
Swedish Volunteer Corps, 156
Switches, altimetric, 135

*M/S Tai Shan*, 210, 211
Talvela, General, 204
Tamm, Admiral, 26, 94
*Tapperheten*, 234
Taranto, attack on, 121, 230, 236
Tass, 63, 255
Taub, Walter, 61, 153; Lux, 61
*M/S Taurus*, 210, 211
Tedder, Air Marshal Lord, 264
Telecommunications, 26, 31, 34; arranged breakdown, 211; cut, with Sweden, 113
Telegrams, 8, 151, 205; terms for Italian Navy, 237; from Prytz with Butler's peace-feelers, 182-3, 206
Telephones, 26
Telephone tapping, 151, 232, 241. *See also* Intercepts, Security Service
Tennant, Ernest (cousin), 10, 202; Frank (son), 11, 46; Hellis, née Fellenius (wife), 2, 3, 5, 83, 135, 254, 255, 270; Lotta (daughter), 11; (Sir) Peter (author), and Boheman, 126-7; at Cambridge, 2-3; home life in Stockholm, 38-48; appointed Lecturer in Scandinavian Languages and Literature, 3-4; marries Hellis Fellenius, 3; appointed Press Attaché in Stockholm, 8;

recruited into SOE, 133; visits UK, 35; Suzie (daughter), 46, 270
Terboven, Reichscommisar Josef, 171
Territorial waters, Norwegian, 119, 175; Swedish, 14, 27, 29, 30, 123
*Text och Bilder,* 116
Theatres, 87-9
*Things English,* 124
Thompson, Mrs, 108
Thomsen, Dr Hans, 96
Thörnell, General Olof, 25, 28, 29, 31, 32, 33, 34, 54, 86, 101, 151, 161; pro-German attitude of, 157
Thornley, Robert, 146
Thornton, Wing-Commander Bill, RAF, 35, 52
Thornton, Dr Grace, 117
Thorsing, Oscar, 10, 47, 93, 127
Three Power Pact, 28
Thulstrup, Dr Åke, 79, 83
Thunberg, Professor Sven, 70
Tidningarnas Telegrambyrå, 97
Timber, 15, 21
*Times, The,* 53, 61, 81, 120, 121, 123, 267
*Time and Life,* 63, 78
*Times Weekly, The,* 81
Tingsten, Professor Herbert, 80
*Tirpitz,* 29, 121
Todt organisation, 172
'Torch' landings, 30
Torture, 86. *See also* Atrocities
Tower, Pamela, 55, 145
Trade, Swedish, with Britain, 19, 21; with Germany, 19, 21-2, 30; with USA, 21. *See also* Ball bearings, Blockade, Iron ore, War Trade Agreements
Trade Union Movement, 13, 61, 89, 107, 108
Translations, 116
Transit traffic, through Sweden, Allied, 18, 20, 130, 266; German, 14-15, 20, 26, 27-8, 29, 30, 31, 86, 88, 91, 111, 119, 122, 143, 151, 233, 244, 271; abrogation of, 28; numbers of troops carried, 27
Treaty of Paris, (1856), 17
Trelleborg, 27
*Tribune,* 63
Trofelt, Captain Ewert, 167, 172
Trondhjem, 27, 92, 171, 203, 204, 207
*T R Signal,* 99
*Trots Allt,* 79, 86, 116, 131
von Trott zu Stoltz, Adam, 83, 106, 174, 180, 267
Tuesday Club, the, 76-80, 82, 131, 157; anonymous accusations against, 158-60
Turnbull, Ronnie, 55, 105, 145; Teresa, 145
*Tyska Röster,* 99
Tysklands Vänner, 103

U-Boats, 131, 136, 137; training in Sweden, 101
'Ultra', 4, 253
Unconditional surrender, of Germany, 94, 111, 122, 179, 180. *See also* Casablanca, War Aims
*Undra* (yacht), 39, 109
Undset, Sigrid, 84
Union, of Sweden and Norway, 16, 18
Universities, 86, 115; Berlin, 82, 103; Cambridge, 2-3, 6, 9, 52; Edinburgh, 6; Heidelberg, 86; London, 3, 9; Lund, 85, 262; Munich, 82; Oslo, 2; Oxford, 51, 61, 137, 177, 208; Uppsala, 82, 85, 262; U P (United Press), 63, 69
Urch, R O G ('Olly'), 61, 121, 123

Urquhart, G A, 8, 50
USA, approach to German anti-Nazis, 174; threatens to bomb Sweden, 23, 225; steel production, 23; trade with Sweden, 21; in World War I, 94; enters World War II, 27, 220
Ustvedt, Hans, Jacob, 147

Valéry, Bernard, 62
*Valkyrian* (yacht), 16, 39, 109, 163
Vaněk, Vladimir, 76, 80, 90, 162
*Varbergs Posten*, 69
*Vår kamp*, 103
Värmland, 29
*Västmanlands Läns Tidning*, 117
*Veckans PM*, 70
Venn, Dr, J A, 9
Venosta, Marchese Riri Visconti, 239
Venlo Incident, 176, 177
Vichy, 62
Victoria, Queen of Sweden, 91
Viksberg (family house), 7, 38, 39, 40, 41-3, 151, 164. See also Fellenius, Tennant
Vinde, Victor, 79
Virke, Mrs Britt, 108
Vold, Terje, 166
Volunteers, in Finland, British, 25, 108, 145, 214, 253, 265; Swedish, 19, 25, 26, 156-7, 169
V2 rocket, 121, 263-4
Vougt, Alan, 78, 181

Wagner, Dr Hans, 33, 35, 148, 249
von Wahlert, Commander Paul, 218
Wahlström, Professor Lydia, 79
*HMS Wallace*, 218
Wallenberg, Jakob, 13, 31, 76, 93-4, 232; contacts with German resistance, 25, 34, 180; Marcus, 13, 31, 76, 93-4, 183, 205, 236; friendship with Mallet, 57, 58; Raoul, 37
Walter, John H ('Karlsson'), 74, 75, 76, 229-33, 235-8, 240. See also Italian Navy
Ward, Barbara (Lady Jackson), 108, 117, 120, 267-8
Wars, civil in Finland, 19; Danish-Prussian, 17; declaration of, by Britain and France, 16; by Italy, 240; Finnish/Soviet, 88, 110, 130, 252; Franco-Prussian, 17; World War I, 19, 20, 94; World War II, 19, 90, 95, 153. See also Invasion, Neutrality
War aims, Allied, 110, 111, 122, 175; of German resistance, 176-7. See also Unconditional surrender
Waring, Ann, 55, 206, 210; H W A (Bill), 50, 206; Patrick, 46, 206
War Office, the, 92, 133
Warner, Sir Christopher, 11
Warnings, of British mine-laying, 25; of attacks, 29, 34, 151, 253-4
War Trade Agreements, 16, 22, 23, 52, 226, 266, 272
*Waste Land*, 267
*Waterloo Bridge*, 106
*We Usually Shoot Englishmen*, 61
Weapons/War Material, 19, 20, 24, 26, 28, 135, 168, 214, 221, 229; British, for Finland, 52, 109, 134; from Czechoslovakia, 231; Swedish, for Finland, 19
Weaver, Denis, 60, 121
von Weizsäcker, Ernst, 183
Welchman, Gordon, 4
Welin, Dr Malte, 103
Welles, Sumner, 174, 179, 220
*Welt-Dienst*, 100
'Weserübung', Operation, 25
Westin-Silverstolpe, Gunnar, 113
Westman, K.G., 70
*Weyers Taschenbuch der*

*Kriegsflotten,* 231
Wheeler, Mike (Sir Charles), 201, 226, 266
White books (British), 130
White papers (British), 116
White, Ken, 50, 204
*Why Britain Went to War,* 68
Wickman, Johannes W, 71, 83
zu Wied, Prince Victor, 25, 153
Wigforss, Harald, 79, 114, 120
Wilhelm, Prince, 74, 90
Winchester College, 51, 56, 61
Wiskeman, George, 266
Wissenschaffliches Institut, 99
*With Seaplane and Sledge in the Arctic,* 200
Wollweber, Ernst, 89, 181
Woburn Abbey, 63, 135, 137
Workers Educational Association, 115
Wright, Sergeant-Major, 52, 129; Dinky, 52

*A Yankee Flies to London,* 107
York, Carl, 106
Young, Gordon, 60-1, 62
Yugoslavia, 65

Zaba, Norbert, 63
Zdhanov, Andrei, 259
Zetterquist, Police Chief, 88
Zimmerman Telegram, 94
Zurich, 98